# Table of Contents

# Chapter 4: Sentence Structure and Punctuation    133

# Chapter 5: Punctuation     206

# Chapter 6: Developing Ideas     249

# Writing Together

## Sentence and Paragraph Basics

Claire McKenzie
Norma DePledge
University of Victoria

**Canadian Cataloguing in Publication Data**

McKenzie, Claire, 1941-
    Writing together: sentence and paragraph basics

Includes index.
ISBN 0-13-020908-2

1. English language - Sentences. 2. English language - Paragraphs. 3. English
language - Composition and exercises. I. DePledge, Norma Elizabeth, 1946-  . II.
Title.

PE1439.M34    2000    808'.042    C99-931758-X

Allyn and Bacon, Inc., Needham Heights, MA
Prentice-Hall, Inc., Upper Saddle River, New Jersey
Prentice-Hall International (UK) Limited, London
Prentice-Hall of Australia, Pty. Limited, Sydney
Prentice-Hall Hispanoamericana, S.A., Mexico City
Prentice-Hall of India Private Limited, New Delhi
Prentice-Hall of Japan, Inc., Tokyo
Simon & Schuster Southeast Asia Private Limited, Singapore
Editora Prentice-Hall do Brasil, Ltda., Rio de Janeiro

ISBN 0-13-020908-2

Vice President, Editorial Director: Laura Pearson
Acquisitions Editor: David Stover
Associate Editor: Susan Ratkaj
Production Editor: Alex Moore
Copy Editor: Nancy Carroll
Production Coordinator: Peggy Brown
Art Director: Mary Opper
Cover Design: David Cheung
Page Layout: B.J. Weckerle


1 2 3 4 5    04 03 02 01 00

Printed and bound in Canada

Visit the Prentice Hall Canada web site! Send us your comments, browse our
catalogues, and more at www.phcanada.com. Or reach us through e-mail at
**phabinfo_pubcanada@prenhall.com**.

Every reasonable effort has been made to obtain permissions for all articles and data
used in this edition. If errors or omissions have occurred, they will be corrected in
future editions provided written notification has been received by the publisher.

# Preface

## To the instructor:

The purpose of this book is to provide a Canadian composition textbook that can be used in college and university English courses, including those where native English speakers and ESL (English as a Second Language) speakers work side by side in the same classroom.

Many classrooms across Canada already use a workshop approach to teaching composition, a process that we applaud, believing that students learn to write by writing and that honing their analytical skills is essential. We want to provide the primary tools—an understanding of parts of speech, basic punctuation and grammar, organizational and developmental strategies, and diction and idiom—for writing in college or university.

We, Norma and Claire, are the audience as well as the authors of our book as we have a great deal of experience in working in such classrooms. We, like you, have found that most texts seem to fit into one of two categories: texts aimed exclusively at ESL learners, or texts aimed at native-born English speakers. In the latter case, at best, there may be a token addendum that minimally addresses the needs of ESL learners. Inspired by our experience and our commitment to all the students in our classes, *Writing Together* gradually took form.

Colleges and universities across Canada recognize that the Canadian classroom has changed dramatically. Andy Hargreaves, director of the International Centre for Educational Change, Ontario Institute for Studies in Education at the University of Toronto writes, "In many urban schools, more than half the students speak English as their second language." ["A wrong-headed approach to educational reform." *The Globe and Mail*. A 23, Nov. 11, 1997].

Hargreaves' comment clearly shows the challenges facing college and university students and instructors as we move into the 21st century. All across Canada, instructors recognize the need for a text that serves the diverse needs of native-born English speakers and of the recent immigrants or second-generation students sitting next to them.

*Writing Together* presents an integrated approach to developing writing skills. The nine chapters of *Writing Together* present discrete lessons, exercises, and activities to help students acquire the skills involved in writing clear and effective essays. The chapters address not only the needs that are common to ESL and native speakers, but also the *parallel* needs of both groups.

To increase the text's effectiveness, we believe that both those whose first language is not English and native-born English speakers should keep a log of spelling, idiomatic, and grammatical errors, memorizing the former and analyzing the latter. Such logs put the keepers in a position of power, for they will see the patterns and be able to monitor their own improvement.

Because research indicates that there is little automatic transfer of skills from exercises to independent writing, and experience demonstrates that the transfer of grammar skills must be made explicit, *Writing Together* includes the middle step, thereby taking students from exercises to independent writing.

## To the student:

### Our Partnership

We welcome the opportunity to be partners with you, whether English is your first, second, or third language. We have provided you with a mix of rules, examples, exercises, and activities that will help guide you in the process of writing. We recognize that, in large part, you will be learning to write by writing. Therefore, your instructor, our other partner, may make your progress easier by writing things in the margin, within the text, or at the end of your paper that draw attention to certain areas that need improvement. Working together as your partners, we will strengthen your abilities in a subject that will have a lasting impact on your life: written communication.

You need a guide to the kinds of remarks that your instructor may include on your papers. Your instructor may have a special system that he or she will explain to you, but most of us use something like the list that we have included for you on pages xi–xii. Learning the names of the various errors is obviously helpful, but knowing a name without being clear about its meaning won't make it easier to avoid the same structure the next time you write. We have, therefore, included a second list on pages xii–xiii with examples of the errors so that you can see them in action. When your instructor has identified an error that you have made, you can find an example, and then check the page reference for further help.

Early in the book, we have included a section on Parts of Speech that will ensure that you share with us a vocabulary that allows us to talk about errors and how they can be corrected using language that we all understand. We will also be able to discuss your style and how you can make it more effective. You will find much to explain punctuation, sentence structure, modifier, and idiom problems as well as exercises designed to reinforce your new knowledge.

We will remind you now and then of the benefits of creating a personal spelling list, of the necessity of proofreading carefully, and of the value and difficulties of using a spell checker. We will also include a list of Spell Checkmates, those troublesome words a spell checker cannot help you with. Similarly, although we cannot possibly cover all the possibilities that create a great "awk," our focus on being clear, concise, and concrete should mean that the great awk becomes extinct.

In partnership with your teacher and with us, you can gain expertise and confidence in your writing.

## Symbols that Appear in the Margin or the Text of Your Papers

| | |
|---|---|
| p | Punctuation is needed or should be omitted (Chapter 5) |
| prc | Pause rule comma (incorrect) (page 208) |
| wgw | Comma needed after words preceding independent clause (page 210) |
| ss | Sentence structure (Chapter 4) |
| frag | Fragmentary, incomplete sentence (page 171) |
| cs | Two sentences wrongly joined by comma (page 173) |
| run on | Two or more sentences joined without punctuation |
| non // | Sentence elements are not parallel (page 169) |
| [ ] | Leave this out |
| sp | Spelling (pages 420–436) |
| D | Make this a small, lower case, letter |
| ^ | Add a word or words here |
| ? | Not clear or understandable/not readable |
| ¶ | Begin a new paragraph here |
| w | Correct a word |
| ww | Incorrect word, malaprop |
| agr / | Lack of agreement between subject and verb, or pronoun and antecedent (Chapter 3) |
| tense | Verbs have changed tense or are faulty (Chapters 3 and 5) |
| dm | Dangling modifier (page 189) |
| mm | Misplaced modifier (page 192) |
| awk | Awkward phrasing |
| ref? | Weak pronoun reference, unclear antecedent (pages 122–124) |
| logic? | Faulty logic |
| ambig | Ambiguous |
| trans? | Transition needed between ideas or paragraphs (pages 135–136) |
| ⌐ | This should be two words |
| idiom | An error that offends custom (Chapter 8) |

cn          This word can be counted (pages 34–38)

ncn         This word cannot be counted (pages 34–38)

## Examples of Errors and their Symbols

p           Sam liked fast cars, hard rock loud sports shirts and quiche.
            It's weight doubled.

prc         Peggy's two sisters and her cousin Barbara, planned to meet
            her in Quebec.

wgw         After eating the cat Peter gave me fell asleep on my sweater.

ss          Never she drinks coffee without lots of milk and sugar.

frag        Especially a full moon!

cs          Sarah was angry, Sam went home.

run on      Our car is old we need a newer one.

non//       You can get to Penticton by car, bus, or fly.

[  ]        Sam's tie was [very] unique.

sp          Sarah drank alot of tea.

/           I really love Spinach.

^           Peter wanted ^ book about motorcycles.

?           Sam likes movies better than Sarah.

¶           Sarah's interests are more sensuous.

w           I arrived two month ago.

ww          They had a fun time.
            Barbara became a star, and that was a great constellation to
            her mother.

agr         Sam drink coffee more often now.
            Everyone should try their best.
            One should try your best.

tense       She falls and broke her ankle.
            Sarah had been born in 1959.

dm          Walking down the street, her red hat caught everyone's
            attention.
            To be clear, a good vocabulary is necessary.

mm          The cat was in the basket with a mouse in its mouth.

awk         Sarah liked tea for the reason that it was refreshing either hot
            or cold.

ref?        The teachers left the students in the crowded lecture hall, and
            they vowed to complain to the president.

logic?      He was the lecturer, so he was late.

ambig       Tom left the doctor in confusion.

trans?      Barbara was caught in a traffic jam. She was not late for
            dinner.

⌐⌐      She liked the book eventhough her brother found it boring.
idiom   He likes living in here better than in Vancouver.
cn      Steve has a large amount of chairs.
ncn     Sandra loves both pops and popcorns.

## Making Sense of Marks

Although many students think that marks on an English paper are totally arbitrary and subjective, in fact, experienced teachers have a good sense of what differentiates a C from a B. Furthermore, given an idea of what to look for, students themselves recognize effective writing. Claire has had great success with first year composition students whose first essays she grades without putting the mark on them. The students must read the grading criteria, write a comment about their own papers, and assign them a grade. Usually, the papers are within 5 marks of Claire's, a B instead of a B–, for example. Someone who knows what to look for will assign a fair grade.

Below, we present the grading criteria we use, differentiating between grades. Within each category, there is room for expressing further gradations. A paper with superior structure and ideas expressed in correct, sophisticated sentences using a varied vocabulary will probably receive an A+, while one whose ideas are not quite so fully developed and whose sentence structure is varied but contains a few minor grammar or punctuation errors might receive an A–.

Naturally, each instructor has personal preferences that he or she will make clear to you. Therefore, your instructor may provide you with his or her own criteria. As an alternative, he or she may direct you to use the list we have provided with specific additions. You can add them to our list with asterisks beside them. One semester, you may have a teacher who says he or she will fail any paper with the word "alot." Another semester, you may have a teacher who insists that you make transitions to a new paragraph in the final sentence of the previous paragraph. Be glad that you have this information. Add it to the list below, check your drafts against the list and you will be better able to predict the grade that your instructor will assign to your papers.

### The A Paper

- clear subject
- logical organization
- superior ideas and insight
- original thought or perspectives

- clear purpose in each sentence and paragraph
- well-developed ideas
- clear sense of audience
- smooth rather than mechanical transitions
- varied sentence length and structures
- no easy zaps (see pages 86–87)
- precise vocabulary: denotation, connotation, tone, and idiom
- correct spelling
- only very minor grammar or punctuation errors

## The B Paper

- clear subject
- clear organization
- sound ideas, but perhaps limited or vague
- clear purpose in each paragraph
- details in paragraphs
- mostly clearly aimed at audience
- transitions sometimes strained
- sentences quite varied in length and structure
- a few easy zaps (see pages 86–87)
- generally correct word usage, often precise
- generally correct control of tone and idiom
- generally correct in grammar, mechanics, and spelling
- some errors in complex grammar or punctuation

## The C Paper

- observable, but not always clear, focus on subject
- acceptable organization
- rather conventional or incompletely developed ideas
- clear thesis and topic sentences, but not always upheld
- structured paragraphs, but lack of support
- errors in sentence structure *or*

- few errors in sentence structure, *but*
- sentences seldom varied in length or structure
- acceptable, but limited vocabulary
- easy zaps (see pages 86–87)
- some sense of audience
- imprecise and/or monotonous diction
- few major errors, *but*
- mistakes in the fine points of spelling, mechanics, or idiomatic errors

## The D Paper

- passably clear subject
- a sense of organization
- commonplace or unfocused ideas
- undeveloped ideas and/or paragraphs
- lack of unity or coherence
- little sense of audience
- several serious sentence-structure errors
- many easy zaps (pages 86–87)
- imprecise word usage
- little control of tone
- unclear diction
- many or major errors in punctuation, grammar, and/or idiom

## The F Paper

- unclear subject
- little attempt at organization
- unfocused, undeveloped, or superficial ideas
- incoherent, undeveloped, and non-unified paragraphs
- no sense of audience
- many serious sentence-structure errors that hamper understanding
- no attempt to zap isys (see pages 86–87)

- flawed word usage, diction that hampers understanding
- little control of tone or inappropriate tone
- many and major errors in punctuation, grammar, and/or idiom

# Parts of Speech and Word Formation

## Learning Outcomes

**This Chapter will help you to**

- recognize the names of English parts of speech.

- speak with precision about your writing.

- recognize the differing functions of parts of speech.

# Pretest: Parts of Speech

A. Identify the underlined parts of speech by name, i.e., noun
(common, proper, concrete, abstract, collective), pronoun (personal,
interrogative, relative, possessive, intensifier, reflexive), verb
(transitive, intransitive, linking), verbal (gerund, infinitive,
participle), adverb, adjective, coordinating conjunction,
subordinating conjunction, preposition, article (definite or
indefinite), interjection. For nouns, you may need to use two names,
such as "common concrete."

1. <u>Letitia</u> <u>threw</u> the apple <u>at</u> the judge.

   _____   _____   _____

2. <u>He</u> realized that the man <u>who</u> was racing in the <u>lead</u> had the
   cheapest <u>running</u> shoes.

   _____   _____   _____   _____

3. <u>To be fit</u> <u>became</u> her <u>most</u> cherished wish.

   _____   _____   _____

4. <u>Cowabunga</u>! Bart thought of a <u>perfect</u> example for his
   presentation.

   _____   _____

5. Terry <u>skates</u> well, <u>but</u> <u>jogging</u> is her passion.

   _____   _____   _____

6. <u>Who</u> saw Robert sunning <u>himself</u> on <u>the</u> apartment roof?

   _____   _____   _____

7. <u>Because</u> it is <u>early</u>, we will take <u>an</u> apple pie for the <u>team</u>.

   _____   _____   _____   _____

8. She <u>herself</u> had <u>never</u> accepted <u>candy</u> from a stranger.

   _____   _____   _____

B. Identify the **function** of the following words. Use, for example,
"subject of the verb _____," "direct object of the verb _____,"
"object of the preposition _____," "predicate adjective following the
verb _____," "adjective, modifing the noun _____". Look at this
example.

Sam ate the <u>dripping</u> piece of <u>watermelon</u>.

*modifier of the noun "piece"   object of the preposition "of"*

1. Letitia threw <u>this</u> apple at the <u>judge</u>.

   _____   _____   _____

2. <u>To be fit</u> became <u>her</u> <u>object</u>.

   _____   _____   _____

3. <u>That</u> was <u>better</u> than flying.

   _____   _____

4. <u>Fortunately</u>, Philip gave <u>Letitia</u> the <u>car</u> <u>keys</u>.

   _____   _____   _____

5. Cooking <u>is</u> a <u>passion</u> <u>that Philip and Letitia share</u>.

   _____   _____   _____

6. <u>Wandering</u> players moved through the <u>park</u>.

   _____   _____

7. <u>This</u> path <u>wandered</u>.

   _____   _____

8. Philip <u>tripped</u> over the <u>sprawling</u> <u>dog</u>.

   _____   _____   _____

9. <u>These</u> were <u>the</u> buttons that <u>Jeff</u> had been searching for. The dog, <u>however</u>, did not wake up.

   _____   _____   _____   _____

# Parts of Speech

Learning about Parts of Speech will help you in many areas of your writing, from understanding punctuation and creating sentence variety to grasping the grammar and regular idiomatic patterns of English.

You'll understand, for example, why you put a comma after "however" when it begins a sentence but not after "although." You'll find out why your grade four teacher told you not to begin a sentence with "because" and why you will see many sentences that do, indeed, begin with that very word. Because you will know what "gerunds" and "infinitives" are, you will find it easier, if your first language is not English, to recognize idiomatic patterns that follow these words. If your native language is English, learning Parts of Speech will give you a vocabulary to explain to a non-native speaker why certain patterns occur. Finally, you will all benefit when you, your instructor, and your partners (us) share a vocabulary to discuss your writing. Read and work

through the following section to gain the basic knowledge that will put
your writing on a solid foundation.

# Nouns

**denote persons, places, things, or ideas.**

**Types of Nouns:** nouns can be classified in the following ways.

## Proper Noun

a particular noun, e.g., Virginia Woolf, Tokyo, the Vatican, the
Eiffel Tower (note the capitalization of these nouns)

## Common Noun

a member of a class or group of nouns, whether concrete or
abstract, e.g., women, cities, places, monuments, honesty

## Collective Nouns

groups that function as units or a whole, e.g., team, herd, collection,
jury

## Concrete Nouns

nouns that can be perceived by any of the five senses (sight, hearing,
smell, touch, and taste), e.g., door, scream, tree, lemon

## Abstract Nouns

nouns that express a quality, condition, action, or idea, e.g., beauty,
loneliness, inspiration, campaign, democracy, sin, emptiness

## Exercise 1: Types of Nouns

Identify the following nouns by type. (You will find that a noun can be
two types). Look at this example before doing the exercise:

- Put the suitcases in the *Honda*. *(concrete, proper)*

  1. Put the <u>kettle</u> (_____) on to boil.

  2. Please give my <u>regards</u> (_____) to Molly's mother.

  3. Please turn the <u>radio</u> (_____) off.

  4. Where is the shepherd who looks after the <u>flock</u>? (_____)

  5. Sean is now a teacher in <u>Indonesia</u>. (_____)

## Features of Nouns

Nouns change form to indicate possession and pluralization. They also possess countability. Look at the following examples.

### Possession

Michael's car is important to him.

Canada's landscape is incredibly varied.

Beauty's definition can vary from culture to culture and person to person.

### Pluralization

In my grade twelve class, there were three Michaels.

Learning that there were once two Canadas, Upper and Lower, surprises many students.

Both the red and yellow roses were beauties.

### Countable or Non-countable

countable: dishes, boys, countries, children

non-countable: information, help, garbage, equipment

We deal further with this important aspect of nouns, countability, on pages 34–39. In the meantime, look at the following examples that show how certain nouns are countable while very similar nouns are not. Note that the verbs used after uncountable nouns are singular.

The chairs are missing, but the rest of the furniture is here.

Jeremy always carries his own suitcases, but the rest of the luggage goes on the baggage cart.

Although the lyrics are new, the music is from a song that was popular in the forties.

### Activity 1: Features of Nouns

Write sentences that make the nouns exhibit the feature given in brackets.

1. Frog (possessive)
2. Sesame seed (plural)
3. Robbie Burns (possessive)
4. child (plural)
5. women (possessive)

## Exercise 2: Features of Nouns

Identify the underlined noun as countable or uncountable.

1. I need new <u>equipment</u>. _____

2. Where did you put my <u>spider</u>? _____

3. Jeremy bought his sister some new <u>software</u>. _____

4. Find yourself a <u>chair</u>. _____

5. <u>Information</u> is available at the reference desk. _____

## Functions of Nouns

Nouns perform differing functions in sentences.

| | |
|---|---|
| **Possessive:** | Penelope was puzzled by <u>beauty's</u> elusive nature. |
| **Subject of a verb:** | <u>Beauty</u> is the stuff of legend. |
| **Subjective completion:** | Jennifer was a <u>beauty</u>. (a predicate noun or adjective completes the meaning of the subject.) |
| **Direct object of a verb:** | Penelope bought <u>beauty</u> in a bottle. (The direct object is a noun that directly receives the action.) |
| **Indirect object of verb:** | Mary threw <u>Robert</u> the remote control. (Robert received the action only indirectly. He did not get thrown.) |
| **Object of Preposition:** | The pot was full of <u>tea</u>. |
| **Direct address:** | "Would you like some tea, <u>Mary</u>?" |
| **Modifier:** | Nathan took a <u>college</u> composition course; he was given credit for a <u>university</u> course. |
| | The <u>Moon</u> Fesitival is next week. |
| | (When nouns function as modifers, to reduce confusion, you can regard such structures as compound nouns.) |

## Exercise 3: Functions of Nouns

Identify the following nouns by function. Look at this example before doing the exercise:

- Put the suitcases in the <u>Honda</u>. (*object of the preposition "in"*)

1. Put the <u>kettle</u> (_____) on to boil.
2. Give my regards to <u>Mr. Lopinski</u>. (_____)
3. <u>Koji</u> (_____) is enthusiastic.
4. Where is the boy who gave the <u>sheep</u> a bath? (_____)
5. Mandy became a <u>teacher</u> (_____) in Malaysia.

---

**Activity 2: Writing with nouns**

Working as a class, write a list of thirty nouns on the board. Include at least four proper nouns, one collective noun, and four abstract nouns.

Then, writing as individuals, incorporate these nouns into a composition. You may add some nouns in order to make your composition more meaningful.

---

## Exercise 4: Concrete and Abstract Nouns

Identify the underlined words as concrete or abstract. Look at the following example before doing the exercise:

- The <u>taste</u> of the hot and sour <u>soup</u> confused Sean.

  *abstract*                    *concrete*

1. The two <u>boys</u> went to the same elementary <u>school</u>.

   _____            _____

2. The <u>knowledge</u> of the new <u>student</u> was impressive.

   _____            _____

3. The <u>campaign</u> was over in two <u>months</u>.

   _____            _____

4. The <u>counsellor</u> gave her good <u>advice</u>.

   _____            _____

5. <u>Loneliness</u> was a <u>problem</u> during the first month.

   _____            _____

6. <u>Sarah</u> poured another cup of <u>tea</u>.

   _____            _____

7. The <u>smell</u> reminded Sam of his grandmother's <u>house</u>.

   _____            _____

8. The <u>coffee</u> was left in the <u>tree house</u>.

   _____            _____

9. <u>Audrey</u> welcomed the <u>sympathy</u>.

_____     _____

10. Why did you put the <u>tea pot</u> in the <u>microwave</u>?

_____     _____

## Exercise 5: Common and Proper Nouns

Identify the underlined words as common or proper. Look at the following example before doing the exercise:

• The taste of the hot and sour <u>soup</u> made <u>Sean</u> confused.

                               *common*       *proper*

1. The <u>girls</u> planned to go camping at <u>Banff</u>.

_____     _____

2. <u>Pencils</u> and papers lay on the <u>floor</u>.

_____     _____

3. Tom and Pamela bought <u>tickets</u> for the play at the <u>Phoenix</u>.

_____     _____

4. <u>Christmas</u> comes on a <u>Thursday</u> this year.

_____     _____

5. <u>The University of Victoria</u> has a pretty <u>campus</u>.

_____     _____

6. <u>Woody Guthrie</u> wrote some delightful children's <u>songs</u>.

_____     _____

7. Understanding the poetry of <u>William Blake</u> provides a <u>lifework</u> for some people.

_____     _____

8. They used to manufacture <u>Jergens Lotion</u> in <u>Perth</u>, Ontario.

_____     _____

9. Her best <u>friend</u> appeared in the chorus of *La Boheme*.

_____     _____

10. Can you run <u>PowerPoint</u> on your <u>computer</u>?

_____     _____

## Pronouns

Pronouns are words used in place of nouns (their antecedents). Note that some pronouns, however, do not have antecedents, e.g., <u>It</u> is raining. <u>It's</u> a good thing you brought your umbrella.

## Types of Pronouns

| TYPES OF PRONOUNS | A FEW EXAMPLES |
|---|---|
| demonstrative | this, that, these, those |
| indefinite | each, anyone, everybody, either, some |
| intensive | I myself, he himself |
| interrogative | who, which, what |
| personal | you, I, it, they, him, she |
| reflexive | myself, yourself, themselves |
| relative | who, which, that |

## Exercise 6: Types of Pronouns

Identify the following underlined pronouns by type. Look at this example before doing the exercise:

- <u>This</u> (*demonstrative* ) is the best example.

  1. <u>They</u> (_____) put Harry in the back seat.

  2. <u>I myself</u> (_____) am in favour of a four day week.

  3. Yi Ling couldn't decide <u>which</u> (_____) chocolate to eat.

  4. <u>Everyone</u> (_____) took one book to read on the bus.

  5. She gave <u>herself</u> a pedicure. (_____ )

  6. <u>Who</u> (_____) put the gum in the microwave?

  7. This is the programme <u>that</u> (_____) Sophie likes the best.

  8. Throw <u>this</u> (_____) tomato in the compost!

  9. <u>One</u> (_____) should try to remember to proofread.

  10. Yasmine <u>herself</u> (_____) had never eaten a kumquat.

## Functions of Pronouns

Like nouns, pronouns act as subjects, objects, and possessives.

**Subject:**    It is in the eye of the beholder.

**Object:**     She adored it. He loved those.

**Possessive:**     Penelope was puzzled by its elusive nature.

**Adjective:**     When demonstrative pronouns are used before words acting as nouns, they function as adjectives. Contrast "This cookie is good" (demonstrative pronoun functioning as an adjective) and "This is good too" (demonstrative pronoun functioning as the subject of a verb).

Note that a demonstrative pronoun can also function as an object as it does in the second object example above.

## Exercise 7: Functions of Pronouns

Identify the following pronouns by function. Look at this example before doing the exercise:

- Put *them* in the Chevette (*object of the verb "put"*).

  1. <u>Her</u> (_____) last essay was the longest but the easiest.

  2. <u>They</u> (_____) all left the barn before the bull.

  3. Saskia poured the acid over <u>it</u> (_____) and stirred vigorously.

  4. On the final lap, <u>he</u> (_____) managed to take the lead.

  5. <u>Its</u> (_____) final sentence made Geraldo laugh until he cried.

A pronoun must refer clearly to its referent. This is important enough that we devote pages 116–118 to pronoun agreement in its many forms. This following exercise can be thought of as a warm-up.

## Exercise 8: Pronoun/Antecedent

Draw an arrow to the antecedents of the underlined pronouns. After you do this, you may find that some of the sentences are incorrect because the pronouns and the antecedents disagree. Put an X beside any incorrect sentence. Look at this example before doing the exercise:

- I need my thesaurus, but I can't find <u>it</u>.

  1. The students wanted <u>their</u> midterm to be worth 20%.

  2. One of the chairs in the dining room was missing <u>its</u> seat.

  3. Everyone should do <u>their</u> best.

  4. After the young men picked up their luggage, <u>they</u> boarded the new flight.

5. Because it was raining, the cow stayed in <u>her</u> barn.

6. The instructor, together with three graduate students, took <u>his</u> students on the field trip to the Marine Biological Station.

7. Although <u>it</u> seems to save some time, computers can also waste lots of your time.

8. Many of the younger boys were carrying <u>their</u> skateboards under their arms.

9. My neighbour with the wonderful roses wants to have a garden sale in <u>her</u> back yard.

10. The visiting group of international teachers was surprised to see <u>their</u> colleagues wearing jeans in the classroom.

# Verbs

Verbs denote actions, occurrence, or a state of being (existence).

## Features of Verbs

Verb forms change to indicate tense. We devote a large part of Chapter Two to tense, so you can tell that this capability of verbs is an important one in English. For now, we will just mention the basic example of how we usually change present tense to past by adding "ed" to form the past indicative (simple past) and the past participle: *end, ended; type, typed*. However, many important verbs in English form the past indicative and the past participle in irregular ways: *sing, sang, sung; does, did, done; write, wrote, written*. See pages 103–107 for a complete list of irregular verbs.

## Types of Verbs: transitive, intransitive, and linking

## Transitive verbs

- Transitive verbs need objects to complete the meaning.

  ✗ Robert <u>fixed</u>.

  ✓ Robert <u>fixed</u> the <u>teapot</u>.

The action of a transitive verb is directed toward a receiver.

Aladdin <u>poured</u> the <u>jinni</u> out of the lamp.

The <u>jinni</u> <u>was poured</u> by Aladdin.

The action of a transitive verb does not have to be physical.

Mr. Lee <u>bought</u> a <u>motorcycle</u> because he <u>thought</u> that motorcycles were safe, dependable, and economical. He believed <u>that</u> motorcycles were the answer to most transportation problems.

## Exercise 9: Transitive Verbs

In the following sentences, underline the verb with a double line and the object with a single line. Look at this example before doing the exercise:

- Tai <u>fed</u> the <u>cat</u> every morning at seven o'clock.

   1. Put the kettle on to boil.

   2. Herbert mowed the lawn for his elderly neighbours.

   3. The paper carrier always delivered the paper before six thirty.

   4. Griffey hit another homer.

   5. Kim booked passage for a three week cruise to Alaska.

## Intransitive verbs

Examples:

- Intransitive verbs do not need objects to complete the meaning.

   Algernon <u>sniffed</u> a lot.

   Percival <u>smelled</u> a lot.

Most dictionaries will identify verbs as transitive or intransitive, but you will find that these verb types are not invariable: a verb may be transitive in one sentence and intransitive in another.

Examples:

Lightning <u>struck</u>!

Lightning <u>struck</u> the <u>tree</u>.

Robert <u>reads</u> quickly.

Roberta <u>reads</u> *Scientific American*.

   In each of the above examples, the first verb, having no object, is intransitive, while the second, having an object, is transitive.

## Exercise 10: Intransitive Verbs

In the following sentences, underline the intransitive verb with a double
line. Look at this example before doing the exercise:

- Hannah <u>left</u> every morning at seven o'clock.

    1.  The bottle exploded when Harry shook it.

    2.  Helen left Nova Scotia twenty years ago and cried for a month.

    3.  The paper carrier always arrives before six thirty.

    4.  Hing walked in the park at least once a week.

    5.  Before he made supper, Hideki swam to the raft and back.

## Linking Verbs

Linking verbs refer to *states of being*, e.g., *to be, appear, become, seem, grow,
remain* and also refer to the *five senses*, e.g., *touch, look, smell, taste, sound.*

Linking verbs connect the subject of a sentence with a noun, a
pronoun, a verbal acting as a noun, an adjective, or an adverb of place.
A noun following a linking verb is termed a predicate noun, and an
adjective is called a predicate adjective.

Mayumi is <u>a karate student</u>. (predicate noun)

Raoul is <u>tired</u>. (predicate adjective)

The coffee smelled <u>good</u> to Maritza. (predicate adjective)

Her coffee cup is <u>on the counter</u>. (adverb of place)

Lenka is <u>outside</u>. (adverb of place)

Note how the meaning may change if you use an adverb instead of
an adjective following a linking verb. For example, which of the
following roommates would you rather take home to meet your
mother?

Percival smelled <u>bad</u>. Because his roommate, Algernon, had a cold,
and smelled <u>badly</u>, they remained friends.

You'll notice that Percival has an offensive odour while Algernon
merely has difficulty smelling anything. "Badly" modifies the act of
smelling.

Think about what someone would say when she didn't do as well as
she expected on a test. Would she say "I feel bad" or "I feel badly?" She
*should* say "I feel bad about the test." That is, she is describing an
internal emotional state. If, on some other occasion, she says "I feel
badly," she will be modifying the act of "feeling" and saying that she has

difficulty—perhaps because she is wearing mitts. Remember, if you are upset, you feel "bad," not "badly." Whether you use an adjective or adverb after a linking verb can radically alter the meaning of your sentence. Look at some final examples:

Mia sees <u>well</u>. Mia looks <u>good</u>. Mia looks <u>well</u>.

Mia sees <u>good</u> in everyone. (We threw this adjective in just for fun!)

Which of the above is a comment on Mia's appearance, which on her visual acuity, which on her health? Remember that you need to take care using adjectives and adverbs after linking verbs.

## Exercise 11: Linking Verbs

Underline the linking verb with a double line, and, in the brackets, identify what follows it as a predicate noun, a pronoun, a verbal acting as a noun, a predicate adjective, or an adverb of place. Look at this example before doing the exercise:

*   Cultural anthropology <u>is</u> fascinating. (*predicate adjective* )

    1.  Their canoe, along with the two kayaks, is in a boat house on Gorge Road. (_____)

    2.  Luckily, Takashi, unlike his brother, remains calm before his exams. (_____)

    3.  This is it—the best detergent on the market! (_____)

    4.  Dalbir was the chairperson last year. (_____)

    5.  Because he is hungry, Ben wants to go home. (_____)

# Verbals

**Verbals** are forms of verbs used as nouns, adjectives, or adverbs. They are termed **non-finite**. Although finite verbs can serve as the only verb in a sentence, nonfinite verbs (verbals) cannot. They function only as nouns, adjectives, or adverbs.

## Types of Verbals

Verbals can be classified in the following ways:

**Gerunds** end with "ing" and function as nouns.

Parking is expensive. (subject of the verb "is")

He avoided spending money by parking on Cedar Hill Cross Road. (object of the preposition "by")

**Infinitives** usually include the verb (present tense) plus "to." The "to" may sometimes be omitted, forming a "bare infinitive." An infinitive may be used as a noun, an adjective, or an adverb.

To park a van seems difficult. (subject of the verb "seems")

The work to be done is overwhelming. (adjective modifying the noun "work")

To tell the truth, I think that the plan is impossible. (adverb phrase modifying the independent clause)

**Participles** may end with "ing" (present) or, usually, with "d", "ed" or "en" (past). A participle may be used in a verb phrase, as a nonfinite verb, or as an adjective.

The cat had finished almost all its food. (verb phrase)

The baby, crying loudly, grabbed the dish. (nonfinite verb)

The crying baby scared the cat. (adjective)

## Exercise 12: Types of Verbals

Identify the underlined verbals by type and function. Look at the following example before doing the exercise:

- I like swimming better than skiing because it is less expensive.

  *(gerund, object of the verb "like")*

  1. Kuei teaches people to drive. (_____)

  2. Driving aficionados often prefer a stick shift. (_____)

  3. Driving on the freeway in a winter blizzard is not my favourite thing to do. (_____)

  4. The robbers, driving erratically from lane to lane, made their escape. (_____)

  5. The driven snow covered the entrance to the apartment building. (_____)

**Activity 3: Working with verbals**

Use the appropriate verbals to fill in the blanks. Where we want a specific kind, we indicate it after the blank.

_____ is my favourite pastime. Some people prefer _____, _____, or _____, but _____ is more fun. I really like _____ [infinitive] because _____ is _____ [your choice of adjectives] If you want to learn how _____, I can tell you how _____ and _____. I'm sure that you'll want _____ for the rest of your life.

# Adjectives

These words modify (qualify or restrict) the meaning of nouns or words acting as nouns (pronouns, verbals).

She and the wine looked <u>perfect</u>. (predicate adjective following linking verb "looked")

She wore a <u>long</u> <u>white</u> gown. (modifier of noun "gown")

The wine was <u>red</u> and <u>dry</u>. (predicate adjectives following the linking verb "was")

To pour the wine seemed <u>easy</u>, but he was <u>nervous</u>. (predicate adjectives following linking verbs "seemed" and "was")

<u>Quick</u> mopping with his napkin saved her dress. (modifying the gerund "mopping")

They were <u>excited</u>. (predicate adjective following linking verb "were")

## Forms of Adjectives

Possessives and articles are always adjectives.

<u>The</u> dinner was a success.

<u>Their</u> excitement made other people happy.

**Activity 4: Working with adjectives**

Working in pairs, think of at least two adjectives for each of the following adjective endings.

- Record the class' collection of adjectives on the board.

- Add new words to the original lists.

Here are some common adjective endings. We discuss adjective endings at further length on page 420.

| | |
|---|---|
| al | ing |
| ary | ish |
| able | ive |
| ed | less |
| en | ly |
| ful | like |
| ian | ous |
| ible | wise |
| ic | y |

## Features of Adjectives

Demonstrative pronouns function as adjectives. They can, however, also function as subjects or objects.

This room is a mess! (adjective modifying "room")

These bottles are empty. (adjective modifying "bottles")

These are full of dry, red wine. (subject of the verb "are")

She wants these. (object of the verb "wants")

---

**In English, adjectives appear in the order listed below:**

1. Articles (determiners) or Possessives

2. Opinions (judgments)

3. Measurements

4. Shapes

5. Age

6. Colours

7. Nationalities or Religions

8. Material

---

Look at the two examples below:

✗ a Canadian, nylon, old, red and white flag

✓ an old red and white nylon Canadian flag

## Exercise 13: Adjectives

In the following sentences, underline the adjective with a double line and the word it modifies with a single line. Look at this example before doing the exercise:

- Mike fed the <u>ravenous</u> <u>cat</u> before anyone else got up.

    1. The peanut butter is completely natural.

    2. My favourite number is five.

    3. Slow dancing goes in and out of fashion.

    4. The print was easy to read.

    5. A cohesive plan took hours to hammer out.

# Articles

The articles, "**a**," "**an**," and "**the**," come before nouns and are sometimes called determiners. As we mentioned before, they function as adjectives. Native-born English speakers, when asked to think of an article rule, can usually come up with one from the distant past: "You use 'a' before a word starting with a consonant and 'an' before a word starting with a vowel."

Their confidence, however, often wavers when they are presented with "an uniform" or "an university." Soon, though, they modify that rule they remembered from grade four to recognize that when the "u" sounded like "you," they have always used "a" before it. Thus, they happily go back to writing about "an unusual occurrence" or "a usual situation," ignoring the one "rule" that they knew.

New speakers of English know that Article Rules are actually much more complex and that native-English speakers unknowingly and unerringly apply them every time they speak or write. To help those who must learn Article Rules rather than intuit them, we deal with them on pages 27–30 and supply many exercises to reinforce the learning process.

# Adverbs

These words modify verbs, adjectives, adverbs, verbals, phrases, and independent clauses.

Examples:

She and the red wine looked <u>quite</u> perfect. (modifies the adjective "perfect")

He poured the wine <u>nervously</u>. (modifies the verb "poured")

The wine splashed out <u>very</u> quickly. (modifies the adverb "quickly")

Mopping <u>frantically</u> with his napkin, he saved her dress. (modifies the gerund "mopping")

<u>Although only half the wine was spilled</u>, he ordered another bottle. (adverb subordinate clause modifying the independent clause)

This wine, <u>however</u>, was white. (modifies the independent clause)

The white wine was not as pretty as the red; <u>fortunately</u>, it tasted fine. (conjunctive adverb joining two independent clauses)

## Types of Adverbs

Adverbs appear in many forms and accomplish much more than simply modifying verbs.

**manner** (how): slowly, well, happily

**time** (when): usually, infrequently, often

**place or direction** (where): inside, downtown, south

**cause, result, purpose** (why): because she ran, that she won

**degree:** so fast, not done, more slowly

**conjunctive** (used to join independent clauses): moreover, therefore, however

## Features of Adverbs

Many adverbs end in "ly": commonly, swiftly, frequently. Remember two things, however; some adverbs do not end in "ly," (often, well, quite) and some other parts of speech do (lovely, deadly, family). Clearly, you can use "ly" as a clue, but not a conclusion about a word's identity as adverb. Other endings for adverbs are "ward(s)," (backwards, frontwards), and "wise," (lengthwise, crabwise.)

Adverbs can move within a sentence (sometimes changing the meaning slightly).

Examples:

He ran quickly to the finish line.

Quickly, he ran to the finish line.

He, quickly, ran to the finish line.

He ran to the finish line quickly.

In contrast, subordinating and coordinating conjunctions cannot move within a sentence.

 Examples:

Because he ran fast, he won.

He ~~because~~ fast ran, he won.

He ran fast ~~because,~~ he won.

He ran fast, he won ~~because~~.

He ran fast, so he won.

He ~~so~~ fast ran, he won.

He ran fast, he ~~so~~ won.

He fast ran, he won ~~so~~.

## Common Conjunctive Adverbs

| | |
|---|---|
| consequently | meanwhile |
| finally | moreover |
| furthermore | nevertheless |
| hence | nonetheless |
| however | therefore |
| in addition | thus |

## Exercise 14: Functions of Adverbs

Underline the adverbs in the following sentences and identify their function. Look at this example before doing the exercise:

* He ate the goldfish <u>really</u> quickly. (*modifies adverb "quickly"*)

    1.  Koji never teaches people to drive. (_____)

    2.  The confused seagull crashed clumsily into the mailbox. (_____)

    3.  The robbers, driving erratically from lane to lane, made their escape. (_____)

    4.  After the snowplow passed, the snow covered the entrance to the apartment building. (_____)

    5.  Mandy graduated; therefore, she went back to Malaysia. (_____)

> ### Activity 5: (Purple) Writing with adjectives and adverbs
>
> Write a paragraph of 100-150 words. Modify each noun with at least one adjective, at least one adjective with an adverb, and each transitive verb with an adverb.

# Prepositions

These words always have objects: together the preposition and its object are called a prepositional phrase. The following sentence has three prepositional phrases: the prepositions are underlined once and their objects twice.

- Sarah, <u>with</u> great <u>vehemence</u>, expressed her love <u>of</u> <u>tea</u> <u>to</u> her <u>aunt</u>.

## Features of Prepositions

Prepositions may follow their objects and come at the ends of sentences, despite stories to the contrary. Apparently, when England's former Prime Minister Winston Churchill, a man renowned for his use of language, replied to someone who had criticized him for ending a sentence with a preposition, he wrote, "This is the sort of English up with which I will not put" to show just how awkward a sentence can be if you insist on applying rules appropriate to Latin to English. He would think that the two examples that follow are perfectly acceptable English.

<u>What</u> is it made <u>of</u>?

<u>What</u> did you do that <u>for</u>?

Prepositional phrases form the basis for many of our idiomatic phrases, and thus present an ongoing challenge for non-native speakers of English as they try to distinguish, for example, between being "on time" or "in time," between "hang on" and "hang up,"or between "sit up" and "sit down." Chapter Eight has lists of the most commonly used prepositional phrases.

## Functions of Prepositions

Prepositions link the object to some other part of the sentence. Prepositional phrases can act as adjectives or adverbs.

## Common Prepositions

| | |
|---|---|
| across, after | in, into, in regard to, |
| around, as, at, | like, near, of, off, |
| because of, | on, on top of, over, |
| before, between, | through, to, |
| below, by, for, | together with, under, |
| from, in front of, | until, up, with |

## Exercise 15: Prepositions

Underline the prepositions in the following sentences with one line and their objects with two. In the brackets, identify the function of the prepositional phrase. Look at the following example before doing the exercise:

- Sam lay the knife <u>on</u> the <u><u>table</u></u>. (*adverb phrase of place* )

  1. In the evening, the wind rose, and they closed all the windows.
     (_____)

  2. Finding a cure for polio saved many lives. (_____)

  3. Mandy has lived in Malaysia for six years. (_____)

  4. The confused seagull crashed clumsily into the mailbox.
     (_____)

  5. They felt pleased that the levels of pollution had declined.
     (_____)

  6. After the snow plow passed, the snow covered the entrance to the apartment building. (_____)

  7. He awoke periodically throughout the night. (_____)

---

### Activity 6: Writing with prepositions

Review the common phrases on pages 341–353 before you begin. Write a 100–150 word beginning of a fairy tale. Use as many prepositional phrases as possible.

Begin with "Once upon a time ...."

---

# Conjunctions

These words function as connectors and are very important as they may connect words, phrases, or whole clauses.

## Coordinating Conjunctions

Coordinating conjunctions connect units of equal value. They can join two words, two phrases, or two independent clauses. Recognizing them will help you a great deal in your efforts to punctuate correctly, and as there are just seven of them, we suggest that you memorize the coordinating conjunctions.

| | |
|---|---|
| but | or |
| yet | for |
| and | nor |
| so | |

(See Comma Rule 4 on page 210 for how to punctuate when coordinating conjunctions join two independent clauses.)

Examples:

Sarah made tea <u>and</u> coffee. (joining two nouns)

He does not like Coke, <u>nor</u> does he like Pepsi. (joining two independent clauses)

To sit down <u>and</u> to take off her shoes was heavenly. (joining two verbals)

Sarah drank tea, <u>but</u> Roberta drank coffee. (joining two independent clauses)

**ESL Note:** When you are making a negative sentence, join the elements with "or," not "and."

✓ Jim liked cats <u>and</u> dogs.

✓ Judy did not like snakes <u>or</u> spiders.

✓ Jamie liked ham and eggs. (one entity)

✗ Jane didn't like guppies <u>and</u> goldfish.

## Exercise 16: Coordinating Conjunctions

Underline the coordinating conjunctions in the following sentences with one line. In the brackets, identify the conjunction's function. Look at this example before doing the exercise:

• Sonya didn't like hiking <u>or</u> canoeing. (*CC joining two verbals* )

1. Why did you add the garlic and the onion after you cooked the tomatoes? (_____)

2.  Wayne wanted pizza, but the rest of the gang wanted lasagna.
    (_____)

3.  After the game ended, Rick and Kevin went to their grandma's
    house. (_____)

4.  Sam enjoyed gardening, so all his neighbours benefited from the
    fresh vegetables. (_____)

5.  "To be or not to be" is just one of the Shakespearean phrases we
    often hear in everyday conversation. (_____)

## Subordinating Conjunctions

Subordinating conjunctions mark dependent (subordinate) clauses and
connect them to the independent (main) clause. Together a subordinate
clause and a main clause make up a "complex sentence." Careful
subordination adds emphasis to your main ideas and helps provide
cohesion as well as sentence variety.

## Common subordinating conjunctions:

| | | |
|---|---|---|
| after | before | until |
| as if | even though | till |
| as | if | when |
| although | since | whereas |
| because | unless | while |

Here are some examples of complex sentences, but for more
information, see page 142 in Chapter 4.

When she got home, to sit down and to take her shoes off was
heavenly.

While Sarah was resting after she came home from work, she read a
short short story until the kettle boiled.

Since Sarah had made tea, Joe had some.

**Note:** Punctuation differs when the subordinate clause precedes the
main clause. (See Comma Rule number 5, page 211) Note the
punctuation difference in the following pair:

Because it rained, Maria left early.

Maria left early because it rained.

## Exercise 17: Subordinating Conjunctions

Underline the subordinating conjunctions in the following sentences with one line. Put an ✗ beside a sentence whose punctuation is wrong. Look at this example before doing the exercise:

✗ <u>Although</u> Sona didn't like hiking or canoeing she loved snorkeling.

1. You always call, when I am in the shower.

2. Since Algernon moved, the parking space is always available.

3. Joseph had found the matches before his sister even realized they were missing.

4. Tai has been working in Ottawa since he graduated.

5. Because she was feeling domestic she made a delicious pumpkin pie.

### Activity 7: Writing with subordinating and coordinating conjunctions

First, read over comma rules 5 and 6 on page 211. Second, write a list containing a combination of coordinating and subordinating conjunctions. Write six of each, but make your list in random order. Third, exchange your list with another student. Finally, using all the words on your classmate's list, preferably in the given order, write 50–100 words beginning "When I returned home..."

Example: The first four words on the list are "but," "because," "so," and "although." You could write: "When I returned home, I was tired, <u>but</u> I still had work to do. <u>Because</u> I was hungry, I checked out the fridge. I found a piece of leftover lasagne, <u>so</u> I felt very cheerful <u>although</u> I'd eaten lasagne ten days in a row."

## Correlative Conjunctions

These conjunctions appear in pairs and must precede the same parts of speech.

Failure to put them before the identical parts of speech means the sentence is non-parallel, a sentence structure error. See pages 168–170 for further discussion of parallelism.

**Common correlative conjunctions:**

both .... and                    neither .... nor
either .... or                    not only .... but also

Examples:

✓ She decided to read **either** *Persuasion* **or** *Emma* over the Easter holiday.

✗ She decided to **either** read *Persuasion* **or** *Emma* over the Easter holiday.

✓ Thomas Hardy wrote **not only** novels **but also** poetry.

✗ **Not only** did Thomas Hardy write novels **but also** poetry.

Sentences that start with "not only," like the Hardy sentence above, cannot be made parallel.

## Exercise 18: Correlative Conjunctions

Underline the correlative conjunctions in the following sentences with one line. Put an ✗ beside a sentence that is non-parallel because the conjunctions precede different parts of speech. Look at the following example before doing the exercise:

✗ Sonya <u>not</u> <u>only</u> loved snorkeling <u>but</u> <u>also</u> scuba diving.

1. Both Sarah and Roberta recycle even when they are camping.

2. Not only does Sarah recycle but also she reuses a great many things.

3. Either Sarah or Roberta will collect the papers.

4. If the weather is fine, George neither stays at home nor goes to work.

5. Both *Brave New World* and *1994* are satires by English authors.


# Interjections

These words not only express emotion or surprise ("Wow!" "Super!" "Rats!" "Ai yahh!" "Fiddlesticks!" "Oh No!" "Oi Veh!"), but also include the famous Canadian "eh?" as in "That was a great game, eh?"

Learning these basic Parts of Speech, already familiar to those of you who learned English in a systematic way, will increase your confidence in writing, whether you are a native-born English speaker or a newcomer to the language. You will now have the tools to help you avoid parallelism errors and pronoun agreement errors, for example. Moreover, you can confidently say to a classmate or workmate whose work you are peer editing "You cannot use 'By studying' as the subject of the verb because it is a prepositional phrase;" or "'Whereas' is a subordinating conjunction like 'because' or 'when,' not an adverb like 'therefore' or 'however,' so you must not begin a sentence 'Whereas, ... .'"

## Using Articles

In Canada, many of us who are native-born English speakers study French and many of us who are native-born French speakers study English. Some people in each situation say that the learned language's articles are arbitrary, illogical, and absurd. Any of us who have learned a second or third language probably know that articles can continue to plague us even after we have learned seemingly much more difficult structures in the new language.

The rules that follow should help guide new learners of English through the minefield of English articles. Native speakers of English, too, should read through the Article Rules. Scanning these Rules will make it much less likely that native speakers will continue to complain about article use in other languages. We believe that they will be not only appalled at the rules' capriciousness, at the exceptions, and at the complexity, but also grateful that they have intuited these rules without being taught even one of them. Nonetheless, it is very important to understand that, ironically, new learners of English can absolutely rely on native speakers, despite their lack of knowing the "rules," when they say, "You need to use 'the' here."

If you, as a new English language learner, are currently writing a paper and need a Band-Aid rather than full treatment, here is our emergency advice. For a full, more effective treatment, when the crisis is over, you can read the rules and do the exercises.

## The Key to Articles

The article you use depends on whether the noun is definite or indefinite.

- If you know its specific identity, the noun is definite.
- If you do not know its specific identity, the noun is indefinite.
- The first time a noun is mentioned, it is usually indefinite.
- The subsequent times, it is usually definite.

## Prescription

**Count nouns**

- Indefinite (first use): Use plural or "a."

- Definite (second use ): Use "the."

**Noncount nouns**

- Indefinite (first use): Do not use "a"or "an." Do not use plural. (Noncount nouns never use "a" or "an," and never form plurals.)

- Definite (second use): Use "the."

- When in doubt, ask a native speaker!

# Articles Rules

## *Definite Article, "the"*

1. **Use "the" if you want a single noun to mean a whole species or group.** [The cat is an independent, intelligent pet.]

2. **Use "the" before**
   - public institutions [the Macpherson Library, the Royal British Columbia Museum],
   - theatres [the Odeon, the Capital],
   - hotels [the Imperial, the Dominion], and
   - newspapers [*The Vancouver Sun*, *The Globe and Mail*].

3. **Use "the" before**
   - unique nouns [the sun],
   - superlatives [the best chocolate],
   - nouns modified by prepositional phrases [the University of Victoria, April 10, but the 10th of April,
   - nouns modified by participles [the finishing touches, the finished product], and
   - nouns made particular in context [She is the teacher I had last semester.].

4. **Use "the" before inventions.** [Who invented the cell telephone?]

5. **Use "the" before musical instruments.** [Kimiko plays the piano.]

6.  **Do not use "the" before**
    *   proper nouns if they are not definite [Easter],

    *   abstract nouns [intelligence],

    *   nouns behaving as abstract nouns [after school], or

    *   plural nouns [Computers are . . .].

        **Exception:** If proper nouns are used as modifiers, use the definite article before them. [the Christmas holidays, the Halloween decorations, the St. Valentine's Day surprise]

7.  **Do not use "the" before**
    *   geographical names of continents [North America],

    *   countries [China], cities [Paris],

    *   lakes [Huron],

    *   individual mountains [Mount Washington, Mount Fuji], or

    *   streets [Pandora, Main].

**Exceptions:**
*   continents [the Arctic, the Antarctic],

*   countries [the former USSR, the USA, the Dominican Republic, the British Isles, the Philippines, the Hawaiian Islands, the Bahamas, the Falklands, the Netherlands],

*   cities [the East End, the Hague, the Bronx],

*   rivers [the St. Lawrence, the Okanagan, the Yangtze],

*   seas [the Indian Ocean, the Mediterranean, the Baltic Sea]

*   mountain chains [the Rockies, the Himalayas],

*   canals [the Suez, the Panama],

*   deserts [the Gobi, the Kalahari], and

*   winds [the Mistral, the Sirocco].

*Indefinite Articles, "a" "an"*

1.  **Do use "a" ("an") before count nouns** [a desk, a cup of rice, an application].

2.  **Do use "a" ("an") the first time that you mention something, but use the definite article thereafter.** [I have a computer. The computer both saves and wastes time.]

    **Exceptions:** Something familiar in a cultural situation is used with the definite article, "the," even though it hasn't been mentioned before. [Please look for <u>the</u> mail. It wasn't there when I picked up <u>the</u> newspaper.]

3. **Do use "a" if you are making a generalization about a whole group or class of things.** [A cat is an independent animal. A car has become a necessity in rural communities.] This use is similar to that of rule #1 under Definite Articles.

4. **Do use "a" ("an") before class (broadly, noncount) nouns modified by adjectives.** [Light moves faster than sound, but A bright light hurts my eyes.] [You need experience, but I had an odd experience.]

5. **Do use "a" ("an") if you mean "a kind of."** [Sarah wants to try a wine she hasn't tried before. Help Joe choose a wine and a cheese to go with it.].

6. **Do not use "a" ("an") before**
   - plural nouns [news, schools],
   - noncount nouns [advice],
   - unique nouns [sun], or
   - superlatives [best writer].

## Exercise 19: Articles

Use "a", "an", "the", or nothing. Be prepared to say which rule you have used.

1. _____ Sahara desert is hot and dry.

2. _____ Ottawa is _____ capital of _____ Canada.

3. Tom was _____ bad boy.

4. Holly liked to investigate _____ nature.

5. _____ human beings are innovative.

6. _____ University of Saskatchewan has _____ beautiful campus.

7. Lee likes to go to _____ plays.

8. Yesterday I saw _____ cute puppy and _____ silly kitten. _____ kitten was washing _____ puppy's nose.

9. Ian always longed to climb _____ Himalayas.

10. Ian climbed _____ Mount Everest _____ last year.

## Exercise 20: Articles

Use "a", "an", "the", or nothing. Be prepared to say which rule you have used.

1. Darren was interested in _____ nature of wasps.

2. At _____ end of _____ paragraph, you should wrap it up.

3. _____ human race is varied and interesting.

4. From _____ Long Beach on _____ Vancouver Island on _____ Pacific coast, you can imagine you could swim to _____ Japan.

5. How do you plan to spend _____ Christmas?

6. "Have _____ good day," she growled.

7. She goes to _____ kindergarten.

8. Sheila Marshall is _____ happiest driver in Delia.

9. _____ answers written in _____ book are incorrect.

10. Did you see _____ moon on _____ Monday evening?

## Exercise 21: Articles

Use "a", "an", "the", or nothing. Be prepared to say which rule you have used.

1. I want to buy _____ red pen because _____ one I have is almost empty.

2. Tai studied _____ music of _____ 18th Century.

3. _____ best solution given came from _____ smallest boy.

4. _____ dog is a faithful and loving pet.

5. _____ Carleton University has _____ good journalism courses.

6. Have you memorized _____ ten provinces?

7. I have _____ good news for you.

8. Terry always jogs at _____ night.

9. Philip is going home during _____ summer holidays.

10. _____ Chinook is _____ warm wind which suddenly makes temperatures warm in _____ Alberta.

## Exercise 22: Articles

Use "a", "an", "the", or nothing. Be prepared to say which rule you have used.

1. _____ Laurentians are _____ beautiful mountains.

2. Mr. Lee is _____ teacher in _____ school where Ms. Thompson is _____ principal.

3. I have _____ glass of milk and _____ dozen cookies. Would you like to share _____ cookies?

4. Does Barbara read _____ Bible in _____ evening?

5. _____ United States is a neighbour of _____ Canada.

6. _____ Canadian North is largely uninhabited.

7. I finished _____ book you gave me _____ last week.

8. _____ computer is gaining wide acceptance.

9. Carol went fishing in _____ Fraser River and sailing on _____ Okanagan Lake last summer.

10. Dawn goes to _____ University of Calgary now, but she wants to get her Master's degree at _____ Harvard University.

## Exercise 23: Articles

Use "a", "an", "the", or nothing. Be prepared to say which rule you have used.

1. _____ history of France and _____ British history cannot be ignored by _____ students of _____ Canadian history.

2. Mary always does _____ homework after _____ dinner.

3. I want to buy _____ red ink.

4. Give him _____ homework that he missed about _____ Confucious.

5. I met him at _____ corner of _____ Portage and Main.

6. How did you spend _____ Easter break?

7. Sam made _____ overlapping magazines look neater.

8. We had afternoon tea at _____ Empress, then went to an early show at _____ Royal.

9. Sarah found similar articles in _____ *Macleans* and in _____ *Calgary Sun*.

10. _____ cookies are _____ easiest dessert to serve.

## Exercise 24: Articles

Use "a", "an", "the", or nothing. Be prepared to say which rule you have used.

1. Could we meet _____ Sunday after next?

2. Irene heard _____ bad news about her last exam.

3. I want _____ coffee with the maximum amount of caffeine.

4. Would you please turn off _____ radio.

5. The baby needs _____ nap.

6. When we go to _____ India, can we go by way of _____ Suez Canal?

7. _____ mice were a continuing problem in Elly's life.

8. When she is in Halifax, Stephanie always reads _____ *Chronicle Herald*.

9. Hong put _____ painted chair back in the living room.

10. He is _____ man who was tailgating me yesterday.

## Exercise 25: Articles

Use "a", "an", "the", or nothing. Be prepared to say which rule you have used.

1. Andrew was interested in finding _____ information about Kenya for his research paper in English 115.

2. Susan needs to get _____ advice about her courses for next year.

3. Ben has _____ good news.

4. Last night, Sam told me _____ good news about your ICBC claim.

5. _____ computer is helpful to us all.

6. _____ human beings have some very strange habits.

7. Is your friend interested in _____ co-op programme at _____ UVic?

8. Get me _____ information in the calendar about how to register.

9. _____ computers are very helpful on campus.

10. _____ computers in A wing of the Saxon Building are all Macs.

## Exercise 26: Articles

Use "a", "an", "the", or nothing. Be prepared to say which rule you have used.

1. _____ Waterloo University has lots of co-op programmes.

2. Many of _____ co-op programmes at _____ University of Waterloo are in sciences.

3. _____ advice that Ben gave me about running was helpful.

4. _____ cat that followed me home yesterday had a collar.

5. Where is _____ newspaper section with _____ comics?

6. I want to see _____ movie about David Helfgott, *Shine*.

7. Would you lend me your notes on _____ math?

8. _____ Chemistry exam is on December 12.

9. I went to the McDonalds on the corner of _____ Pandora and _____ Vancouver.

10. Her son planned to attend _____ University of Montreal.

# Countability

## Countable and Uncountable Nouns

Whether a word is countable seldom concerns native speakers of English unless they are corrected when one of them says something like "I would like less green peppers and less anchovies on my pizza than on my sister's." A grammar-conscious server might repeat the order this way: "Two Petite Palate Pleaser Pizzas to go. One with fewer green peppers and fewer anchovies." To the server, the fact that you can count anchovies is important.

People who learn English as an additional language find more challenges than those concerning "few" and "less." For instance, no sooner do they identify "paper" on a quiz as uncountable than a teacher says, "Hand in your papers." Students see clearly that bricks and stones are countable, but they soon find out that fences are just made of brick or stone, not bricks and stones. Moreover, though a house is never made of woods, the living room floor may have a variety of woods, and the house may have a back gate leading to the woods. People painfully learn, too, that "clothes" and "clothing" mean the same thing, yet clothes always takes a plural verb, although you can never have one of them. Conversely, clothing is always singular. Clearly, the challenges in learning the intricacies of Countable and Uncountable nouns are so numerous as to be almost uncountable.

---

## NONCOUNT NOUNS

**Some of the Most Common Non-count Nouns**

| | |
|---|---|
| air | knowledge |
| advice | laundry |
| change (money) | luggage/baggage |
| clothing | machinery |
| equipment | music |
| furniture | news |
| garbage | pop |
| guidance | popcorn |
| hardware | research |
| help/assistance | software |
| homework | stuff |
| housework | traffic |
| information | transportation |
| intelligence | vocabulary |
| jewellery | weather |
| junk | work |

---

## Exercise 27: Uncountable Nouns

Here is a short paragraph that incorporates seven of the common non-count nouns listed above. Underline the uncountable nouns with one line and underline the verbs connected to them with a double line.

The advice that her friends gave her was ignored. The information that she heard on the radio and television was dismissed. Despite the blizzard, Sandra decided to try to drive to work. Proper clothing was a concern, for the weather was definitely windy, and she needed to get the two feet of snow off her car. Once out of the driveway, she was sure that heavy traffic was not going to be a problem. The whole world was white and silent.

---

### Activity 8: Uncountable nouns

Write a short paragraph of 75–100 words that incorporates five of the common non-count nouns from the list. Underline the uncountable nouns with one line and underline the verbs connected to them with a double line.

---

Some words, frequently food items, like those in the following table are usually noncount, but are countable if you mean "different kinds of them." Usually, the non-countable meaning is "general," while the countable is "specific."

One would write that "Tea is a delightful beverage, and the teas in Murchies are many and varied," or "We had snow last night. The snows in the latter part of this decade have been much heavier than we are used to." Here are some words that are used in this countable or uncountable way.

## COUNTABLE/UNCOUNTABLE NOUNS

| | |
|---|---|
| bread | paper |
| cheese | pop |
| coffee | popcorn |
| flour | rain/snow/hail |
| food | sherry |
| gas | stone |
| ink | sugar |
| meat | tea |
| milk | wine |
| money | wood |

## Activity 9: Uncountable nouns

Write a short paragraph of 75–100 words concerning a picnic, and incorporate five of the usually noncount nouns from the above list.

Remember that, if you mean "different kinds of them," you can make these words plural. Underline the nouns you have selected with one line, and underline the verbs connected to them with a double line.

## ABSTRACT UNCOUNTABLE NOUNS

Note that abstract concepts are often, but not invariably, expressed as non-countable nouns. Here are a few examples.

| | |
|---|---|
| love | work |
| pleasure | beauty |
| pressure | campaign |
| sleep | courage |
| empathy | damage |
| stress | happiness |

Similar to the words in the "Countable/Uncountable" list above, this list of abstract nouns is usually uncountable, but countable if you mean "different kinds of them." Usually, the noncountable meaning is "general," while the countable is "specific." You may, for example, meet the one and only (specific) love of your life this year. We, however, have all known people who have had many "loves" (general). In a like manner, some of us may readily admit to "fear" of heights (specific), but if someone pushes the point, we may admit to many other "fears" (general). Similarly, if we are involved in an accident, we may worry about the "damage" (specific) to our car or bicycle. If, however, we had to go to court, our lawyer might well talk about "damages" (general). Then, because of "pressures," "stresses," and "strains" (general), we might say that we could count on just one hand the few good "sleeps" (general) that we had in the two months before we found out that we had won our case.

Parents are countable, but many people just have two. "Family" is generally regarded as uncountable, so you would say "My whole family—three brothers, two sisters, my parents and my grandparents—is coming to visit me at mid-term." You can, of course, take your family to meet the "families" of your friends, so "family" fits into the Un/countable abstract nouns. As you would with other collective nouns that are regarded as acting as a unit, if the family members act as individuals rather than as a group, you will use a plural verb: "My family **are** going to vacation separately this year." (See Agreement on pages 110–113)

"Work" has its own quirks. You can see "works of art" in a gallery, and if you mean the whole creative output of an artist, musician, or writer, you can speak of "works." Nonetheless, even though you go to college full-time and hold down two part-time jobs, you can never talk about your "works." Moreover, if you have homework in Biology, Math, and Computer Science as well as in English, you still cannot ever have "homeworks;" however, you can celebrate if you finish your homework with "fireworks." Still another useable "works" means a factory: a glassworks, ironworks. Checking with native-born English speakers about whether an abstract term should be countable in your sentence is a good idea. In their absence, your dictionary is your greatest friend, and even Spell Check will question your use of "homeworks."

---

**Activity 10: Uncountable abstract nouns**

Write brief (fewer than 25 words) definitions for three of the abstract terms listed on the previous page.

---

## Countable People

It is strange, but true, that not all nationalities are equal when it comes to countability. People whose nationality ends with an "ian," or an "i," can be counted, but people whose nationalities end with "ese," "ch," "ish," or "sh" cannot. This means, then, that you can have a joke that begins, "There were two Iraqis sitting in a bar, and in came a Canadian ...," but you cannot say "There were two Frenchs sitting in a bar, and in came a Danish...." Here is a partial list of people you can count and those you cannot. Please add to it.

| Countable | | Uncountable |
|---|---|---|
| (South, North) American | Iraqi | British |
| Asian | Italian | Chinese |
| Australian | Korean | Danish |
| Belgian | Malaysian | Dutch |
| Bosnian | New Zealander | Finnish |
| Brazilian | Norwegian | French |
| Bulgarian | Pakistani | Irish |
| Canadian | Persian | Japanese |
| Chilean | Peruvian | Polish |
| Colombian | Puerto Rican | Scottish |
| Dane | Russian | Spanish |
| Egyptian | Rwandan | Swedish |
| German | Scot | Turkish |
| Hawaiian | Somali | Vietnamese |
| Hungarian | South African | Welsh |
| Indian | Thai | |
| Indonesian | Tibetan | |
| Iranian | Zambian | |

## Determining Countability

There are some words whose use depends on your knowing whether a word is countable or not. "Number," for example, will always be followed by a countable noun while "amount" will always be followed by an uncountable noun. "Few" and "fewer" are used with countable nouns; however, "less" is used with uncountable nouns. You may, however, have noticed that many grocery stores ignore this fact in the signs indicating their express lanes: often "Nine items or less" is the lineup you'll have to choose.

Use the following charts to help you choose the correct words to use.

## Exercise 28: Words that Signal Countablity

Choose words from the first column above to make these sentences correct.

1. Unfortunately, Yasu had _____ problems with his car.

2. Andrew wanted to have _____ raisins for his cereal.

3. I want to have _____ perennials because I prefer annuals.

## NUMBER/FEW/A FEW/FEWER/AND MANY

**Use these words with countable nouns**

| | |
|---|---|
| number | You have a *number* of books, pens, chairs, lights, groceries, pictures, cars, cats, carrots, commas. |
| few | Use *few* if you mean *not many*. Fortunately, he made *few* mistakes. She has *few* close friends because she just moved here in September. |
| a few | Use a *few* when you mean some. I have a *few* candies left. Terry had *a few* friends over after the concert. |
| fewer | You have *tewer* books, pens, chairs, lights, groceries, pictures, cars, cats, carrots, commas. |
| many | You have *many* books, pens, chairs, lights, groceries, pictures, cars, cats, carrots, commas. |

## AMOUNT/LITTLE/A LITTLE/LESS/A GREAT DEAL/MUCH/ANY

**Use these words with uncountable nouns**

| | |
|---|---|
| amount | You have an *amount* of advice, knowledge, information, furniture, garbage, stuff, or equipment. |
| little | Use *little* when you mean <u>not much</u>. I have *little* time to finish. Because she studied hard, Pat had *little* problem with the mid-term. |
| a little | Use *a little* when you mean some. I'm glad I have <u>*a little*</u> money. She had <u>*a little*</u> trouble finding it. |
| less | You have *less* advice, knowledge, information, furniture, garbage, stuff, or equipment. |
| a great deal of | You have <u>*a great deal*</u> of advice, knowledge, information, furniture, garbage, stuff, or equipment. |
| much and any (in negative statements) | Use *much* and *any* with non-countable nouns in negative statements, *but not in positive*: I don't have *much* advice. Sarah cannot find *any* information. |

4. Grace was happy to make _____ mistakes in agreement.

5. You can't take _____ suitcases.

Make sure that when you make a positive statement about a non-countable noun, like these below, that you do not use "much" or "any."

✓ Joe has a lot of stuff.

✓ Sarah found lots of information.

✓ Jane will buy a great deal of equipment.

We are giving you this rule about not using "much" or "any" in positive statements because that way you will always be right. Nonetheless, we know that we ourselves have said things such as "Sean has much experience in programming." There seems to be a grey area here, but just follow the rule and be safe.

## Exercise 29: Words that Signal Countablity

Choose words from the first column in the previous table to make these sentences correct.

1. Please give me the same _____ of milk.

2. Sammy has _____ furniture in his basement.

3. Where can Kim find _____ privacy?

4. He hasn't got _____ money for frivolous things.

5. When I get back, I want to see _____ garbage lying around.

## Flexible Words: All/A Lot/Lots/Scads/Most of/Some of

Some words don't signal countability, so you can use them freely with either countable or uncountable nouns.

- You can have <u>lots of</u> information or <u>lots of</u> facts.

- You can have <u>a lot of</u> knowledge or <u>a lot</u> of books.

- You can have <u>scads</u> of money or <u>scads</u> of friends.

- You can have <u>most of</u> the furniture and <u>most of</u> the appliances.

- You can have <u>some of</u> the beer and <u>some of</u> the peanuts.

Countability, whether you are writing an essay or standing in a supermarket lineup, concerns both native and new learners of English.

## Exercise 30: Articles and Non-Count Nouns

Unlike singular count nouns, non-count nouns do not use the article "a" or "an." In the following sentences, you must decide which nouns are count nouns and which are non-count nouns; then, where necessary, use "a" or "an" to fill in the blanks. Do not use "the" in this exercise.

1.  Did Maria buy _____ bottle of milk this morning?

2.  The teacher assigned _____ homework to be done for tomorrow.

3.  Lucy took _____ sandwich and _____ fruit in her lunch today.

4.  Claudia asked her mother for _____ advice.

5.  For graduation, Mark received _____ jewellery, _____ CD player, and _____ piece of luggage.

6.  The boys were standing outside the 7-Eleven when _____ violence broke out.

7.  We must arrange _____ transportation for our vacation.

8.  Jeff asked the waiter for _____ ketchup and _____ serviette.

9.  Do you enjoy _____ wine with your meals, or do you prefer _____ glass of water?

10. The researcher went to the archives to try to find _____ information on the origins of the old building.

## Exercise 31: Articles and Non-Count Nouns

Unlike singular count nouns, non-count nouns do not use the article "a" or "an." In the following sentences, you must decide which nouns are count nouns and which are non-count nouns; then, where necessary, use "a" or "an" to fill in the blanks. Do not use "the" in this exercise.

1.  Jean's mother says if he refuses to eat _____ spinach for his supper, he cannot have _____ piece of cake because she thinks he would eat nothing but junk food if she would let him.

2.  Lindsey just completed _____ new painting of _____ scenery.

3.  Although Mr. Archibald took his complaint to small claims court, he could not get _____ satisfaction.

4.  We studied _____ poetry in class today, and then we had to write _____ poem.

5.  The bakery will purchase _____ equipment for cooling cakes quickly.

6.  There was _____ news tonight about _____ robbery in our neighbourhood.

7. On Friday on the radio, I heard _____ weather report that said the sun would shine all weekend, but then we had _____ awful weather all day Saturday.

8. In order to start making paintings that depicted the effects of industry on our world, the art students studied _____ machinery for two weeks.

9. Ling, who usually paints pictures of rural scenes, gained _____ confidence, so she tackled _____ painting of _____ cityscape.

10. Masa was surprised to find that _____ traffic was _____ problem in Dryden.

## Exercise 32: Countable and Non-Countable Nouns

Choose the appropriate word from the brackets to fill in the space.

1. My teacher often gave me _____ . (advice, advices)

2. When Lise opened the door, all the _____ tumbled out. (equipment, equipments)

3. When Bonnie saw all the _____ she started to laugh. (junk, junks)

4. On the field trip, they visited many factories and saw a lot of _____. (machinery, machineries)

5. At the smorgasbord, Ling and Mary tried _____ from many different countries. (food, foods)

6. One of the best things about movies is the smell of all the _____. (popcorn, popcorns)

7. Tom had to check his _____ right away. (luggage, luggages)

8. The _____ from her Biology, Physics, and Chemistry courses really helped Penny in her summer job. (knowledge, knowledges)

9. Steven thanked his advisor for all his _____ during the past three years. (help, helps)

10. The room looked bare without all the _____ in it. (furniture, furnitures)

## Exercise 33: Countable and Non-Countable Nouns

Choose the appropriate word from the brackets to fill in the space.

1. Joe had a hard time getting all his _____ into his _____ (stuff, stuffs) (luggage, luggages)

2.  Kim was very interested in the development of _____. (software, softwares)

3.  After Lesley received all the _____ about the _____, she went straight home. (information, informations) (homework, homeworks)

4.  If you tune into the campus radio station, you are sure to hear some of the newest _____. (music, musics)

5.  Sarah bought many different coloured _____. (ink, inks)

6.  The _____ on the long weekend made the trip to the ferry very tedious! (traffic, traffics)

7.  Reading magazines was the way Raina used to increase her _____. (vocabulary, vocabularies)

8.  After doing _____, Terry thought doing _____ was a bit of a break. (homework, homeworks) (housework, houseworks)

9.  Please help me pick up all the _____ that the dogs got into. (garbage, garbages)

10. The _____ would be improved if the schedules were changed to avoid rush hour. (transportation, transportations)

## Exercise 34: Variable Countable and Non-Countable Nouns

Using one of the bracketed words, fill in the following blanks in order to make the sentence correct.

1.  Barbara has gone off to the bakery to buy a variety of _____ for the buffet. (bread, breads)

2.  How can we choose from among all the red _____ that Phillipe told us about? (wine, wines)

3.  At the deli, we found _____ from sixteen countries. (cheese, cheeses)

4.  Andrea liked making _____ on cold winter days. (bread, breads)

5.  Her very favourite _____ contains three _____. (bread, breads) (flour, flours)

6.  Simon learned a lot about the properties of _____ in Chemistry. (gas, gases)

7.  Downtown, it seems that every block has a shop selling exotic _____. (coffee, coffees)

8.  Daphne puts too much _____ in her tea. (sugar, sugars)

9. The natural _____ in fruit seldom need much enhancement. (sugar, sugars)

10. _____ and _____ and an apple makes a fast lunch when Myra is in a hurry. (bread, breads) (cheese, cheeses)

## Exercise 35: Indefinite Nouns

Some of the nouns in the following two paragraphs do not become definite even though they are repeated several times. Be alert for indefinite nouns as you decide whether to use an article to complete each sentence.

1. There are many reasons why _____ people criticize others who watch television. They think that if _____ people spend too much time watching television, they may become lazier and lazier. _____ television has a lulling effect on _____ people. It acts like an opiate, taking _____ person's mind off other things like work, study, or goals. Sometimes, _____ people use television to calm their nerves or to make them forget that they are unhappy. By identifying with the characters on television, _____ person can cling to _____ false impression that everything is okay and he or she is part of _____ big happy family. Still another person may watch _____ television for quite another reason: he or she cannot help but feel superior to the dysfunctional characters on the screen.

2. Louisa thoroughly enjoys _____ movies. She went to _____ movie on the weekend. _____ movie was about a group of people who went on a holiday together and became entangled in a series of crimes because of their naïveté. That type of movie is Louisa's favourite. She says _____ movies like that provide her with an escape whereas _____ movies about relationships leave her tired from worrying about the characters. She doesn't like art movies either because _____ movies with slow plots leave her bored. As a result of her taste in _____ movies, Louisa says few of her friends will go with her to _____ movie. They say that _____ movies Louisa enjoys are a waste of time. Louisa says that's not true. Even silly movies often give you something to think about. In fact, Louisa claims, you can learn a lot from _____ movies.

# Clues for Recognizing Nouns and Adjectives

Although there are, of course, "exceptions to the rule," you will find it helpful to know that certain word endings signal whether a word is a noun or an adjective.

## Exercise 36: Distinguishing nouns and adjectives

Identify these words as nouns or adjectives by putting N or A in the box.

| | | | |
|---|---|---|---|
| mountain | ☐ | impressive | ☐ |
| picky | ☐ | imaginary | ☐ |
| independent | ☐ | panic | ☐ |
| spectacle | ☐ | tragic | ☐ |
| effusive | ☐ | dominant | ☐ |
| extravagance | ☐ | gradual | ☐ |
| astonished | ☐ | certain | ☐ |
| pushy | ☐ | memorable | ☐ |
| excitement | ☐ | ticklish | ☐ |
| vibrant | ☐ | concealment | ☐ |
| confidence | ☐ | dubious | ☐ |
| surprising | ☐ | questionable | ☐ |
| wakeful | ☐ | finicky | ☐ |
| concentration | ☐ | dependent | ☐ |
| panelling | ☐ | indelible | ☐ |
| mistaken | ☐ | freedom | ☐ |
| insurance | ☐ | friendly | ☐ |
| effective | ☐ | various | ☐ |
| economic | ☐ | creamy | ☐ |
| comfortable | ☐ | drainage | ☐ |
| fussy | ☐ | forcible | ☐ |
| bother | ☐ | refusal | ☐ |
| attractive | ☐ | similarly | ☐ |
| serious | ☐ | impression | ☐ |
| friendship | ☐ | ability | ☐ |

**Adjective or Noun?**

Before you do the following exercise, notice the ways in which the underlined words below are used. You can differentiate between the noun and the adjective forms of the words by noticing their endings.

A microwave oven is a <u>convenience</u> that I would not want to be without.

A microwave oven is <u>convenient</u> if you don't like to cook.

I have complete <u>confidence</u> that you will do the job well.

I am <u>confident</u> that you will do the job well.

Stan's <u>dependence</u> on his parents for support was uncomfortable for him.

Stan did not like to be <u>dependent</u> on his parents for support.

There is a lot of <u>violence</u> in *Pulp Fiction*.

*Pulp Fiction* is a <u>violent</u> movie.

## Exercise 37: Adjective or Noun?

Fill in the blank in each sentence with the appropriate form of the word in parentheses.

1.  (violent, violence) I think TV has altogether too much _____ .

2.  (confident, confidence) If _____ in the government fails, the government will fall.

3.  (dependent, dependence) I'd hate to be _____ on someone else for my living expenses.

4.  (competent, competence) If Frank were not so _____, the job would never have been completed on time.

5.  (persistent, persistence) Thanks to the committee's _____, every detail was taken care of, and the convention ran as smoothly as silk.

6.  (violent, violence) How do you think parents should handle children who behave in a _____ manner?

7.  (decadent, decadence) Her grandmother said that the awful behaviour of the characters on the soap operas was nothing short of _____.

8.  (confident, confidence) Do you think of yourself as a _____ person?

9.  (convenient, convenience) Having the cafeteria in a different building from the dorms is not at all _____.

10. (confident, confidence)  I wish I had Joan's _____.

ESL speakers should come back to this chapter often, reviewing the parts of speech, the article rules and the exercises. Intensive concentration now can lead to a most desirable payoff, that in years to come they will join their native-born English speaking peers in not knowing any rules but seldom making mistakes.

# 2

# *Verbs and Voice*

## Learning Outcomes

***This Chapter will help you to***

- recognize and use the form and functions of different tenses.

- understand the concept of voice.

- use verb tenses and moods precisely.

- use active and passive voice appropriately.

Any of you who have learned even a handful of survival phrases in a new language in order to travel know that verbs are at the heart of sentences. "Eat" or "comer" or "makan" is often enough to communicate to a stranger that you are looking for something to fill your stomach. "Sleep," or "dormir," or "tidur" may be enough to get you a bed for the night. When a person speaks a foreign language, he or she soon learns the importance of verbs. Therefore, students of English as an additional language rarely have to be convinced of the value of studying verbs.

In contrast, many native speakers cannot recognize a verb in a sentence. Moreover, some cannot see the point in learning to do so. Luckily, those who have a gift for language rarely need to pick out a verb, but those who make sentence errors and wish to eliminate them, or those who want to increase the precision of their language need to focus on verbs. Writers who make **sentence fragment** or **comma splice errors**, for example, can learn to eliminate them by first becoming adept at recognizing verbs.

While native speakers rarely make glaring errors in their use of tense, their use of both tense and voice is frequently imprecise. Many native speakers, for example, overuse **modals**. Instead of "A seasoned hiker takes her feet very seriously," they write, "A seasoned hiker may take her feet very seriously." The former statement is more decisive. The second one waffles. Nuances of meaning such as these affect the precision of a piece of writing.

This chapter describes the form and usage of the most common English tenses and provides exercises and activities that are broad enough in their scope to allow students to tailor their focus, concentrating on form and accuracy of usage or on subtleties of expression, depending upon what is needed.

We begin the chapter with present tenses of verbs and move on to past tense and then to voice. Verbs are the only parts of speech that change tense, so learning about tense is a foolproof method of learning to recognize verbs.

# Verbs

## Tense

### Present Indicative

*Formation*

The present indicative or simple present form of the verb has only one word in it. In almost all cases, that word is formed from the bare infinitive of the verb. It is very important to note that with third person singular (he, she, or it), the present indicative tense of the verb ends in "s."

The following are examples of the Present Indicative:

| | |
|---|---|
| I play | they follow |
| we sail | Seang works |
| we agree | you succeed |
| Kelly asks | she dances |
| they grumble | I laugh |

The verb "to be," which is irregular, is a special case, formed as follows:

| | |
|---|---|
| I am | we are |
| you are | they are |
| he / she is | |

## *Usage*

1. The present indicative describes an action or state of being that happens on an ongoing basis. If you can use the words "often," "always," "usually," or "in general" with the verb, the appropriate tense is probably present indicative.

   Examples:

   My classes (always) start at 9:00 am.

   Summers here are (usually) warm and sunny.

   People who are athletic (generally) enjoy outdoor activities.

2. The present indicative can be used to describe a condition or set of conditions.

   Examples:

   **When traffic is heavy**, tempers flare.

   **After students write an exam**, they often feel physically as well as mentally tired.

   **Since your car needs a tune-up**, we will drive mine.

3. The present indicative can suggest the future. Students whose first language is French need to pay particular attention to this usage.

   Examples:

   **When I win the lottery**, I will treat you to a vacation.

   **If you accept the job**, you will be working in the same office as I.

   **We have** a practice tomorrow.

4. Present indicative can be used in the place of present progressive to create an immediacy, even suspense, especially when it describes a series of ongoing events. The following is an example:

**Cold Beads of Sweat**

A sinister man in a trench coat **enters** a building on the ground floor, **walks** across the lobby to the elevator, **presses** the button for the penthouse, and **waits**. Seconds tick by as the red floor indicator light **indicates** the slow passage of the elevator between floors. The desk clerk **busies** himself behind the counter as usual. He **gives** no outward show of being tense or more than usually alert. However, if an observer were astute, she might notice that the clerk repeatedly **snatches** glances in the direction of the manager's office and that his colour has blanched. His lips **are** almost white and beads of cold perspiration have begun to glisten on his forehead.

### Activity 1: Present indicative

Using the above paragraph as a model, write a paragraph of your own on one of the following topics. Most of the verbs in the paragraph will use the present indicative tense.

a. Describe an average day in the life of a custodian in the House of Horrors in a wax museum.

b. Describe a student's adventures on the first day of school.

c. Describe lottery winner Joan Smith's preparations for an exotic vacation or for her final encounter with her boss.

### Activity 2: Writing suspense fiction

Reread "Cold Beads of Sweat." Notice the somewhat unusual use of present indicative in that passage. Using the passage as a model, write the first paragraph of your own who-dun-it.

**Possible settings:**

a. Night time at a bank machine: a lone person is withdrawing money.

b. Winter, on the deck of a ship deep in a fjord somewhere in Canada's north: the deck is covered with a thin film of snow, and a single set of footprints crosses it.

c. At home alone on a November night: the door creaks open.

d. Hiking the Bruce Trail on a hot summer day, thunderheads build, threatening a storm.

## Present Historic

Academic essays primarily use the present indicative tense to talk about literary works. In those cases, the tense is called present historic. Students, too, are expected to use the present historic to write essays about literature. The following is an example:

> Jane Newby's novel, *Cold Beads of Sweat*, **opens** with a scene that is typical of a who-dun-it. In the first pages of the book, "a sinister man in a trench coat **enters** a building on the ground floor, **walks** across the lobby to the elevator, **presses** the button for the penthouse, and **waits**." Oddly, despite the conventional nature of the text at that point, the reader **feels** genuine suspense mount as Newby **stretches** time, and seconds **tick** by. She **describes** the details of the scene: the red, floor indicator light, which **records** the slow passage of the elevator between floors; the desk clerk, who **busies** himself behind the counter. Though the clerk **gives** no outward show of being more than usually alert, Newby subtly **establishes** in the reader an awareness that the clerk repeatedly **snatches** glances in the direction of the manager's office and that his colour has blanched. Though Newby **doesn't dwell** on the clerk's appearance, the reader **is** left with a strong memory that the man's "lips **are** almost white and beads of cold perspiration have begun to glisten on his forehead."

### Activity 3: Academic writing

Imagine that the who-dun-it you just wrote is now being studied in literature classes across the country. Using the above paragraph as a model, write a short analytical composition about your own who-dun-it. This exercise gives you an opportunity to examine closely the techniques you have used to make your fiction suspenseful. Remember, the analysis will primarily use the present indicative tense. When referring to yourself, use either your complete name or your family name only and the pronoun "he" or "she."

Writing the analytical composition may lead you to decide that you would like to make some revisions to your who-dun-it before you continue to the next exercise.

### Activity 4: Analysing what you've learned

Exchange your who-dun-it with that of someone else in the class, preferably someone whose writing you do not know well. You are more likely to have some interesting surprises that way.

Write an analysis of your peer's fiction, once again using the present historic tense. Take particular notice of good verbs and concrete details that your peer used to achieve suspense. Also, watch for techniques that you might be able to use to improve your own who-dun-it.

### Activity 5: Analysing what you've learned

1. Working with the person whose fiction you analysed, quickly decide which of you will be the Critic and which the Author for the first half of this exercise. Once the decision is made, the Critic should read aloud the Author's who-dun-it and then the Critic's own analysis of it. Then complete the following questions.

   a. Question for the author of the who-dun-it:
   What did I learn about my who-dun-it from hearing my partner's analysis?

   b. Question for the author of the analysis:
   From reading it aloud, what have I learned about my analysis? For example, does it have a clear focus? Is it well organized? Does it read smoothly? Does it need more or better transitions?

   c. Question for both of you working together:
   Are the tenses correct and consistent in both the fiction and the analysis? If not, discuss necessary changes.

2. Switch roles and repeat the process.

3. Now make any revisions that you would like to the who-dun-its and the analyses.

### Activity 6: Summarizing your knowledge

Without refering to the text, summarize what you know about the formation of the present indicative tense, its usage, and its effects. If you are unable to summarize this information clearly, chances are that you still need clarification of some aspect of the present indicative form of the verb.

## Present Progressive

*Formation*

The present progressive form of the verb has two words in it, the present of the verb "to be," and the present participle of the main verb.

The following are examples of the present progressive:

| | | |
|---|---|---|
| I am playing | Kelly is asking | They are following |
| We are sailing | They are grumbling | Seang is working |
| You are succeeding | I am thinking | She is dancing |

The verb "to be" is no exception.

I **am being** admitted to the bar tomorrow.

The dog **is being** a nuisance.

*Usage*

1. The present progressive tense expresses an action or state of being that is in progress right now. It focuses on the present moment, rather than leaving a more general sense of time.

   Examples:

   I am eating my supper (right now).

   Jean's business is growing by leaps and bounds.

   I am feeling lucky (tonight).

2. Some verbs are almost never used in the present progressive tense. For second language learners of Asian backgrounds, the following verbs are worth memorizing as examples that DO NOT form present progressive.

   | | |
   |---|---|
   | **appear:** | It ~~is appearing~~ that he is arriving. |
   | **believe:** | I ~~am believing~~ you. |
   | **belong:** | My niece ~~is belonging~~ to your choir. |
   | **contain:** | This book is ~~containing~~ all the information you need. |
   | **hear:** | ~~I am hearing~~ an odd noise. |
   | **know:** | ~~Are you knowing~~ the answer? |
   | **like:** | She ~~is liking~~ him very much. |
   | **love:** | She ~~is loving~~ him very much. |
   | **need:** | ~~Are you needing~~ any help with your assignment? |
   | **taste:** | This pie ~~is tasting~~ delicious. |
   | **think** (when it is transitive): | ~~I am thinking~~ that you look very nice. |
   | **understand:** | I do not think you ~~are understanding~~ the question. |
   | **want:** | This boy ~~is wanting~~ to go to the movie. |

## Past Indicative

*Formation*

The past indicative or simple past form of the verb has only one word in it. Usually, the past indicative is formed by adding "ed" to the root of the verb. If a new verb, for example, enters English, this is the way we will form the past indicative. Think, for instance, of "spell-checked" and "bolded."

The following are examples of the past indicative:

| | |
|---|---|
| I play**ed** | They follow**ed** |
| We sail**ed** | Seang work**ed** |
| We agre**ed** | You succeed**ed** |
| Kelly ask**ed** | She danc**ed** |
| They grumbl**ed** | I laugh**ed** |

Some verbs form the past indicative or simple past form of the verb in irregular ways.

The following are examples. For a more complete list, see pages 103–107.

| | |
|---|---|
| Joe **did** | It **fell** |
| You **went** | Koji **ran** |
| Jakob **put** | We **thought** |
| They **sang** | Mandy **took** |
| The cat **drank** | He **was** |

## Usage

1.  The past indicative normally describes an event that took place at a specific point in time in the past. The point in time may be specified in words, implied by context, or suggested by words such as "just" or "recently."

    Examples:

    I **baked** a cake this morning.

    The cake **was** delicious.

    We **went** to Banff last summer.

    I just **saw** a man riding a tricycle down the corridor.

2.  The past indicative usually describes an event that is over and done with.

    Examples:

    When I **was** a kid, I **loved** ketchup sandwiches.

    Penelope **had** a very unhappy weekend, but she is happy now.

    The blanket of snow **covered** the scarred road.

3.  The past indicative is used when the passage of time is not important.

Examples:

We **won**!

The sun **shone**.

The leaves **fell**.

Note that the use of the past indicative tense is very common in narrative writing. Ethel Wilson's short story, "Fog," for example, begins "For seven days fog settled down upon Vancouver. It crept in from the ocean, advancing in its mysterious way in billowing banks which swallowed up the land."

### Activity 7: Present indicative to past indicative

Rewrite the following passage, changing present tense to past.

Lying on her side in the noonday sun, the kitten seems like a small grey pool, serene and motionless. Suddenly, though, her gold-green eyes blink open, and she yawns twice, showing her delicate pink tongue. Thoroughly awake now, she begins to tidy herself up. When she washes herself with that suddenly functional tongue, she begins with the back of her right paw. When it feels right, she raises that paw to wash the left side of her face, reaching the paw up and pulling it down toward her mouth. The paw goes right over her ear, turning it almost inside out. After half a dozen swipes at the left side of her face, she starts on her sleek grey body, not just licking, but nuzzling hard with her sharp teeth and pulling as though she finds huge tangles in her inch-long fur. Then she repeats the process on the left side, screwing her eyes shut in concentration. Finally, she pushes herself to a sitting position, and after attending to the right side of her face, does her best to wash under her chin. Every so often her tongue catches on her flea collar, and she looks momentarily puzzled. Back down she falls, raising her right hind leg high in the air and turning so that her tawny, apparently very dirty stomach is revealed. She attacks it vigorously. She then takes the last few long swipes at her tail, and the bath is done.

### Activity 8: Past indicative

Write a paragraph that makes use of the past indicative tense. If tense is easy for you, focus on your selection of verbs. Find verbs that work hard on their own, describing actions in concrete and specific ways.

**Suggested topics:**

- Your first day at high school/university/your job

- The first time you drove a car/a motorcycle/a bicycle /an airplane

- The first time you used chopsticks/a knife and fork/a weed-eater/a chain-saw

## Present Perfect

*Formation*

The present perfect is formed by using the present tense of the verb "to have" and the past participle of the verb in question. The past participle usually ends in "ed," though not in the case of irregular verbs.

The following are some examples of regular verbs in present perfect:

| | |
|---|---|
| I **have** play**ed** | They **have** follow**ed** |
| We **have** sail**ed** | Seang **has** work**ed** |
| We **have** agre**ed** | You **have** succeed**ed** |
| Kelly **has** ask**ed** | She **has** danc**ed** |
| They **have** grumbl**ed** | I **have** laugh**ed** |

The following are some examples of irregular verbs in present perfect:

| | |
|---|---|
| Joe **has done** | It **has fallen** |
| You **have gone** | Koji **has run** |
| Jakob **has put** | We **have thought** |
| They **have sung** | Mandy **has taken** |
| The cat **has drunk** | He **has been** |

*Usage*

1.  The present perfect tense is used most commonly to describe events that took place in the past but for which no time or date can be specified.

    Examples:

    According to the newsletter, the housing committee **has decided** to increase the rents.

    **Has** your tiger **eaten** yet?

    Our team **has improved** a great deal since last year.

2.  The present perfect tense can be used to describe an action taking place over a period of time if the action extends to the present.

    Examples:

    Kim **has lived** in Victoria for three years.

    I **have worked** since eight o'clock this morning.

    Ling **has been** on the phone for twenty minutes.

3. Occasionally, the present perfect tense can indicate the future.

Examples:

When you **have finished** your homework, you can watch TV.

They will, of course, return the video after they **have watched** it.

When Sarah **has made** tea, we can take a break.

4. Present perfect stresses the passage of time. As a result, the present perfect is often needed after the subordinate conjunction "since."

Examples:

He **has driven** that car for as long as I can remember.

We **have** finally **completed** the department review.

Since the new shipment arrived, we **have sold** almost twice as many Night Vision glasses as we expected.

## Exercise 1: Present Perfect Tense

If necessary, correct the following sentences that use the present perfect; be prepared to say why the sentence is correct or incorrect.

1. I have moved to Victoria six months ago.
2. Elaine has started her final essay last Monday.
3. The roof has been damaged by snow last night.
4. Because it has been frosty, the flowers look depressed.
5. Rolf has left home three years ago.
6. I have lived in Victoria for three years.
7. When Sean has completed the project, he can return your mice.
8. The snow has damaged the roof.
9. Jane has done her assignment for three days.
10. Has Tai written his exam?

## Exercise 2: Present Indicative, Past Indicative, or Present Perfect

The tense in most of the following sentences is incorrect. Name the verb tense used in each sentence, but make changes only where they are necessary.

1. Michelle is popular ever since she was a little girl.

2. The principal of the school taught mathematics until he retired.

3. After we have a party, we are always sleeping for at least 12 hours.

4. Gail is only 12, but she smokes for two years.

5. The woman I introduced you to used to be my old high school teacher. She has taught in Montreal until last year, when she has moved to Quebec City.

6. In Calgary, the famous Calgary Stampede is taking place every summer about the first week of July.

7. Right after breakfast this morning, the girls have gone down to the creek to fish.

8. My dentist is very committed to his patients. He is working six days a week without fail.

9. If the teacher asks for volunteers to build the stage sets, I would offer to make the mural.

10. Since the weather began to improve, we are going to the park every Saturday for a picnic.

## Exercise 3: Present Indicative, Past Indicative, or Present Perfect

Fill in the blanks with the appropriate tense.

1. Joe _____ (live) in the same house for ten years.

2. Jane _____ (be) neat her entire life. Her house _____ (be) always tidy.

3. Since they got married, Sean _____ (try) to become neater.

4. Last spring, Mrs. Norris _____ (give) the children's used winter clothes to her church.

5. Every spring for the last seven years, Mrs. Norris _____ (give) the children's used winter clothes to her church.

6. It _____ (be) more than two years since my cousin Louis _____ (come) to town.

7. Two and a half years ago, my cousin Louis _____ (be) here.

8. Young adults often _____ (appreciate) innovative music that their elders don't even know exists.

9. The young _____ (be) musical innovators for much of the twentieth century.

10. Over time the music of each new generation _____ (enter) the mainstream listened to by people of all ages.

## Exercise 4: Present Indicative, Past Indicative, or Present Perfect

Fill in the blanks with the appropriate tense.

1. Mary and her family are in a hurry tonight. As a result, when they sit down at the table, Mary's mum says to Mary, "When we _____ (finish) supper, would you mind doing the dishes and making a few sandwiches?"

2. When the new owner came to inspect the plant, Tom's boss introduced them, saying: "I'd like you to meet our floor manager, Tom Berwick. He _____ (work) here for 15 years."

3. My neighbour who has cancer _____ (undergo) ten radiation treatments. He still has eight to go.

4. My neighbour who had cancer _____ (undergo) eighteen radiation treatments before he was fully cured.

5. Since we first broadcast our radio show, we _____ (receive) over 200 letters of congratulations.

6. After our first broadcast, we _____ (receive) over 200 letters of congratulations.

7. My sister _____ (always be) neat and tidy whereas my brother _____ (be) messy and disorganized ever since he was a little boy.

8. On the other hand, my mother _____ (be) tidy and always _____ (to be).

9. I _____ (live) in that town for three years after graduation.

10. I _____ (live) in this town for three years, ever since I came to high school.

## Exercise 5: Present Indicative, Past Indicative, or Present Perfect

Fill in the blanks with the appropriate tense.

1. During the 1930s, Zora Neale Hurston_____ (write) five major works.

2. Almost immediately after Jennie graduated, she _____ (find) a job.

3. When the circus _____ (come) to town, there's so much traffic that it's faster to walk than to drive a car.

4. Did you know that polls _____ (reveal) that most people fear making oral presentations more than they fear death?

5. When you _____ (give) an oral presentation, you should remember that you _____ (have) interesting information that the audience would like to hear.

6. If you _____ (watch) your friends do presentations, you know that people generally _____ (do) better than they _____ (think) they have done.

7. Ralph Zapinsky _____ (be) in my room in grade ten at J. R. Helmiston High School, but since then he _____ (moved) seven times.

8. After the sun _____ (set), you can turn the lights on.

9. Dennis _____ (leave) school before ten o'clock yesterday.

10. Since Frank _____ (take) Tai Chi, he _____ (become) more flexible and coordinated.

## Activity 9: Present perfect, present indicative, or past indicative

Read the following paragraphs, taking note of the movement back and forth between the present indicative, past indicative and present perfect tenses.

Then write a short essay of about the same length (250 words) beginning with the sentence: *I have wanted to take up _____ for a long time.*

I **have wanted** to take up kayaking for a long time. I didn't do it in the past, because I couldn't afford to. Recently, however, I met a friend who has a kayak, and she allowed me to borrow it several times. The first time I used it, I spent the entire session just learning how to get into and out of the boat without tipping it. The second time, I felt much more confident, so I decided to paddle a little way up the coast.

What I saw really surprised me. From the vantage point of a kayak, the scenery is very different than it is from the shore. The land looks so much bigger—and wilder too.

Because the city **has grown** so much in the last few years, when I travel across town to go to a beach, I am completely unaware of the ruggedness of the terrain we live on. It seems as if someone **has paved** or **landscaped** every square inch of the land or covered it with some kind of structure. Even when I'm at the beach, I'm always aware of the apartment buildings only a few metres behind me and the traffic buzzing along the network of roads. However, from a kayak, a person can get some idea of what this land **must have looked** like many years ago. I'm very happy that I **have taken up** kayaking. It **has given** me a different perspective on the place where I live.

**Activity 10: More topics for practising present perfect**

Drawing on the knowledge you have gained in writing the previous essay, write another composition on one of the following topics. These topics will, once more, require that you make use of the present perfect in some sentences.

- Computers have changed the way we live.
- The changes that have occurred during the last century are more dramatic and widespread than any that have occurred before.
- Women's drive for equality has affected the way both women and men think about their lives.

## Exercise 6: More Paragraph Practice

Read the following paragraphs, taking note of the movement back and forth between the present indicative, past indicative and present perfect tenses. Identify the tense of each of the bolded verbs, and be prepared to explain the reason for each tense.

My life **has changed** (_____) dramatically in the past five years. Five years ago, my parents and I **moved** (_____) from Cornerbrook, on the west coast of Newfoundland, to the city of St. John's. At first, I **was** (_____) very unhappy. I **found** (_____) the city to be impersonal and too fast-paced. People **walked** (_____) by me on the street and didn't even look me in the eye. No one **seemed** (_____) to have the time or the inclination to stop and say hello. At school, I **didn't know** (_____) anyone and **didn't want** (_____) to. I **thought** (_____) all the other students **were** big city snobs who **didn't have** (_____) time for a country bumpkin like me. I hated all of them, and I really **hated** (_____) St. John's. I just **wanted** (_____) to go home.

Then I **met** (_____) Ti. What a friend! We **started** (_____) doing everything together. We **joined** (_____) the hiking club and the soccer team, so we met other people. As it turned out, there **were** (_____) actually quite a few people in our school who weren't snobs. I **was** (_____) just too shy to get to know them.

Ti and I **have been** (_____) inseparable for the past four years. Like me, Ti came from somewhere else, so right from the start, we understood each other because each of us **knows** (_____) what it feels like to be homesick and not to fit in. In our last year of high school, we applied to the same university. We even enrolled in some of the same classes. In the past five years, Ti and I **have gone** (_____) over some rough roads together, but we've **had** (_____) lots of good times along the way too.  Now we've **decided** (_____) that once we've **finished** (_____) university, we're going to travel for six months. I never would have had the nerve to do that before. It seems as if the world **has become** (_____) less intimidating in the past five years, but actually, I know that it's me that **has changed** (_____).

---

### Activity 11: Essay with present perfect

Write a short essay of about the same length (250–300 words) as the one above. Begin with the sentence: _____ *has changed dramatically in the past five years.*

---

## Present Perfect Progressive

### *Formation*

The present perfect progressive (also called present continuous) is formed from the present perfect of the verb "to be" plus the present participle of the verb in question. The following are some examples:

I **have been playing**

I **have been falling**

We **have been sailing**

Koji **has been running**

They **have been agreeing**

You **have been thinking**

Mandy **has been taking a course**

They **have been grumbling**

## Usage

The present perfect progressive (continuous) expresses an action that began in the past, has continued up to the present, and is probably still going on. It stresses the continuity of the action. When a person says, "I've been working here since last summer," she means she has worked continuously at this place.

As you already know, the present perfect tense, like the present perfect progressive, can be used to describe an action taking place over a period of time where the action extends to the present. In those cases, the present perfect and the present perfect progressive are interchangeable. For example, "I've worked here since last summer," and "I've been working here since last summer," have virtually identical meanings.

On the other hand, when the present perfect tense describes events that took place in the past but for which no time or date can be specified, or when it suggests the future, the present perfect progressive cannot take its place.

For example, in the following sentences, the present perfect progressive cannot replace the present perfect:

✓ Is it true that John has accepted the job in Calgary?

✗ Is it true that John has been accepting the job in Calgary?

✓ I've seen that movie at least three times.

✗ I have been seeing that movie at least three times.

✓ When you have finished eating, give me a call.

✗ When you have been finishing eating, give me a call.

## Exercise 7: Present Perfect Progressive or Present Perfect

Complete the sentences by using either the present perfect or the present perfect progressive form of the verb in parentheses. You will find that even where the present perfect progressive works well, the present perfect could be used in its place. The reverse, however, is not always true.

1. At last, at the age of twenty-three, after much investigation and uncertainty, Jasmin _____ (decide) to pursue a career in photography.

2. Over the years, she _____ (receive) a great deal of encouragement from her grandmother, who _____ (be) a successful photographer for twenty years.

3. Jasmin_____ (think) about photography ever since she was in grade seven when her teacher took the class to a professional slide show.

4. Jasmin never doubted her commitment to making images, but from time to time, she _____ (express) concern that it may be difficult to make a good living as a photographer.

5. Three months ago, her mind was made up when one of her photographs won the first prize in a prestigious competition. Ever since then, she _____ (talk) about beginning her own photography business to everyone who will listen.

6. At the same time, she _____ (investigate) schools, courses, business plans, market potential, and even the possibility of a travelling studio.

7. She says that she _____ (avoid) this decision for far too long, and now that she _____ (make) it, she's never been happier.

8. On the day the decision was made, her grandmother gave Jasmin a camera that was given to her by her grandfather, an enthusiastic amateur photographer. A few days later, Jasmin remarked to her mother, "I _____ (count) the number of photographers in this family."

9. "It makes me realize that photography _____ (be) in this family's blood for a long, long time."

10. Once Jasmin _____ (graduate) from her course, she plans to set up a business in her home town.

## Past Perfect

*Formation*

The past perfect is formed by using the past tense of the verb "to have" and the past participle of the verb in question.

Examples:

| | |
|---|---|
| I **had played** | It **had fallen** |
| We **had sailed** | Koji **had run** |
| They **had agreed** | You **had thought** |
| Kelly **had asked** | Mandy **had taken** |
| They **had grumbled** | We **had been** |

*Usage*

1. The past perfect is a relational tense. That means that it expressly describes one event in the past in relationship to another event in

the past. The action which is past perfect happened <u>before</u> the other event in the past.

Examples:

By the time Mark arrived, Mary **had** already **left** for the meeting.

We **had finished** the preparations before the committee even arrived.

The boat **had** already **docked** when we woke up.

2.  When the word "if" precedes the past perfect form of the verb, the sentence means that the converse of what is stated is true.

Examples:

If you **had eaten** your supper, you would not be hungry now. (This sentence means that you did not eat your supper, so you are hungry now.)

If only I **had** not **been** so greedy, I would have some brownies left to share!

If Pete **had studied** for the exam, he would have passed.

3.  Do not use the past perfect if the actions in the past occurred at the same time.

Examples:

When they found the apartment, it was brown inside and out.

When the princess saw the frog, she was amazed.

When Tai hit the ball, Kim ran to third.

Look at the following diagram. It depicts two events and shows their relationship to each other and to the imaginary present which, in this case, is 1999.

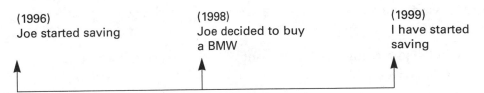

(1996)
Joe started saving

(1998)
Joe decided to buy
a BMW

(1999)
I have started
saving

Joe **had** already **started** saving when he **decided** to buy a BMW.
        past perfect                              past indicative

Joe **had** already **saved** $6000 when he **decided** to buy a BMW.
        past perfect                              past indicative

Joe **had been saving** for 2 years when he **decided** to buy the car.
    past perfect                                past indicative

When Joe **decided** to buy his car, I **had** not yet **started** saving, but
           past indicative                      past perfect
I have started saving now.

## Exercise 8: Past Perfect Tense

Using the two diagrams below as prompts, write sentences that contain
verbs in the past perfect tense.

| (January)<br>Paula started to<br>learn to ski. | (March)<br>Paula won a trip to<br>Whistler. | (June)<br>Present time from<br>which the speaker<br>is looking back. |
|---|---|---|

1. _____

   _____

| (Two days before<br>Jiki's birthday)<br>Jiki had a party. | (One day before<br>Jiki's birthday)<br>Jiki had another<br>party. | (September 19th)<br>Jiki's birthday<br>arrived. | (Two days after<br>Jiki's birthday)<br>Jiki had a party. |
|---|---|---|---|

2. _____

   _____

## Exercise 9: Past Perfect

If necessary, correct the following sentences, which use the past perfect
tense.

1.  They had already lived in Toronto for three months when their
    uncle arrived.

2.  She had tried this method three years ago.

3.  They had joined the chess club three years before Sam had joined.

4. Sarah had studied French in school after she had learned some Spanish.

5. They had moved to St. John's, Newfoundland before their uncle arrived in June.

6. Jane had moved to Edmonton six months before she bought a condo.

7. For months, they had been unable to decide what car to buy, but they finally bought a Mazda.

8. They had finished the exercise.

9. After the term ended in April, Terry and Susan had driven over the Hope-Princeton highway three times.

10. Penelope wrote three letters before Patricia had written one.

## Exercise 10: Present Perfect or Past Perfect

Complete each of the sentences below by writing the correct tense of the verb in the blanks.

1. After we _____ (complete) the plans for the conference, we began to send out letters of invitation.

2. When you _____ (finish) your homework, please hand in a typewritten copy.

3. Julia_____ (work) in the same factory as John for years before he was even aware that she existed.

4. Julia _____ (work) in the same factory as John ever since the place opened.

5. As far as I know, the contractor _____ (paint) all the storage sheds now. The only building that remains unpainted is the garage.

6. If the club members _____ (cooperate) with each other, the problems that arose would never have happened.

7. If you _____ (have, negative) measles yet, you should get the vaccination.

8. I don't suppose you _____ (stop) to think who is going to pay for all this.

9. I can't believe how much you _____ (grow) since I last saw you.

10. I _____ (give up) all hope that you were coming to Noranda.

## Activity 12: Past perfect

Read the following paragraphs, taking note of the movement back and forth between past indicative tenses and past perfect tenses. Then write a short essay of about the same length (250–300 words) beginning with the sentence: If I had known _____.

If I **had known** how important that phone call was, I would have recorded it.

Just after nine, on a January morning about five months ago, I received the call from my former boss. She **had laid** me **off** three weeks earlier, just before Christmas, because things at the office were slow. Then, a week into January, she received a big order, so she said she needed my help.

Although my mind was in turmoil, I said that I would come. Of course, after Christmas I needed the money. I **had** not **received** even one EI cheque yet. There was, however, a big problem. The night before, **we'd had** an ice storm. In the brilliant sunshine, the roads shone like well-used children's slides. Just before my boss's call, I **had seen** the paper carrier gliding over the road as though he were skating. In those conditions, I knew I could not drive.

Wearing my most rugged boots, I slithered rather than glided to the bus stop. I **had** not **taken** the bus for years, and I was feeling anxious rather than eager. The crowded bus arrived just as I got to the stop. On I got, cheeks glowing with the sense of accomplishment as well as the brisk, cold wind. There I stood with half a dozen others hanging onto the rail. My doubly mittened hand bumped a black leather glove. As I turned to apologise, I saw, to my surprise, Jamie Buxton, my old flame from grade three. Thanks to this unexpected meeting, we rekindled our old friendship. The outcome of the coincidence is that we are now planning our wedding, which will take place on the Number 3 bus in September, just three months from now.

Just imagine: if there **had** not **been** the special order, if there **had** not **been** the phone call, if there **had** not **been** an ice storm, and if the bus **had** not **been** running twenty minutes behind schedule, the valentine card in my grade three folder, Forever Thine, My Valentine, would be just a memory, not a prophecy.

# Mood

Although we have not yet mentioned mood in this chapter, we have actually been using verbs in the indicative mood. The indicative is used to express an action or describe a state **as a fact**. The following six sentences, in six different tenses, all use the indicative mood of the verbs to state facts:

The man is crossing the street.

Tourists flock to Peggy's Cove, Nova Scotia in the summer.

I spent $300 having my car fixed.

The clothes were flapping in the breeze.

Many companies have hired computer technicians.

I will call you on Saturday.

Verbs in English, however, do not always state facts. They can issue commands (imperative mood), suggest possibilities or desires (subjunctive mood), or describe actions or states that are contingent upon other actions or states (conditional mood).

## Conditional

### *Usage*

The conditional mood of the verb **does not state a fact**. It expresses a hypothetical action, that is, an action or situation conditional upon something else. The action or state expressed by a conditional verb may seem to be imaginary. For example, the statement "My ideal vacation **would be** a Caribbean cruise," does not describe an actual cruise; rather, it suggests an imaginary one, a hypothetical cruise. If the writer were to continue to write about the cruise, most of her verbs would necessarily be conditional because they would describe imaginary events as part of an imaginary cruise, rather than real events.

### *The "If" Clause*

Often the condition upon which a conditional verb depends appears in a clause that begins with the word "if."

If I had the time, I would join you in a round of golf.

If he caught the eleven o'clock bus, he would arrive at one-fifteen p.m.

### *Formation*

The conditional mood of the verb uses the word "would" or "could" plus the bare infinitive.

If John decided to quit school, I think he **would be** sorry.

If you came to our house after school, you **could ride** to the game with us when my mom gets home.

We decided that Mary **would drive** the van, Jake **would ride** the bicycle and pull the wagon behind it, and Louanne and I **would take** the bus.

*The "If/Were" Construction*

When the "if clause" contains the verb "to be," it creates a special case.

If he were a child, he could get in for half price.

If I weren't so hungry, I would wait to have supper with you.

For a full explanation of this special case, see page 72.

## Exercise 11: Conditional Verbs

Complete the following three sentences by writing clauses that use verbs in the conditional mood.

1.  If we had some onions and garlic, _____

    _____

2.  If it were not so cold out today, _____

    _____

3.  If you finished your essay this afternoon, _____

    _____

Look at the completed "cruise" paragraph below. Then complete the following activity.

> My ideal vacation would be a Caribbean cruise. The first thing each morning, I **would go** for a swim in the big swimming pool located on the upper deck. It **would be** crowded with many families splashing in the water and lounging in the sun at poolside. Each afternoon, I **would walk** around the promenade deck or **play** games in the video arcade. In the evening, I **would go** to my stateroom, where my evening wear **would already** be **laid out** on the bed. I **would take** a leisurely shower, **get dressed**, and **get** ready for dinner.

---

### Activity 13: Mood: Practising the conditional

Using the cruise paragraph as a model, write paragraphs beginning with each of the following sentences:

1.  If I won the lottery, I would . . .

2.  If I could have a dream house, it would be . . .

---

Read the following letter, which L.M. Ramsey wrote to City Council to suggest changes to the bylaws governing public gatherings. When L.M. Ramsey describes the effects that the changes would make, he or she uses the conditional mood of the verb because, at this point, the changes are hypothetical.

---

701 Rose Petal Way
Blossomtown, British Columbia
X1Y 2Z3

July 9, 2000

T.P. Ooling
Chairperson, Canada Day Celebration
City Council
12 - 345 Lilac Row
Blossomtown, British Columbia
X1Y 4Z5

Dear T.P. Ooling:

Congratulations and thank you to all the members of your committee on the success of last weekend's Canada Day celebrations. The event was well organized, well advertised, and well run. As a result, the turnout was larger than it has ever been before, yet I understand that there were fewer problems with cleanup than there have been in the past.

The only criticism that I have of the event is the effect on traffic flow into and out of the city. While hundreds of citizens and tourists remain in town explicitly to take part in the celebrations, those individuals who do not wish to enjoy the parade or wander through the street markets are inconvenienced by the traffic tie-ups in the maze of clogged or closed streets. I wish to recommend some changes that **would alleviate** the traffic problems:

- A temporary "ring road" **could be established** to channel all bypass traffic from the point at which the highway enters town at the north end. The "ring" **would follow** Bougainvillea Boulevard, Wisteria Way, and then Lily Lane through to the south end where traffic **would** again **join** the highway. Truckers, travellers, and other drivers who wish merely to pass through the town **would be saved** the inconvenience and irritation of hour-long waits just to drive a few kilometres.

- Billboard sized maps at the north and south entrances of town could clearly identify the parade route, the ring road, the market sites, and the park-and-ride lots. These measures **would inform** out-of-towners as well as local people about what to expect.

- Market sites **would be limited** to the fair grounds, the Clocktower Square, downtown, the schools' playing fields, and the arena complex parking areas. When make-shift markets pop up in almost every inter-section, as they have done in the past two years, the whole town grinds to a halt. Limiting market sites to a few locations **would allow** most of the town's streets to remain passable.

Once again, thank you for your work in making the celebrations a success. I look forward to hearing your response to my recommendations.

Yours sincerely,

*L. M. Ramsey*

L.M. Ramsey

## Activity 14: Mood: using the conditional present mood

Select one of the three topics below and write a 250- to 300-word letter using the full block (left justified) format illustrated here. This activity provides additional practice in forming and using the conditional and in developing a convincing argument while attending to the impact of verb forms on rhetoric.

1. Making school sports facilities available to a greater number of students.

2. Using people who more closely resemble the ordinary citizens of Blossomtown when casting actors and models for television.

3. Making the cafeteria a more pleasant place to eat lunch.

## A Special Case: The subjunctive of "to be" in the "if clause"

As we have discussed in the previous pages, the condition, or the hypothetical situation, upon which a conditional verb depends, often appears in a clause that begins with the word "if." That is, it is the "if clause" that sets up a situation that is either imaginary or improbable.

Situations that are not real (wishes, for example) or that are unlikely to come to pass are sometimes expressed by the subjunctive mood. Luckily, there are only a few circumstances in which this rule affects the form of the verb in English; unluckily perhaps, the use of the verb "to be" in an "if clause" is one of those circumstances.

## Form of the subjunctive mood of the verb " to be"

Present tense: **be** ( I be, you be, he or she be, we be, they be)

Past tense: **were** (I were, you were, he or she were, we were, they were)

Read the following ten sentences paying particular attention to the bolded verbs. In each case, the bolded verb is the subjunctive verb "to be."

Examples:

1.  If I **were** you, I would write a letter explaining my side of the story.
2.  If I **were** not so cold, we could go for a ride in the rowboat.
3.  If he **were** two years older, he could get the seniors' discount.
4.  If only she **were** able to move to Thunder Bay!
5.  If you **were** to be offered the job, would you take it?
6.  Why not relax and act as if the job **were** already yours.
7.  I wish I **were** home now.
8.  Imagine the look on Sue's face if we **were** to drop in unexpectedly.
9.  Larry would burst with delight if he **were** to win.
10. Suppose Marianne **were** your supervisor, not Martine's. How would you handle the problem?

## Exercise 12: Subjunctive of "To Be" in the "If Clause"

Complete each of the following sentences by filling in the blank with either the subjunctive or the indicative form of the verb "to be."

1.  If I _____ (be) a sailor, I would buy a boat.
2.  Since Jeremy _____ (be) a sailor, he bought a boat.
3.  Suppose you _____ (be) invited to the party; would you go?
4.  If Hemi _____ (be) invited to the party, do you think she would go?
5.  When Clara _____ (be) invited to the party, did she go?
6.  If the weather _____ (be) to turn nice, you could have the party on the lawn.
7.  If you _____ (be) to buy some onions and garlic, we could make a pizza.
8.  If I _____ (be) lucky enough to win a Caribbean cruise, I would splurge on a new swimsuit.
9.  Michael relaxed because he felt sure that the job _____ (be) already his.
10. He was happy that he _____ (be) home.

## Past Conditional: The "No-Such-Luck" Mood of the Verb

*Formation*

The past conditional mood of the verb uses the conditional of the verb "to have" (would have or could have) plus the past participle of the verb in question.

Examples:

If John had decided to quit school, I think he **would have been** sorry.

If you had come to our house after school, you **could have ridden** to the game with us.

We **would have made** an offer on the house if we had arranged a pre-approved mortgage beforehand.

*Usage*

So far, we have been studying the present tense of the conditional, so we have been describing situations that we can imagine and that we might hope for, if certain conditions occurred. You may have noticed that when the "if" clause uses the past indicative tense of the verb (simple past), the independent clause almost always uses the conditional present. Most of the sentences above fall into that pattern.

If I won . . . , I would . . .

When the "if" clause uses the past perfect tense of the verb, the independent clause almost always uses the past conditional. Instead of describing a simple imaginary or hypothetical situation, the sentence describes a reversal of meaning: an imaginary situation which did not come to pass.

If I had won . . . , I would have . . . .

When you write, "If I had won the lottery, I would have bought a boat," what we understand is that you did not win the lottery, so you did not buy a boat.

Examples:

If I **had started** to save in 1994, I **could have afforded** a BMW.
     past perfect               conditional perfect

If you **had called**, I **would have waited** for you.
     past perfect     conditional perfect

If the bus **had not been** late, the accident
          past perfect
**would not have happend**.
     conditional perfect

## Exercise 13: Charlie Carp's Conditional Blues

The following exercise is about "Bad Luck Charlie." None of the hoped-for events of Charlie's life came to pass. As a result, his biography is littered with the conditional past mood of the verb.

In some sentences, you will need to supply the "if" clause with the past perfect form of the verb. In other cases, you will need to supply the independent clause with the past conditional form of the verb.

If Charlie Carp had been the baby of the family, he believes he

_____ (be) much luckier. Instead, he was the middle child. He

claims that middle children tend to be overlooked, so they develop less

confidence, and, as a result, their lives are much more difficult than

those of their luckier siblings. If his parents had not overlooked him,

Charlie is convinced that he _____ (rocket) to success.

Charlie had an older brother, Dan, and a younger sister, Louise.

Both of them are much luckier than Charlie. Louise, for example, is

adored by everyone around her. If Charlie had been like Louise, that is,

if he had been the baby, he too _____ (be) lucky in love, he claims.

In Charlie's opinion, the reason that everyone loves Louise is that she is

so pretty, an asset that she owes to birth order.

Charlie says he has personally done studies that prove that each

successive child in a family is more attractive than the last. If a family

had ten children, the final one would be downright dazzling, he says.

Sadly for Charlie, he was the second child, so he is rather plain.  The

result is that he has never had many friends. If he _____ (be) more

handsome, people _____ (love) him as well, he says.

Even without good looks, Charlie believes he _____ (appeal) to

more people if he had secured a better job. After all, Dan is very

popular even though he looks so much like Charlie that the two of them

are often mistaken for twins. However, what makes Dan popular,

Charlie says, is that Dan, the first-born, has a six-figure salary and all

the material possessions that go with it. Charlie thinks that being the

first-born gives an individual drive, something that Charlie doesn't have.
If he _____ (have) the advantage of being the first-born, he is sure
he would have been as popular and lucky as Dan because drive brings
with it its own kind of luck.

Charlie _____ (study) to be a lawyer or an architect if he had
been the first-born. In fact, as first-born, he might even _____
(enter) politics and become the Prime Minister of Canada. As it was, he
dropped out of school because, without drive or good looks, he never
felt like trying out for teams, studying for exams, or putting any extra
effort into assignments. "It just isn't worth it," he said. The way he
figured it, there was no point breaking his back if he was never going to
come first anyway.

Dan's best friend, Roget, is a middle child like Charlie. Everyone
agrees that Roget is a funny looking guy. He has a crooked nose that
didn't heal properly after he broke it playing street hockey when he was
about six. It slopes off to the right, and makes him wheeze. As if that's
not enough, his hair is all cowlicks. To top it off, Roget's family is dirt
poor. For years, he wore Dan's hand-me-down clothes, and since Dan is
four inches shorter than Roget, Roget's legs and arms dangled about
four inches below his cuffs.

Charlie says it isn't at all strange that Roget has always been the
most popular kid in town. He's had the advantage of having nowhere to
go but up. If Charlie had had such severe liabilities as Roget, he
_____ (turn) them to advantages too. Take Roget's hair, for
example. Roget makes fun of his hair before anyone else gets a chance.
Charlie _____ (make) fun of his hair too if he had had the kind of

hair Roget has, but Charlie's hair isn't half bad, so he _____ (not gain) any advantage by drawing attention to it.

Roget's wheezing is another example. Roget practised wheezing strategically until he could whistle through his nose, which gained him a lot of admirers because everyone found him to be funny. Charlie _____ (wheezed) through his nose too, except that he didn't have the advantage of having adenoid problems like Roget did.

As for Roget's poverty, Roget started rolling up his pant legs to exaggerate the gap between his pant cuffs and his ankles, and the next thing you know, every guy in town started rolling up his pant legs too. Charlie _____ (roll) up his pant cuffs, but he never thought of it because his family was quite well off so he got new pants that fit whenever he needed them. If Charlie had had the luck to be born poor, he's pretty sure he _____ (be) popular like Roget too.

Poor ol' Charlie spends most of his time in a downright conditional mood. He's not likely to get out of it unless he gives up feeling so dependent on his imperfect past.

---

### Activity 15: Using the "no-such-luck" tense

Write a 250- to 300-word essay about either of the following people:

1. Whining Willy, the younger of Charlie Carp's two children
2. (or if you feel up to a challenge) Cheerful Chloë, Charlie's uncharacteristically optimistic offspring

---

## Review: Patterns of Use

Some fairly stable patterns govern the use of tense and mood in sentences in which there is an "if" clause. There are, of course, exceptions—as is so often the case in English. However, if English is your second or third or fourth language, you may find the chart below helpful because it covers most situations.

| | |
|---|---|
| **VERB CHART: "IF" CLAUSES AND CONDITIONAL** | |
| **"If clause"** | **Main clause** |
| **Present tense** | **Present**<br>**Future**<br>**Imperative** |
| If you drive a car... | ...you need insurance |
| If you need the car... | ...you will have to phone me. |
| If you need the car... | ...phone me. |
| **Past indicative** | **Conditional** |
| If you listened more carefully | you would understand |
| **Past perfect** | **Conditional perfect** |
| If you had listened more carefully... | you would have understood |

Examples:

If I win the lottery, I will treat you to a trip around the world.

If I win the lottery, come on a trip around the world with me.

If I win ten dollars on the lottery, I always buy more tickets with my winnings.

If I were to win ten dollars on the lottery, I would buy more tickets.

If I won the lottery, I would treat you to a trip around the world.

If I had won the lottery, I would have treated you to a trip around the world.

## Exercise 14: Tense and Mood

Use the correct tense and mood in the independent clause in each of the sentences below. The appropriate verbs are in brackets.

1. If they don't complete the renovations of the classrooms before classes begin in September, what _____ (happen) to the students.

2. If she hadn't had so much difficulty with the exam, she probably _____ ( not become) depressed.

3. If they had the choice, I think they _____ (prefer) to spend their holiday in Greece.

4. If were an astronaut, I _____ (make) Milky Way commercials.

5. If she had been ready, the accident _____ (not happen).

6. If they have enough money, they _____ (fly) first class.

7. If Joe had had a head start, he _____ (beat) Sarah.

8  If they are first in line, they _____ (have) a chance to buy the concert tickets.

9. If he passes English 099, he _____ (celebrate) all night.

10. If they have received delivery of their new car by Saturday, they _____ (come) to the family reunion.

## Exercise 15: More "If" Clauses

Use the correct tense and mood in the independent clause in each of the sentences below. The appropriate verbs are in brackets.

1. If they had not had a hide a bed, they _____ (negative, have) enough room for the two children.

2. If he were not a computer science whiz, he _____ (be) a great chef.

3. If he had not become a computer whiz, he _____ (be) a great chef.

4. If she had not had a headache, she _____ (finish) the game.

5. If he had had a bigger car, the six passengers _____ (be) more comfortable.

6. If she wins the 649, she _____ (buy) a new house.

7. If the sun had come out, they _____ (go) to Beacon Hill Park.

8. If they had looked at the sun, they _____ blind. (become)

9. If there were to be an eclipse, we _____ (be) in the dark.

10. If there had been an eclipse, we _____ (be) in the dark.

## Exercise 16: Still More Practice

In Exercise 5, you will notice that the "if" clause is not always the first clause in the sentence.  Nevertheless, the same rules apply.

Use the correct tense and mood in the independent clause in each of the sentences below.  The appropriate verbs are in brackets.

1. _____ (call) me at work if you decide to go out for supper tonight.

2. If I don't hear from you, I _____ (call) you when I get home.

3. By the way, if you want something uplifting to do when your cousin Joe comes to visit next week, _____ (go) see the movie that's playing at the Jewel Cinema.

4. I _____ (be) happy to water your plants for you if you decide to go and visit your aunt for a week when Joe returns home.

5. If I had realized that you were going to be away last winter, I _____ (water) your plants for you then.

6. If Yasu announces that he is engaged, nobody _____ (surprise).

7. It _____ (be) fun to give them a surprise party if they made an announcement of their engagement.

8. If you gave me a list of names before the end of the week, I _____ (phone) and try to get things organized.

9. I would have talked to Sean and Jane about this last Sunday if I _____ (know).

10. _____ (not forget) to give me a call if you find out anything more.

## Exercise 17: The Tense Preoccupations of Mr. Bains

In the previous four exercises, you have been required to supply the appropriate tense and mood for the verb in the independent clause only. In Exercise 17, you will have to supply the verb in either the dependent or the independent clause. This exercise is not limited to the use of the conditional mood in the main clause. Therefore, you may wish to glance at the "If clauses and conditional" chart on page 78 again.

1. Mr. Bains recently observed to his colleagues, "If I had my way, I _____ (regulate) every minute of what appears on television."

2. Mr. Bains' arch-rival, Mr. Mortimer Motley, turned up his nose and replied, "If you chose your television programmes as carefully as you choose your beer, Mr. Bains, I'm sure you _____ (choose) very carefully, indeed."

3. "If I _____ (drink) beer, Mr. Mottley, which I do not," said Mr. Bains, "my choice would not be affected by what I see on television because I _____ (ban) beer commercials altogether."

4. "Fortunately, you are not in a position to make such decisions. People like you _____ (ruin) all chances of commercial success if government agencies had ever allowed you to interfere."

5. "On the contrary," huffed Mr. Bains. "If people like me had been given free rein to organize television advertising, we _____ (train) the public to enjoy what is good for them."

6. "If you had more respect for the public, Mr. Bains," replied Mr. Motley, "you _____ (defend) people's right to make choices for themselves."

7. "I would be the first person to respect the members of the public, Mr. Motley, if I _____ ever _____ (observe) people making wise choices."

8. "If you had ever observed anything at all, Mr. Bains, you _____ (know) that your last statement is rubbish."

9. "Mr. Bains and Mr. Motley, if I have to listen to one more of these rancorous arguments," interrupted Ms. Eugenia, "I _____ (scream)."

10. "Thank you, Ms. Eugenia," said the boss, arriving unexpectedly on the scene. "If you had not stepped in to stop this nonsense, I think I _____ (lost) my temper and fired them."

Students often complain that, although they know the grammar rules and get all the answers right in exercises, when they write an essay, the old errors creep back in. In order to master correct forms, learners must *consciously* transfer the knowledge they have about grammar to new writing situations.

### Activity 16: Theory to practice

Reread L.M. Ramsey's letter, pages 71–72, and "Charlie Carp's Conditional Blues," pages 75–77. Many of the verbs in L.M.'s letter use the present tense of the conditional; in "Charlie Carp's Conditional Blues," verbs use the past conditional.

From the prompts that follow, select two; then write one paragraph on each, using present conditional in the first and past conditional in the second. Remember that the point of doing these activities is to reinforce what you have learned and help you to make the transfer from knowledge of grammar rules to their application in real writing. As you write, think consciously about the grammar you have learned. Doing so will help you to accomplish the transfer.

Students who are learning English as an additional language may find it helpful, once again, to refer to the "If clause and conditional chart" on page 78.

Prompts:

- If I could be anything I wanted, I think I would be . . .
- If I could meet any historical figure past or present, I would choose to meet . . .
- If I could change anything in the world, I would change . . .
- If I had turned off my computer when the storm started, I wouldn't be in such a mess now.
- If we had received the letter from the bank, we would have dealt with the problem immediately.
- If we had packed immediately, instead of partying, we would have caught the earlier bus and missed the storm.

For more practice in using verb tenses consistently, see Chapter Four, pages 125–128.

# Voice

The voice of a verb is either **active** or **passive**. A verb is active when the subject does the action. It is passive when the subject receives the action.

**Active:** Sarah **phoned** Joe. (Sarah, the subject, does the phoning).

**Passive:** Joe **was phoned** by Sarah. (Joe, the subject, does not do the phoning; instead, he receives the action).

**Active:** Interest rates **concern** all of us. (Interest rates, the subject, cause the concern).

**Passive:** We **are** all **concerned** by interest rates. (We, the subjects, do not cause the concern).

## Formation

The passive voice always uses a form of the verb "to be" **plus** a past participle.

The verb "to be" can occur in any tense. The following are a few possibilities:

| | |
|---|---|
| **Present:** | am, is, are, |
| **Past indicative:** | was, were |
| **Conditional:** | would be |
| **Present perfect:** | has been, have been |
| **Past perfect:** | had been |

| VERB | ACTIVE VOICE | PASSIVE VOICE |
|---|---|---|
| recover | He recovered the money. | The money was recovered. |
| scandalize | They scandalized the press. | The press was scandalized. |
| gain | We will gain access. | Access will be gained. |
| recognize | She recognized him. | He was recognized. |

Sometimes writers use the passive voice because they believe that it sounds academic or intellectual. Instead, however, when used in situations that do not call for passive verbs, it frequently creates confusing or awkward sentences. As a general rule, the active voice of the verb is clearer and stronger. The passive voice, which often omits telling the reader who did the action, can create ambiguity.

## The Key to Passive Voice

### Some verbs never form the passive:

| | | |
|---|---|---|
| **happen** | ✗ | An accident was happened by Lori speeding. |
| **depend** | ✗ | My mark is depend on how well I study. |
| **occur** | ✗ | A problem is occurred. |
| **belong** | ✗ | The car was belonged to Sam. |
| **exist** | ✗ | This community is existed for a long time. |
| **lack** | ✗ | He is still lacked three credits. |
| **become** | ✗ | The choir is become well respected in the city. |

### Some verbs form the passive very rarely:

| | | |
|---|---|---|
| **survive** | ✓ | The deceased man is survived by his wife and two sons. |
| | ✗ | Fortunately, everyone in the village is survived the storm. |

### Some verbs are awkward or wordy in the passive voice, so the use of the passive with these verbs should be avoided:

| | | |
|---|---|---|
| **resemble** | Awk: | June is resembled by her daughter, Mary. |
| | Better: | Mary resembles her mother, June. |
| **suit** | Awk: | His speech was suited to the occasion. |
| | Better: | His speech suited the occasion. |
| **fit** | Awk: | The course has been fitted to the students' needs. |
| | Better: | The course fits the students' needs. |
| **suffer** | Awk: | Hardship was suffered by everyone in the region. |
| | Better: | Everyone in the region suffered hardship. |
| **look** | Awk: | The problem was looked into. |
| | Better: | The committee looked into the problem. |
| **agree** | Awk: | It was agreed by everyone that the meeting should adjourn. |
| | Better: | Everyone agreed that the meeting should adjourn. |

## Exercise 18: Active and Passive

Underline the verb(s) in each sentence. Then, in the blank, identify the voice of the verb(s) as active or passive. Finally, rewrite each sentence, changing the voice of the verb. Because an "actor" does the action of an active verb, you will have to provide an actor, if one is not already present, in order to change passive verbs to active ones.

1. The author of *All the Planks in the Platform* tells a humorous tale of electioneering in Canada. _____

2. All the political parties that have ever campaigned in Blossomtown are mercilessly satirized in the novel. _____

3. Julien Nostram, the writer, spent fifteen years of his life in politics at the municipal and provincial levels. _____

4. Nostram, therefore, capitalizes on insider knowledge to spin a convincing yarn. _____

5. No doubt, the incidents in the book are exaggerated. _____

6. For example, in the novel, Pearlie Lightfinger, who is a thinly disguised reproduction of Mayor June Brightlight, is locked in a file room for ten hours on election day. _____

7. The press would have reported such an event, if it were true. _____

8. Mr. Nostram's book has enjoyed enormous success. _____

9. It was promoted to the top of the best seller list last week. _____

10. I recommend it to you as a light-hearted, humorous read. _____

### Activity 17: Voice: active and passive

Write sentences that use the following verbs in the passive voice:
- block
- teach
- hurt
- declare

Write sentences that use the following verbs in the active voice:
- ask
- embarrass
- annoy
- depress

## Exercise 19: Passive to Active

The following sentences are awkward or confusing and ambiguous because they use the passive voice when the active voice would be preferable. Rewrite the sentences making the passive verbs active. You may need to insert an actor to do the action.

1. Self-reliance and tolerance of difference is developed by young people during their teenage years.

2. Self-reliance was gained by me by driving a bicycle rickshaw for a summer in Winnipeg.

3. Important knowledge about how to get along successfully in the world was learned by having to keep my own accounts and pay rent on the pedicab.

4. Interesting information about my city was also gained by driving tourists to nooks and crannies that I didn't know before.

5. Mistaken assumptions about tourists were also exposed.

6. Tourists are often criticized for being ignorant about the places they visit.

7. However, many of the people I taxied were revealed to be extremely well-informed about Winnipeg and its history.

8. I was entertained with unfamiliar stories of incidents and individuals.

9. Every minute of the experience was enjoyed, even the hours of bad weather.

10. A more tolerant and respectful view of the world was acquired because of my peddling summer.

### Activity 18: Active and passive

Below are the first three paragraphs of a short essay. Many of the verbs in the essay are passive. They do not tell the reader who is doing the action. In addition, most of the ideas expressed are abstract or vague. When unknown actors act upon vague ideas, the results are ambiguous or downright confusing.

Select one paragraph from the essay, and edit it so that it uses active verbs and concrete images. In many cases, you will have to make major sentence changes. Your objective is to produce a final draft that is correct, clear, and strong. Work in pairs if you would like to.

1. For most students, the idea of being well-liked is welcomed with open arms; but being popular can create difficulties for the

continued

## Activity 18: Active and passive (continued)

person in question. For these problems to be controlled, the disadvantages must be turned into advantages. That way, the outcomes will be handled effectively, and the best of both worlds will be achieved.

2. Being popular is taken to mean having a lot of friends. Having a lot of friends means that disruptions can be caused which are a detriment to homework. To do homework effectively, concentration is needed to complete the work quickly and accurately. Too many interruptions mean that important information may be missed and exams may be failed.

3. Personal development can also be affected by being popular. Sometimes to maintain popularity, a back seat may be taken by personal development in favour of image. As a result, great unhappiness can be caused, even resulting in unpopularity. Then the original goal of being well-liked is not achieved.

For more exercises on the formation and use of the passive voice, see pages 166–168 in Chapter Four.

# "Isys"

The verb "to be" is probably the most important verb in the English language so it would be foolish and detrimental to one's writing to avoid it altogether. However, lazy writing often overuses the verb "to be" instead of using active, vivid verbs. We refer to the overuse of the verb "to be" as "isys." Your writing will be stronger and more effective if you greatly reduce or "zap" their numbers.

Here are the verbs to watch out for: on the left, the verb "to be," and on the right, some less easily recognized passive verbs that point to weak constructions.

| | |
|---|---|
| is | seem |
| am | appear |
| are | become |
| was | remain |
| were | |

Four common uses of the verb "to be" are the constructions "there is," "there are," "it is," and "it was." Generally speaking, these are weak constructions. Often, a writer can eliminate wordiness and increase clarity by getting rid of them.

We will remind you in the chapters on sentence structure and in the chapter on diction about how your writing can be made more clear, concise, and concrete simply by eliminating needless "isys." If you start zapping needless "isys," you will automatically write more active sentences, where the doer of the action forms the subject of the sentence.

Perhaps you have noticed that government publications and pamphlets favour the passive, "isy" sentence. This happens partly because, in such sentences, the doer of the action is not clear. For example, when someone intones, "It is regrettable that civilian collateral damage has been incurred," the speaker conveniently leaves out the doer of the action. Saying "Unfortunately, we killed a lot of civilians" is more clear, more concise, more concrete, and more disturbing.

If you return to "Exercise 19: Passive to Active," on page 85, you will notice that when you revised the sentences, you in fact removed the "isys."

You sometimes get a bonus for zapping "isys," the correction of dangling modifiers. "Working as a group, the project was finished by Friday," provides an example of a dangling modifier as, clearly, the project cannot "work as a group." If you zap the "isy," the sentence will read something like this: "Working as a group, we finished the project by Friday." Although we didn't reduce wordiness, we eliminated a serious sentence structure error. Clearly, zapping "isys" can help you be a more effective writer.

## Exercise 20: Eliminating *Isys*

Revise the following sentences eliminating the verb "to be" where possible. Where appropriate, insert a stronger, more active verb. You may need to add other words or phrases to the sentences too. Compare the number of words in revised sentences with the numbers at the end of the sentences.

1. There are many people who enjoy playing cards.  8

2. As I looked out the window, there was a ship pulling into the harbour.  14

3. It is true that a reader is able to figure out word meanings because of context.  16

4 There will be sales right after Christmas.  7

5. This situation is a reflection of the climate of unrest.  10

6. When they are at university, it is not unusual for students who are athletic to join sports teams.  18

7. It was because he was afraid of failing that John was unwilling to try out for the basketball team.  19

8. The consensus of opinion is that the exam was too difficult.  11

9. The club will be in need of a new secretary if it is the case that the old secretary is unable to complete his term of office.  27

10. Lack of confidence can be the result of being made fun of when a person is young. 19

## Exercise 21: Zapping *Isys*

As in Exercise 20, revise the following sentences eliminating the verb "to be" where possible, and—where appropriate—inserting a stronger, more active verb into the sentence. Here also, you may need to add other words or phrases to the sentences. Once again, compare the number of words in your revised sentences with the number at the end of the sentences.

1. It is clear that the new procedure is working well.  10

2. The manager is keeping the employees in suspense. She is continually talking about "downsizing."  14

3. He was nineteen, and he felt that he was very mature.  11

4. As I was walking past the park, the band was playing "Scarborough Fair."  13

5. Rob was a man of principle. He was happy to go to jail over such an issue.  17

6. Approval was given to remove the tax on tobacco.  9

7. Matt is of the opinion that schools are neglecting the basics.  11

8. The small rabbit was being chased across the road by a big dog.  13

9. The participants were experts in this field. Their solutions to the problem were surprising.  14

10. It is very likely that you may find that you may actually like the exam because of the fact that you learn something new as you are synthesizing the material that you have learned during the course. 37

## Modal Auxiliaries

Modals belong to a class of verbs called auxiliaries or helping verbs. Auxiliary verbs include the major English verbs **be**, **have**, and **do**, which also function independently as main verbs.

**Be**, **have**, and **do** take many forms. For example, look at some of the variations of the verb **be**:

| | |
|---|---|
| **Present forms:** | am, is, are |
| **Past forms:** | was, were |
| **Future forms:** | will be, will have been |
| **Conditional forms:** | would be, would have been |
| **Perfect forms:** | have been, had been |

In contrast, **modals** are invariable; that is, they have only one form regardless of whether the subject is singular or plural. Moreover, they can be used only in conjunction with a main verb. A modal is always followed by the bare infinitive of the main verb. In the following sentences, the modal is in bold, and the bare infinitive is underlined.

You **must** <u>eat</u> properly if you hope to stay healthy.

He **must** <u>eat</u> properly if he hopes to stay healthy.

The race **will** <u>begin</u> at the second narrows.

The races **will** <u>begin</u> at the second narrows.

You **should** <u>consider</u> putting sliced tomato on your peanut butter sandwich.

They **should** <u>consider</u> putting sliced tomato on their peanut butter sandwiches.

## Usage

Modal auxiliaries express necessity or obligation, capability, possibility, permission, and probability. Notice that they may express more than one of these meanings.

| | |
|---|---|
| **necessity or obligation:** | must, should, ought to |
| **capability:** | can, could |
| **possibility:** | may, might |
| **permission:** | may |
| **probability:** | shall, should, will, would |

The correct use of modals rarely presents a problem for native speakers of English, with one exception: the use of ***can*** or ***may***. As noted above, *can* expresses capability. *May* expresses permission. "Can I take the car to the ball game?" literally means "Am I capable of taking the car to the ball game? Do I have the ability to drive?" In contrast, "May I take the car to the ball game?" means "Will you give me permission to take the car?"

## Prescription

**Modals in Brief**

- Modals are invariable.
- They can be used only with a main verb.
- They are followed by the bare infinitive.

We suggest that students of English as a second or additional language classify **do** (also **does** and **did**), and **make** with modals. Technically, they are not modals. For one thing, they have different forms for singular and plural. Also, they can be used independently as main verbs. However, they are frequently used as auxiliary verbs, and in those cases, they are followed by the bare infinitive, not by a past or present participle. Notice that "make" requires an object before the bare infinitive.

**Do** you <u>enjoy</u> car racing?

Father **makes** me <u>clean</u> my room.

## Exercise 22: Finding the Right Modal

Complete the following sentences by using modals that express the meaning given in brackets.

1.  (capability) Dogs _____ communicate their affection in a number of ways.

2.  (possibility) We _____ win this game after all though it certainly didn't look promising at halftime.

3.  (obligation) According to the user's manual, you _____ never use the catalytic heater in an unventilated space.

4.  (probability) The fudge _____ be cool enough to eat now.

5.  (permission) Liam wants to know if he _____ borrow your paddle for the race.

## Exercise 23: Using Modals

In the blanks, write an appropriate modal auxiliary for the verb in parentheses.

1. If the committee is short of helpers, I _____ (have) to serve at the banquet.
2. You _____ (not drive) the car because you don't have a licence.
3. If they finish the work on time, they _____ (be able) to leave early.
4. The bus driver explained that she _____ (not allow) a passenger to disembark anywhere but at a bus stop.
5. The director announced that all the actors _____ (arrive) at least an hour and a half before the performance.

## Exercise 24: Appropriate Precautions

In each blank, write the appropriate form of the verb in brackets. Some of the verbs will need modal auxiliaries; others will not.

To travel safely and enjoyably in the back country, hikers and campers

_____ (keep) three features in mind when choosing equipment:

weight, reliability, and comfort. Although a hiker _____ (be) able to

carry 20 kilos around the back yard without much discomfort, she

_____ (experience) such a load to be crippling after 15 to 20

kilometres over rough terrain. Therefore, every gram counts.

Fortunately, manufacturers now _____ (produce) light-weight

tents, mattresses, sleeping bags, stoves, and even food.

Reliability _____ (be) the second essential feature of good

equipment. A camp stove, for example, _____ (light) when you

need it, even at high altitude. Straps, fabric, and stitching on backpacks

_____ (be) sturdy enough to withstand prolonged hard use. A hiker

whose equipment is not reliable _____ (place) himself or herself

and companions in danger.

While comfort _____ (seem) like a luxury not to be expected in

the back country, in fact it is an essential consideration. Admittedly,

campers _____ (not need) lounge chairs or silk sheets, but they

_____ (need) comfortable footwear and a well-fitting pack.

Equipment that does not fit comfortably _____ (cause) blisters. In

the comfort of home, a blister _____ (represent) little more than a

short-term irritant, but miles from the trailhead, blisters _____ (be)

serious. If they _____ (become) infected, they _____

(immobilize) you and_____ (threaten) your safety. A seasoned hiker

_____ (take) his or her comfort very seriously.

## Activity 19: Modals commuting

The following paragraph uses the indicative voice to make generalized statements about how experienced commuters behave. Read the
paragraph, then revise it, using modals to direct a novice commuter
in how to commute with flair.

Enculturated commuters arrive carelessly at a bus stop, 46.3 seconds before the bus is due to arrive. They slide into a posture of
absorbed boredom. Their eyes glaze over and their faces take on
an appearance of studied vacancy. Regardless of the provoca-
tion, they do not, under any circumstances, let on that other life
forms are in the vicinity. A belch of black fumes coughed out of
the tail pipe of a passing truck, a scurvy cat yowling into the
waste can beside the bus shelter, a child in full tantrum, thrum-
ming on the wooden bench and screaming for ketchup potato
chips, none of these enters the consciousness of the commuter
in the advanced stages of enculturation.

## Activity 20: Here's my advice

Write a paragraph of 100–150 words in which you offer advice or
directions. Incorporate some of the following modal auxiliaries:

| | |
|---|---|
| might | may |
| can | must |
| ought to | should |
| do not | would |

Here are some possible topics:

1. You are the author of an advice column. Respond to an individual who has written to you complaining that his or her spouse
refuses to pick up his or her socks and dirty laundry.

2. You are the owner of a restaurant. You are instructing your summer staff on how to improve business by being customer-friendly.

*continued*

> **Activity 20: Here's my advice (continued)**
>
> 3. You are a grandparent. You are offering your grandchild advice on how to convince his or her parents to allow him or her to learn to drive the car.

# Gerunds and Infinitives

In Chapter One, we talked about participles, gerunds and infinitives, the three types of verbals. Here we will concern ourselves with gerunds and infinitives only.

Many verbs in English, as in most languages, can be followed by another verb. In some languages, like French, the form of the second verb is invariably the infinitive, for example, "Je voudrais t'**accompagner**"; or "Il a décidé de **conduire**"; or "Elle préfère **prendre** le train."

In English, a verb may be followed by an infinitive, a noun or pronoun plus an infinitive, a gerund, or a bare infinitive. Sometimes, the choice doesn't matter, but sometimes it does. Native speakers rarely make mistakes in this area because the right choice *sounds* right to them. In contrast, because these patterns are idiomatic, the choice of infinitive, noun or pronoun plus infinitive, or gerund can be very confusing for second language learners.

Students of English as a second language simply have to memorize the differences. The good news is that you will find that you already know many of them. The objective of the pretest is to enable you to identify which ones you don't know. Those should be compiled in the learning log provided at the end of this chapter.

## Pretest

Complete each sentence using the appropriate form of the verb in parentheses: an infinitive, a gerund, or a pronoun plus infinitive. In the latter case, you will have to supply the noun or pronoun. This test includes the majority of the most commonly used verbs in each of these patterns.

1. William admitted _____ (eat) the plums that his roommate was saving for breakfast.

2. Being a music student, my friend appreciates _____ (hear) good music.

3. The registrar advised _____ (register) early.

4. Lise avoided _____ (study) until the last minute.

5. Have you agreed _____ (help) your aunt with the children?

6. The police allowed_____ (return) to our homes as soon as the danger was past.

7. I suggest that you ask _____ (borrow) the car.

8. The heat caused_____ (faint).

9. Jotham denied _____ (feel) angry.

10. The children begged _____ (go) to the lake for a picnic.

11. One of the jurors claimed _____ (know) the suspect.

12. The council decided _____ (accept) the contractor's bid.

13. The general commanded _____ (hold) the position.

14. The kindergarten class enjoyed _____ (visit) the bakery.

15. I have _____ (improve) my eating habits.

16. Michelle convinced _____ (vote) for her.

17. Did you escape _____ (get) caught in traffic?

18. We hope _____ (complete) the project tomorrow.

19. The chef encouraged _____ (try) a little of each dish.

20. The foreman managed _____ (convince) the owners to listen to the workers.

21. Have you finally finished _____ (sell) raffle tickets?

22. Imagine _____ (win) a dream vacation to Barbados!

23. I don't think he meant _____ (hurt) your feelings.

24. The teachers instructed _____ (leave) the building when the fire alarm rings.

25. Now that she's so far away, I miss _____ (spend) Saturday mornings with my sister.

26. Have they postponed _____ (buy) a house?

27. Be sure to practise _____ (stop) before you leave the bunny hills.

28. The sergeant ordered _____ (run) to the mess on the double.

29. Did the salesperson persuade _____ (buy) the spot remover?

30. I need _____ (get) to bed early tonight.

31. The company offered_____ (pay) the costs of the repairs.

32. Please remind _____ (take) the film to the drugstore to be developed.

33. Many universities now require _____ (take) placement tests.

34. I put off _____ (fix) my car for as long as I could.

35. The person at the information desk told _____ (phone) this number for information on parking.

36. The government plans _____ (maintain) lighthouse keepers in some of the lighthouses along our coast.

37. The children pretended _____ (be) pirates.

38. The vacuum cleaner has quit _____ (work).

39. Due to the water shortage, the municipality has urged _____ (not water) our lawns.

40. Do you recall, as a kid, _____ (play) crack the whip?

41. Government sponsored advertisements on TV urge _____ (not smoke).

42. I promise _____ (remember) your birthday this year.

43. Despite being exhausted, the children resisted _____ (fall) asleep.

44. The soldiers warned_____ (not cross) the border.

45. Abdi refused _____ (play) without his companions.

46. I recommend_____ (take) the scenic route along the coast.

47. The travel agent also suggests _____ (take) that route.

48. We do not tolerate _____ (fight) at this school.

49. I think I can help _____ (learn) how to ski.

50. It seemed as if they waited for ever _____ (receive) the results of their exams.

51. What do you feel like _____ (do)?

52. It's really difficult _____ (stop) smoking.

53. My friend had difficulty _____ (stop).

54. Your mother wants _____ (be) home before midnight.

55. Both teaching and being a student mean _____ (have) to work a lot of weekends.

56. I don't think this gadget is worth _____ (buy).

57. Would you please teach _____ (use) this programme?

58. Rover seems _____ (think) there is something unusual in the basement.

59. He tried _____ (wedge) the door open with his nose, and now he's barking.

60. He is obviously trying hard_____ (get) our attention.

61. The entrance requirements do not permit _____ (enroll) without all the prerequisites.

62. Lucia spends a lot of time _____ (clean up) after the children.

63. Drivers are responsible _____ (abide) by the posted speed limits.

64. Droond ended up _____ (lose) his credit cards.

The verbs in the Pretest are listed on the following three pages. The lists are not exhaustive; however, they represent the majority of the verbs that cause problems for students of English as a second language.

## Verbs and Expressions that Use Infinitives

Idiomatically, some verbs must be followed by infinitives. Many of those verbs convey a sense of the future. Here is a list and some examples.

| VERBS + INFINITIVES | | | | |
|---|---|---|---|---|
| agree | decide | manage | pretend | wait |
| ask | expect | mean (intend) | promise | want |
| beg | have | need | refuse | wish |
| claim | hope | offer | seem | |
| choose | learn | plan | try | |
| it is hard | (See Chapter Four for more information on "it is hard," "it is easy" and similar expressions.) | | | |
| have a chance | | | | |

Examples:

I agreed to help with the preparations.

We asked to borrow the vacuum cleaner.

The boy begged to accompany his father.

The woman claimed to know the suspect.

They decided to accept the proposal.

I don't think he meant to hurt your feelings.

## Verb + Noun or Pronoun + Infinitive

Some verbs must be followed by a noun or pronoun (or another word acting as a noun) and then an infinitive. Many of these verbs convey a feeling of instruction, advice, or command.

Here is a list and some examples.

| VERB + NOUNS OR PRONOUN + INFINITIVE | | | |
|---|---|---|---|
| advise | | permit | urge |
| allow | have the responsibility | persuade | warn |
| cause | help | remind | |
| command | instruct | require | |
| convince | let (+ bare infinitive) | teach | |
| encourage | order | tell | |

He advised **me** to register early.

Please allow **her** to join the swim club.

The heat caused **the wax** to melt.

The colonel commanded **the troops** to march.

The teacher convinced **the students** to come to the meeting.

## Verbs and Expressions that Use Gerunds

Some verbs must be followed by a gerund. Here is a list and some examples.

| VERBS + GERUNDS | | |
|---|---|---|
| admit | finish | quit |
| appreciate | have difficulty | recall |
| avoid | imagine | resist |
| deny | mean (express) | risk |
| feel like | miss | spend time |
| spend time | postpone | suggest |
| discuss | practise | tolerate |
| enjoy | put off | (to be) worth |
| | | waste time |

He admitted taking the book.

She appreciates listening to music.

We avoided doing our homework.

They denied <u>having</u> the stolen goods.

We enjoyed <u>visiting</u> with you.

Both teaching and being a student mean <u>having</u> to work a lot of weekends.

## Exercise 25: Verbs Followed by Nouns Plus Infinitives

Fill in the blanks with the appropriate form of the given word.

1. On the first day of the fall semester, Daniel convinced Ting _____ (arrive) an hour early.

2. He encouraged her _____ (get) all her books ready the night before.

3. He reminded her _____ (set) her alarm for seven o'clock, which is pretty hard when she had slept in until eight all summer.

4. Her summer job had permitted her _____ (choose) her own hours as long as she worked six of them.

5. Nonetheless, Ting's boss urged her _____ (start) at 9:00 so that she would miss the heavy traffic both coming and going.

6. Daniel also warned Ting _____ (make) her lunch before going to bed.

7. He told her _____ (put) the tomato for her favourite sandwich in a plastic bag so that the bread wouldn't get soggy overnight.

8. Chef Peter Piccolo himself taught Daniel _____ (do) that when he had worked at Pizza Palace and got tired of pizza.

9. Chef Peter persuaded Daniel _____ (make) a lunch at home but to use a plain brown wrapper when he carried it into the restaurant.

10. His good experience with making lunches encouraged Daniel _____ (plan) to use the school cafeteria only in emergencies.

## Exercise 26: Verbs Followed By Nouns Plus Infinitives

Fill in the blanks with the appropriate form of the given word.

1. As soon as they arrived at school, Ting advised Daniel _____ (take) both their locks and secure lockers while she tried to find a parking space.

2. She convinced him _____ (try) to get one of the tall lockers, even though he thought there was little chance of success.

3. While Daniel was scouting for lockers, Ting found to her surprise that regulations now permitted students _____ (park) right in front of the main entrance of Blair Hall.

4. This parking change caused her _____ (beat) Daniel to the tall lockers, and she was bravely standing in front of two of them when he came in the building.

5. A couple of large paper clips had allowed her _____ (create) two rather primitive locks, but she was very relieved to see Daniel.

6. As he fastened the real locks, Daniel encouraged Ting _____ (keep) the paper clips as a souvenir of the first success of the day.

7. Ting had convinced Daniel _____ (keep) a diary last semester, and he enjoyed reading over their adventures.

8. Therefore, she urged him _____ (start) a journal of the new semester and _____ (mention) how well-organized people, who made their lunches the night before, kept tomato sandwiches from becoming soggy and how well-equipped people could fashion locks from material found in their pencil cases.

9. These ideas gave him a head start in English class that afternoon when he was instructed _____ (write) a 400–500 word essay on what he had learned at school on the first day.

10. The class encouraged Daniel _____ (update) his diary regularly since the entries turned out to provide useful material for the essays he had to write.

## Exercise 27: Practice With Verbs Followed by Gerunds, Infinitives, or Nouns (or Pronouns) Plus Infinitives.

Fill in the blanks with the appropriate form of the verb in parentheses. In some cases, you will need to include a noun or pronoun to complete the sentence.

1. We persuaded _____ (come) to the party.

2. Have you practised _____ (parallel park)?

3. Fred and Ollie admitted _____ (be) bored.

4. The judge promised _____ (consider) all the evidence.

5. You risk _____ (have) a heart attack if you continue to smoke.

6. We've finished _____ (cut up) the vegetables.

7. The label on the bottle warns _____ (not ingest) the contents.

8. I don't recall _____ (order) a pizza.

9. We expect _____ (fly) to Montreal.

10. Did you instruct _____ (lock) the doors?

## Exercise 28: More Practice With Verbs Followed by Gerunds, Infinitives, or Nouns Plus Infinitives

Fill in the blanks with the appropriate form of the verb in parentheses. Remember that some of the verbs in these sentences will require that you include a noun or pronoun before an infinitive.

1. We encourage _____ (sip) the wine slowly.

2. She didn't offer _____ (pay) for the damages.

3. We will need _____ (supply) the students with exam booklets.

4. I must remind _____ (bring) her walking shoes.

5. His parents let _____ (drive) the car.

6. The campers probably resist _____ (walk) that far.

7. The rules of the game permit _____ (ask) three questions.

8. I suggest _____ (borrow) the book from the library.

9. She had difficulty _____ (learn) to spell.

10. Did you mean _____ (say) that?

## Exercise 29: The Memorable Second Date of Joe and Sarah, With Gerunds, Infinitives, and Nouns Plus Infinitives

Fill in the blanks with the appropriate form of the given word. Where necessary, also include a noun or pronoun.

1. Joe and Sarah could not escape _____ (go) out again.

2. On the first day, they hadn't expected _____ (enjoy) each other's company so much.

3. However, they seemed _____ (get along) famously from the start.

4. On their second date, Teresa invited _____ (join) her and Sam to make a foursome.

5. She suggested _____ (try) the new restaurant in Sidney.

6. She wanted _____ (know) whether or not it was as good as she had heard.

7. The two couples planned _____ (meet) at the restaurant.

8. Joe had difficulty _____ (find) the new restaurant.

9. He admitted to _____ (have) no sense of direction.

10. Fortunately, before they left, he warned _____ (be) patient.

Chapter 2 | Verbs and Voice

## Exercise 30: More of the Memorable Second Date of Joe and Sarah, With Gerunds, Infinitives, and Nouns Plus Infinitives

Fill in the blanks with the appropriate form of the given word. Where necessary, also include a noun or pronoun.

1. Sarah tried _____ (appear) relaxed, even when they were lost.

2. She resisted _____ (tell) Joe to go and ask directions at a gas station.

3. Eventually, she persuaded _____ (consult) the map.

4. She certainly appreciated _____ (have) a map in the glove compartment.

5. Sarah managed _____ (not give) too much advice while Joe read it.

6. He spent a long time _____ (read) under a street light.

7. Sarah didn't offer _____ (read) it for him.

8. She did remind _____ (consider) that their reservation was at seven, and it was almost eight.

9. Joe denied _____ (need) glasses.

10. They ended up _____ (be) one hour late.

## Exercise 31: Chapter Three of the Memorable Second Date of Joe and Sarah, With Gerunds, Infinitives, and Nouns Plus Infinitives

Fill in the blanks with the appropriate form of the given verb. Where necessary, also include a noun or pronoun.

1. Teresa and Sam had already finished _____ (eat) their appetizers and salads when Sarah and Joe arrived.

2. They had postponed _____ (order) as long as they could.

3. Once the meal was finally underway, Teresa encouraged _____ (choose) four different dishes in order to try a range of foods from the menu.

4. Unfortunately, everything was very spicy, and Sarah cannot tolerate _____ (eat) food with jalapeno peppers.

5. Teresa urged _____ (pick) the peppers out, but Sarah said she could still taste them.

6. Joe was forced _____ (eat) most of Sarah's dinner.

7. Sam felt like _____ (have) a big dessert.

8. Sarah promised _____ (try) a little of it since she had not eaten much dinner.

9. Joe, who had eaten for two, could not imagine _____ (eat) any more.

10. In the end, though, he risked _____ (taste) a small bite of Sam's apple cobbler.

---

**Activity 21: Applying what you've practised**

Using the above pattern, write sentences containing the following words:

1. advise

2. warn

3. spend time

4. discuss

5. convince

6. refuse

7. order

8. help

9. mean

10. miss

**Activity 22: Drill Sergeant (verb plus noun or pronoun plus infinitive)**

As noted on page 97, many of the verbs that are followed by nouns or pronouns plus infinitive convey a feeling of instruction, advice, or command. Therefore, in this activity, you are a drill sergeant, or the director of some organization which prides itself on tough, uncompromising discipline. Use verbs from the list on page 97. Your assignment is to write the lecture of 150–200 words that you plan to deliver to the new members of your organization.

**Activity 23: Dream a little dream**

As noted on page 96, many of the verbs that are followed by infinitives suggest the future. Therefore, in this activity, you are to write a letter of 150–200 words to a grandparent who wants to know all about your plans and dreams. Tell him or her both your real and your fantasy plans for the next ten years. Use verbs from the list on page 96.

# Irregular Verbs

The vast majority of verbs in English fall into a regular pattern, that of adding "ed" to the bare infinitive, as they form the past indicative (simple past) and the past participle. As we mention in Chapter Nine on diction, when new words enter the language, we make them conform to this pattern. Small children, too, recognize this pattern. A three-year-old might say "I doed a good thing." or "I goed to the store with my mum!" An adult hearing this kind of sentence might well reply "You did a good thing? That's great!" or "Really? You went to the store with your mum?" These gentle corrections eventually show the child the irregularities in the pattern he or she has intuited.

Only a few of the irregular verbs give adult native-speakers any difficulty. One common problem, however, is the "lie", "lay", "lain" sequence. This "lie" means to recline, to lean back, to relax, and this verb is intransitive. For example, you **lie** on your air mattress. You **lay** on a foamie last week. You have not **lain** on a real bed since you left home two weeks ago.

This verb sequence is often confused with "lay", "laid", "laid." This verb is transitive: the verb must have an object. A hen, for instance, **lays** an egg. It **laid** two eggs yesterday. Since last Monday, it **has laid** a full dozen. Someday you can **lay** a towel on the sand where nobody ever

**laid** one before. After it **has been laid** there, you can think of it as your personal flag.

Yes, irregular verbs can be a challenge, but there are not very many of them, and you can even find a pattern among them to make learning them easier. We'll show you one big regularly irregular pattern, and you can look for others—one, for example, in which vowels change in a regular way.

## Regular Irregulars

*Words With the Same Simple Past and Past Participle*

In this list, we have included a few verbs, for example, "get" and "prove," that follow this pattern but that have alternate past participles. Either will be correct.

| Simple Present | Simple Past | Past Participle |
| --- | --- | --- |
| (a)wake | (a)woke | (a)woke |
|  | (a)wakened | (a)wakened |
| bend | bent | bent |
| bleed | bled | bled |
| bind | bound | bound |
| breed | bred | bred |
| bring | brought | brought |
| build | built | built |
| buy | bought | bought |
| catch | caught | caught |
| deal | dealt | dealt |
| dig | dug | dug |
| dream | dreamt | dreamt |
|  | (dreamed) | (dreamed) |
| feed | fed | fed |
| feel | felt | felt |
| fight | fought | fought |
| find | found | found |
| get | got | got |
|  |  | (gotten) |
| grind | ground | ground |
| hang (an object) | hung | hung |
| hang (a person) | hanged | hanged |
| have | had | had |
| hear | heard | heard |
| hide | hid | hid |
|  |  | (hidden) |

| Simple Present | Simple Past | Past Participle |
|---|---|---|
| hold | held | held |
| keep | kept | kept |
| kneel | knelt | knelt |
|  | (kneeled) | (kneeled) |
| lay (intrans. put) | laid | laid |
| lead | led | led |
| lean | leant | leant |
|  | (leaned) | (leaned) |
| leave | left | left |
| lend | lent | lent |
| light | lit | lit |
|  | (lighted) | (lighted) |
| lose | lost | lost |
| make | made | made |
| mean | meant | meant |
| pay | paid | paid |
| proved | proved | proved |
|  |  | (proven) |
| read | read | read (These look the same, but the second two are pronounced "red," not "reed.") |
| say | said | said |
| seek | sought | sought |
| sell | sold | sold |
| send | sent | sent |
| shine | shone | shone |
|  | (shined) | (shined) |
| shoot | shot | shot |
| show | showed | shown |
|  |  | (showed) |
| sit | sat | sat |
| sleep | slept | slept |
| slide | slid | slid |
| speed | sped | sped |
| spend | spent | spent |
| spin | spun | spun |
| stand | stood | stood |
| stick | stuck | stuck |
| sting | stung | stung |
| strike | struck | struck |
|  |  | (stricken) |
| swing | swung | swung |

| Simple Present | Simple Past | Past Participle |
| --- | --- | --- |
| teach | taught | taught |
| tell | told | told |
| think | thought | thought |
| weep | wept | wept |
| win | won | won |
| wring | wrung | wrung |

## Real Irregulars

You'll find that the following list has some of the most important verbs in the English language, and that you already know many of them simply because you hear them so often. There are eighteen verbs commonly regarded as being the core of English verbs: *be, come, do, get, give, go, have, keep, let, make, may, put, say, see, seem, send, take,* and *will.*

Of the eighteen verbs, only one is regular, "seem," some are regularly irregular, and the great bulk are *really* irregular.

| Simple Present | Simple Past | Past Participle |
| --- | --- | --- |
| be | was/were | been |
| bear | bore | borne |
| begin | began | begun |
| bite | bit | bitten |
| blow | blew | blown |
| break | broke | broken |
| choose | chose | chosen |
| (be)come | (be)came | come |
| dive | dove (dived) | dived |
| do | did | done |
| draw | drew | drawn |
| drink | drank | drunk |
| drive | drove | driven |
| eat | ate | eaten |
| fall | fell | fallen |
| forbid | forbade | forbidden |
| forget | forgot | forgotten |
| freeze | froze | frozen |
| go | went | gone |
| grow | grew | grown |
| know | knew | known |
| lie (intrans. recline) | lay | lain |
| ride | rode | ridden |
| ring | rang | rung |

| Simple Present | Simple Past | Past Participle |
| --- | --- | --- |
| rise | rose | risen |
| run | ran | run |
| see | saw | seen |
| shake | shook | shaken |
| shrink | shrank | shrunk |
| sing | sang | sung |
| sink | sank | sunk |
| speak | spoke | spoken |
| spring | sprang | sprung |
| steal | stole | stolen |
| swear | swore | sworn |
| swim | swam | swum |
| take | took | taken |
| tear | tore | torn |
| throw | threw | thrown |
| wear | wore | worn |
| weave | wove | woven |
| write | wrote | written |

## Learning Log: Gerunds and Infinitives

When you have completed the Pretest on verbs followed by gerunds, infinitives or nouns/pronouns plus infinitives, use this page to record those verbs that you need to memorize.

Verbs followed by gerunds

_____

_____

_____

_____

_____

_____

_____

_____

_____

_____

_____

Verbs followed by infinitives

_____
_____
_____
_____
_____
_____
_____
_____
_____
_____
_____

Verbs followed by a noun or pronoun plus infinitive

_____
_____
_____
_____
_____
_____
_____
_____
_____
_____
_____

**3**

# Agreement

## Learning Outcomes

*This Chapter will help you to*

- recognize and correct errors in subject-verb agreement.

- recognize and correct two of the ten most common errors made in college/ university writing: errors in pronoun-antecedent agreement, and unclear or faulty reference.

# Agreement

## Pretest: Agreement

Correct the following sentences.

1. Everybody who comes to the games (wants, want) our team to win.

2. All of the teams that will play in this tournament (has, have) already won in their own districts.

3. Each of the adults in the organization (expects, expect) to act as president of the committee for one year.

4. The faculty (contributes, contribute) to the United Way every year.

5. Neither the students nor the teachers' union (wants, want) to see a strike.

6. The old wrecked car, which has only three unbroken windows, (looks, look) as if it has been in a fire.

7. There (seems, seem) to be no end to the cousins in Louise's family.

8. There (is, are) so many presents under the Christmas tree that they are spilling out into the rest of the room.

9. For me, three hours (plods, plod) during some of the three hour movies, but in an exam, three hours (go, goes) quickly.

10. All of the information (is, are) available at the front desk.

11. The keys to a student's success in a university career (includes, include) self-discipline, effective study skills, and a supportive group of friends.

12. Most of the computers in the office where Mary works (requires, require) a password before a user can gain access.

13. Though people have been asking questions for months now, government officials have refused to divulge any information about planned changes. Therefore, when the government (announces, announce) the revised policies next week, the news (promises, promise) to generate a lot of discussion among members of the public.

14. The Wilson family (has, have) bought a new house in Fredericton.

15. Why (has, have) the team broken up after playing together for three years?

## Subject-Verb Agreement

The rule for subject-verb agreement sounds very straightforward: the subject of the sentence or clause must agree in number with the verb. For example, in the sentence, "The boys eat a lot of watermelon in the summer," the subject "boys" is plural and the verb "eat" is also plural. If you wrote about one boy, "The boy eats a lot of watermelon in the summer," you would have a singular verb as well as a singular subject. Subject-verb agreement is an area that speakers of English as an additional language need to pay special attention to. Underlining the verbs and drawing a line to their subject when proofreading will produce an immediate improvement in this area, and soon such a mechanical strategy will not be necessary.

Here are special cases of subject-verb agreement that all people writing in English must watch for.

1.  When you have any of the following pairs of words, the verb will be singular.

    | | |
    |---|---|
    | each of | every one of |
    | one of | which one of |
    | either of | neither of |

    Examples:

    <u>One</u> of the books <u>is</u> missing.

    <u>Either</u> of the recipes <u>makes</u> a great cake.

    <u>Which</u> one of the classes <u>does</u> Sam find most helpful?

    Another way to look at this rule is just to remember that **you will never find the subject of a sentence in a prepositional phrase.** Despite the fact that, in the above sentences, "books," "recipes," and "classes" are the words closest to the verb, they are NOT the subjects of the verbs.

2.  When you use correlative conjunctions, the verb will agree with the nearest subject.

    either/or

    neither/nor

    not/but

    Be careful to distinguish this list from the one that Rule 1 covers. In this case, when we are using correlative conjunctions, the verb will not necessarily be singular. It will agree with the nearest subject. For example, look at the following four correct sentences:

Either the students or the <u>teacher</u> <u>has</u> to contact the museum before Friday.

Either the teacher or the <u>students</u> <u>have</u> to contact the museum before Friday.

Not the dogs but the <u>owner</u> <u>is</u> to blame.

Not the owner but the <u>dogs</u> <u>are</u> to blame.

In the above sentences, the subjects are joined by **either/or** and **not/but**. Therefore, the verbs agree in number with the nearest subject.

The difference between the words governed by Rule 1 and Rule 2 is that, in Rule 1, words like *either*, *each*, and *neither* function as subjects of verbs. In Rule 2, the pairs of words, *either/or*, *neither/nor* and *not/but*, are actually **correlative conjunctions**, which clearly cannot act as the subject of a verb. Only the words that they are joining can act as subjects.

3. Words concerning distance, time, weight, mass, or money take singular verbs.

   Examples:

   Ten <u>miles</u> <u>is</u> a long walk.

   Twenty <u>pounds</u> <u>seems</u> a lot for a cat to weigh.

   I think that <u>$50</u> a ticket <u>is</u> too much!

   Twenty-five <u>minutes</u> was a long time to wait on hold.

4. In sentences beginning "There is/are" or "Here is/are," the subject follows the introductory phrase, and the **verb** agrees with that subject.

   Examples:

   There <u>is</u> a large grey <u>cat</u> sitting in the doorway.

   Here <u>are</u> the <u>turtles</u> that I found in your bathtub.

   Similarly, in sentences that are questions, the subject follows the verb.

   Where <u>is</u> the <u>cat</u> now?

   What <u>are</u> <u>we</u> going to do about the turtles?

5. If you have a collective noun that acts as a unit, you use a singular verb. If the members of the collective noun act individually rather than as a unit, you use a plural verb. Here are some common collective nouns:

| | |
|---|---|
| audience | panel |
| class | public |
| committee | staff |
| family | team |
| flock | tribe |
| herd | |

These sentences containing collective nouns are both correct:

The <u>jury</u> <u>is</u> unanimous.

The <u>jury</u> <u>have</u> disagreed, so there must be a new trial.

You can avoid writing sentences that are correct but awkward by rewriting them. The second sentence above, for example, can be rewritten to read:

The jury members have disagreed, so there must be a new trial.

Here is another example of making a correct sentence less awkward:

The team are travelling to different cities to give motivational speeches.

↓

The team members are travelling to different cities to give motivational speeches.

6. When you use an auxiliary verb, you must make sure that the main verb is the bare infinitive:

The boy runs, *but* The boy can/might/will/does/has <u>run</u>.

Sarah waits, *but* Sarah can/would/may/does/should <u>wait</u>.

## Exercise 1: Subject-Verb Agreement

In the following sentences, underline the subject once and the verb twice. Some of you will find it easier to identify the verb before you find the subject. Correct any incorrect subject-verb agreement errors. A couple of sentences have more than one main clause, so be sure to check both clauses.

1. A fax transmission use telephone lines to send pictures of whole pages.

2. A fax, in fifteen or twenty seconds, can travels coast to coast in Canada.

3.  Twenty seconds are not very long, and many people enjoy the instant nature of facsimile transmissions.

4.  In addition, costing the same as a phone call, fax transmissions transmits complex information with ease.

5.  Moreover, one of the fax's advantages are that you can send graphics as well as text.

6.  Unlike faxes, which use telephone lines, e-mail messages use computers to transmit messages.

7.  In a business, the staff use e-mail to communicate with each other.

8.  Electronic messages are either stored on the computer or printed and saved as hard copies.

9.  Of course, either e-mail or faxes raises the question of privacy, and with either kind of message, senders should be aware that what they write may be read by more than just the intended receivers.

10. Both e-mail and faxes are part of everyone's life as Canada moves into the new decade.

## Exercise 2: Subject-Verb Agreement

Most of the following sentences have errors in subject-verb agreement. Make the necessary corrections.

1.  I can be sitting in front of my computer with paper scattered all around, and Algernon will asks me to let him play a game.

2.  We must all make a ten-minute presentation next week, and ten minutes are a very long time to speak about how we plan to pass this course.

3.  There is a lot of problems with the programme that Norman wrote, but at least he got it done on time.

4.  Either the salads or the dessert have to be put in the other refrigerator.

5.  Why do you think the instructor would wants to mark thirty 5000-word essays?

6.  Not the bakery, but Kerry and Shauna make the best gingerbread houses.

7.  Only ten of the 400 people was from Newfoundland, but they sang the loudest.

8.  The main sources of income for Alberta was oil and wheat.

9. The herd of cows that was near the oak tree have moved closer to the barn.

10. Which one of the players are your favourite?

# Pronoun-Verb Agreement

A pronoun must agree with its verb. This rule is very straightforward and can be broken down into subsections that will make it likely that fewer *agrs* will appear in the margins of your papers.

## Words That Signal Singular

### *Body, One, and Thing*

A helpful rule to remember is that, with all **words ending "body," "one," and "thing,"** you use a singular verb. These are the words that you should watch out for:

| | |
|---|---|
| one | someone |
| anyone | somebody |
| anybody | something |
| anything | no one |
| everyone | none |
| everybody | nobody |
| everything | nothing |

Examples:

Although it is only 7:45, <u>everybody</u> <u>is</u> here, so the meeting can begin.

<u>Something</u> <u>has been gnawing</u> at the wiring, but <u>nobody</u> <u>is</u> doing anything about it!

### *Each, Either, and Neither*

Another group of words also takes singular verbs, "each," "either," and "neither;" naturally, they also take singular pronouns.

Example:

The twins are going on a picnic. Each <u>is</u> responsible for picking up garbage. Neither is happy about this, but either <u>is</u> bribable if you happen to have bubble gum.

# Pronoun-Antecedent Agreement

An antecedent is something that precedes or goes before. A pronoun's antecedent is the word (usually a noun) that is replaced by the pronoun. That word almost always precedes the pronoun; thus, the name "antecedent." For example, in the sentence "Jane paid for the **book** and then left **it** in the store," "it" is the pronoun, and "book" is the antecedent.

You can also call the antecedent "the referent": the word to which the pronoun refers. If you have found your papers returned with *ref??* written above "this," "that," "these," or "those," making sure that your pronoun clearly refers to its referent provides the key to removing this notation from your work.

A pronoun must clearly agree with its antecedent or referent.

## Body, One, and Thing

One mistake that many people make is using the pronouns "their" and "them" to refer to the antecedents "everybody" or "everyone." Although you may hear "**Everybody** wants to get **their** homework done early tonight so **they** can catch the playoff game," using "they" to refer to "everyone" or "everybody" is colloquial and does not belong in academic, business, or technical writing.

Actually, part of your mind knows that "everyone" and "everybody," like the rest of the words ending with "body," "one," and "thing" are singular. Nobody, not even the most informal person, has ever walked into a room and said, "Wow! Everybody are here!"

## Body, One, and Thing plus Gender Neutrality

Most colleges and universities want their students to use gender-neutral language. If you use "everybody," "everyone," "anybody," or "somebody," the pronouns you use must agree with these antecedents and must also be gender-neutral.

Therefore, if you write a sentence with "everyone," you will be expected to write "his or her," "himself or herself," or "he or she" when you refer to that pronoun. We would then write "Everybody wants to get his or her homework done early tonight so he or she can catch the playoff game." We have been gender-neutral, but we readily admit that what we wrote is not a pretty sentence. Fortunately, just as we change awkward sentences when members of collective groups act as individuals, we can change awkwardness when we use gender-neutral pronouns.

We could, for example, modify the sentence to read "All students want to get their homework done early tonight so they can catch the playoff game." This sentence avoids the problem by using the plural, a good strategy.

Using a second strategy, we can simply reduce the numbers of gender-neutral pronouns. If we, for example, were drafting an incident report and accidentally wrote the following sentence, we could soon fix it up.

> Judging from the muddy footprints and bloody fingerprints, the police believe that one individual broke into the washroom and that he or she cut himself or herself when he or she broke the small window above the radiator.

↓

> Judging from the muddy footprints and bloody fingerprints, the police believe that one individual broke into the washroom, receiving a cut after he or she broke the small window above the radiator.

If we wanted to go to extremes, we could do away with all questions of pronoun-antecedent agreement and all questions of gender neutrality:

↓

> Judging from the muddy footprints and bloody fingerprints, the police believe that one individual broke into the washroom, receiving a cut after breaking the small window above the radiator.

Of course, gender-neutrality is an issue that moves beyond indefinite pronouns. For centuries, people wrote and read sentences such as "The gardener must treat his soil with respect, or he risks starving his plants," and understood it to mean that both male and female gardeners must be conscientious about maintaining the quality of their soil. Now such sentences seem odd and old-fashioned. It is no longer acceptable to think of the "male" as representing both male and female genders. Fortunately, over the years, we have all become more graceful at being gender-neutral.

## Exercise 3: Pronoun-Antecedent Agreement

The following paragraph contains pronoun-antecedent agreement errors. Remember that a pronoun must clearly point to its referent or antecedent.

In this exercise, first, circle the pronouns and draw arrows to their antecedents. Second, and this is very important, after reading the paragraph through again, **devise a strategy** and then correct the errors in the most efficient, effective way.

---

Everybody looks forward to Reading Break, but they all have their own reasons. Teachers, for example, have good reasons to be happy. Using Reading Break to catch up on marking or, without pressure, to plan for the following weeks give a teacher reasons to be happy about their break. This break can help them survive the following weeks and allow them more time to spend with panicky students who are trying to cram three months into one week at end of term. If he or she is already such a hard-working and organized person that all their planning and marking are done, then Reading Break can really be fun. Similarly, a student who has all their assignments and reading up-to-date may take a couple days to relax or visit their friends and families. Reading Break, for them, is a pause that refreshes. In contrast, a student who is behind or disorganized can use Reading Break to save themselves from disaster. If they are sinking in a sea of undone assignments and readings, Reading Break is like a lifeline they can use to pull themselves away from certain doom. Is it any wonder that, no matter whether you speak to a teacher or a student, they can always tell you when Reading Break will be?

---

## Pronouns and Consistency

### Person Agreement

If someone writes "One must always try your best," we admire the sentiment rather than how it is phrased. In this sentence, we have one indefinite pronoun and one personal pronoun. To be consistent (and parallel), we can write either "One must always try one's best" or "You must always try your best." Clearly, the latter sentence has a more personal tone. Mixing pronouns in a sentence or a paragraph can not only disconcert your reader but also affect the tone of your paper and, ultimately, your mark.

If, for instance, you begin an essay using "one," your reader feels very disturbed if, part way through the essay, you suddenly begin using "you." If, with a light tone, you are writing an essay clearly meant to amuse, then switching part way through from "you" to "one" would be just as upsetting. Similarly unsettling is switching from writing of "the reader—he or she" to "the readers—they." Pronouns must be consistent through a passage of writing. Consistency is one of the signals of competence in writing.

## Exercise 4: Pronoun Consistency

In the following paragraph, the pronouns switch back and forth. Make the necessary changes to correct the inconsistencies. Begin by underlining the pronouns and their antecedents.

> One reason some teenagers quit school is to work to support their families. If he or she is the eldest child, the teen may feel an obligation to provide for the family, so they look for a minimum wage job. Unfortunately, the student often must work so many hours per week that they cannot give much attention to schoolwork. As a result, he or she grows discouraged and drops out. If teenagers feel that their families need more financial support, they should speak to their counsellors about the problem. Counsellors can provide proper referrals to appropriate services so that the student does not jeopardize his or her future for the sake of the family's present.

## Exercise 5: Pronoun Agreement

Read the following passage, and (1) change the protagonist to Daniel and insert the necessary pronoun changes, or (2) change the protagonists to the twins Natalie and Noel and insert the necessary pronoun changes.

> For twelve months, Diana dreamt about getting her driver's licence. She turned sixteen months later than Pat and Terry, her best friends. She had wanted to get her licence as soon as possible, so she was pleased when, on her birthday, her big, and only, brother Darren gave her a cheque to get it. She was pleased, but she was also a bit surprised. "Cool," she said, "I was afraid that you had had it with Diana the Dreadful!"
>
> For weeks before her birthday, Diana had been studying the driver's manual every night after doing her homework. Disappearing into her room promptly after nine o'clock to study the book, she had been confident that she knew it all after just a week.
>
> Then she had started phase two of the learning process. During the next few weeks, whenever her brother or either of her parents took the car out, she had asked to go along, asked her dad to drop her off at her friend Pat's house on his way to his poker game, asked her mother if she could go and watch her get a haircut, and asked her brother if she could go to a movie with him and Winona, his girlfriend. Some days, she managed four trips, and, on all the trips, she watched everything the driver did.
>
> During these trips, much to her delight, Diana could point out all the mistakes Darren and her parents made. She had warned her
>
> *continued*

father three times to watch out for cyclists as he made a right turn, explained to her mother how to turn the wheels when she parked uphill on a street without a curb, and told Darren, who had been driving only four years, the penalty for driving only one kilometre above the speed limit in a school zone.

On the morning of the fourth day of phase two, when Diana, whistling cheerily, had gone down to breakfast, she found a bus pass and a certificate in her cereal bowl. The certificate read "Official Back Seat Driver's Licence." Under the official-looking red seal, her parents and Darren had signed as witnesses. It wasn't the kind of driver's licence she had dreamt of.

## Words That Signal Plural Verbs

Be very careful with any "of" construction such as **"both of," "each of," "either of," "many of,"** or **"one of."** These words are signposts. The noun that follows the "of" will be plural. If you use a sign post, your reader knows there must be a plural ahead.

## Words That Can Signal Both Plural and Singular Verbs

Be similarly careful with words, many of them indefinite pronouns, such as **"all," "a lot of," "hardly any," "more," "the majority/minority of," "most"** or **"most of," "none," "plenty of," "scarcely any," "some"** or **"some of."**

Either countable nouns or uncountable nouns can follow these words. You can have some luggage or some suitcases. You can also have none of the information or none of the documents. Check with care the words following these ambiguous signals.

## Pronouns Used With Collective Nouns

If a collective noun acts as a unit, you will choose a singular pronoun to refer to it. For instance, a reporter might write, "The jury has begun deliberations." This means that the jury acted as one, a unit, so the singular verb is appropriate. The article could continue by saying, "It will be sequestered until the verdict is reached." Clearly, as the jury, the antecedent, is acting as a unit, the article should refer to it using a singular pronoun.

Ten days later, the same reporter might write, "The jury have not been able to reach an agreement." As the jury are no longer acting as a unit, the plural verb is correct. The writer might continue by saying

"They are going to be dismissed with the judge's thanks, and a new trial will be held in September." Therefore, because the group now are acting as individuals, using a plural pronoun is correct.

## Exercise 6: Pronoun Agreement

Choose a form of the verb in the brackets to fill in the blanks. If the verb is "to be," use present tense; if not, you will subvert the idea of the exercise. Look at this example before doing the exercise:

- One of the examples ____*is*____ (to be) taken from a real document.

  1. Every one of the girls _____ (to have) a red bicycle.

  2. Everyone _____ (to want) to get a good mark on the mid-term.

  3. Some of the information _____ (to be) missing.

  4. Everyday, someone _____ (to let) the bird out of the cage before breakfast.

  5. Each of the men _____ (to plan) to start his own business.

  6. Everybody _____ (to need) to get a ride home before ten o'clock.

  7. Although he appears year after year standing silently at the graveside, no one _____ (to see) through his disguise.

  8. All of the students _____ (to leave) their coats in their lockers, so a sudden rainstorm is not a problem for long.

  9. Some of the calculators _____ (to have) a graphing capability.

  10. Each of the boys _____ (to have) skateboards.

## Exercise 7: Pronoun-Verb Agreement

Choose a form of the verb in the brackets to fill in the blanks. If the verb is "to be," use present tense; if not, you will subvert the idea of the exercise. Look at this example before doing the exercise:

- The herd ____*is*____ (to be) much smaller than the one Al sold last year.

  1. None of the newspaper accounts about the economy _____ (to be) cheerful.

  2. I can tell that someone _____ (to be) home because of the noise.

3. The jury is not sequestered, but it _____ (to discuss) the case only in the jury room.

4. The team is finally ready, and it _____ (to have) boarded the plane.

5. Anyone who expects an A+ _____ (to be) in for a surprise.

6. The Board of Directors meets on the last Wednesday of the month, except during July and August when it _____ (to communicate) only by fax or e-mail.

7. Everyone, even the Superintendent of Nursing, _____ (to wear) casual clothes on Friday.

8. Each of the Russian ships _____ (to contain) a thousand men, so the welcoming committee should prepare lots of sand-wiches.

9. A lot of problems _____ (to occur) when your computer crashes just before you have to leave work.

10. Either of the answers _____ (to be) right, so everyone should be happy.

## Unclear or Faulty Reference

As we discussed on pages 116–117, an antecedent is sometimes referred to as the referent: the word to which a pronoun refers. Almost all pronouns must have an antecedent or referent. The above exercises deal with agreement between the pronoun and its referent or antecedent.

In contrast, the following exercises deal with the problems that occur when it is not clear what word a pronoun refers to. Look, for example, at the *ref* error in the following sentence:

✗ At this university, **they** insist that students write a placement exam.

The sentence provides no referent for the pronoun "they." To correct the problem, you would need to provide an appropriate noun.

✓ At this university, **the administration** insists that students write a placement exam.

### Exercise 8: Providing a Referent

In the following sentences, the bolded pronouns either lack referents or have unclear referents. In order to eliminate the errors, replace the bolded segments with appropriate nouns. You may also have to change other words in order to create smooth sentences.

1. The audience at the rock concert was searched for drugs, but they didn't need to do **it** because no one had any.

2. Mark was a hockey fanatic though he had never been to a live **one**.

3. Though she is only fourteen, Louisa has already performed a successful piano concert. When she goes to university, **that** will be her field of study.

4. It had been raining for two months before the sun finally came out **which** made a lot of people really depressed.

5. The woman's only concern was for her child. **She** risked her life saving him.

6. When Ray's car wouldn't stop stalling, they checked the carburetor, the fuel line, and the alternator, but **it** was still unclear.

7. Yumi and Nicole had made **her** aware that she had misunderstood the lecture in class.

8. At the meeting after church, **they** ran out of coffee.

9. Maurice is fascinated by war movies and never misses one, which seems strange to me because **it** terrifies him.

10. The employees' morale was low because management kept making decisions like changing seniority regulations without informing **them**, and **it** should not have happened.

## This, That, These, Those, and It

You may have had papers returned with *ref??* written above "this," "that," "these," or "those." To correct this error, make sure that your pronoun clearly refers to its referent.

Make sure that words like "it" and "this" refer clearly to something else that you have written. This will ensure that your meaning is clear. "This" in the preceding sentence refers to the idea that you need clear referents.

You can use "this" or "that" to refer to ideas or clusters of ideas. Look at the following quotation:

> "Many students hate making mistakes. They often restrict their vocabulary and their sentence structure so as to avoid making errors. <u>This</u> is an unfortunate way to look at mistakes that have such potential to improve their way of expressing themselves."

"This" refers to the cluster of ideas that suggests that restricting how you express yourself to avoid making mistakes is a harmful practice.

You could use "that" in place of "this" in the quotation, but it would be awkward because of the second "that." Therefore, "this" is a better choice. The italicized *"it"* refers to replacing "this" with "that." *"That"* refers to the awkwardness of repeating "that."

"It" usually refers to one specific object or thing rather than a cluster. For example, William Wordsworth, a British Romantic Poet, wrote, "Poetry is the spontaneous overflow of powerful feelings: it takes its origin from emotion recollected in tranquillity." "It" refers specifically to "Poetry."

When Dorothy Parker, an American writer of poetry and short stories, wrote many years after Wordsworth, "Sorrow is tranquillity remembered in emotion," this was a parody of Wordsworth's famous line. "This" in the previous sentence refers to the words that Dorothy Parker wrote. The antecedent is more than just one word.

## Exercise 9: Pronoun Reference

Use "it" or "this" or "that" in the following blanks.

1. I finished the book on logic that you lent me. _____ was very helpful.

2. City Council has decreed that nobody can obstruct downtown sidewalks by sitting, squatting, or lying on them from 8 a.m. to 9 p.m. _____ is a strategy that has already been tried in Seattle.

3. There used to be a bench on the corner of Yates and Government. _____ is gone now.

4. I read the chapter on making presentations twice, and _____ was very helpful when I had to fill in at the meeting as chair.

5. Giovanni found an opera ticket and turned it in at the box office, missing a chance to hear Richard Margison. _____ is typical of his honest nature.

6. Kevin found a goat on New Year's Eve. _____ was accompanied by a big dog.

7. Irina has a mysterious past and never stops talking about _____.

8. When I finished the newspaper articles, I had changed my mind about the whole issue. After thinking one way for so long, _____ was a big surprise.

9. Because Kim recommended the book, Barbara read _____ on the bus going home.

10. It became clear that he was losing his hearing, so _____ was the deciding factor in his early retirement.

# Verb Tense Consistency

Tense and mood should be consistent throughout a piece of writing. Achieving consistency, however, is easier said than done. Students often ask, "If I start the paragraph in present tense, should I use present tense throughout?" The whole problem would be resolved if the answer were "Yes." It is not.

Tense must change when a logical shift in time occurs. Look at the verbs in the following sentences:

> I finally <u>arrived</u> at the airport in Toronto after a four-hour delay. I <u>thought</u> I would never find my sister in that huge place. Toronto's airport is at least three times as big as the one in Vancouver.

The shift in tense here is logically necessary. The arriving and thinking happened in the past and then were finished. Toronto's airport, however, remains larger than Vancouver's. Here is a further example taken from an exercise in Chapter Four:

> While it <u>was</u> daylight, the little hedgehog <u>spent</u> most of its time curled up in a tea cozy, because hedgehogs <u>are</u> really nocturnal animals.

Because hedgehogs are always nocturnal animals, the use of present tense in the subordinate clause is essential. When we describe the past actions of the particular little hedgehog, we use past tense.

Consider another example. If a writer is describing the place where she lives, she might write most of the passage in the present tense. However, if details of the description remind her of an experience that she had as a child, she will change to the past tense to describe that experience.

The following example demonstrates this kind of shift. When the writer describes the boardwalk, she uses the present indicative tense. When she begins to describe a childhood dream, however, she switches the tense to past.

> I always enjoy the stroll along the boardwalk that stretches from West Bay Marina all the way into town. In places, the path cantilevers out over the water. In those spots, you can lean over the rail and gaze down into the nodding sea grass. It <u>reminds</u> me of dreams I used to have as a child, slow, safe, rocking dreams, underwater dreams in which all sounds were muted and gentle, and breathing was more satisfying.

Notice that we highlighted the word "reminds." The verb "remind," like "remember," is worthy of note because it frequently causes problems for students of English as a second language. In this passage, "remind" is present tense for a logical reason: the act of remembering takes place in the present even though the memory is in the past. We can use "remembered" only if we are recounting an act of remembering that occurred at a point in the past:

> When I was seven, I remembered how scared I was the year before to be entering the "real school," so I was kind to my little brother, Sam, when he started grade one.

The following paragraph includes inexplicable or illogical shifts in time.

> I always <u>enjoy</u> the stroll along the boardwalk that <u>stretches</u> from West Bay Marina all the way into town. In places, the path <u>cantilevers</u> out over the water. In those spots, the <u>grasses were undulating</u> so they <u>made</u> me feel dizzy.

In the above paragraph, there is no logical reason to switch from present to past tense. The paragraph begins by signalling that the writer will describe a habitual experience. However, when she switches to "the grasses were undulating," she is no longer describing a habitual experience. Unless she wishes to change her description to a specific occasion in the past **and clearly signals that change to the reader**, she must not change tenses.

## Shifts Between Indicative and Conditional

One verb shift that commonly causes problems for native speakers of English is the shift between the indicative and conditional voice. We deal with the conditional voice in detail in Chapter Two: Verbs and Voice, so here we will touch on it only briefly.

The conditional voice of the verb is expressed by the words "would" or "could" preceding the bare infinitive; for example, "Linda **would help** with the baking if she had the time." In fact, Linda probably will not help with the baking because, apparently, she does not have the time. The act of helping is dependent or "conditional" upon another factor: time.

To summarize, the conditional voice is used to describe an act or situation that would happen only if something else happened.

Like all other shifts in verbs, a shift from one voice to another must be logical. Look at the following examples. The verbs that are underlined once are present or past indicative. Those underlined twice are conditional.

If I <u>could stroll</u> along the boardwalk from West Bay Marina into town, <u>I would stop</u> along the way to lean over the rail and gaze into the water. I <u>used</u> to walk there when I was a child. I <u>remember</u> that in places, the path <u>cantilevers</u> out over the water. In those spots, you <u>can lean</u> over the rail and <u>gaze</u> down into the nodding sea grass. If I <u>could walk</u> there again now, I <u>would lean</u> out over the water as I <u>used</u> to do.

Conditional verbs, like those in the above passage, do not describe actual events; rather, they describe actions that would happen if particular circumstances prevailed. In the above passage, the conditional verbs describe events that the speaker would like to have happen, but they depend on her being able to stroll along the boardwalk from West Bay Marina.

The following passage contains illogical shifts in voice.

I <u>walk</u> to work every morning, and I <u>take</u> the boardwalk from West Bay Marina into town. I <u>don't have</u> time to stop. Nevertheless, when I <u>cross</u> the section that <u>cantilevers</u> out over the water, I <u>would always think</u> about standing there as a child. However, I <u>would hurry</u> past because I <u>am</u> usually late.

In Chapter Two, we deal with tense in great detail. Here, we include only a short exercise to remind you that tense agreement is an area of concern. For more exercises and a fuller treatment of this problem, see Chapter Two.

## Exercise 10: Identifying Illogical Shifts in Tense

In the following exercise, put an ✗ in the blank preceding those paragraphs that contain illogical shifts in tense or voice. Be prepared to suggest corrections.

1. _____ Jamie finalized his class schedule this afternoon though he is not very happy with it. He now has a class every morning at 8:30, followed by a three-hour break. He wanted to have all his classes back to back, but his timetable did not work out nearly as conveniently this term as it did last term.

2. _____ Some students prefer to have big gaps in their schedules. They claim that, if their schedule keeps them at school all day, they tend to go to the library and study when they are not in class. If they went home, they did not get anything done.

3. _____ For them, if they went home, there are always too many distractions. They can spend a whole afternoon talking on the

phone or flipping through the channels on television. They did not get any homework done if they do those kinds of things.

4. _____ Jamie, on the other hand, knew that, if he had all his classes scheduled together, he went home before anyone else in his family got home from work. That way, he got his studying done when there are no distractions.

5. _____ Jamie's friend, Bob, arranged to have big gaps in his schedule because he has a part-time job. Unlike Jamie, he finds the four-hour gap to be very convenient because he works right on campus. He says the break gives him time to make a few dollars and to get away from his studies for a while.

We end this chapter with exercises that contain agreement errors in subject-verb and pronoun-antecedent agreement as well as errors in pronoun-reference.

## Exercise 11: General Disagreement

Most of the following sentences have errors in either subject-verb or pronoun agreement. Make the necessary corrections. Sentences may have more than one error.

1. I can be standing in front of my car with parts scattered around my feet, and someone will ask me to give them a ride.

2. Sven knows that thirty kilometres are too much to expect a novice hiker to cover.

3. The police officer removed the knife from the tree and then photographed it.

4. The settlers' lifestyle was particularly difficult; they had to clear acres of trees and cope with an extreme climate.

5. The undergraduate students elect their executive board tomorrow.

6. The undergraduate student body elects their executive tomorrow.

7. The settlers had to clear acres of trees and rocks as well as cope with an extreme climate, and it was difficult for them, regardless of their country of origin.

8. Ten of the 40,000 people was from Newfoundland, and they carried flags.

9. The main sources of income for Alberta are oil and wheat.

10. If anyone notices any suspicious activity, they should report it to Traffic and Security.

## Exercise 12: General Disagreement

Most of the following sentences have errors in either subject-verb or pronoun agreement. Make the necessary corrections.

1. Patricia, together with ten of her best friends, are going to *Smoke Signals* again.

2. Verbs in Chinese is not conjugated in the same way that English verbs are.

3. By the final curtain, 90 percent of the audience had voted with their feet.

4. Each of the acrobats take a turn on the high wire in every performance.

5. Two hours are enough time to write a 500-word essay and proofread it.

6. Nearly everyone on the panel favour a temporary moratorium on cod fishing in Newfoundland.

7. Fortunately, all of the luggage are waiting for you in your room at the motel.

8. Some of the information were available in glossy brochures.

9. One of the grammatical features that are likely to cause problems is articles.

10. At the seminar, the morning was spent in review and the afternoon in hearing about the new material, but it meant that the committee was tired when they should have been most alert.

## Exercise 13: General Disagreement

Most of the following sentences have errors in either subject-verb or pronoun agreement. Make the necessary corrections.

1. Both Joe and Sarah has asked Jane to run for president.

2. There is cantaloupe, watermelon, and grapes in the fridge.

3. My favourite games are Pictionary and Battleship.

4. Cats are my favourite animal.

4. Crosbie said that he was glad that some of the delegates was upset.

6. At MGM, the wonders of movie making comes alive.

7. She is the only one of our professors who emphasize the role of the student in learning.

8. The key programme of Alcoholics Anonymous are the Twelve Steps to Recovery.

9. Five top students applied for the scholarship, each one hoping that it would look impressive enough on their résumé to land them a job.

10. Tutors are very helpful as it gives us the opportunity to learn more.

## Exercise 14: General Disagreement

Most of the following sentences have errors in either subject-verb or pronoun agreement. Make the necessary corrections.

1. Thirteen weeks are actually quite a short term.

2. All work and no play make Jack a dull boy.

3. Algernon is the only one who ever think of how to get in for nothing.

4. Neither Kim nor his parents plans to attend the wedding.

5. Either Joe or his sisters goes home to Truro, Nova Scotia every year.

6. I found a mistake in the programme; this had caused all the confusion.

7. There is lots of flowers on the balcony.

8. Either the thesis or the topic sentences has to be changed.

9. Everyone should get their lockers on the first day.

10. The most important criteria in real estate is location.

## Exercise 15: General Disagreement

Most of the following sentences have errors in either subject-verb or pronoun agreement. Make the necessary corrections.

1. Toast and raspberry jam were Joe's favourite breakfast.

2. The Vancouver Canucks was the first on the ice.

3. The other team was first on the ice.

4. A lot of the advice were vague, so Penelope stopped reading the daily horoscope.

5. Farmer Brown has noticed that a lot of the chickens escape into the field behind the shed if the gate is left open.

6. Stress and rhythm makes the Polish language very musical to listen to.

7. There are lots of luggage in the back seat, so I think I'll take the bus and meet you at the hotel.

8. Three months are a long time for the ships to be at sea, so everybody took their cameras to see all the ships sail into the harbour.

9. Tom, together with his two brothers and his sister Susan, are going to rent a townhouse on Mt. Washington in early December.

10. In the United States, the word "aspirin" have been trademarked; the word must be capitalized, and it mean only aspirin made by the Bayer Corporation.

## Exercise 16: General Disagreement

Most of the following sentences have errors in either subject-verb or pronoun agreement. Make the necessary corrections.

1. The Toronto Blue Jays is having a tough year again, and, in Victoria, the team is losing fans to the Seattle Mariners.

2. Be sure to visit old Montreal, where they have outdoor cafés and street musicians.

3. Neither Victoria nor Vancouver have much snow in the winter.

4. The cherries in that blue bowl is sweeter than the ones in the green bowl.

5. Each of the instructors have six new pieces of chalk, and they are very excited.

6. In Canada, we can use the word "aspirin" to mean one of the many aspirin compound on the market.

7. Both of these books contains information about how to use articles.

8. Is there any questions?

9. Sarah prefers a dentist who doesn't ask her questions when there is a drill in their hands.

10. Jeremy made a great deal of money selling cold drinks to the people waiting for the parade to begin, and it allowed him to buy the bike he had always wanted.

## Exercise 17: General Disagreement

Most of the following sentences have errors in either subject-verb or pronoun agreement. Make the necessary corrections.

1. Each of the first- and second-level courses are plagued with long waiting lists.

2. Many of the puppies are already spoken for, and it is a great relief to Mrs. Reid, if not to Richie.

3. Basic to this course are the development of machine skills and safety awareness.

4. Economics are my favourite subject.

5. One of the chairs is missing their seat.

6. Some of the students forgot to wear their bike helmets.

7. Bacon and eggs are a very popular North American breakfast.

8. A number of ducks were swimming in the fountain.

9. Either of the movies are suitable for children under twelve.

10. Three dollars are a lot to pay for an ice cream cone.

## Exercise 18: General Disagreement

Most of the following sentences have errors in either subject-verb or pronoun agreement. Make the necessary corrections.

1. One of the most famous pain killers, aspirin, celebrated a birthday in 1997, but not many people noticed it.

2. Aspirin can soothes migraine headaches and arthritis.

3. Aspirin is one of the most widely used medication in the world.

4. Neither doctors nor patients thinks about how versatile aspirin really is.

5. Some people claim that there is many uses such as preventing colon cancer, reducing the chance of heart attack, and even treating Alzheimer's disease.

6. Some of the claims are scientifically backed, and some of the information are anecdotal.

7. Aspirin, however, is just a chemical form of a painkiller and anti-inflammatory made by many cultures from willow bark.

8. About a hundred years ago, a 29-year-old German chemist named Felix Hoffman figured out how to make the chemical equivalent of willow bark.

9. Now there is four dozen chemical compounds called non-steroidal anti-inflammatory drugs (NSAIDs), but aspirin is the original.

10. Tylenol, one of the other popular painkiller, is not a NSAID.

# Sentence Structure and Punctuation

## Learning Outcomes

***This Chapter will help you to***

- write correct sentences.

- write a variety of sentence structures to add interest to your writing.

- recognize and employ varying sentence patterns.

## Pretest

Join the following sentences as instructed. Use the given words and only **one** other. Be very conscious of punctuation. Given: Percival yelled. Penelope left.

For example, if the directions are to use a subordinating conjunction to show that Percival embarrassed Penelope, we could write "Since Percival yelled, Penelope left," or "Penelope left because Percival yelled." You can intuit from the sentences we wrote that Percival had embarrassed Penelope, so she left.

Notice that we have used only the given words plus one other, a subordinating conjunction. Notice, also, that we have carefully followed the comma rules.

1. Use a subordinating conjunction to show that the two actions occurred simultaneously.

2. Use a coordinating conjunction to show that Percival's action angered Penelope.

3. Use a subordinating conjunction to show that Penelope's leaving angered Percival.

4. Use a conjunctive adverb to show that both actions were negative.

5. Use a coordinating conjunction to show that Penelope went home despite Percival's anger.

6. Use a subordinating conjunction to show that Penelope went home in spite of Percival's anger.

7. Use a subordinating conjunction to show that Penelope's leaving didn't make Percival less angry.

8. Use a conjunctive adverb to show that Penelope left despite Percival's anger.

9. Use a coordinating conjunction to show that the witness is not sure which of the actions occurred.

10. Use a conjunctive adverb to show that Percival embarrassed Penelope.

## Sentence Variety

Although you can express ideas adequately if you write simple sentences that follow a single pattern, you will express them more effectively if you introduce a variety of sentence patterns. To avoid monotony and to present your ideas vividly and effectively, you should use a variety of sentence structures. The pretest allowed you to join two simple ideas in a variety of ways to create different meanings. You can do much more. You can vary long sentences with short ones, mix simple ones with complex or compound ones, and use an occasional absolute or appositive. You can be adventurous!

Before you can create a pleasing variety of sentence structures, you have to be thoroughly comfortable with the different kinds of transitions that we use in English. These are the words that will fit your ideas together so that the reader follows your ideas easily.

# Transitions

Nestling up against other "C words," such as "clear," "concise," and "concrete," all of which are important in writing, we find the word "coherent." To "cohere" means to cling together, to hang together, to stick together. In writing, it's your ideas and paragraphs that must cling, hang, and stick together. If they do not, obviously your audience will read consecutive sentences or paragraphs but not understand their meaning. Have you heard someone described as "in**coher**ent"? Clearly, this was someone whose muddled or jumbled ideas didn't get through to the audience.

Look at the following paragraph. We have put transitional words linking the ideas in bold.

> Summer is a time of inspiration **and** perspiration in the garden. We, **for example**, decided to give some shrubs away. **On the one hand**, they were growing very well where we had them. **On the other hand**, they grew so well that they blocked the sun from the other plants. **Therefore**, we decided to find them a new home **in order to** save the rest of the garden. **After** we dug up the three big plants and wrapped the root balls in burlap, we tried to put them in the big blue wheelbarrow. The plants, **however**, tipped out and lay there looking depressed. Was this a Freudian tip? Were we making a big mistake? **Admittedly**, they had been happily growing in our yard for years. Shouldn't they be allowed to grow in peace? We began to reconsider. **Nonetheless**, we **finally** reminded ourselves that other plants with just as much right to life were being stunted. **Furthermore**, we had a friend with a big back yard that needed some plants to break up its vast expanse. **Thus**, we pressed onward with our plan and delivered the shrubs. **As a result**, two gardens now look better: a good day's work.

Here's a paragraph without transitions. Does it make sense?

> Smoking is not an anti-social activity. Smokers are anti-social because they endanger not only their own lives but also others' and should be ostracized, socially expelled. Non-smokers can remove themselves from danger, just as they can avoid a cholesterol-laden buffet table. In many Canadian cities now, smokers can't indulge themselves in restaurants. Smokers are far from

isolated. They have been banned from many public places, including restaurants. On balconies, patios, sidewalks, and outside theatre lobbies, smokers meet others that they otherwise may never have met. Smokers always have two passports to conversation: "Gotta cigarette?" or "Gotta light?" Smoking is still a social activity.

There are about a hundred words in that paragraph, but what does it say? What is its main point? How was the paragraph developed? Do its ideas stick together?

We have a clue about the main point because of the topic sentence and the wrap-up sentence. The main point seems to be that smoking is a positive social experience. As far as the developmental strategy goes, it seems to be mostly a pro-con approach, mentioning negative points, but undermining them. The idea that smokers are now isolated, for example, is countered by the idea that they now meet others they may never have met before. The ideas in this paragraph, however, do not stick together. The paragraph and ideas are incoherent.

Here is the paragraph again with the addition of some transitional words and phrases that glue the ideas together.

Smoking is not an anti-social activity. **Some non-smokers say** that smokers are anti-social because they endanger not only their own lives but also others' and should be ostracized, socially expelled. Non-smokers, **however**, can remove themselves from danger, just as they can avoid a cholesterol-laden buffet table. **Of course**, in many Canadian cities now, smokers can't indulge themselves in restaurants, **yet** smokers are far from isolated. **Although** they have been banned from many public places—including restaurants—on balconies, patios, sidewalks, and outside theatre lobbies, smokers meet others that they otherwise may never have met. **Moreover**, smokers always have two passports to conversation: "Gotta cigarette?" or "Gotta light?" Smoking is still a social activity.

Transitions carry the reader from idea to idea, reason to reason, example to example, and paragraph to paragraph. When you want to guide your reader using transitions, you must understand that they fulfill differing functions and that they appear in differing kinds of sentence structures. This knowledge will set you on the path to pleasing sentence variety.

## Exercise 1: Transitions

Arrange the following words into these categories: Addition/Sequence; Contrast/Change of Direction; Illustration; Time; Space; Conclusion; Concession.

| | |
|---|---|
| above | meanwhile |
| across | moreover |
| admittedly | naturally |
| after | nearby |
| after all | nevertheless |
| also | next |
| although this may be true | next to |
| and | nonetheless |
| as | nor |
| as a result | now |
| as an illustration | of course |
| at the same time | on the contrary |
| before | on the opposite corner |
| beside | on the one hand |
| besides | on the other hand |
| but | otherwise |
| consequently | presently |
| conversely | second |
| currently | shortly |
| during | similarly |
| eventually | since then |
| finally | soon |
| first of all | specifically |
| for example | still |
| for instance | subsequently |
| for one thing | such as |
| furthermore | the third reason |
| hence | then |
| however | thereafter |
| in addition | therefore |
| in contrast | thus |
| in front | to begin |
| in like manner | to the left |
| in summary | while |
| later | yesterday |
| | yet |

Transitions carry the reader from idea to idea, reason to reason, example to example, and paragraph to paragraph. However, they do not just carry out differing functions: they are different parts of speech. This reality means that punctuation differs depending on the kind of transition you use, a fact that probably occurred to you when you did the pretest about Percival and Penelope. Knowing a transition's part of speech is an invaluable aid to help you understand the mysteries of punctuation.

## Exercise 2: Transitions Arranged As Parts of Speech

Arrange the following transitions under the following categories:
subordinating conjunctions, coordinating conjunctions, adverbs, and
prepositions. Some may fit into more than one category.

| | | |
|---|---|---|
| above | finally | presently |
| across | for | shortly |
| admittedly | furthermore | similarly |
| after | hence | since |
| also | however | so |
| although | later | soon |
| and | meanwhile | specifically |
| because | moreover | subsequently |
| before | naturally | still |
| beside | nearby | then |
| besides | nevertheless | thereafter |
| but | next | therefore |
| consequently | nonetheless | thus |
| conversely | nor | unless |
| currently | now | when |
| during | or | while |
| eventually | otherwise | yet |

The punctuation for each sentence pattern varies. For example, when
you use a conjunctive adverb such as "therefore" to join two clauses, you
will also need to use a semicolon whereas, when you use a coordinating
conjunction, you will need only a comma. See comma rules 4 and 5 on
page 210 and semicolon rule 1 on page 222, for helpful advice.

# Sentence Patterns

## Pattern 1. Simple Sentence

The basic pattern is subject (S), verb (V), object (O) or subject (S), verb
(V),  subjective completion (SC). Remember that if you are using an
intransitive verb, however, you need nothing to complete the meaning.

The following sentences have intransitive verbs. The sentences do
not need objects; they are complete.

Sarah relaxed. Sarah smiled. Sarah giggled.

The following sentence has a transitive verb. The sentence needs an
object to complete the meaning.

Sarah drank tea.
S      V     O

The following sentence has a linking verb. The sentence needs a predicate adjective (or predicate noun or an adverb of place) to complete the meaning.

Sarah was content.
S      V     SC

These sentences are correct, and this fundamental pattern is obviously useful; nonetheless, they all follow the same pattern, have the same length, and are ultimately boring. A paragraph composed of a dozen such short machine-gun bursts would kill the reader's interest.

## Pattern 2. Simple Sentence with Phrases or Modifiers

Groups of words can precede a simple structure of subject (S), verb (V), object (O) or subject (S), verb (V), subjective completion (SC). The result is still a simple sentence.

Here are a couple of sentences that follow this pattern. Note that the many words that precede the underlined independent clause are not a clause themselves. You should remember that the length of a group of words has nothing to do with whether it is a clause or not. The words preceding these independent clauses have neither the S V O, S V SC, nor SV(intrans) pattern that marks an independent clause. Neither are they subordinate clauses, where the same patterns are headed by subordinating conjunctions. They are just a long group of phrases.

Long, long ago, in a cavern studded with diamonds far beneath the earth's surface, there lived a strange little man and his lovely daughter, Aurora.

Standing in the corner of the lobby, shifting from foot to foot, looking at his watch every two minutes, Jay waited for intermission so that he could take his seat.

You will notice that the following sentence is not **Pattern 2**, for what precedes the underlined independent clause is a subordinate clause.

While he waited for intermission so that he could take his seat, Jay stood in the corner, shifting from foot to foot, looking at his watch every two minutes.

If you took away its subordinating conjunction, you would have an independent clause:

He waited for intermission so he could take his seat.

---

**Activity 1: Pattern 2**

Add groups of words to precede the given independent clause. Double-check to make sure that you have not written a subordinate clause.

1. Mr. Cavanaugh rented a large tent to erect in the back yard.

2. The moon sent a silver path over the water toward the dock.

3. The runner raced toward second base.

4. Paul Revere went out for a midnight ride.

---

# Pattern 3. Compound Sentence

The third pattern involves joining the simple sentences by a comma plus a coordinating conjunction (CC): *but, yet, or, nor, for, and,* and *so.* The joining results in a **compound sentence**.

Sarah drank tea, <u>so</u> she was content.

Barbara drank the tea, <u>yet</u> she was content.

## Exercise 3: Sentence Structure Pattern 3:

Use different coordinating conjunctions to join the following sentences.

1. The sun came out. They decided to go on a picnic.

2. It started to rain. They went on a picnic.

3. Sam appreciated getting e-mail. He actually *loved* to get hand-written letters.

4. On the highway, Ming saw a large dark shape. He decided to slow down.

# Pattern 4. Compound Sentence with Semicolon

A fourth pattern, like the third, joins two simple sentences, giving equal weight to closely related ideas, but it uses a semicolon instead of a conjunction. Patterns 3 and 4 result in compound sentences. Note that unless the word following the semicolon is a proper noun, it is not capitalized.

She was exhausted; Sarah needed a break.

Sarah drank tea; she was content.

The following attempts at creating compound sentences do not work because the ideas are not related.

✗ Sarah drank tea, and there was a rainbow.

✗ Sarah drank tea; there was a rainbow.

An important variation on this pattern of compound sentences uses a conjunctive adverb, such as "therefore," "however," "moreover" or "instead," together with the semicolon.

I wanted to finish the essay; nonetheless, I went to the movie.

Meg wanted to finish the essay; therefore, she locked herself in her room.

## Exercise 4: Sentence Structure Pattern 4

Use a semicolon to join the following sentences.

1. It looked like rain. John wondered why Ahn Yi had left the umbrella in the car.

2. The squirrel leapt on top of the bird feeder. It swung there precariously.

3. The mid-term projections for profit had not been reached. The directors were not pleased.

4. Ralph got B+'s in English. He got A's in History.

## Exercise 5: Sentence Structure Pattern 4

Use a semicolon and a conjunctive adverb to join the following sentences.

1. Jane was late picking him up. Sean eventually called a taxi.

2. Debbie started to giggle. Frank began to laugh.

3. The train pulled in an hour ahead of time. Ling was at the station waiting.

4. Daisy felt a cold coming on. She decided to go to bed.

# Pattern 5. Complex Sentence

The fifth pattern involves the use of subordinating conjunctions, such as "although," "because," "unless," "if," "after," or "when," to give one idea more emphasis than the other. This pattern creates a **complex sentence**.

Note the significant differences in the following pairs of sentences.

Sarah drank tea because she was content.

Because Sarah drank tea, she was content.

After she received the postcard from Singapore, Kimiko ripped up Sam's picture.

Kimiko received the postcard from Singapore after she ripped up Sam's picture.

Although we have used the same subordinating conjunction in each pair of clauses, both the punctuation and the meaning change dramatically depending on which clause is subordinated. In which case do you think that Sam and Kimiko's relationship has a chance of continuing?

Note, too, that sentence elements introduced by subordinating conjunctions depend on the main or independent clause to complete the meaning: that is why we often refer to them as **dependent clauses**.

**Subordinate** or **dependent clauses** used by themselves are sentence fragments because, even though they do have subjects and verbs, they are not complete grammatical thoughts.

## Exercise 6: Sentence Structure Pattern 5

Use a subordinating conjunction to join the following sentences.

1.  It looked like rain. John wondered why Ahn Yi left the umbrella.

2.  The squirrel leapt on top of the bird feeder. He swung there precariously.

3.  Jane was late. Sean eventually called a taxi.

4.  Debbie started to giggle. Frank began to laugh.

5.  The train pulled in an hour ahead of time. Ling was there waiting.

6.  Daisy felt a cold coming on. She decided to go to bed.

## Pattern 6. Compound-Complex Sentence

The sixth pattern, compound-complex, combines, as you might expect, a compound sentence and a complex sentence.

### Examples:

Sam sent the postcard, and Kimiko finally received it, although not quite in the manner he expected.

After Kimiko received the postcard from Singapore, she ripped up Sam's picture, and she fed the pieces to her parrot.

After Kimiko ripped up Sam's picture, she sent him a postcard, but he didn't receive it.

A few days ago, Kimiko met a woman, Naylin, who had known Sam in Singapore, and she had owned a shop that sold postcards.

When Sam and Kimiko thought about it years later, neither could remember how the relationship ended, so neither of them realized that the whole problem could have been resolved if they had used e-mail.

## Exercise 7: Sentence Structure Pattern 6

Make the following groups of sentences one compound-complex sentence. You may modify the order of the words or change them if necessary.

1. Hing saw the car accident. Later, he called the owner of the red car. Moreover, he notified his lawyer.

2. Joe ate a pizza. It was a large. Later, he felt very full. He fell asleep.

3. Pierre bought a new software programme. He had bought a similar one two years ago. This new package was cheaper and had more features.

4. Monique had a job interview. She felt very prepared. She had researched both the business and its competitors.

## Pattern 7. Sentences Containing a Series of Modifiers

The seventh pattern involves putting adjectives or verbs in a series. If you have a series of bullet-like sentences concerning the same subject, this pattern will be a helpful one.

Here is an example of using adjectives in a series to combine short sentences:

**Original:** The teapot was very old. It was blue. It was unusually round. It fell from its special dining room shelf.

The teapot, blue, very old, and unusually round, fell from its special dining room shelf.

Although you have used five fewer words in the second example, you have written a more interesting sentence. Here is another example using a series of adjectives in a sentence:

The teapot landed unharmed on the chunky, multicoloured rag rug.

Finally, here is an example using a series of verbs in a sentence:

The teapot fell on its side, rolled to the edge of the shelf, teetered, and dropped to the floor.

# Pattern 8. Sentences with Absolute Phrases or Clauses

The eighth pattern involves using absolutes. An absolute is a noun or word acting as a noun. It acts as a modifier but has no grammatical connection to the word it modifies; rather, it just sits next to it. An absolute is often used with a participle and is often used to modify the whole sentence. Using absolutes provides one interesting way to zap needless isys.

Here are some examples showing how absolutes can combine sentences and reduce needless words. Although the first example uses an absolute that contains a participle, the second example does not.

**Original:** Jennifer was elated. The presentation had gone very well.

The presentation having gone well, Jennifer was elated.

**Original:** The book is poetic, pathetic, and powerful. It is Belliveau's first novel.

Poetic, pathetic, and powerful, the book is Belliveau's first novel.

## Exercise 8: Sentence Structure Pattern 8

Join the following groups of sentences by using an absolute.

1.  The battery was dead. Toby and Henrietta needed a lift to the nearest garage.

2. The instructor was fifteen minutes late. Many members of the class had left.

3. They established their place in the line-up with camp stools. They then went off to look for food.

4. Brendan had the longest string of hits. The team made him captain.

## Pattern 9. Sentences with Appositives

The ninth pattern involves using appositives: words renaming or restating the idea of a neighbouring word.

You'll notice that appositives, as well as providing sentence variety, also work to reduce wordiness and to zap an isy or two. Here are some examples of sentences joined by using appositives.

**Original:** Mrs. Chan is a great gardener. She is my neighbour on the right.

Mrs. Chan, a great gardener, is my neighbour on the right.

**Original:** My car is a real lemon. I've had it in for repairs five times in six months.

I've had my car, a real lemon, in for repairs five times in six months.

### Exercise 9: Sentence Structure Pattern 9

Join the following groups of sentences by using an appositive.

1. I need to replace my battery. It was a Supertuff Roadking.

2. You can save more money if you shop at warehouses. These stores reduce their staffing costs by leaving the products in packing boxes.

3. Yvonne needed a clearer thesis. She needed something to alert the reader to the main thrust of her argument.

4. Tom really admires his manager. She is a great communicator, a stickler for the rules, and a fantastic shortstop.

# Forming Questions

In English, we form questions using a number of methods. These methods differ depending on whether we are speaking or writing.

## Pattern 1: Forming Questions with Who, What, Where, When, Why, or How

In speaking, if we start a question with "Who," "What," "Where," "When," "Why," or "How," we do not generally raise our tone at the end of the sentence. "Where is my piece of pizza?" we'd say, or "How on earth do you expect us to be done by tomorrow?" Although we are clearly asking a question, perhaps with a great deal of emotion, our tone at the end of the sentence does not rise. In this oral pattern, one of the above words is followed by a verb, often a form of "do," "can," or "to be." In the following list we have put the "who" question last for a special reason. You will find the reason on page 148.

- What do you think they are talking about?

- Where did you put the tape recorder?

- When did these batteries run out?

- Why has she got a water gun?

- How do we get out of here?

- Who is on the phone?

## Pattern 2: Forming Questions with Tone

In speech, however, we can turn any statement into a question just by raising our tone at the end of a statement. We'd say, for example, "You ate the whole pizza?" or "You said we'd be done by ten o'clock?" The word order, SVO or SVSC, shows that these sentences are statements. It's only our raised tone (and perhaps raised eyebrows) that alerts the listener that we are actually asking a question, requesting affirmation or confirmation.

## Pattern 3: Forming Questions with Auxiliary Verbs

In expository prose, as opposed to fiction where we would attempt to reproduce realistic dialogue, the way we form questions is quite rigid. Often, we use an auxiliary verb.

If we make a question out of a statement containing an auxiliary verb, we shift the auxiliary verb to the beginning of the sentence. For example, we can make a question out of the following statements in this way.

John <u>has done</u> very well on his mid-term.

<u>Has</u> John done very well on his mid-term?

We <u>have been looking</u> for the cat.

<u>Have</u> you been looking for the cat?

Note that the subject and the auxiliary verb have switched places in sentence one, but in sentence two, just the first word of the verb phrase precedes the subject. Look at the following example: again, only the first word of the verb phrase precedes the subject.

Percival <u>should have been</u> doing the dishes.

<u>Should</u> Percival have been doing the dishes?

## Pattern 4: Forming Questions with Forms of "Do"

If a statement has no auxiliary verb, we can form a question using the present or past tenses of "do."

English contains words from many other languages.

<u>Does</u> English contain words from many other languages?

Kunikiyo left his calculator at home.

<u>Did</u> Kunikiyo leave his calculator at home?

Robert and Josephine have many recipes for chocolate chip cookies.

<u>Do</u> Robert and Josephine have many recipes for chocolate chip cookies?

Note that, in the above sentences, the word order remains the same. The verb must change if the tense demands it, but the word order in the question beginning with a form of "Do" is the same as it is in the statement.

## Avoiding the Use of Question Word Order in a Statement

Students whose first language is not English should look particularly carefully at embedded questions. A common error when writing statements or questions with embedded questions occurs when students use normal question word order in the embedded clauses.

This phenomenon occurs often with the **Who, What, Where, When, Why,** or **How** pattern that we discussed above. Look again at the first five questions under that section. If you make statements that contain these questions, the word order must change:

I asked what they thought they were talking about.

Every week, I have to ask where you put the tape recorder.

Jeremy asked when these batteries ran out.

Jennifer asked if Ruth has got a water gun.

He asked me how we get out of here.

☞ I wonder who is on the phone.

When we form a statement from the last question, "Who is on the phone?" the word order doesn't change because "who" is acting as subject of the verb "is."

Similarly, if you make questions containing these questions, the normal question word order must change:

Do you have any idea what they thought they were talking about?

How many times do I have to ask where you put the tape recorder?

Do you know when these batteries ran out?

Did Jennifer find out if Ruth has got a water gun?

Have you got the map showing how we get out of here?

☞ Do you know who is on the phone?

Avoiding the use of question word order in embedded interrogative clauses is extremely important for all speakers of English as a second or additional language.

## Exercise 10: Question Word Order

Using the cue word, make questions that would result in the following statements.

Example:

* Daphne wants to go to Salmonier.

   Where *does Daphne want to go?*

   or

   Does *Daphne want to go to Salmonier?*

1. Sheila needs to find the flour sifter.
   **What** _____

2. Crawford is having a lot of trouble finding the programme that he
   has written.

   **Is** _____

3. The fence is eight feet high.

   **How** _____

4. The cat is on the hot tin roof.

   **Where** _____

5. Yumiko put the helmet carefully in her locker.

   **Where** _____

6. If we are lucky, the daffodils should appear in February.

   **When** _____

7. Martha's mother does not like figgy duff.

   **Does** _____

8. Kam went downtown about four o'clock.

   **What** _____

9. Paul put the mouse pad in the wash.

   **Did** _____

10. Yvonne and Vinh left early because it was raining.

    **Why** _____

## Exercise 11: Question Word Order

Make questions that would result in the following statements.

1. Brian set up his new computer on the corner of the dining room
   table.

2. After work, Wing found shopping at Fabulous Foods on Fort Street
   was most convenient.

3. The hummingbird feeder was attached to the kitchen window.

4. Thomas saw the first snowdrops.

5. I have two cats.

6. The butter is on the table.

7. I know what time it is.

8. David's car has been at the garage since last Monday.

9. The most enjoyable book was a series of linked short stories.

10. I chose the music.

## Exercise 12: Question Word Order

Make statements or questions that embed the following questions. For example, "How often does the iguana get in the drain?" becomes "He asked how often the iguana gets in the drain," or "Will you please tell me how often the iguana gets in the drain?"

1.  Where did he find the tarantula?

2.  How is his mother feeling now?

3.  When did the rain stop?

4.  Who did the decorations in the gym?

5.  Why did the elephant paint its toenails red?

6.  What is Sam's new postal code?

7.  What has Gerry done with the stapler?

8.  When does the next bus get in?

9.  How can you fix broken fingernails?

10. Where is the best Hungarian restaurant?

## Exercise 13: Question Word Order

Make statements or questions that embed the following questions. For example, "Where has Joe put my luggage?" becomes "I asked where Joe had put my luggage," or "Do you know where Joe put my luggage?"

1.  How old is she?

2.  When did the Christmas lights go up?

3.  What have Frank and Josephine done with all the walnuts?

4.  Where is the dog I got for Christmas?

5.  Why is that squirrel staring at me?

6.  What country does Craig want to visit next?

7.  Did you put the timer on?

8.  Have you tried the newest version of *Alcazar*?

9.  Why is Tom's book sitting in the dryer?

10. Why is there no number eleven?

# Additional Sentence Structure Elements

## Subordination

The concept of subordination is important for everyone who communicates in written English. Many native English speakers, for example, need to understand the difference between a subordinate (dependent ) clause and a main (independent) clause. If they don't, they make mistakes in punctuation, particularly with semicolons and colons. They may also write fragments, not recognizing them as subordinate clauses.

Non-native English speakers, many of whom learned English in a more structured way than native-born speakers, may be less likely to write fragments or comma splices. Nonetheless, our experience shows that many such students have difficulty joining two ideas by subordinating one of them.

We have already pointed out Sentence Pattern 5, the complex sentence, as one of the ways to achieve sentence variety, but all students should also know how subordinating one idea can give emphasis to another. Students then move beyond creating sentence variety into creating style and influencing content.

You need to remember that a subordinate clause has a subject, a verb, and, if the verb is transitive or linking, something to complete the meaning, a predicate adjective, predicate noun, an adverb, etc. What then stops it from being an independent clause or, essentially, a sentence? It's the subordinating conjunction.

A subordinate clause is dependent: it cannot stand alone. Imagine someone saying the following:

"Algernon failed his driver's exam again."
    subject    verb        object

"Oh," you think, "poor Algernon!"—or "Stupid Algernon!" Although your reaction to the statement can vary, the main idea is clear: there is an independent clause.

In contrast, think about someone saying

"Because Algernon failed his driver's exam again."

"Although Algernon failed his driver's exam again."

"After Algernon failed his driver's exam again."

What is your reaction? It is probably "What happened?" The main idea is not clear. These clauses need an independent clause to complete the idea.

The above three examples are fragments, incomplete grammatical thoughts. The subordinating conjunctions created fragments even though the clause had a subject, "Algernon," a verb, "failed," and something to complete the meaning, the object, "his driver's exam."

## Exercise 14: Recognizing Subordinate Clauses

Underline the subjects and verbs that you find in the following sentences. Then circle any subordinating conjunction.

1. Since the snow had not stopped falling, Mrs. Yeager shovelled the walk again when she took the garbage out.

2. After the dance was over, Lucia and Norman started for home, but they were late because they missed the 12:00 bus.

3. When it was night, the little hedgehog came out of the tea cozy where it spent the daylight hours, because hedgehogs are really nocturnal animals.

4. When the vote was taken, although they had spoken strongly against the motion, only three of the members bothered to vote.

5. Since the project would take place over three weeks, when Jeanne was asked to participate, she had to reschedule her vacation plans.

6. In the five minutes before the meeting was called to order, Sean and Patrick accomplished a great deal.

7. Lying in a puddle behind the neighbours' car, Bruce, the dog, gleefully wallowed in the mud.

8. Until we get the binoculars fixed, we won't be able to see whether the neighbours have put up their bird house.

9. As soon as they got up, before they had got dressed, one of them had to go and feed the cat; otherwise, she drove them crazy because she wound around and around their feet purring.

10. Unless you are very quick indeed, you will need the whole class to finish the exam because two of the questions require answers in paragraph form.

## Exercise 15: Recognizing Subordinate Clauses

Underline the subjects and verbs that you find in the following sentences. Then circle any subordinating conjunction.

1. Sarah would have liked to start playing Christmas carols when the stores put up their decorations at the beginning of November, but she waited a whole month before she actually did play them.

2. While Janet played on the swing, Judy played on the merry-go-round, and Jim played on the slide.

3. In the cupboard on the right over the stove, you will find candles and matches.

4. After we saw the movie, Peter and Jeanette read the book because they felt that they had missed some of the best lines when people were laughing so hard.

5. If you come over after supper, we can work on the project until we get tired, probably about ten o'clock.

6. Since Gianni moved, Marina has been able to play the country music that she loves.

7. If you have difficulty reaching us by phone, please try e-mail because we check it six times a day.

8. Throughout the lecture, including the two intermissions, the curly-headed blond man in the front row slept.

9. Even though the dishwasher is broken, we should go ahead with the wedding.

10. Whereas Ping wrote long, interesting paragraphs filled with concrete details and errors, the young woman sitting next to her wrote dull, perfectly correct ones.

## Relative Clauses

We have talked previously about the use and usefulness of subordinate clauses in helping you provide sentence variety. Remember that sentence elements introduced by subordinating conjunctions depend on the main or independent clause to complete the meaning, and that is why we often refer to them as **dependent clauses**.

We are now ready to look at a new use of subordinate clauses. Like the ones that we looked at previously, these clauses have a subject, a verb, and, unless the verb is intransitive, something to complete the meaning: a predicate noun, adjective, adverb of place, or object.

These new clauses are called relative clauses. Usually, they begin with a relative pronoun: "that," "which," "who," "whom," or "whose." Some relative clauses, however, begin with "when" or "where." **Relative clauses function as adjectives.**

There are two important characteristics to remember about relative pronouns and the clauses they introduce:

1. Like all pronouns, a relative pronoun takes the place of a noun and, therefore, must have an antecedent.

2. A relative pronoun, like other nouns and pronouns, can function as the subject of the verb, the object of the verb, or the object of the preposition.

A correct relative clause must contain a subject and a verb. It may contain an object. In order to ensure that your relative clauses are correct, you need to be able to verify that they have these elements, and that the elements work together to make sense. Therefore,

1. if you identify the antecedent of the relative pronoun, you can verify that the antecedent would make sense if it were substituted for the relative pronoun, and

2. if you identify the function of the relative pronoun in the sentence (is it a subject or an object?), you will be able to verify whether or not the clause has all the components it needs.

Look at these examples of relative clauses functioning as adjectives that modify a noun in the main, independent, clauses:

Under the chesterfield, I found the pie <u>that</u> was missing.

Noriko rode the biggest horse, <u>which</u> was also the most gentle.

This is the nurse <u>who</u> looked after me in the emergency room.

These are the books <u>whose</u> bibliographies suggest that they will be useful, reliable sources.

This is the time <u>when</u> we should act.

After driving around for hours, Hing found the house <u>where</u> he had lived when he was two.

Relative clauses can create problems for both native speakers and second language learners. Native speakers often have difficulty with the punctuation of restrictive and nonrestrictive relative clauses. Second language learners are more likely to have problems with the sentence structure of relative clauses.

Look at the following example of a problem with relative clauses:

✗ I define a true friend as a friend that he or she will always be there for you when you need.

The first clause in this sentence is correct, but the second is wrong because the verb has two subjects: "that" and "he or she." The third clause is also wrong because the transitive verb "need" has no object.

✓ I define a true friend as a friend that ~~he or she~~ will always be there for you when you need one.

In order to correct difficulties with relative clauses, you must first be able to recognize them and know how they are structured.

In the nine sentences below, the relative clauses have been set off in brackets. Note that, in the first three sentences, the relative pronoun acts as subject, but in the next three, it acts as an object. In the final three, we use "when" and "where." In all cases, these relative clauses act as adjectives.

## Exercise 16: Analyzing Relative Clauses

Circle the relative pronouns in the relative clause below and draw an arrow back to the antecedents.

1.  One of the people (*who* lives on my block) has four Dalmatian dogs.
    subject verb

2.  The oldest dog, (*which* is now close to thirteen years old), is the
    subject verb
    mother of the three others.

3.  Because there was no insurance on the car (*that* caused the accident)
    subject verb object
    the driver is faced with severe financial penalties.

4.  May I please borrow the book (*that* I gave you for your birthday)?
    object subject verb

5.  The hat (*that* the man wore) made me wonder what he did for a
    object subject verb
    living.

6.  Your friend, (*whom* I met yesterday), is in my chemistry class.
    object subject verb

7.  Paul leaves the day (*when* the new term begins).
    subject verb

8.  When you find the room (*where* the food is, tell Aaron).
    subject verb

9.  Chanukah is an occasion (*when* family and friends get together).
    subject verb

10. Jay found a black toque, (*which* <u>exuded</u> quite a different <u>feeling</u> than
                subject   verb                        object

his yellow one).

If you have difficulty with the sentence structure of relative clauses, you can verify that a clause is correctly formed by replacing the relative pronoun with its antecedent. Look at number one, for example. The antecedent for "who" is "one of the people." If you replace "who" with "one of the people," the clause makes sense:

<u>One of the people</u> <u>lives</u> on my block.
      subject        verb

If the relative pronoun acts as an object instead of a subject, the process is slightly more complicated. You must replace the pronoun with the antecedent and change the word order. The subject must come first, followed by the verb, and then the object. For example, in number four, the antecedent for "that" is "the book" (<u>that</u> <u>I</u> <u>gave</u> you for your birthday).
                                         object subject verb

If you replace the relative pronoun and change the word order, the clause reads, "I gave you the book." This makes sense, so the relative clause is correct.

In the following exercise, parentheses have been placed around the relative clauses. We ask you to underline the relative pronoun in each relative clause and classify it as either subject or object. Then, underline its antecedent twice. Finally, substitute the antecedent for the relative pronoun.

Example:

Pierre invested in a well-equipped, second-hand <u>bike</u>, (<u>which</u> has a
                                            antecedent   subject of the
                                                      verb "has"

rack, panniers, a headlight and taillight, and safety reflectors).

You can see if you substitute "bike" for "which," you get "The bike has a rack, panniers ..." In other words, you get a sensible sentence. Therefore, the relative clause is correct.

## Exercise 17: Analyzing Relative Clauses

Underline the relative pronoun in each relative clause, and classify it as either subject or object. Then underline its antecedent twice. Finally, substitute the antecedent for the relative pronoun.

1. The most expensive car in the show (which rides so smoothly it seems to float) costs more than twice what I make in a year.

2. The team won the game (that assured it a place in the finals).

3. The student (who was chosen to be valedictorian) was poised and self-assured as she gave her speech.

4. Because the house (that was damaged by the explosion) was fully insured, the family was fully compensated.

5. Hervé is the fellow (who is apprenticing to be a butcher).

6. Our friends were upset by your cousin Bill, (who behaved strangely during the whole ceremony).

In the above exercise, you will have noted that all the relative pronouns function as subjects of the verb in the relative clause.

As we noted on pages 155–156, when the relative pronoun functions as the object of the clause, the order within the clause will be altered. The normal order of a declarative clause in English is Subject - Verb - Object. In relative clauses in which the relative pronoun is object, the order is Object - Subject - Verb.

Consider this example:

Pierre recently invested in a well-equipped, second-hand bike,
antecedent

(which he has already decided to sell).
object

The antecedent of the pronoun "which" is "bike." If you substitute "bike" for "which," you get "The bike he has already decided to sell." When the relative pronoun functions as an object, you have to change the word order to verify that the relative clause is correct. Put the object of the verb in its normal position: "He has already decided to sell the bike." That makes sense, so the relative clause is correct.

## Exercise 18: Analyzing Relative Clauses

Parentheses have been placed around the relative clauses. Underline the relative pronoun in each relative clause, and classify it as either subject or object. Then underline its antecedent twice. Finally, substitute the antecedent for the relative pronoun.

1. Will you please return the books (that I lent you last term)?

2. The outfit (that the man wore) made the children stare.

3. Mr. James' philosophy class (which I take at 8:00 in the morning) is always full.

4. The story, (which the teacher read aloud to the class), brought tears to Lianne's eyes.

5. Most of our students, (whom we expect to arrive on Saturday), will need help unloading their luggage.

6. Do you have any further comments about the incident (that you witnessed last night)?

## Exercise 19: Relative Pronouns as Subjects or Objects

Underline the relative pronoun. Write subject or object above it and draw an arrow to its antecedent.

1. Joel's dad gave a ride to all the kids who happened to be in our yard when we were heading to the playground.

2. The mid-term that I wrote in October did not count toward the final mark.

3. The staff that is on the development team for the new product arrive at work an hour early each morning.

4. The holidays, which we spent helping our grandmother settle in to her new home, flew by before we had time to relax.

5. After the heated discussion that dealt with the increase in the strata fees, the head of the Complex Police made a motion that everyone take a break.

6. The council members, who have a good sense of humour, gauged the mood of the meeting correctly.

7. If we can use up the old paint that we bought for the bedroom, we won't have to worry about how to dispose of it.

8. After we escaped the traffic jam caused by the parade, we scrapped the plans that we had made to attend the jamboree.

9. The butter tarts, which I froze because I wanted to keep them long enough to take them to the picnic, had mysteriously disappeared from the freezer when I went to get them.

10. My son Pete, who swore he hadn't been the only midnight marauder, assured me that the tarts were as delicious frozen as they were thawed.

## Exercise 20: Analyzing Relative Clauses

Underline the relative pronoun in each of the sentences below. Identify the pronoun as either the subject or the object of the relative clause, and draw an arrow to its antecedent. Use the process outlined earlier in this chapter to check that each clause is correctly formed.

1. He gave a ride to the children, which was really very nice of him.

2. The quizzes that we complained about last week will not count toward our final marks.

3. All of the individuals that are on the team must be at the gym by seven o'clock.

4. Marianne is planning to buy a bike with the money that she gets from delivering papers.

5. The club members decided to take a recess after the discussion, which is why nobody was present for the second half of the meeting.

6. Can you lend me the vacuum cleaner that has the long hose?

7. If we sell all the tickets that we printed for the raffle, we will make enough money to pay for the new ball uniforms.

8. After our trip to the Caribbean, which was our third, the plans that we had for a cruise to the Mediterranean were dropped.

9. The Moon Festival was the time when Li-Ahn had the most fun that year.

10. Did Jeremy see the house where the quintuplets lived?

The following sentences contain sentence-structure errors in the relative clause. In particular, these sentences contain the types of errors that second or additional language learners often make. Now that you have had practice analyzing relative clauses and observing what their components and functions were, we think that you will make fewer of these errors.

## Exercise 21: Relative Clauses

Underline the relative pronoun, draw an arrow to its antecedent, and where there is an error, correct it. You will need to identify the subject and verb in order to check the structure.

1. If you give me the cheque that wrote for the groceries, I will pay the bill.

2. I need the letter that in the mail yesterday.

3. Do you know the child lives next door to me?

4. What time is the bus goes uptown?

5. There are some apartments in Charlottetown are more than fifty years old.

6. Most of the people living in the apartments are poor people have very little money for repairs.

7. This book tells a story happened in the 1950s.

8. When there is an unknown person comes to my house, my dog barks.

9. A forensic scientist examined the discarded papers and the clothing contained the evidence about the crime.

10. Some of the papers contained cryptic symbols appeared to be ancient writing.

## Exercise 22: Relative Clauses

In each relative clause below, identify the subject and the verb. Where necessary, use "which," "that," or "who" to correct the errors in sentence structure in the subordinate (relative) clauses. You will need to insert subjects or verbs in some cases.

1. If I lend you the shirt that gave me for my birthday, please give it back.

2. After they finish the courses are prerequisites, students will enroll in elective courses.

3. Actually, her brother borrowed the video was due back this morning.

4. Many of the students ate in the cafeteria served the tainted turkey.

5. He hopes to settle in a city has lots of theatres.

6. Mr. Simms was impressed by the workers that hired to do the detailed finishing work.

7. Mary-Lynne and Angie often disagree about the steps need to complete their project.

8. Bus drivers agree that kneeling buses improve access for all transit riders are a very good addition to the fleet.

9. Most people welcome newcomers bring new ideas and a fresh view of the world.

10. My next-door neighbours are newcomers come from the West African country of Senegal.

## Exercise 23: More Relative Clause Review

Each sentence in this exercise contains at least one faulty clause. First, identify the correct clause or clauses in each sentence. Then put brackets around the faulty clauses. Those clauses may lack a subject or object, or may have an extra subject or object. Make the necessary corrections.

1. If I can have one or two true friends in my life is worth it.

2. There were only three of us from my grade on the team, which including me.

3. Do not buy the jeans, which we looked at yesterday, because too expensive.

4. There is an exercise programme that sign up for in the Physical Education building.

5. Jack plays on the team won the finals.

6. The car drive to work every day is in the garage.

7. The briefcase, which combination lock, is in the back seat of the car.

8. The computer programme use to do word processing is very easy to learn.

9. Where is the lamp that bought yesterday for the living room?

10. People watch a lot of TV say there are many educational programmes.

## Exercise 24: Ensuring That the Relative Clause Has a Subject

Correct the following sentences when necessary. Underline the verb in each relative clause. Ensure that the relative clause has a subject for the verb.

1. I met many students wore shorts and heavy jackets today.

2. There are many bookstores in downtown Regina sell second-hand books.

3. I saw a book had a much better explanation of what happened.

4. This is the woman gave me the right answers.

5. Colleen knows some friends took a bus to Chemainus.

6. This is the book was on the bestseller list for nine months.

7. Do you know where the wing has computers is?

8. There are many stores downtown that sell books.

9. Every day I see a man goes for a walk up Mount Doug.

10. Did you read about the pit bull rescued a little girl?

## Exercise 25: Ensuring That the Relative Clause Has a Subject

Correct the following sentences when necessary. Underline the verb in each relative clause. Ensure that the relative clause has a subject for the verb.

1. Sam met a man has a 1960 red Cadillac convertible.

2. The Okanagan is a valley has lots of orchards and vineyards.

3. This is my cousin took me to see *Men in Black*.

4. Did you see the cloud looked like an elephant?

5. Put the papers have the right answers in this pile.

6. There is the lectern has a picture of superman on it.

7. There are many tourists visit Quebec City every year.

8. Last winter I had a friend got stuck in her house for a whole week during the blizzard.

9. Let us see the book has all the autographs in it.

10. Where is the boy looks after the sheep?

# Restrictive and Nonrestrictive Clauses

Restrictive and nonrestrictive are terms that describe two types of relative clauses. Restrictive clauses restrict the meaning of the word they modify. If you were to remove a restrictive clause, you would change the essential meaning of the sentence. For example, look at the sentence "People who break the law will be punished." If you were to remove the relative clause, "who break the law," instead of being a warning to lawbreakers, the sentence would express a threat that people in general will face punishment. We have used both of these kinds of clauses in the sentences in the above exercises. Perhaps you wondered why we used commas sometimes and not others.

# Punctuation of Restrictive and Nonrestrictive Clauses

You must put commas around information not essential to the meaning of the sentence. That is,

Nonrestrictive clauses are surrounded by commas.

Restrictive clauses are not surrounded by commas.

Examples:

Students who fail for the third time must see the dean.

Mark, who has failed for the third time, must see the dean.

In the first example, only students who fail for the third time must see the dean. If we removed the relative clause, the sentence would suggest that the dean will be a very busy person. Indeed, she may be busy and very annoyed. In the second example, the dean will have only one appointment—with Mark.

## Exercise 26: Restrictive/Nonrestrictive Clauses

In the following sentences, put commas around nonrestrictive relative clauses.

1. I have five cousins. The one who owns the red Ferrari is very rich.

2. That cousin buys a different car every year. The one that he drove to the family reunion two years ago was my favourite.

3. That car which wasn't nearly as expensive as the Ferrari wasn't even new. In fact, it was an antique, an old 1960 Mustang.

4. Of course, he also drove up with a new girlfriend which is what happens every year.

5. The girl said that the Mustang was a car that said everything she wanted to hear about a man.

6. My mum who loved the Ferrari best said the Mustang was cute, but if it were in a contest with the Ferrari, there was no contest.

7. I said I'd settle for a moped if I could just get wheels, so Mum who likes to spoil me if she can afford it came through when I graduated.

8. My birthday Volvo which is dung brown and flat out at eighty kilometres per hour is not pretty, but I love it dearly.

9. It has a bumper sticker that says "Slow and Safe Wins the Race."

10. My Volvo which I call Valerie takes me as far and as fast as I need.

## Exercise 27: Restrictive/Nonrestrictive Clauses

Here are more restrictive and nonrestrictive clauses. You can tell that we think they are important. Once again, insert commas around nonrestrictive relative clauses. Do not add commas to restrictive clauses.

1. Sunday night, I delivered my lasagne to the potluck supper which was at the church hall.

2. I decided long in advance to bake lasagne for the supper, but I have two recipes and couldn't decide which one to use. The recipe that calls for ground beef is very tasty, but wouldn't suit people who are vegetarian.

3. I called my grandmother and asked for her lasagne recipe that had the most drips and spatters on it.

4. I liked the recipe that my grandmother gave me, but it called for fresh spinach which was out of season.

5. Luckily, I remembered that Sally's Super Saver Market which is only six blocks away had frozen spinach on special.

6. On the way to the church hall, I had to slam on my brakes to avoid hitting a stray dog that ran out into the middle of the road.

7. The lasagne which was on the seat beside me flew off and splattered all over me and the dash.

8. Fuming, I pulled over, opened the door which was draped with a fat lasagne noodle and stepped out.

9. The dog that I nearly hit was apparently a big fan of frozen spinach dishes because he took a quick lick at my pant legs, smiled the way dogs do, and leapt into the car where he began wolfing down my contribution to the church supper.

10. I was so grateful to have the mess cleaned up that I adopted the dog which I now call Lucky-to-be-Alive, or Lucky, for short.

In the above exercises, have you discovered that you have been putting commas around clauses that begin with "which" but not those that begin with "that"?

Although not all grammar books agree, we think that it is useful to maintain the following pattern: if a clause is restrictive, essential to the meaning of the sentence, begin it with "that." If a clause is helpful or interesting but not essential to the meaning, non-restrictive, put commas around it.

## Exercise 28: Restrictive/Nonrestrictive Clauses

Here are yet more restrictive and nonrestrictive clauses. Consider whether the relative clauses are essential and, once again, insert commas around nonrestrictive relative clauses.

1. Charles Smith who is ten years old won the car.

2. My eldest sister who married a doctor lives in Kaleden.

3. People who live in glass houses should not throw stones.

4. A child who screams for attention should be ignored.

5. Andrew whom you considered meek is very temperamental.

6. Men thought to be meek and mild often act like heroes.

7. Bess had waited impatiently for the taxi which was twenty minutes late.

8. The fall exercise schedules which are a little late this year should arrive in the mail tomorrow.

9. Lin's elder brother who is coming for a visit has never been on a plane.

10. The parking restrictions which were revised in June have been changed again.

## Exercise 29: Restrictive/Nonrestrictive Clauses

Return to exercises 26, 27, and 28. Punctuate them properly, using the rules for restrictive and nonrestrictive clauses. You will find that, in some cases, the clause could be either restrictive or nonrestrictive depending upon the meaning you wish to give it. Be prepared to defend your punctuation.

### Activity 2: Writing—Putting theory into practice

Now that you can recognize and punctuate relative clauses correctly, write a short composition of about 250 words in which you focus on relative clauses. To make the task easier, begin by making a chart containing details that you can use in the composition.

☆ (We have set up the exercise so that you can write about cars. However, if you don't have much interest in cars, follow the same process but write about shoes, apartments, or reclining chairs.)

a) On the chart, list five cars. Two of them must be the same make and model.

b) Then list five locations where you saw those cars. You might use the names of real car dealerships; you might list imaginary street addresses of cars advertised for sale in a newspaper; or you might make up the names of salesrooms.

c) Finally, list a minimum of three details about each car. You might include colour, price, type of upholstery, condition, type of transmission (manual or automatic), type of stereo system, etc.

*continued*

**Activity 2: Writing—Putting theory into practice (continued)**

| Names of cars | Locations | Details |
|---|---|---|
| _____ | _____ | _____ |
| _____ | _____ | _____ |
| _____ | _____ | _____ |
| _____ | _____ | _____ |
| _____ | _____ | _____ |
| _____ | _____ | _____ |

Once your chart is complete, write a comparison and contrast composition in which you focus on using relative clauses correctly. Since at least two of the cars on your list are the same make and model, it should be easy for you to use at least one restrictive clause.

Start your composition with the following sentence:

*Last Saturday, I went shopping for cars.*

## Passives

Although we deal with Passives in Chapter Two: Verbs and Voice, we also want to mention it here. The passive is a structure with some great drawbacks but a few useful features.

In a passive sentence, the object of the action is the subject of the sentence. "The ball was thrown to first base by the pitcher," is a passive sentence that no sportswriter would use. The sentence is dull and cumbersome. It emphasizes the ball rather than the pitcher who picked up the bunt and got the ball to first. A sportswriter would write, "The pitcher hurled the ball to first base," an active sentence where the doer of the action is the subject of the sentence.

Perhaps you noticed that the original sentence contained an "is," and if the sportswriter was in the habit of zapping isys, he or she would automatically have written the active sentence. If your writing contains few needless isys, you can be sure that it also has few passive sentences.

Passive sentences are, in general, weak, wordy, and indirect. Business and technical writing courses now emphasize the desirability of active sentences. Even some government departments have got on the active bandwagon. In the past, they have been eager users of the passive, probably because passive sentences, with no doers of the action or with de-emphasized ones, allow bureaucrats to evade responsibility for actions. "It is regrettable but necessary that taxes will be raised next year," neatly avoids saying who exactly will raise the taxes. You can be sure, however, that the opposition parties will clear up the omission.

The following activity will familiarize you with the passive form.

---

### Activity 3: Writing a paragraph in the passive

From the list below, select ten verbs to use in a single paragraph. Form the passive of those verbs by putting "was," "were," "is," "are," or "will be" in front of each one and changing the verb itself to the past participle.

For example, if you chose the first two verbs on the list, the past participles would be" caused" and "guaranteed." Using those two verbs, you could form any of the following passive forms:

Violence **is caused** . . .
Accidents **are caused** . . .
Our happiness **was caused** . . .

The appliance **is guaranteed**. . .
The dates **are guaranteed**. . .
The workers' support **was guaranteed**. . .

The disagreements **were caused** . . .
A drop in temperature **will be caused** . . .

Our tickets **were guaranteed** . . .
His safety **will be guaranteed**. . .

**Verb list**

| | | | |
|---|---|---|---|
| cause | dismiss | find | track |
| guarantee | include | develop | turn |
| dedicate | decide | experience | drive |
| convert | refer | resolve | pilot |
| invite | expect | concern | propel |
| prepare | control | untangle | manoeuvre |
| fire | clear up | abandon | steer |
| insult | share | overcome | launch |
| distract | make | leave | aim |

---

### Activity 4: Changing passive to active

Rewrite the paragraph you just completed, using the same verbs but changing them from passive to active. You may need to think of "actors" to do the action of the verbs. If, for example, you said, "Our tickets were guaranteed," you might change the sentence to say, "The ticket agent guaranteed our tickets."

---

The next activity, seemingly by a bureaucrat-in-training, uses the passive voice to conceal information and, thereby, evade responsibility.

## Activity 5: Passive voice

**Nobody-Dun-It**
**A Mystery in the Passive Voice**

The following mysterious note was discovered on the kitchen table by an unidentified father one Saturday morning. Rewrite the note, using active voice and names to identify the characters in this drama. (You may also wish to eliminate some of the clichés.)

Dear Mum and Dad,

Unfortunately, the family car was involved in a minor traffic accident yesterday afternoon and was slightly damaged. (Nothing that cannot be repaired, you will be pleased to know!) Due to lateness and rush-hour traffic, schedules were upset, so it was collectively decided to take a shortcut through the alley behind the Mayhurst Shopping Centre. As ill luck would have it, the lane appeared to be tightly constricted by a delivery van. It was decided by someone with a clear view out the back window that backing up would be a good idea, so the car was put in reverse, but, in the meantime, another van, which was not noticed at first, had been driven into the lane. Thus, the car was bumped (very gently) into the second van before it was apparent that the car was sandwiched between two vehicles.

Because exams were scheduled for Friday afternoon, and it was unanimously agreed that parents would be very irritated if the exams were missed, it was voted that the car be squeezed past the first van. It was while the squeezing was taking place that the paint on the car became slightly damaged.

The twelve dollars in the envelope, which is all that could be dug up by the individuals who were present at the time of the mishap, has been donated as a gesture of apology and goodwill.

Love,

An individual present
at the time

# Parallelism

Parallelism creates problems for native speakers and second-language learners alike. Both second-language learners and native speakers improve their writing when they eliminate errors in parallelism and begin to use parallel structure to generate powerful sentences.

Native speakers often make errors in parallelism when they are unaware of the impact of style on their writing. Their problem is not that they cannot make one phrase parallel to another; rather, it is that they concentrate on content to the exclusion of form, thereby losing much of the power of language. A native speaker, for example, *might* write "The purpose of this mission is to look for new places as well as seek new life; we're going to go where people are living in different ways. Also we plan to be very bold about travelling where nobody else has gone." In contrast, another native speaker, very conscious of the power of parallel structure to affect style, *did* write "These are the voyages of the starship, Enterprise, its continuing mission: to explore strange new worlds, to seek out new life and new civilizations, to boldly go where no one has gone before." Clearly, the second version has much more power to convince than does the first.

In contrast to native speakers, second-language learners often make errors in parallelism, but they frequently do so because they are unfamiliar with particular forms. Sometimes they lack vocabulary; sometimes they need help to acquire unfamiliar structures. For example, a second-language learner may know the noun forms "goal" and "plan," but she may not know the noun "perseverance." Therefore, instead of writing "A successful individual has a goal, a plan, and perseverance," she might write "To be successful, an individual needs a goal, a plan, and keep on working even when it is hard."

The first sets of exercises should familiarize both groups of students with simple parallel structures. The second set gives students an opportunity to play with the rhetorical effects of purposefully used parallel structures. In brackets after each entry, we have named the grammatical forms in each series so that students who need to acquire a better understanding of the forms may do so. As students learn to use parallelism, they will notice an increase in conciseness and clarity: a combination of style and substance.

## Parallel Structures: Form

1. When you have items in a series, they should all have the same structure: that is, they should all be nouns, or verb phrases, or adverbs, or subordinate clauses, etc.

   ✗ She enjoyed <u>playing golf</u>, <u>riding</u> dirt bikes, and <u>to swim</u> at Elk Lake.   gerund   gerund   infinitive

   ✓ She enjoyed <u>playing</u> golf, <u>riding</u> dirt bikes, and <u>swimming</u> at Elk Lake.   gerund   gerund   gerund

   ✗ In the summer, they read *Emma*, *Jane Eyre*, and   noun   noun

   <u>finished *Return of the Native*</u>.   verb + noun

✓ In the summer, they read *Emma*, *Jane Eyre*, and
                                   noun      noun
*Return of the Native*.
        noun

2.  When you have correlative conjunctions such as *not only/ but also*, *either/or*, *neither/nor*, *whether/or*, *both/and*, they should be followed by words of the same grammatical structure. If, for example, the first part of the correlative expression is followed by adjectives, then the second part must be as well. If the first is followed by noun phrases, the second must be followed by noun phrases. If the first is followed by verbs, the second must be followed by verbs, and so on.

✗ Joe *not only* liked maple walnut ice cream *but also* strawberry.
               verb + adjective                  adjective + elided noun

✓ Joe liked *not only* maple walnut *but also* strawberry ice cream.
              adjective + elided noun           adjective + noun

✓ Joe *not only* liked maple walnut *but also* loved strawberry.
          verb                   verb

✗ Sarah wanted *either* to go water skiing *or* sky diving.
             infinitive            gerund

✓ Sarah wanted *neither* to go water skiing *nor* to go sky diving again.
              infinitive        infinitive

## Exercise 30: Parallelism

Make necessary changes in the sentences to ensure that items in a series or words following correlative conjunctions are parallel structures.

1.  Joe preferred listening to CBC rather than to listen to CKNW.

2.  At the basketball clinic, Sam learned self-confidence, new skills, and being a good sport.

3.  The group not only saw the baby lions but also the new stork.

4.  Andy found sand in the shoes, the pants, and in the jacket.

5.  The doctor was knowledgeable, quick, and she talked a lot.

6.  Good analytical skills are necessary in not only studying science but also literature.

7.  Eugene preferred to rent a house rather than buying a condo.

8.  Eleanor thought that the car was too old, too ugly, and it cost a lot!

9. Frank wanted to take both the chemistry course and physics.

10. Sam had not decided whether to take the bus or hitchhike.

## Exercise 31: Parallelism

Make necessary changes in the sentences to ensure that items in a series or words following correlative conjunctions are parallel structures.

1. Barbara likes people who have a good sense of humour and a good car.

2. Sarah admires people with gentle personalities, but they have firm ideas.

3. He would rather play than to sing at the concert.

4. You can get to St. John's by boat, ferry, or fly.

5. Unlike Linda, Pat neither likes knitting nor to crochet.

6. Jeremy ran up the steps, laughing, panting, and with a struggle to keep his knees straight.

7. Patrick's best friend likes listening to music, to watch television, and to play video games.

8. The dog was not only long legged but also he had a short tail.

9. You will have a smooth sauce if you use medium heat, stir regularly, and you should add the liquid slowly.

10. Samantha told her friend that she expected courtesy, tolerance, and he should be honest.

# Problem Sentence Patterns

## Fragments

Fragments are regarded as very serious sentence-structure errors, but knowing about a subordinate clause and about what differentiates it from an independent clause should help you to avoid this error. After you thoroughly understand fragments and never ever write one accidentally, you may choose to use them occasionally to create a certain effect.

A fragment masquerades as a sentence because it has a capital letter and some kind of end punctuation. Here, for example, is a particularly brilliant fragment. It begins Aldous Huxley's novel *Brave New World*:

"A squat grey building of only thirty-four storeys."

Of course, by the time Huxley wrote this fragment, he had already written dozens of books and knew exactly what he was doing. You don't have to wait quite that long, but waiting until you are finished your formal education would be a good idea, and if you are in business or any occupation that requires standard English, you will have to wait longer. If you are writing dialogue, of course, you will use fragments, particularly in response to questions.

"Horace!" she screamed. "How on earth did you get here?"

"Camel train, s-s-sweetheart," he said, spitting sand out through the "s."

A fragment may lack a subject, or it may lack a verb. The Huxley quotation, for example, lacks a verb. Sometimes, as we mentioned before, a fragment may have a subject and a verb and whatever is needed to complete the meaning, but it is a fragment because the clause begins with a subordinating conjunction. Because that's the way it is. Remember that length does not signal a fragment; a fragment could occupy four lines but still be a grammatically incomplete thought.

## Exercise 32: Recognizing Fragments

Put an ✗ by any of the following that are fragments.

1. ___ The last one being the best, of course.

2. ___ After he got home from work.

3. ___ Then, the bomb exploded.

4. ___ The trees swaying, the birds gliding on the air currents, and, underneath the shelter, the team members readying their kites.

5. ___ When the boy jumped, and after his sister jumped in after him.

6. ___ Over on the far right, past the small stream, and further still to the edge of the distant village.

7. ___ Since it was gone, Tatsu left.

8. ___ Such as the software package and the size of the hard drive, not to mention whether the screen was an active dot matrix.

9. ___ Driving a car without a licence being really stupid.

10. ___ Wanting not only the salsa but the guacamole.

## Exercise 33: Recognizing Fragments

Put an ✗ by any of the following that are fragments.

1. ___ Penelope wept.

2. ___ Joanne had a short rest after she got home from school.

3. ___ Because, for example, Blaise Pascal and Pierre de Fermat stated the theory of probability in the mid-seventeenth century.

4. ___ *The Cure for Death by Lightning* coming out in 1996 and, on the other side of the country, *Fall on Your Knees* coming out in 1997.

5. ___ Once they had found the building, the classroom, and the washrooms.

6. ___ On the left lay a decrepit barn.

7. ___ Suffering from scurvy and other preventable diseases.

8. ___ Store-bought tomatoes being pale, hard, and tasteless.

9. ___ Especially hard to believe considering that in 1914 only 16 cities had a population of more than a million.

10. ___ Peeking under the hanging branches that hung to within six inches of the ground and looking like tiny blue stars.

# The Comma Splice

Recognizing what is and what is not an independent clause will help you with another very serious sentence-structure error besides the fragment, the comma splice. "Splice" means "to join" or "to connect." What is being joined by a comma in a comma splice are two independent clauses. In the chapter on punctuation, we state our position that commas are not strong enough glue to hold independent clauses together, no matter how "short" the clauses may be. We regard a comma between any independent clauses as a comma splice and, therefore, a grievous error.

Fortunately, we have five common ways to correct a comma splice. Some of these you used in the pretest when you dealt with Percival and Penelope and their tumultuous relationship. Let's use the unhappy couple again. If we write "Percival yelled, Penelope left," in these clauses, the verbs are intransitive and do not need anything to complete the meaning. We have, therefore, two independent clauses joined by just a comma, and we have, therefore, created a comma splice.

## Prescription

### The comma splice

1. Don't join independent clauses with just a comma.

2. Separate two independent clauses with a period.

3. Join two independent clauses with a semicolon.

4. Join two independent clauses with a semicolon and a conjunctive adverb.

5. Join two independent clauses with a comma and a coordinating conjunction.

6. Join two independent clauses with a subordinating conjunction.

Let's follow the prescription with Percival and Penelope. All of the following sentences are correct.

Percival yelled. Penelope left.

Percival yelled; Penelope left.

Percival yelled; **therefore**, Penelope left.

Percival yelled, so Penelope left.

**Because** Percival yelled, Penelope left.

Try the same sequence using other conjunctive adverbs and other conjunctions. You see, correcting a comma splice is easy if you recognize the problem. If you have honed your ability to recognize independent clauses, you will quickly spot and correct comma splices. You may even be able to use an absolute to correct a comma splice: **Percival having yelled, Penelope left.** When you look at the many ways that you can correct comma splices, you may begin to look upon correcting them as an opportunity to add sentence variety to your writing.

## Exercise 34: Spotting the Comma Splice

Put an ✗ beside any comma splice in the following sentences.

1. In 1859, Karl Marx wrote *Critique of Political Economy*, John Stuart Mill wrote "Essay on Liberty."

2. When John saw the mouse, he was startled, he jumped back so fast that he lost his footing and fell into the compost pile.

3. A four-year-old girl was the first person to receive gene therapy, she lacked the adenosine deaminase gene.

4. It took thirty-three years to complete the Netherlands Delta Flood Protection project, it was finished in 1986.

5. Bob Geldorf did a great deal for famine relief, so he was knighted.

6. Wole Soyinka won the Nobel Prize for literature, despite world-wide protests, he was later executed for treason in Nigeria.

7. Cameron enjoys walking, whether the weather is fine or not.

8. I really need mosquito repellent, a mosquito net, candles, and a slingshot.

9. Wendy couldn't believe it, in *Curtain*, Agatha Christie killed off Hercule Poirot.

10. When readers stop to think about it, they realize that the hallmarks of English detective fiction all started with *The Moonstone*.

## Exercise 35: Spotting the Comma Splice

Put an ✗ beside any comma splice in the following sentences.

1. I can't believe that my computer just told me that things that go away by themselves can come back by themselves, I think that is untrue, especially with computers!

2. Pele was a superstar soccer player from Brazil, a country that takes its soccer very seriously.

3. Brazilians are also very interested in politics, as are many people in other South American countries.

4. To many students from other countries, Canadian instructors at first seem disorganized and lackadaisical, then they begin to understand that there is more than one way of teaching.

5. Kami thought that one difference was that in Japan teachers focused on memorizing, while Canadian teachers focused more on understanding.

6. Steve went shopping, he was looking for a birthday present for Jennifer, but he came home empty-handed.

7. She loved cooking, cleaning up the kitchen was another matter.

8. When Jordan returned to work after his three week holiday, there were 306 e-mail messages to read.

9. Putting topic sentences in the first sentence of a paragraph seems the most logical, effective place, so you should place them elsewhere only when you are trying to create a special emphasis, perhaps using inductive reasoning or even trying to create suspense.

10. I really like an African proverb that my friend Kenzi told me: it says you can leave a log in the water as long as you like, it will never be a crocodile.

---

### Activity 6: Correcting the comma splice

Combine the following incorrectly spliced sentences in three ways each: one, using a conjunctive adverb, two, using a coordinating conjunction, and three, using a subordinating conjunction.

1. Molly and Ling planned a picnic, it rained on the day that they set.

2. Rob studied hard for his economics exam, he expected to do well.

3. Debbie wanted to try engineering, Vera wanted to try philosophy.

4. The cat was hungry, it stood patiently in front of the fridge.

5. She loved to drive fast, she collected a lot of tickets to put on her wall.

6. Marcus wrote the introduction, conclusion, and recommendations, Oksana wrote the body.

7. The scouts saw the sailboat heeling over, they called 911.

8. Many immigrants do quite different jobs than they did at home, many of them feel frustrated by this situation.

9. Canadians spell most words like the British do, they spell some like Americans do.

10. The bowl was empty, Oliver asked for more congee.

---

## Negative Sentence Pattern

When you use certain negative words in English, after the negative word or words, you must invert the subject and the auxiliary verb. Here are some examples. Note that many of the negative words are adverbs of frequency.

Hardly <u>had</u> he left when the mail came.

Only by changing the system <u>can</u> she succeed at the job.

Never before <u>had</u> Joan driven the car.

Scarcely had Sam poured the tea when the doorbell rang.

Nowhere can you find better muffins.

Rarely do students see dragon flies on campus.

She has not learned to swim; neither has she learned to fly.

They won't help the bird, nor will they harm it.

Never again will you meet such friendly people.

Only by making mistakes can you make progress.

Nowhere have I seen such nice peaches.

Seldom does she finish before nine o'clock.

Hardly had the car stopped when he jumped out.

Only at this time can we complete the letter.

Under no circumstances should you go.

**"Not only/but also" are not part of this pattern.** Do not ever start a sentence with "not only" unless you are explaining the rule!! You cannot make such a sentence parallel. "Not only"/"but also" are correlative conjunctions and should appear before the same parts of speech, an impossibility when you begin a sentence with "not only." In the following example, the "not only" is followed by a verb, but the "but also" is followed by a pronoun.

✗ Not only do nurses need to provide care, but also they need to provide understanding.

The sentence should be changed to read

✓ Nurses need to provide not only care but also understanding.

In the second example, the correlative conjunctions are followed by the same parts of speech: nouns, the second noun being a gerund. Here is another incorrect example followed by the corrected sentence:

✗ Not only do I want cake but also ice cream.

✓ I want not only cake but also ice cream.

## Exercise 36: Negative Pattern Sentences

Change these sentences so that they begin with a negative word, e.g., She never drinks pop. ➜ *Never does she drink pop.*

1. John seldom saw children in the park.

2. We rarely go to matinees.

3. Joe doesn't make mistakes in spelling often.

4. David never ate eggplant.

5. Jane didn't see whales anywhere.

6. Mary did her homework only when she was coaxed.

7. They seldom went to the park on Bay Street.

8. I didn't see the elephant anywhere.

9. He took time off only in July.

10. Sarah wouldn't ride the camel under any circumstances.

## Exercise 37: Negative Pattern Sentences

Create correct sentences beginning with the following words and underline the **subject** and the auxiliary **verb**:

1. Only when

2. Rarely

3. Not often

4. Under no circumstances

5. Never again

6. Nowhere

7. Scarcely

8. Never

9. Only infrequently

10. Never before

# Redundant Pronouns

Do not begin a sentence with a prepositional phrase in which the object of the preposition is also the antecedent for the subject of the sentence. This error most commonly occurs in sentences beginning with the prepositions "by," "with," "for," "in," "on," and "at." To correct the problem, simply eliminate the preposition and the redundant pronoun.

Examples:

✗ By the word average, it means ordinary, normal, or typical.

✓ The word average means ordinary, normal, or typical.

✗ To an unskilled person, he may care more about the cost of the camera than the innovative technology.

✓ An unskilled person may care more about the cost of the camera than the innovative technology.

## Exercise 38: Redundant Pronouns

Correct the following sentences, all of which contain redundant pronouns and problem prepositional phrases.

1. With many people, they have trouble making decisions.
2. For students, they need somewhere quiet to study.
3. In a good marriage, it requires that people be considerate of each other.
4. By cleaning out your desk drawers, it will get you off to a fresh start.
5. On well-planned assignments, they should include criteria explaining how the finished work will be evaluated.
6. With a lot of checkout clerks, they have health problems caused by repetitive movement syndrome.
7. By reading a short story twice, it will give you time to think about the author's technique and consider how he or she creates such condensed meaning.
8. For an athlete, she should recognize the need for a healthy diet to nourish an active body.
9. With Alice Munro, she is best known for her short fiction.
10. By renting a video, it will be much less expensive, and you can make your own popcorn.

## Exercise 39: Redundant Pronouns

Correct the following sentences, all of which contain redundant pronouns.

1. At a party, it should have good food and enjoyable music.
2. In some movies, they have so many special effects that very little attention is paid to a good script.
3. In a murder mystery, it often creates suspense by using music written in minor keys.
4. By checking the forecast, it will give you a clue about whether to pack your bathing suit.
5. With a new puppy, it can make people revise their opinions about what is chewable and what is not.

6. For a language like English, it often has a variety of ways to spell the same sound.

7. By checking your e-mail often, it will save you time in the end.

8. On the title page, it should include in addition to your name, your instructor's name, the course and section number, and the date.

9. After Christmas at the museum, it had long lineups for the Leonardo Da Vinci exhibit.

10. For the winning team, they just looked as though they could easily play another two periods, but we were exhausted.

## *It Is Easy; It Is Hard,* etc.

These two expressions—exceptions to the rule that pronouns must have antecedents—present problems for many speakers of English as an additional language. We dedicate a whole section to these expressions because they are so commonly used that students who have not mastered them often make at least one or two of this type of sentence-structure errors in every essay.

These expressions work in one of four ways:

1. It is hard to study when the weather is beautiful.

2. It is hard for some people to study when the weather is beautiful.

3. Beautiful weather makes it hard to study.

4. Beautiful weather makes it hard for some people to study.

In each sentence, there is an action or experience that is hard. We refer to that action as "the activity." The activity is always expressed as an infinitive. "The activity" in the above sentences is "to study."

The sentence *may or may not* include a person or thing for whom the activity is hard. We refer to such a person or thing as "the actor." Sentences two and four include actors. Those actors are "some people."

These sentences also may or may not include "the cause" of the difficulty. In sentences three and four, the cause of the difficulty is "beautiful weather."

### Diagnostic Exercise: *It Is Easy; It Is Hard*

Put an ✗ beside sentences that are wrong and a ✓ beside those that are correct.

1. ___ In tropical countries, the climate is hard to stay dry because there is so much humidity.

2. ___ Many people are very hard to learn a second language.

3. ___ The internet is easy to communicate with people all over the world.

4. ___ Nevertheless, it is easy to understand why people enjoy visiting tropical countries.

## Exercise 40: *Hard* or *Easy*

Using the information in the chart at the end of this exercise, construct sentences based on one of the four sentence patterns modelled above. Remember, "the activity" must be expressed as an infinitive.

The first sentence is done for you.

1. *It is hard to swim against a current.*

   *It is easy to swim against a current.*

2. _____

   _____

3. _____

   _____

4. _____

   _____

5. _____

   _____

6. _____

   _____

7. _____

   _____

8. _____

   _____

9. _____

   _____

10. _____

    _____

| THE CAUSE | THE ACTOR | THE ACTIVITY |
|---|---|---|
| | | swimming against a current |
| | teenagers | understanding their parents |
| | someone without a car | enjoying the tourist attractions<br>swallowing bad-tasting medicine |
| high housing prices | newly married couples | buying a home |
| car fumes | people with asthma | breathing comfortably<br>getting a job |
| high cost of tuition | some students | paying for higher education<br>eating sensibly every day |
| traffic jams | commuter | getting home quickly |

In the previous exercise, you were asked to use only "It is hard," or "It is easy." However, this pattern is not restricted to those two expressions. The following expressions all follow the same pattern as the one you have just practised.

It is important.                    It is difficult.
It is useless.                      It is fun.
It is delightful.                   It is dangerous.
It is glorious.                     It is challenging.
It is possible.                     It is common.
It is impossible.                   It is unusual.
It is sensible.                     It is convenient.
It is foolhardy.                    It is inconvenient.

## Exercise 41: *Dangerous, Inconvenient,* and *Downright Impossible*

Using the information in the second chart below, select an appropriate expression from the list above and construct sentences based on one of the four sentence patterns you practised in Exercise 40. Remember that "the activity" must be expressed as an infinitive.

| THE CAUSE | THE ACTOR | THE ACTIVITY |
|---|---|---|
| | | living right next to a bus stop |
| | teenagers | enjoying different music than their parents |
| | a determined person | succeeding despite great odds<br>eating wild berries if you don't know what kind they are |
| infrequent buses | people in the suburbs | taking the bus to work<br>sitting on the rock beside the ocean on a summer's day |
| | Bassett hounds | being bad-tempered |
| student loans | students without many savings | attending university |
| | | eating sensibly every day |
| traffic jams | commuter | getting home quickly |

1. *It is convenient to live right next to a bus stop.*

2. _____

3. _____

4. _____

5. _____

6. _____

7. _____

8. _____

_____

9. _____

_____

10. _____

_____

---

**Activity 7: Excuses, excuses, excuses**

Write a 75- to 100-word paragraph, in which you use the sentence patterns just practised to come up with every excuse in the book to rationalize why you should be excused from doing this exercise.

---

## Recommend, Advise, Insist, Suggest, Ask, etc.

Here is a list of words that express recommendation, resolution, or demand:

| | |
|---|---|
| demand | suggest |
| recommend | ask |
| advise | require |
| insist | move |

"It is essential," "it is necessary," "it is imperative," and "it is important," are also part of this pattern. "Advise," however, does not fit this pattern, though it means much the same as "recommend" or "suggest." See Chapter Two, page 97.

Students whose first language is not English frequently use words of recommendation or demand incorrectly in sentences. Here are some typical errors.

✗ I suggest them to see this great movie.

✗ He recommended me to go to Arts and Science Advising.

However, you must remember two things:

1. When words express a recommendation, resolution, or demand, you use what is called the subjunctive. This means that no matter whether the subject is singular or plural, you will use the same bare infinitive.

2. Words of recommendation, resolution, or demand must be followed by a "that" clause that uses the subjunctive.

The following sentences are correct: they have a "that clause," and they use the subjunctive.

✓ I suggest <u>that</u> Patrick and Valerie <u>see</u> this great movie.

✓ He recommended <u>that</u> I <u>go</u> to Arts and Science Advising.

Note that you can change the nouns or pronouns that are the subject of the verb in the "that" clause without changing the verb.

✓ I suggest <u>that</u> Patrick <u>see</u> this great movie.

✓ He recommended <u>that</u> they <u>go</u> to Arts and Science Advising.

Examples:

1. Joan insisted that they eat their breakfast before leaving for school.
2. She insisted that Jane eat her breakfast before leaving for school.
3. He demanded that John leave before ten o'clock
4. Ivan demanded that the students leave before ten o'clock.
5. I move that the resolution be adopted.
6. I move that the resolutions be adopted.
7. Jan required that the top margin be one inch.
8. Giovanni required that all margins be one inch.
9. Shauna asked that the baby be taken to work.
10. Shauna asked that the babies be taken to work.
11. It is essential that I finish before 6:30.
12. It is essential that we finish before 6:30.
13. It is necessary that Ian do all the exercises.
14. It is necessary that Ian and Juan do all the exercises.
15. It is important that Juanita know this pattern.
16. It is important that we know this pattern.

Some of the above list of words can also be followed by gerunds.

I <u>suggest</u> finishing quickly.

They <u>advocate</u> catching the three o'clock ferry.

She will <u>recommend</u> cancelling the Thursday meeting.

The recipe <u>required</u> using all the chocolate chips.

## Exercise 42: *Recommend, Advise, Insist, Suggest, Ask*

Correct the following sentences if necessary.

1. I recommend you to fix the car.

2. Jane suggest me to read the text book.

3. The counsellor demanded me to finish the application before April 30.

4. Joe recommended me to start a garden.

5. I suggest you to study on the ferry.

6. It is necessary for us to eat the leftovers today.

7. Sarah required Joe to water the garden.

8. Joe insisted Sarah to help him.

9. Joe insisted them to help him.

10. I move the meeting to adjourn.

## Exercise 43: *Recommend, Advise, Insist, Suggest, Ask*

Correct the following sentences if necessary.

1. It is imperative that James write the test again.

2. Sam recommends Teresa to take a sociology course.

3. The course demands us to do a lot of reading.

4. She asked that the people have their pens ready.

5. I suggest you to study this carefully.

6. It is important that the singers control their movement.

7. The Academic Advisor suggested me to take Honours.

8. The usher insisted them move to the front row.

9. The dentist recommends me to change my toothpaste.

10. Shelagh asks that he finishes the book before Tuesday.

## Exercise 44: *Recommend, Advise, Insist, Suggest, Ask*

Finish the following sentences using the correct pattern.

1. I recommend that you

2. It is important that they

3. Sean suggested that Kimiko

4. Adrienne advocated that we

5. She asked that Anick

6. Joe insisted that Barbara

7. It is necessary that the meeting

8. Yasu insisted that his friends

9. It is essential

10. She suggests that

## *So* as an Intensifier

When you use "so" as an adverbial intensifier, you must follow it with a "that" phrase. For example, saying "My brother got a present that was so big," is incorrect. "My brother got a present that was so big that we had to take the front door off its hinges," is correct. You cannot use "so" as you would use "very," another adverbial intensifier. "Very" needs no "that" phrase to complete the sentence correctly. Using "very," you could say "My brother got a present that was very big," and you would be perfectly correct.

### Exercise 45: *So* and *Very* as Intensifiers

Put a ✓ beside sentences that correctly use intensifiers.

1. ___ My new bike goes so fast, even up steep hills.

2. ___ At fifteen pounds, Aidan weighs so much that you would never believe he is only three months old.

3. ___ Whenever it rains, our basement gets so wet.

4. ___ Whenever it rains more than three hours, our basement gets so wet that we have to use a pump.

5. ___ Whenever it rains, our basement gets very wet.

6. ___ During the ballgame, Phoebe, Chloë, Penelope, and Daphne cheered so much.

7. ___ When the game was over, their throats were so sore that they mixed up a pitcher of hot honey and lemon punch.

8. ___ By studying fifteen minutes every night, you can do so well.

9. ___ Using a highlighter to mark the main ideas will make studying so easy.

10. ___ The box was so bulky that Percival could not get it on his motorcycle.

## Exercise 46: *So* and *Very* as Intensifiers

If necessary, change the following sentences in order to make them correct.

1. The swimming pool was so cold.

2. The manuscript was very old but well-preserved.

3. Trinh is dating a boy who is so tall.

4. On the other side of the room, the fire made the room so warm.

5. Where is the essay that the teacher said was so good that it should be published?

6. After the mid-term, Steve felt so relieved.

7. Because of all the nuts and chocolate chips, the cookies were very delicious.

8. Josephine was so glad when she received a new cookie sheet for her birthday.

9. Robert was so glad about the number of cookies they sold.

10. The descent was so steep, so Mr. Chan was glad to have his walking stick.

## Exercise 47: *So* and *Very* as Intensifiers

If necessary, change the following sentences in order to make them correct.

1. Gordon was so hungry.

2. Peter was very glad that he had eaten before the concert.

3. Penelope was so happy.

4. On the way downtown, Yoshi and Elaine saw a very big accident involving three cars.

5. The new Zamboni driver was so proud.

6. The speaker's "uhms" and "uhs" made it so hard to listen to the content of the presentation.

7. When he finally got on the ferry, Sasha felt very relaxed and ready to begin his adventure.

8. Proofreading a printed document is so important.

9. The water was so hot that the plastic cup warped and shrank.

10. Ever since the blizzard, Mac was so conscious of carrying proper equipment.

## Dangling and Misplaced Modifiers

Making your reader smile or laugh is admirable—if the subject warrants it, and you have done it on purpose. If you inadvertently dangle or misplace a modifier, however, you will create not only smiles or laughs, but also errors that can gravely affect the tone of your written work and your mark for mechanics.

### Dangling Modifiers

Dangling modifiers may come either at the beginning of the sentence or at the end. Trying unsuccessfully to hold onto the subject of the sentence, they dangle. A great many dangling modifiers are participles, which, you may remember, can act as adjectives.

Here is an example of a dangling (participle) modifier:

<u>Driving</u> down Government Street, a cougar ran right in front of us.

You'll see that the subject of the sentence is "a cougar." The modifier that precedes the subject should modify it, but clearly does not. It is not the cougar that is doing the driving. The modifier dangles helplessly as it is not properly attached to the subject of the sentence. To correct the sentence, you must supply a subject that can support the modifier.

Driving down Government Street, **we** saw a cougar run right in front of us.

As **we** drove down Government Street, a cougar ran right in front of us.

Now you can look at an example of a dangling modifier that dangles at the end of a sentence:

The report was finally put together working as a group.

You must supply a subject that can support the modifier because in the given sentence nobody is there "working as a group." Here are two corrected versions of this sentence:

Working as a group, **Jim, Bonnie, Franklin, and Rachel** finally put together the report.

**Jim, Bonnie, Franklin, and Rachel,** working as a group, finally put together the report.

If you have already begun zapping needless isys in your sentences, you may have noticed a bonus as you looked at the corrections of the modifiers that dangled above. If the writer had zapped isys in the original sentences, he or she would have automatically corrected the dangling modifiers.

Finally, look at this example of a dangling modifier that is not a dangling *participle*:

As a student, a mid-term exam is helpful, for it forces me to review.

The subject of the sentence is "a mid-term exam." The modifier that precedes it should modify it, but it clearly does not. You know that "a mid-term exam" is not "a student." Again, the modifier dangles helplessly as it is not properly attached to the subject of the sentence, and to correct the sentence, you must supply a subject that can support the modifier.

As a student, **I** find a mid-term exam helpful, for it forces me to review.

A mid-term exam is helpful, for it forces **a student** to review.

Check your work carefully to eliminate dangling modifiers, for you want to make your reader smile on purpose, *with* you, not at you.

## Exercise 48: Dangling Modifiers

In the following sentences, correct any modifiers that dangle.

1. Preparing breakfast on Sunday, the waffle iron burst into flame.

2. Driving the car at 100 km, the direction sign zipped past before it could be read.

3. While waiting for the dentist, magazines with humour sections relieve the tension.

4. At age three, the barber gave John his first haircut.

5. Riding his bike too close to the curb, George had an accident.

6. Not having practised, the oral presentation was a pain rather than a pleasure.

7. As a coach, a first-aid kit is a priority.

8. My computer is my greatest friend as a student.

9. Sending e-mails, stamps now seem to last forever.

10. Climbing through the dense bush and rocky terrain, the hill was formidable.

## Exercise 49: Dangling Modifiers

In the following sentences, correct any modifiers that dangle.

1.  Amazed at the good marks, the test was a success from the students' point of view.

2.  Working as a sales representative, a good smile is a necessity.

3.  As teachers, neatly typed papers are a pleasure.

4.  Walking through the Natural History Museum, the dinosaurs made the greatest impact.

5.  Being an essay writer, a good thesaurus is helpful.

6.  As a lover of vegetables, my favourite is peas fresh from the garden.

7.  When making oral presentations, notes are much better than whole sentences.

8.  Twice when she was three, Mariaye's mother took her to *Cinderella* in a theatre.

9.  A mouse scampered out while cleaning the closet.

10. While cleaning storm gutters, a sturdy ladder is a necessity.

## Exercise 50: Dangling Modifiers

Correct the following sentences to fix any modifiers that do not correctly modify the subject.

1.  Running through the forest, the trees reached out bony fingers to catch us.

2.  Comparing the two cities, Churchill is more exciting.

3.  The research paper was easier to write having done the research.

4.  Despite their lack of knowing any article rules, new learners of English can absolutely rely on native speakers when they say "You need to use 'the' here."

5.  Although rotted and decrepit, they crossed the bridge to safety.

6.  Feeling headachy, an aspirin seemed like a good idea.

7.  Galloping down the street, the horse caught everyone's attention.

8.  As a manager, customer satisfaction must come first.

9.  Putting a foot through the floor boards, the reason for the low price became clear to Yoko.

10. Wanting to be first in line, a sleeping bag and a thermos of coffee would be a good idea.

## Misplaced Modifiers

To correct the dangling modifiers, we added a subject that the modifiers could hang onto. With **misplaced modifiers**, errors that also create inadvertent humour, we make corrections by placing the modifier close to the word that it should modify. We don't need to add something to the sentence; we just need to rearrange the words. You will find that not just words, but phrases and whole clauses can be misplaced with surprising results.

Words that are often misplaced are "almost," "nearly," and "only." Look at the differences in meaning in the following sentences:

Stan **almost** ate the whole pie. (But he didn't eat any.)

Stan ate **almost** the whole pie. (He ate a great deal of it.)

In the first example, the adverb "almost" is modifying the verb "ate," while in the second, it is modifying the adjective "whole." Both these sentences could be correct, depending on how hungry or ethical Stan was, but if you write one when you mean the other, you have created a misplaced modifier.

**"Nearly"** works in a similar manner. "When the program froze, I nearly lost my whole document" is not nearly as dire as "When the program froze, I lost nearly my whole document."

Similarly, **"only,"** depending on its placement in your sentence, can create shades of meaning that you must be aware of. Look at the following examples and the way that the meaning of the sentence changes.

**Only** we sent the brochures to Pocket Printers. ("Only" modifies the pronoun "we." The competition sent their brochures to Priceless Printers or Print and Pay.)

We **only** sent the brochures to Pocket Printers. ("Only" modifies the verb "sent." (This sentence may not say what the writer meant.)

We sent **only** the brochures to Pocket Printers. ("Only" modifies the noun "brochures." We sent the newsletters to Priceless Printers or Print and Pay.)

We sent the brochures **only** to Pocket Printers. ("Only" modifies the noun "Pocket Printers." We never sent them anywhere else.)

We sent the brochures to Pocket Printers **only**. ("Only" modifies the noun "Pocket Printers." We never sent them anywhere else.)

You can see that when you use words like "nearly," "almost," or "only," you must carefully determine where to place them to create the meaning you intend.

Like the above words, phrases can be misplaced in ways that create meanings that are different or unclear to the reader. For example, "The employees agreed **in July** to take two weeks off" is unclear because of the modifier "in July." Does the writer mean "**In July**, the employees agreed to take two weeks off," or "The employees agreed to take two weeks off **in July**?" Obviously, the placement of the phrase affects the meaning of the sentence.

Clauses, like words and phrases, must be placed carefully to ensure that the reader receives the message that you intend. Look at these two examples:

> Mr. Wattanabe gave the transparencies to the students **that needed more detail**.

> Mr. Wattanabe gave the transparencies **that needed more detail** to the students.

In the first sentence, Mr. Wattanabe thinks that the students need help, while in the second sentence, he thinks that they can be of help. Remember, while to correct a dangling modifier, you provide an appropriate subject for the sentence, to correct a misplaced modifier, you move it next to the word that it modifies. Using modifiers correctly helps you to write sentences that are clear, unambiguous, and humorous only when you intend them to be.

## Exercise 51: Misplaced Modifiers

Correct the following sentences to fix any modifiers that are out of place.

1. Did Mr. Lau give that large bowl to the dog containing the leftover congee?

2. When Craig came home from tree planting, he put a load of clothes in the machine that he had worn for a whole week.

3. Sarah found a new kind of candy bar in the junk food dispenser made of coconut.

4. Fred saw a man reading a book while riding his bike.

5. After the double-header was over, the team got on the bus wearing the championship jackets.

6. Last week, I almost read all of *A Fine Balance* because everyone recommended it.

7. I've been looking for the missing marmot with my binoculars.

8. I handed in a drawing of a girl to my teacher, Mrs. Howard, who wore pigtails and had a wart on the end of her nose.

9. I need a title for the book that contains two short words beginning with "W."

10. Una left the dress in the suitcase that she had worn to graduation.

## Exercise 52: Misplaced Modifiers

Correct the following sentences to fix any modifiers that are out of place.

1. She wore a barrette in her hair made of woven strands of platinum and small rubies.

2. Wanted, a three-bedroom house by a recent immigrant with a large backyard, a vegetable garden, and fruit trees.

3. Kim was unhappy that Koji returned the book to the library about communication.

4. The pint-sized poodle stopped in front of the car with a nine-inch bone in its mouth.

5. In Newfoundland, Ling and Elaine visited the place where the ancient Vikings landed last summer.

6. The cat lay on the bed with its paws neatly tucked under its chin.

7. I only want to eat the red candies, so you can have the rest.

8. Jason could see the rampaging bulls looking out his grandma's window.

9. He found a toothbrush with a clear, hollow plastic handle with little fish that looked as though they were swimming in the drugstore.

10. I almost slept for ten hours, so I feel great.

## Exercise 53: Misplaced Modifiers

Correct the following sentences to fix any modifiers that are out of place.

1. He left the pen on the desk that the Prime Minister had used to sign the treaty.

2. While Joe cut the front lawn, in the backyard, Sarah weeded the beds with a hoe that contained the flowers and vegetables.

3. Samson ordered a purple alligator leather wallet from the catalogue with a secret pocket, space for thirty cards, and a built-in calculator.

4. The boy carried a basket under his arm with a six-foot cobra hiding in it.

5. I'd like you to review the police report on the March 15 accident which I had the opportunity to see on June 8.

6. The use of photo radar in my mind reduces accidents.

7. We plan a direct mail campaign targetting members with over $5000 on deposit and no RRSPs between the ages of 30 and 50.

8. Mercedes resolved to create a garden with both flowers and vegetables on January 1.

9. Deborah served Nanaimo bars to the guests on a bed of raspberry coulis.

10. I finally found a compact shrub that likes shade and is evergreen in a new gardening book.

## Question Word Order in a Statement

As we noted earlier in this chapter, avoiding the use of question word order in a statement is extremely important for all speakers of English as a second or additional language.

Before doing the following exercise, reread the section entitled "Avoiding the Use of Question Word Order in a Statement" on pages 147–150. Notice that "who" creates an exception to the rule.

### Exercise 54: Embedded Questions

Rewrite the following sentences correcting the sentence structure where necessary.

1. I don't know when are you going on vacation.

2. Can you please tell me how can I get to Dawson City?

3. Your brother wants to know where is the book he lent you.

4. The team members refused to reveal who was responsible for the damage to the locker room.

5. Doctor, can you tell me why is the fever so high?

6. I wonder what can I buy my father for his birthday.

7. Do you know why is he crying?

8. I think we should consider how are we going to pay for all these presents if we buy them.

9. The coach wants to know who is planning to attend the awards banquet.

10. We still haven't discussed where will the banquet be held.

# Using Sentence Structure for Rhetorical Effect

Using sentence structure purposefully is one of the keys to effective writing. Through sentence variety, we can achieve emphasis or sophistication. Effective sentence structure can even bolster the writer's argument because thoughts expressed well are (perhaps unfairly) taken more seriously than thoughts expressed weakly.

## Subordinating to Achieve a Rhetorical Effect

The first, and perhaps simplest, way of purposefully achieving the rhetorical effect you desire is to decide which ideas are central (main) and which ideas are secondary (subordinate).

Consider the following sentences:

> Dorothy Livesay died in Victoria, BC, where she lived and wrote during the final years of her life. In her obituary in *The Toronto Star*, Livesay was described as "one of the most widely read of modern Canadian poets."

As the above two sentences stand, the ideas they contain are presented as equally important. In fact, however, these two sentences—the first sentences in a short essay about Dorothy Livesay—are **not** of equal importance. Rather, the second sentence contains the idea that will be developed throughout the essay. Weak sentence structure—not weak content—makes the opening of this essay unfocused.

Now consider the following revision:

> When Dorothy Livesay died in Victoria, BC where she lived and wrote during the final years of her life, her obituary in *The Toronto Star* described her as "one of the most widely read of modern Canadian poets."

In the second version, Livesay's death is subordinated to the description of her widespread appeal as a poet. When the first sentence was presented as equal in importance to the second one, it seemed irrelevant to the topic. In contrast, once the fact of Livesay's death was subordinated to her stature as a poet, the relevance of the first sentence became clear. In the new version, the fact of Livesay's death provides a background detail or contextual point—in other words, a subordinate idea.

## Exercise 55: Subordinating the Subordinate Idea

Each of the groups of sentences below represents the first two sentences of an essay. Select the idea that seems most reasonably to express the topic of the essay. Rewrite the sentences as a single complex or compound-complex sentence in which you subordinate all minor details to the main idea.

1. Wicca has a reputation for being about black magic. It is a religion based on harmony with nature and its seasons.

2. Most of us read and write every day of our lives. Literacy is crucial to success and even to survival in our society.

3. Natural disasters often come without warning, so people are unprepared. Disasters bring out the best in people.

4. Within the next few years, many of our landfills will become full. We must find innovative ways to deal with our garbage problems.

5. Music is the language of love. Music is at the heart of love poetry.

## Loose Sentences for Rhetorical Effect

Loose sentences, which are constructed in the same way as most of our oral sentences, start with the subject and verb, thereby giving the reader the essential information right at the beginning. Following the subject and verb, loose sentences "accumulate" bits of loosely attached additional information. The writer could place a period at several points before the end of the sentence without leaving the reader feeling that the main idea was incomplete.

---

**LOOSE AND LYRICAL**

Notice the following loose sentence from Heather Menzies' essay, "When Roots Grow Back into the Earth":

"I worked the ground with my bare hands: scratching among gravel and stones, finding the edge of rocks and prying them out, then foraging around for handfuls of precious soil, sweet black humus with which to cover the roots of ten-inch nursery trees."

---

Loose sentences tend to meander. If you want to slow down the pace of a paragraph, deliberately use a loose sentence. To establish a pensive mood, consider a loose sentence. Loose sentences can be lyrical because their structure eliminates suspense.

On the downside, we sometimes write loose sentences, not by design but by default. Lazy sentences tend to be loose sentences, stringing together one idea after another without much thought to the relationship between those ideas. A loose sentence made up of a series of clauses linked with coordinating conjunctions sounds not only weak or lazy, but immature.

The following sentence is an example of a weak, loose sentence.

---

### LOOSE AND LAZY

High protein diets may include specially prepared drinks and packaged foods, but these may be very expensive and an individual can get most of his or her dietary needs met without eating dietary supplements.

---

## Periodic Sentences for Rhetorical Effect

In contrast to loose sentences, periodic sentences save the essential information until the last and, thereby, keep the reader in suspense until she or he arrives at the period. As a result, periodic sentences tend to be emphatic, teasing the reader along toward a climax.

---

### TEASING

The second chapter of Margaret Atwood's *Alias Grace* begins with a periodic sentence:

"On Tuesday, about 10 minutes past 12 o'clock, at the new Gaol in this City, James McDermot, the murderer of Mr. Kinnear underwent the extreme sentence of the law."

---

### Activity 8: Consciously choosing your sentence structure

Rewrite the following paragraph using periodic sentences to make the effect more suspenseful and to give some punch to the details. You may find it useful to break some of the sentences.

The storm hit at about 4 o'clock, just as we came out of the mall and headed toward the car. It seemed later than 4 o'clock because the sky was black and ominous, and we could hardly see across the parking lot but finally we managed to get back to the car in the blur of pelting rain. Visibility was so poor that we didn't even notice a van backing out just as we stepped into the red glow of its tail lights. Fortunately, the driver saw us at the last second and jammed on the brakes.

## Pace-Breaking Sentences for Rhetorical Effect

Pace-breaking sentences create emphasis by suddenly, and substantially, changing sentence length. Often, a pace-breaking sentence may be only three to five words long. Such a sentence, after a series of long sentences, comes as a surprise to the reader and forces his or her attention to rest on the idea expressed.

---

**PACE-BREAKING**

In her essay, "Hooked on Trek," Dawn Hanna quotes Joseph Campbell, who talks about the functions of myth. Notice the pace-breaking sentence at the end of the excerpt from Hanna's essay:

> "The third function [of myth] is the sociological one—supporting and validating a certain social order—the laws of life as it should be in the good society. The fourth function of myth is the pedagogical function, of how to live a human life-time under any circumstance. Myths can teach you that."

---

**Activity 9: Using a pace-breaking sentence to achieve emphasis**

Write a short paragraph on one of the following topics. End the paragraph with a pace-breaking sentence.

- A warning against drinking and driving.
- Tips for maintaining your sanity while studying for exams.
- An argument in favour of television as our window on the world.

---

## Fragments for Rhetorical Effect

Earlier in this chapter, you were warned about the use (or abuse) of fragments. The inadvertent use of a fragment is considered a serious sentence-structure error. However, fragments are used to great effect by many writers. As we noted earlier, Aldous Huxley begins his 1933 novel *Brave New World* with a brilliant fragment:

> "A squat grey building of only thirty-four storeys."

## FABULOUS FRAGMENS

E. Annie Proulx's novel, *The Shipping News*, is filled with fragments, many of them brilliant. The following short paragraph provides five examples:

"A great damp loaf of a body. At six he weighed eighty pounds. At sixteen he was buried under a casement of flesh. Head shaped like a crenshaw, no neck, reddish hair ruched back. Features as bunched as kissed fingertips. Eyes the color of plastic. The monstrous chin, a freakish shelf jutting from the lower face."

Fragments used well do remarkable things for writing. They shoot images at the reader, images that seem unattached to a writer's pen. Fragments can insist in a way that few other sentence structures can. They ignore the rules that normal sentences have to follow, so they can be more free and, potentially, wilder than other writing. But good fragments require skill. They are not merely sentences in which someone forgot the verb. If you think of them as being harder to write well than other sentences are, you will be more likely to develop your skill at using them.

### Activity 10: Using a model to write good fragments

Using the E. Annie Proulx excerpt above or one of the two excerpts below as a model, write a 50- to 75-word paragraph on one of the topics given.

"Edberg has already sidled past the edge of your vision, down a side alley and away. Country urban: prairie town. A coyote slinking along the too-populous section lines, tail down and muzzle hesitant. A porcupine, lumbering into coppice. Retiring, ready to lapse quietly into the deep breathing of forget."

Aritha van Herk
*Places Far From Ellesmere*

"Nothing. I said nothing. Piled small bowls, dishes, tokkuri, ochoko, ivory ohashi, cluttered to the kitchen. Too tired, too angry to heat water to wash them, only left to harden in the tub, scurry of cockroach, one cockroach seen meant ten unseen, Keiko tugging my sleeve, my obi, Makoto crying so weak like Otosan, Keiko tugging, and me saying nothing nothing NOTHING."

Hiromi Goto
*Chorus of Mushrooms*

*continued*

**Activity 10: Using a model to write good fragments (continued)**

**Topics**

- Using the Proulx model, describe someone with striking features.

- Using the van Herk model, describe the backyard of the place where you grew up or mountains the first time you saw them.

- Using the Goto model, describe a moment when you were frustrated.

# Parallelism for Rhetorical Effect

As you now know if you did the exercises on parallelism earlier in this chapter, what makes a structure parallel is its syntax. What you may not know—but what writers and speech makers have known for centuries—is that parallelism works. In the same way that some musical motifs have the power to stick in our heads and go around and around for days, so some parallel structures have the power to stick in our brains. Their rhythms and their repetitions seem to strike a primitive chord somewhere deep inside us; they deliver not only information but also an emotional jolt. You can use that jolt to bolster the impact of your writing.

To use parallel structure to your advantage, it is worth knowing one more thing about parallelism: the sense or meaning of word groups within parallel constructions may be **equivalent**, **complementary**, or **antithetical**. You will notice in the following examples that these categories sometimes overlap. We understand that you may categorize some of the quotations differently than we have done.

## Equivalent Parallel Meanings

Imagine the following scenario: Melissa is sick of her little twin sisters' going into her room without her permission, so when she gets home from school to find them rifling through her tennis equipment once again, she responds in a way designed to leave a clear message. Though she may not be aware of it, Melissa uses the age old rhetorical strategy of repetition through the use of a sequence of parallel structures that carry equivalent meanings: "Get out of my room," she says. "What are you doing in here? I told you before, I don't want you in here. Out! Now! Remove yourselves. Leave. Do Not Come Into My Bedroom, Ever Again, As Long As You Live, Period. Am I making myself clear?

Get your prying fingers out of my stuff! Get your snooping noses out of my life! Get lost!"

As a general rule, human beings seem to take things more seriously if they are repeated, so although Melissa really only said one thing, she said it approximately nine times. Interestingly—and apparently spontaneously—while not all of Melissa's phrases were parallel, several of them were. We believe that that is because there is something deep in our bones that has an affinity for parallel structures.

Both John F. Kennedy and Winston Churchill were masters of the parallel construction, so a number of their well-known sentences are included below. Think of Melissa when you read the ones that use equivalent meanings. Here are some examples of equivalent meanings.

A rose is a rose is a rose.
_____
Gertrude Stein

When we let freedom ring, when we let it ring from every village and every hamlet, from every state and every city, we will be able to speed up that day when all of God's children ... will be able to join hands and sing in the words of the old negro spiritual, "Free at last! Free at last! Thank God almighty, we are free at last!"
_____
Martin Luther King, Jr.

In the past we have had a light which flickered, in the present we have a light which flames, and in the future there will be a light which shines over all the land and sea.
_____
Winston Churchill, *Speech in the British House of Commons*, December 8, 1941

## Exercise 56: Equivalent Meanings: You Try It.

Build on the following two prompts to write parallel structures with equivalent meanings. You can make good use of your thesaurus in this exercise.

1. Music is a language that lightens our mood, _____
   _____ .

2. Dedicated to competition, _____
   Elvis Stojko embraced the challenge of Nagano as he had faced all earlier challenges, refusing to be defeated by sickness.

## Complementary Parallel Meanings

In contrast to parallel structures of equivalent meaning, parallel structures of complementary meaning list ideas that support, rather than repeat each other in order to make a point. If Melissa said to her sisters, "You've made a mess of my closet! You've broken my tennis racket! You've ignored my direct order never to come into my room again! You are now on my revenge list!" she would be using three supporting reasons to make her main point, which is still, "Get out of my room!" Here are some other examples.

> Light then dark, then light again. Day then night, then day again. A meadow lark sings and it is spring. And summer comes.
> A year is done.
> Another comes and it is done.

W.O. Mitchell, *Who Has Seen the Wind*

> That's one small step for a man, one giant leap for mankind.

Neil Armstrong, On first stepping on the moon, July, 1969

> Who's on first, what's on second, I don't know is on third.

Abbot and Costello, *The Naughty Nineties,* 1945

> Take care! Kingdoms are destroyed by bandits, houses by rats, and widows by suitors.

Ihara Saikaku (1642-1693) *The Japanese Family Storehouse or The Millionaire's Gospel Book I*

> For it is in giving that we receive; it is in pardoning that we are pardoned; and it is in dying that we are born to eternal life.

St. Francis of Assisi (1181-1226)

> "My view is, without deviation, without exception, without any ifs, buts, or whereases, that freedom of speech means that you shall not do something to people either for the views they have or the views they express or the words they speak or write."

Judge Hugo Black, *Speech before the American Jewish Congress, 1962*

## Exercise 57: Complementary Meanings: You Try It

Using the following three prompts, write parallel structures with complementary meanings.

1. He had limited money, few belongings, and _____

2. When the first light of dawn sketched an outline of the hills in the east, and _____, Jack crept out of the tent and headed for the lake.

3. Clive wore a ten-gallon cowboy hat, _____.

# Antithetical Parallel Meanings

Parallel structures that use antithetical meanings contrast opposing ideas in order to make a point. These types of parallel structures include an interesting play of tensions, which makes them challenging to write.

Never in the field of human conflict was so much owed by so many to so few.

Winston Churchill, *Tribute to the Royal Air Force, British House of Commons*, August 20, 1940

Without belittling the courage with which men have died, we should not forget those acts of courage with which men ... have lived.

John F. Kennedy, *Profiles in Courage*, 1956.

A fanatic is someone who can't change his mind and won't change the subject.

Author unknown

## Exercise 58: Antithetical Meanings: You Try It

Build on the following two prompts to write parallel structures with antithetical meanings. Tools such as a thesaurus or a dictionary of antonyms can help you to find words that mean the antithesis of those used in the prompts.

1.  She commended their intentions but _____

2.  If we do not have the entitlement to say "No," _____
_____.

## Exercise 59: An Antithetical Tale

The following passage (with omissions) is the first sentence from Charles Dickens' Victorian novel, *A Tale of Two Cities*. Try your hand at completing the text. Then compare your prose with that of the original, which you'll find in the answer key. You may discover that you are the twenty-first century's answer to one of the big names of literature.

It was the best of times, _____, it was the

age of wisdom, _____, it was the époque

of belief, _____, it was the season of Light,

_____, it was the spring of hope _____

_____, we had everything before us, _____,

_____, we were all going direct to Heaven, _____

_____.

# Specialized Forms of Parallel Structure

## Balance

A balanced sentence contains only two parallel elements. Often the meaning in the first element "balances" the meaning in the second.

He's a rich man in dollars, a beggar in love.

Her disguises unmasked, her plan was undone.

## Chiasmus

Chiasmus is a specialized form of balanced syntax. The order of the elements in the first phrase is inverted in the second.

They arrived empty-handed; empty-hearted they left.

A place for everything and everything in its place

Isabella Mary Beeton (1836-1865), *The Book of Household Management* (1861)

Those who have compared our life to a dream were right.... We sleeping wake and waking sleep.

Montaigne (1533–1592), *Essays, Book II*

## Exercise 60. You Try It

Build on the following prompts to write balanced structures or parallel structures that use chiasmus.

1. Sorrow at his leaving, _____.

2. She was a creative genius, _____.

# Punctuation

## Learning Outcomes

**This Chapter will help you to**

- recognize and apply basic punctuation rules.

- avoid five of the ten most common errors made in college/ university writing.

Without punctuation we'd be lost in a maze of words. Have you ever tried to read even one paragraph lacking punctuation? If not, take our word that it is a time-consuming, wearisome business.

Think of punctuation marks as signposts for your readers. End punctuation—periods, exclamation points, and question marks—signal for example, the end of a complete idea, but clearly they suggest differing meanings. Readers would be influenced a great deal by punctuation in sentences like these:

I passed my mid-term?

I passed my mid-term.

I passed my mid-term!

One student sounds matter-of-fact, another incredulous, and the other ecstatic. The words, you see, do not change, but the signposts set us off in the right direction and, in this case, establish attitude. For our book title, we wanted to include an exclamation point for that very reason: we want to communicate our enthusiasm for writing together.

Less flamboyant punctuation also acts as signposts. **Colons** such as the one preceding the above list and the one at the end of this clause also act as a kind of pointer: they signal the readers that something else will surely appear. **Dashes**—two typed hyphens—can also signal that something is coming up. In addition, dashes (like **parentheses**) can be used as we just did to separate something not essential to the meaning of the sentence from the rest of the sentence. We recommend that you limit your use of dashes and parentheses. We do not, however, feel as strongly about **hyphens** as Winston Churchill, who thoroughly disliked them. We find them helpful in telling us that the joined words should be regarded as a unit. In contrast to our view, Churchill said, "One must regard the hyphen as a blemish to be avoided wherever possible." Now we have an example of another signpost. You recognize, because of the **quotation marks**, that those are Churchill's exact words, not a paraphrase or a summary.

We should also mention **semicolons**, most often used to signal the end of an independent clause. Of course, we must mention **commas** too, the most used and misused piece of punctuation. We'll say right now that, as far as we are concerned, a comma does not signal the end of an independent clause. Finally, we should mention the abused **apostrophe**, a device that signals contraction, possession, and very seldom, plurals.

On the following pages, we will deal in depth with this important aid to clarity, punctuation.

# Internal Punctuation Rules

## The Big Six Comma Rules

If you are currently writing a paper and need a "comma band-aid" rather than full treatment, here is our emergency advice. For a full, more effective treatment, when the crisis is over, you can read the rules and do the exercises.

---

## Prescription

1. Never use the pause rule.

2. Never use a single comma to separate subject and verb, or verb and object (or subjective completion)

3. Use commas to separate items in a series of three or more.

4. Use commas before a coordinate conjunction joining two independent clauses.

5. Use a comma after a group of words introducing an independent clause.

6. Use commas to separate words not essential to the meaning of the sentence.

---

We believe that you can get along very well in your written work if you learn these six comma rules, but we will briefly mention a few others to use on special occasions. (See page 212.)

## 1. Don't use the pause rule.

The "pause rule" causes a lot of grief and red ink. We pause a great deal in English, sometimes for emphasis and sometimes because we have run out of breath. If you put commas where you would normally pause when you read the sentence, your reader will have a bumpy ride.

## 2. Never separate subject and verb, or verb and object (or subjective completion) by only one comma.

Separating subject and verb, or verb and object (or subjective completion) by only one comma is what often happens when you use the "pause rule," and it will always be a mistake. If you read the first example below out loud, we think that you will naturally pause after the word "painted," but if you put a comma there, you have separated the subject "house" from the verb "shone" by only one comma, a mistake. In the second and third examples, the comma separates the verb "offers" from the object "new products, new prices, and new delivery policies." This, too, is a mistake.

### Exercise 1: One Comma Separating Subject and Verb, or Verb and Object

In the main clauses, underline the subject or object of the verb with one line and the verb with two, and cross out the comma if it separates subject and verb, or verb and object by only one comma.

1. The house which was newly painted, shone brightly in the sunshine.

2. Fortunately, the new catalogue offers, new products, new prices, and new delivery policies.

3. The principal announced, that there would be a bake sale on Thursday.

## 3. Use commas to separate items in a series of three or more.

Probably you use commas in lists of three or more without any difficulty except that one instructor may tell you to put the comma in before the coordinate conjunction joining a list of three or more words, phrases, or clauses, and another may tell you to leave it out. This is a fact of life that we all have to get used to. Norma was taught to leave the comma out; Claire was taught to leave it in. We decided that because, about once in a hundred sentences, the meaning might be unclear without the comma, in this book we would put the comma in. In Norma's novel, however, she's going to live dangerously. The following is an example of one of the (many) sentences in which she leaves out the comma before the third verb in a series.

"Clive's tattoo starts on his neck, spreads across his shoulders and fans out over his arms like folded wings."

In contrast to Norma's sentence, here are some examples of commas separating all the items in a series.

On Tuesday night, the moon was huge, orange, and round.

Sam was late getting up, catching the bus, and arriving at work.

I knew he would win when I first saw him, when I heard him speak, and especially when I saw him smile.

As an academic writer, choose one pattern or the other, and be consistent throughout each piece of writing.

## Exercise 2: Commas Separating Items In a series

Following the rule, put commas in the appropriate places.

1.  Where you go where you live and where you buy your eggplant is strictly up to you.

2.  Honga found a pencil a red plastic toy truck a pair of handcuffs and two loonies under the couch cushion.

3.  Potato salad corn on the cob hot dogs and hamburgers fit nicely into the cooler under the pop cans.

**4.  When independent clauses are joined by a coordinate conjunction (*for, and, nor, but, or, yet, so*), put a comma before the conjunction.**

Joining two independent clauses by using coordinate conjunctions is such an important and frequently used sentence pattern that we think you should memorize the seven coordinate conjunctions. If you see them joining independent clauses, you'll know what to do: put commas before them. The acronym FANBOYS will help you remember them.

Here are three examples of independent clauses joined by coordinate conjunctions. Note the inversion of the subject and auxiliary verb in the second example. (See page 176 for more on inversion.) If you change the word order, you will recognize the independent clause. The second independent clause in the last sentence is in normal question word order.

Sarah likes chocolate, but Joe likes caramel.

We cannot afford the rent, nor can we afford to move.

My history book is missing, so can I borrow yours?

## Exercise 3: Commas Before a Coordinate Conjunction Joining Two Independent Clauses

Following the rule, put commas in the appropriate places.

1. The sheep is in the meadow and the cow is in the corn.

2. It has started to rain so I think that we need to borrow an umbrella.

3. I have worked here five years yet the secretary never remembers how to spell my name.

**5. Use a comma after a word or group of words introducing an independent clause.**

It doesn't matter if we use one word or a whole subordinate clause before the independent clause, the rule is the same: put a comma after it.

Examples:

Naturally, Sue bought a chocolate ice cream cone.

Within seconds, the ice cream began to melt.

After the cone started to drip, Sue went back for more napkins.

## Exercise 4: Commas After Introductory Words

Following the rule, put commas in the appropriate places.

1. If you find my hedgehog call me right away.

2. After the fire the dinner party became much more interesting.

3. Nonetheless we must decide on the colour before your birthday.

**6. Use commas to separate from the rest of the sentence a) words not essential to the meaning of the sentence or b) words that mean the same thing as something else.**

This useful rule takes in a lot of territory. If you learn it well, you don't have to learn, for example, that you separate a) direct address, b) nonrestrictive modifiers, c) nonrestrictive appositives, d) parenthetical expressions, e) absolutes, f) contrastive or comparative expressions, or g) interjections or tag questions from the rest of the sentence with commas. We explain more about punctuation of restrictive and nonrestrictive clauses on page 162, but you will recognize that these commas come under this rule. If you just follow this rule and forget about all the smaller rules that it embraces, you will still use commas correctly. The following seven examples correspond to the smaller rules listed above.

You see, Sam, we have a success on our hands.

Mr. Warren Betenko, a figure of imagination, became a celebrity.

Yuki read *Anne of Green Gables*, the first in the series, during the long weekend.

Victorians, of course, enjoy rain.

Vancouverites, their umbrellas at the ready, enjoy more rain.

He ate six, not seven. The bigger they were, the faster he ate.

Well, this is a pretty useful rule, eh?

## Exercise 5: Commas Separating Non-Essential Material.

Following the rule, put commas in the appropriate places.

1. Put the kettle on Polly.

2. He lived in Penticton a city at the south end of Okanagan Lake.

3. Frank wanted cereal not eggs in the morning.

4. Rats I forgot to bring my camera!

5. Margaret Laurence's first book *The Prophet's Camel Bell* was about Africa.

6. The committee agreed therefore to postpone the August meeting.

# Additional Comma Rules

The above rules will get you through everyday writing projects, but there are a few more that we'd like to explain for use on special occasions.

## Commas and Paired Adjectives:

If you have two or more adjectives in a row, then apply two tests:

1. try reversing the order

2. try putting "and" or another coordinate conjunction between them.

**If both versions "sound right,"** then separate them with a comma. You can tell, however, from the "sound right" part that this rule is not particularly helpful for speakers of English as a second or additional language.

Non-native speakers will find the following advice more helpful: when deciding whether the comma is necessary or not, you must decide whether the first adjective gives you information about the noun or about the second adjective.

Examples:

A light, red scarf would be an ideal accessory for your summer outfit.

A light red scarf would be an ideal accessory for your winter outfit, too.

In the first case, the scarf is light-weight, perhaps made of silk. In the second case, the colour of the scarf, red, is light. When a pair of adjectives is separated by commas, both adjectives separately modify the noun.

In the following sentences, you can apply the two tests, or you can ask yourselves whether the words "restless," "favourite," and "crowded" modify the adjectives or the nouns following them. When you do, you'll see that you should add commas to the first and last sentences to make them correct.

Sarah had a restless dream-filled sleep.

Bring me my favourite green blanket.

The crowded smoky room repelled him.

## Exercise 6: Commas and Paired Adjectives

Put commas where needed in the following sentences:

1. A large shiny alien moved ponderously toward the lectern.

2. No one in the audience could understand a word of its long tedious lecture.

3. After a full eight hours, most of the audience had drifted off to sleep.

4. The main gist of the lecture seemed to be that the normal biological clock of the alien was slowed down under the powerful pull of the earth's gravitational field.

## Commas and Quotations:

If the last words in an introductory phrase have quotation marks, the comma goes inside the quotation marks. Look at the comma placement in this example taken from what we wrote above on paired adjectives:

If both versions "sound right," separate the adjectives with a comma.

- Use a comma to separate the introduction to a quotation from a direct quotation:

  Tai said, "I've finally finished revising my resume."

- Do not, however, use a comma before an indirect quotation. You can remember that this error breaks Rule 2, for you would separate the verb and its object by only one comma.

  Example:

  ✗ Tai said, that he had finally finished his resume.

- If the quotation is interrupted by a phrase, put a comma after the phrase:

  "Finally," said Tai happily, "I've finished my resume."

## Exercise 7: Commas With Quotations

Put commas where needed in the following sentences:

1. "In the eyes of its mother, every beetle is gazelle" says a Moroccan proverb.

2. "A mother is not a person to lean on," said Dorothy Canfield Fisher "but a person to make leaning unnecessary."

3. A "mother load" never runs out.

See more on quotations on pages 241–244.

## Commas and Restrictive/Non-Restrictive Words

- Put commas around information that is not essential to the meaning of the sentence. These words are non-restrictive. You have remembered, we're sure, that this rule actually falls under our useful Rule 4.

- If the words cannot be removed without changing the essential meaning of the sentence, they are restrictive and are not set apart by commas.

## Exercise 8: Commas With Restrictive/Non-Restrictive Words

Put commas where needed in the following sentences.

1. Students who ride their bikes should wear helmets.

2. My eldest sister who married a doctor lives in Kaleden.

3. People who live in glass houses should not throw stones.

4. A child who screams for attention should be ignored.

5. Charles Smith who is ten years old won the car.

## Commas and Absolute Phrases

• Put commas around absolutes, phrases usually containing a noun and a participle or complement. We discuss them further in the section on sentence variety. See page 144.

Examples:

Peter, his face a mask of concentration, ignored his fellow students.

Having written the mid-term, he went out to celebrate.

## Exercise 9: Commas With Absolute Phrases

Put commas where needed in the following sentences.

1. Wanting to get the most for their money students sometimes buy recycled texts.

2. The cat a study in concentration sat in front of the birdcage.

3. The expanded library already a success plans to hold a membership drive.

4. The agency lacking funds for new staff decided to move to a four-day week.

5. The presents opened Erin immediately put the wrapping paper in the mixed-paper recycling bag.

## Commas and Dates

• Separate multiple elements in dates with commas.

Examples:

The baby had been expected on April 1. (one element)

Jakob was born on April 7, 1999. (two elements)

We bought Jem, a green singing finch, on Friday, July 23, 1998, after investigating yet another pet store that carried birds. (three elements)

- If the date is preceded by a preposition, do not use a comma.

Examples:

Please reply *by* December 2001.

I received the reply *on* 10 June 2000.

## Exercise 10: Commas With Dates

Put commas where needed in the following sentences.

1. The trade agreement was signed on March 20 1999.

2. On Friday July 17 1959 in Victoria, the 2nd Battalion of the Princess Patricia's Canadian Light Infantry trooped the colours for Queen Elizabeth II.

3. Cupcake was born at 6:24 a.m. Thursday October 1 1998 at Victoria General Hospital, but he quickly became Aidan.

## Commas and Addresses

If you are writing an address within your text, you separate the elements with commas, with the exception of the postal code.

Example:

You must now reach Mr. Janicki at 1486 Table Terrace, Prince Albert, Saskatchewn, S0J 2L9 as he no longer lives at 23916 Alpha Romeo Drive, El Centro, CA 922242 USA.

## Exercise 11: Commas With Addresses

Put commas where needed in the following sentence.

1. He lived for seventeen years at 225 Palmerson Avenue Toronto ON M6J 2J3.

2. Because you are sending the letter out of the country, write the return address this way: 55 Galt Crescent Freont Manitoba W8H 4P6 Canada.

Before you move on to exercises that allow you to use commas in a variety of useful ways, we want you to remember what we have said about commas and independent clauses. Some texts suggest that commas can be used to join independent clauses *if* the independent clauses are very short. This kind of waffling, we think, leads to unnecessary anxiety. Two-word independent clauses are definitely short, but how about three- or four-word ones?

Our position is that commas are not strong enough to hold independent clauses together, no matter how "short" the clauses may be. We regard a comma between any independent clauses as a comma splice and, therefore, a grievous error. You can bear this in mind when you read later about the functions of semicolons; then, in the chapter on sentence structure, we show the number of ways that you can avoid making comma splices.

Exercises 12–16 reinforce your knowledge of the six basic rules that we have given you in our prescription. The final exercise reminds you of the additional rules that we included for your use on special occasions.

## Exercise 12: Comma Review

Put commas in the following sentences where necessary. Above each of the commas, put the rule that you are applying.

1. After the ball was thrown Alicia ran home.

2. July 1 now known as Canada Day was once called Dominion Day.

3. The good news which was hardly unexpected still made everyone cheerful.

4. The good news that Enio had won made everyone cheerful.

5. Naturally everyone watched the newscast.

6. The purse contained keys glasses pictures but no identification.

7. Although the people attending the meeting thought the room was claustrophobic the brochure had described it as cozy.

8. The brochure had described it as cozy but the room seemed claustrophobic.

9. Jerry Jacobs one of the computer trouble-shooters will be here in five minutes and he will look at your machine.

10. In 1791 the British parliament divided Canada into two provinces Upper Canada and Lower Canada.

## Exercise 13: Comma Review

Put commas in the following sentences where necessary. Above each of the commas, put the rule that you are applying.

1. I think therefore that we should plan to give an interview.

2. Sarah pulled the plug and Sam pushed the machine into the other room.

3. Because the bus was late and the elevator wasn't working Fred was ten minutes late for the meeting.

4. Everyone who reads the book will want to try hypnosis.

5. Fred Coate who spoke so eloquently to us last year will be here any minute.

6. Fiona left at 5:00 but Matthew stayed until 6:00.

7. Fred was ten minutes late for the meeting because the bus was late the elevator was broken and the room number on his invitation was incorrect.

8. Her old bike tires worn and slender made riding over the sidewalk grates an adventure.

9. Terry cooked the burgers and Leslie made the salads.

10. Frances always gave the newspaper to Marge Quinlan the woman next door.

## Exercise 14: Commas

The following sentences have a variety of comma errors. Some sentences may be correct, while others may have more than one mistake. Commas may be missing or incorrectly used. Correct as needed.

1. In 1791 the British parliament divided Canada into two provinces, Upper and Lower Canada.

2. Canada Day formerly called Dominion Day is on July 1, Claire Tony and the twins' birthday.

3. In Ottawa on July 1, 1867, church bells rang and there was a twenty-one gun salute.

4. On Canada's first birthday in 1867 Quebec, Ontario, New Brunswick and Nova Scotia were its only provinces.

5. The early Fathers of Confederation included Cartier Galt Macdonald Tilley and Tupper.

6. Joey Smallwood the last Father of Confederation was premier of Newfoundland when it became a province.

7. British Columbia joined Confederation in 1871 and both Alberta and Saskatchewan joined in 1905.

8. In honour of Alberta and Saskatchewan entering Confederation thousands of people including Prime Minister Wilfred Laurier attended ceremonies in Regina and Edmonton.

9. While New Brunswick and Nova Scotia became provinces in 1867 Prince Edward Island waited until 1873.

10. Manitoba preceding British Columbia joined Confederation in 1870.

## Exercise 15: Commas

The following sentences have a variety of comma errors. Some sentences may be correct, while others may have more than one mistake. Commas may be missing or incorrectly used. Correct as needed.

1. In 1790 Admiral Quimper claimed Vancouver Island for Spain.

2. Although Vancouver Island had been governed by the Hudson's Bay Company it became a British colony in 1849.

3. Its first governor stayed about eight months before he returned to England.

4. The Hudson's Bay Company in 1849 leased Vancouver Island back from the British government.

5. James Douglas chief factor of the western division of the Hudson's Bay Company became governor of Vancouver Island.

6. The Hudson's Bay Company had a trading monopoly but it had to pay defence costs and encourage settlers.

7. Because gold was discovered along the Thompson and Fraser rivers Douglas asked the British government to send troops in order to preserve order.

8. Some of Vancouver Island lies under the 49th parallel Canada's border with the United States.

9. When the legislature of Vancouver Island opened in 1856 it was the first one west of the Great Lakes.

10. Vancouver Island's major city Victoria British Columbia's capital was incorporated in 1862.

## Exercise 16: Commas

The following sentences have a variety of comma errors. Some sentences may be correct, while others may have more than one mistake. Correct as needed.

1. In general the best time to prune any woody plant is just before new growth starts.

2. Pruning in late winter or early spring while a plant is dormant won't adversely affect its vigour but pruning at other times can rob it of stored food energy.

3. Severe pruning during or just after active growth in spring only wastes stored energy.

4. Such pruning can retard stunt or dwarf a plant and is not recommended unless a dwarfing effect as in bonsai is the goal.

5. Photosynthesis is most active during summer, when plants produce abundant food and new growth.

6. As the days shorten in late summer growth slows and sugars collect in the leaves.

7. Before the foliage drops the food moves from the leaves into the woody branches.

8. Pruning in fall or early winter, exhausts the stored food reserves needed to initiate spring growth.

9. Since many decay fungi produce spores in fall autumn is also the time when open wounds are most likely to become infected.

10. Later in the dormant season sugars move farther down the plant and they are less likely to be affected.

## Exercise 17: Commas For Special Occasions

Put commas in places where they should be and be prepared to say why the ones in place are correct.

1. "Great! I'm done the project" said Brenda "I feel like a new man! Do you know one?"

2. In your video store, you should look for *Tampopo*, an amusing appetite-stimulating noodle western.

3. Wall climbing which we had never heard of twenty years ago currently has many advocates.

4. The next time my parole officer says "Have a nice day" I may decide to return to prison.

5. Both couples were married on Friday September 13 1957; they exchanged partners a year later, remarried, and recently celebrated their 40th anniversaries together.

6. Wah Lee an excellent student also excels at basketball.

7. In 1859 a French tightrope walker Charles Blondin crossed Niagara Falls.

8. Lashmi spent an hour committing her new address to memory: 7063 Flemming Crescent Calgary Alberta T3H 0X4 Canada.

9. In the Prelude to his novel *The Egoist* George Meredith writes "[comedy] is the ultimate civilizer, the polisher."

10. Leaping down the stairs two at a time Pierre got to the door before the courier rang the bell.

11. Her curly long blonde hair was hidden under a beret.

12. Mary said that she would pick up the hot dogs and buns on her way home.

13. "The combined essences of heaven and earth" wrote Lui An in the second century B.C. "became the yin and yang, the concentrated essences of the yin and yang became the four seasons, and the scattered essences of the four seasons became the myriad creatures of the world."

14. Kelly Kramer is a fast-talking super-slick salesperson.

15. The phone call finished Martin breathed a sigh of relief.

## Activity 1: Commas

Insert commas into the following story using any rule except the pause rule. (See page 119 for correct punctuation.)

For twelve months Diana dreamt about getting her driver's licence. She turned sixteen months later than Pat and Terry her best friends. She had wanted to get her licence as soon as possible so she was pleased when on her birthday her big and only brother Darren gave her a cheque to get it. She was pleased but she was also a bit surprised. "Cool" she said "I was afraid that you had had it with Diana the Dreadful!"

For weeks before her birthday Diana had been studying the driver's manual every night after doing her homework. Disappearing into her room promptly after nine o'clock to study the book she had been confident that she knew it all after just a week.

Then she had started phase two of the learning process. During the next few weeks whenever her brother or either of her parents took the car out she had asked to go along asked her dad to drop her off at her friend Pat's house on his way to his poker game asked her mother if she could go and watch her get a haircut asked her brother if she could go to a movie with him and Winona his girlfriend. Some days she managed four trips and on all the trips she watched everything the driver did.

During these trips much to her delight Diana could point out all the mistakes Darren and her parents made. She had warned her father three times to watch out for cyclists as he made a right turn explained to her mother how to turn the wheels when she parked uphill on a street without a curb and told Darren who had been driving only four years the penalty for driving only one kilometre above the speed limit in a school zone.

*continued*

**Activity 1: Commas (continued)**

On the morning of the fourth day of phase two when Diana whistling cheerily had gone down to breakfast she found a bus pass and a certificate in her cereal bowl. The certificate read "Official Back Seat Driver's Licence." Under the official looking red seal her parents and Darren had signed as witnesses. It wasn't the kind of driver's licence she had dreamt of.

# Semicolon Rules

1. **Use a semicolon to separate independent clauses; a semicolon can replace a period.**

   When you use a semicolon to join two independent clauses, the word following a semicolon will be a capital only if it is a proper noun.

   Joe loved caramel; Sarah adored chocolate.

   When Sarah came home, she made cocoa; Joe brought marshmallows.

   They had leftover marshmallows; therefore, they "roasted" some in the microwave.

2. **Use a semicolon *occasionally* as a kind of major comma if you have a lengthy list with internal punctuation.**

   Both rules two and three are simply ways to make navigating through your sentences more simple for the reader. Although you will seldom write sentences using these patterns, knowing that you can if you want to is gratifying. Your intricate sentence structure will be easier to understand if its major divisions are clear. You'll understand what we mean if you try to envision the following sentence without its semicolons signalling the major divisions.

   Joe planted tomatoes, because Sarah loved them; peas, because he preferred them fresh, an impossibility to find in a supermarket; potatoes, because the Food Bank needed them; and carrots, because his father said that they would make his hair curly.

3. **Use a semicolon *occasionally* as a kind of major comma if you have independent clauses joined by a coordinate conjunction when one or both clauses contain internal punctuation.**

   Joe, inexperienced but hopeful, was, to Sarah's delight, a great gardener; but, despite his success, he decided to abandon the garden in favour of raising guppies.

## Exercise 18: Semicolons

Following the rules, put semicolons in the appropriate places.

1. Interest was rising, inflation was rampant.

2. You should remember to buy candles, cards, and paper at the drugstore, blueberries, whipping cream, and icing sugar at the grocery, and a cake pan, cake rack, and measuring cup at the hardware.

3. Grudgingly, after a long debate, the committee agreed with the chair's idea, so the August meeting was postponed until September, after the renovation would be completed.

## Exercise 19: Semicolons

Put a check mark beside any sentence in which you see the correct use of a semicolon. Correct the punctuation in the incorrect sentences.

1. *The Phantom of the Opera, Les Miserables,* and *Cats* have all been great successes as musicals; two of them began as novels, and one as a book of poetry.

2. Charlotte Bronte wrote *Jane Eyre*; although Emily Bronte wrote *Wuthering Heights*.

3. Here are some of the borrowed words that you use everyday without thinking about it: *cotton, mattress,* and *spinach* from Arabic; *umbrella, stucco,* and *casino* from Italian; *dingy, verandah,* and *shampoo* from Punjabi.

4. Your letter to the editor should be clear; concise; and courteous.

5. Alexis read the speech; therefore, with a great deal of feeling.

6. Joe was engrossed in making his spaghetti sauce; therefore, Sarah made the Caesar Salad.

7. One twin has read *Fear and Loathing in Las Vegas*; the other one has just seen the movie.

8. Advertisements are regarded by many as a loud bore; however, many of them are more imaginative, more skillfully filmed, and more memorable than the programmes they sponsor.

9. Mr. Wong had retired after many years as an accountant; so he volunteered to keep the books for a non-profit agency that helped the homeless.

10. Her dictionary, weighing at least three pounds, didn't contain what she needed; she found her big new thesaurus more helpful, though she had to be careful about connotation.

## Exercise 20: Semicolons

Put semicolons in the following sentences where necessary. Above each of the semicolons, put the number of the rule that you are applying.

1. Nobody is absolutely sure who the first Europeans to visit Canada were Norsemen, Icelanders, and the Irish all visited what became known as Newfoundland.

2. Joe, whose father's family was of Icelandic descent, and Sarah, whose mother was born in Norway, but who was herself born in Ireland, have some lively discussions about history, so you should drop by for the latest rumours.

3. John Cabot landed in Newfoundland in 1497, he was in the employ of the British.

4. Another explorer accomplished something exciting in 1497, Vasco da Gama rounded the Cape of Good Hope, and in 1498 he discovered the sea route to India.

5. Also in 1497, Perkin Warbeck, a pretender to the British throne born in Flanders, aided by the Scots King James IV, landed in Cornwall and attempted to capture Exeter, but he was eventually captured at Taunton, and he was finally executed for treason in 1499.

6. On our way home, we are going to buy kidney beans, hamburger, and a large can of diced tomatoes for the chili, romaine, a lemon, and garlic for the salad, and bananas, ice cream, and chocolate sauce for the dessert.

7. Christopher Columbus, like his fellow explorers John Cabot and Vasco da Gama, was also active in 1497, he reached the Orinoco River.

8. We are going to need the following in the report: an executive summary, less than a page, an introduction outlining why solving this problem is important to the company, your proposal, along with a brief discussion of the alternatives that you rejected, an analysis, preferably with graphs, and, finally, your conclusions and recommendations.

9. Mount Fuji, an extinct volcano, is a major tourist attraction in Japan, the last time it erupted was in the 18th century.

10. Watercress, a peppery herb often used in salads and occasionally in sandwiches in British detective novels, grows well in wet conditions, so it is a bit of a surprise to find that it is related to the nasturtium, which seems to do perfectly well in dry conditions.

## Exercise 21: Semicolons

Put semicolons in the following sentences where necessary. Above each of the semicolons, put the rule that you are applying.

1. Canada's most famous ship is the *Bluenose*, it was launched in Lunenburg, Nova Scotia.

2. When you proofread a paper, check for any changes that should be made in your thesis or topic sentences, make sure that all ideas are developed well, that the paragraphs wrap nicely, and that the essay ends strongly, and finally, proofread for the more mechanical details, like spelling, punctuation, and grammar, for example, and check that you have included a pleasing variety of sentence structures.

3. Although Tai wanted to play badminton, Andrea wanted to play tennis.

4. Home to the Pacific Fleet, Esquimalt has an excellent harbour, an important naval base, a shipyard, and a drydock, which Norma can see from her deck.

5. The weather became cooler the cats began to seek fleeting patches of sun.

6. Major League Baseball now has two representatives in Canada, the Toronto Blue Jays and the Montreal Expos, interestingly, both Toronto and Montreal were previously represented in a long-running international league, Montreal for 55 years and Toronto for 78 years.

7. The end of the war, 1945, saw some comic masterpieces, with *Harvey* by Mary Chase, *The Pursuit of Love* by Nancy Mitford, and *The Thurber Carnival* by James Thurber, some people would also include *Animal Farm* by George Orwell in this list, although it is a satire.

8. In 1981, the Nobel Prize for Physics was won by Kai Seigbahn, from Sweden, and Nicolaas Bloembergen and Arthur Schawlow, from the USA, the Nobel Prize for Chemistry was won by Kenichi Fukui from Japan and Roald Hoffman from the USA.

9. American spelling has got rid of a few of the "oughs" that British spelling retains, for example, "plough" and "hiccough" have been simplified to "plow" and "hiccup."

10. In some words, however, it is the British or Canadian person who writes a shorter form, while the American writes "learned," "dreamed," and "spelled," for example, the British or Canadian person often writes, "learnt," "dreamt," and "spelt."

## Prescription

If you use a colon with a sentence, make sure that you have an
independent clause before it.

## Colon Rules

Use a colon following an independent clause to introduce amplification:
examples, a list, or a quotation.

The concept of an independent clause, a complete grammatical
thought, is vital to using colons correctly. What precedes a colon must
be capable of standing on its own as a sentence, in other words, an
independent clause.

She admired his speech on one of the issues: inflation.

He hated three things: spinach, spiders, and speeches.

The announcer asked a silly question: "Do you know where Noah's
bees came from?"

## Exercise 22: Colons

Following the rules, put colons in the appropriate places.

1.  Thomas Carlyle quoted a Swiss aphorism "Silence is golden."

2.  You have forgotten the following things candles, cards, cream, a
    cake pan, and cake rack.

3.  The committee agreed quickly on only one thing adjournment.

## Exercise 23: Colons

Put a check mark beside any sentence in which you see the correct use
of a colon. Correct the punctuation in the incorrect sentences.

1.  In the preface to *Major Barbara*, Shaw writes that: "The greatest of
    evils and the worst of crimes is poverty."

2.  A Polish speaking person may have difficulty differentiating between
    these words: "sit" and "seat," "bait" and "bet," and "should" and
    "shoed."

3. These are a few of my favourite books by Canadian authors: *The Stone Angel, Fifth Business, The Cure for Death by Lightning, A Fine Balance*, and *Fall on Your Knees*.

4. Janina loved both her literature course and her computer science course, but she struggled with one thing: time management.

5. In *Northanger Abbey* by Jane Austen, eighteen-year-old Catherine Morland explains her surprise that she is not more fond of history: "the speeches that are put into the heroes' mouths, their thoughts and designs—the chief of all this must be invention, and invention is what delights me in other books."

6. She could have just said: "no," but instead, we got a ten minute lecture.

7. The Mock Turtle mentions the following: "Reeling," "Writhing," "Ambition," "Distraction," "Uglification," and "Derision."

8. She knew it was a mall, but Carol was still surprised after she ordered a Tempura Combo to be asked: "Would you like fries or rice with that?"

9. I want to know just one thing: where the washrooms are.

10. A Cantonese speaking person may have difficulty differentiating between the words: "sheep" and "ship," "back" and "bag," and "flight" and "fright."

## Exercise 24: Colons

Put colons in the following sentences where necessary. Although there are places that a comma would do as well, remember that this is an exercise in using colons.

1. This is my favourite line in Austen's *Sense and Sensibility* "'It is not everyone,' said Elinor, 'who has your passion for dead leaves.'"

2. At the market, you can find many inexpensive items such as T-shirts, purses, sandals, and watches.

3. In *The Moonstone*, we find a delightful character Gabriel Betteredge.

4. You'll need the following before you can apply for your licence your birth certificate, a piece of picture ID, and two pieces of correspondence addressed to you at your current address.

5. I think that the line that epitomizes Thomas Hardy comes from *The Woodlanders* "And yet to every bad there is a worse."

6. The boss seems to feel that the new receptionist, although skillful, lacks one thing personality.

7. At the end of the table, the opened gifts piled up sheet sets, towel sets, dishes, glasses, toasters, a router, cookware, and flatware.

8. Medvedev would agree with this point for he wrote the following "Science and technology, and the various forms of art, all unite humanity in a single and interconnected system."

9. If you are interviewing someone of another culture, consider these things the level of courtesy, the use of body language, including eye contact, and the level of directness usual in his or her culture.

10. Martin Luther King stressed that "injustice anywhere is a threat to justice everywhere."

## Apostrophe Rules

The use of the apostrophe, particularly in the use of possessives, is currently under attack. Therefore, students at institutions of higher learning have an obligation to use the apostrophe correctly, restoring it to prominence in possessives as well as in contractions and not succumbing to the virus that has apostrophes inserted in so many plurals.

Few students have problems with contractions, perhaps partly because they have been told to use formal English and, therefore, avoid contractions as they do slang, clichés, etc. Look at these examples of contractions and the letters or numbers that have been omitted:

there's = there is

she'd = she would

it's = it is

Grad of '99 = grad of 1999

in the '70s = in the 1970s

Note, in the immediately above example, that 1970s can also be written 1970's. Similarly, you can write "two B's or not two Bs," "her isys" or "her isy's." This, it seems to us, is where the problem of using apostrophes in plurals begins, as students take a specific rule and broaden it to embrace all plurals. In order to reduce students' confusion, we have stopped using "isy's" as a plural. For a similar reason, you may want to ignore the next rule, after you thoroughly understand it, and not use apostrophes in plurals.

## Plurals

1.  **Use an apostrophe plus "s" ('s) to form plurals of letters, numbers or words referred to as words.**

    As we noted above, this rule about apostrophes used with plurals may account for the virus that has students randomly putting apostrophes in plurals. Therefore, although the following examples are correct, we recommend that you not use apostrophes in these cases.

    If you do choose to use apostrophes, note that the rule is specific, applying only to letters, numbers or **words referred to as words**.

    Examples:

    She was happy with two A's.

    He had to mind his P's and Q's.

    The 8's and 3's in that font are hard to differentiate.

    All of his grandparents were born in the 1930's.

    You should try to eliminate needless isy's.

    He uses "but's" to begin half his sentences!

## Exercise 25: Apostrophes For Plural Letters, Numbers, and Words

Put apostrophes in the appropriate places in these sentences.

1.  Remember to dot your is and cross your ts.

2.  Students receiving Ds need either to reduce the number of serious errors or to increase the development and organization of ideas.

3.  Work on reducing the number of "uhms" and "uhs."

## Possessive

2.  **Use an apostrophe plus s ('s) to show possession or ownership.**

    If a singular noun (or a word acting as a noun) not ending with s possesses something, use an *apostrophe plus s* to signal that possession.

    If an irregular plural not ending in *s*, such as "children," "teeth," or "mice" possesses something, also use an *apostrophe plus s* to signal that possession.

Use one of the following two methods to verify whether the apostrophe is in the right place:

a) Underline that noun that owns something. The apostrophe follows that noun.

Examples:

I've lost the <u>boys</u>' shirts. (The apostrophe follows the *s* because the shirts belong to the <u>boys</u>.)

I've lost the <u>boy</u>'s shirt. (The apostrophe follows the *y* because the shirt belongs to one boy.)

b) Read the apostrophe as saying "of" to check whether the apostrophe is in the right place.

Examples:

Evan's holidays usually start in the second week of July. (the holidays of Evan)

Everybody's favourite was the corn on the cob. (the favourite of everybody)

Jogging's popularity seems to have waned slightly. (the popularity of jogging)

The mice's favourite hiding place was under the stove. (the hiding place of the mice)

## Exercise 26: Apostrophe *s* For Possessives

Put apostrophes in the appropriate places in these sentences.

1. After she left the ball, Cinderellas glass slipper was lost.

2. The catalogues prices are demonstrably cheaper!

3. Now, Yoko finds sewings big advantage to be the way she can tailor each dress to fit perfectly.

4. The Womens Caucus is meeting at 7:00 in the Frontenac Room.

**3. Use just an apostrophe (') with a singular noun ending with *s* or a plural noun ending with s.**

When a noun, such as "biomass," "Charles," or "cats," ends with *s* or double *s*, you will generally leave off the *s* of the *apostrophe plus s* when you form the possessive. Note the difference between "the cat's dish" and "the cats' dish." Keep reading the apostrophe as saying "of" to check whether the apostrophe is in the right place.

Examples:

Robbie Burns' songs can easily bring tears to many Scots' eyes. (the songs of Robbie Burns) (the eyes of Scots)

In the cats' absence, the mice will play. (the absence of the cats)

Ironically, the boss' self-confidence needed a boost. (the self-confidence of the boss)

Putting an *apostrophe plus s* on one of the above possessors is not wrong, but it offends our aesthetic taste. For instance, you can see that "the boss's self-confidence" looks pretty strange, with four *s*'s in a row. (Did you notice that we just used an apostrophe to make a letter plural?)

## Exercise 27: Apostrophes For Possessive Words Ending in *s*

Put apostrophes in the appropriate places in these sentences.

1. After months of letting the animals become accustomed to humans, the biologists were able to put a video camera right in the foxes den.

2. When they returned, the birds nest was empty, and the three babies were gone.

3. Sometimes you have to trudge for a long time before you come across a brilliant bit in Charles Dickens novels.

4. You'll find that the knives sharpness is a mixed blessing.

5. Ross lecture notes are both lively and informative, so be sure to read them.

---

## Prescription

To check whether the apostrophe in a possessive is in the right place,

- read the apostrophe as the word "of".

- or underline the word that does the owning. That word will be followed by the apostrophe.

---

4. **Do not use an apostrophe with the possessive of *it*.**

Because of the epidemic of problems with the possessive of it, we are devoting a whole rule to it. As you will recall, it is one of the personal pronouns, and no possessive personal pronoun has an apostrophe. Think about *my, his, their,* and *our*—none of these possessive personal pronouns has an apostrophe, and neither do the rest, including *its*.

*It's* means one thing, and one thing only: *it is*. Another *it* problem does occur, however. Some people insist that *its'* is the plural possessive of *it*, but if they thought about it a little longer, they would remember that the plural of *it* is *they*. One chair is *it*, but six chairs are *they*.

## Exercise 28: Differentiating Between *Its* and *It's*

Put apostrophes in the appropriate places in these sentences.

1. Its clear that its conclusion should be strengthened.

2. Its length makes its analysis more difficult for Mr. Leung.

---

### Activity 2: Apostrophes

Make the following words possess something:

| | |
|---|---|
| Henry Streeter | woman |
| women | the company |
| Monica Dickens | it |
| printers | children |
| sea | group |

---

## Exercise 29: Apostrophes and Possession

Place apostrophes where appropriate in the following sentences.

1. Apparently, Spains rain falls mainly on the plain.

2. The fragile glass stem broke when she put the glass back on the tray.

3. Its capital is Bogota.

4. Its going to take a long time to proofread its conclusions and recommendations, so take the report home.

5. Gladys mother will return from Denmark on Thursday at 6:00 a.m.

6. Hong wants to borrow Bryans calculator.

7. *Tetris* problem is its addictive nature, or, rather, I suppose that is *my* problem.

8. Using his dads car, Shane will pick Robert up at the airport.

9. The mouses ball became quite dirty, and Wei-Kuo had to take it apart to clean it.

10. "Oh, for goodness sake!" she cried, "Can't you eat just one more?"

## Contractions

Compared to possessives, contractions present few problems. You should simply remember not to use them when you are writing a formal paper or a formal report. We have chosen to write this text in an informal style, so you may have already noticed that we use contractions. If you are in doubt about the level of formality that your instructor or employer expects, be sure to ask.

1. To show that letters or numbers have been omitted, use an apostrophe.

   You won't very often use the apostrophes with numbers, but just be aware that some people do. For example, you might read a sentence like "Recently, we've seen people dressed like people of the '70s dancing to music of the '40s and sipping the drinks of the early '50s."

   Here are a few examples of contractions showing what has been omitted:

   | | | | |
   |---|---|---|---|
   | I'm | (a) | there's | (i) |
   | you're | (a) | would've | (ha) |
   | the '40s | (19) | it's | (i) |
   | what's | (i) | o'clock | (f the) |
   | shouldn't | (o) | he'll | (wi) |

## Exercise 30: Apostrophes and Contractions

Place apostrophes where appropriate in the following sentences.

1. Shed barely reached the finish line before the rain started.

2. When he speaks, hell begin with a short, amusing anecdote.

3. Isnt it a strange thing that Harriet is now going out with Algernon?

4. Take this calculator because its battery is new, and its easy to fit the case into your shirt pocket.

5. After theyve graduated, theyre going on a cross-Canada trip, from Victoria to St. Johns.

6. Shell be taking Chemistry 301 in the fall, but hell wait until spring and borrow the text.

7. "No," hed said, "Playing *Tetris* until one oclock isnt any more admirable than playing *Solitaire*."

8. "Oh, for goodness sake!" shed cried yet again, "Cant you eat just one more?"

9. Youre the first caller, so youve won a trip for two to the West Edmonton Mall.

10. Lets get a couple of Hazels Chocolate Chunk Cookies and have a coffee and cookie break before we start the next exercise.

### Exercise 31: Apostrophes: Contractions and Possessives

Place apostrophes where appropriate in the following sentences.

1. Johns fathers laptop computer was stolen from the trunk of his car last night.

2. The dogs driving me crazy. Wheres the ointment to put on its bites?

3. Hed promised to be here at eight oclock, but its nearly nine.

4. Were going to a concert, so shell come with us if we can get another ticket.

5. Archimedes principle always fascinated Denis.

6. Kenichi got two As and three B+s.

7. Sarah said that shed never seen such a bizarre sight.

8. Joe didnt want to argue, but shed said that at least twice before about different things.

9. Its been a long time since youve seen your brother and sister, hasnt it?

10. Denis preoccupation with Archimedes led him to pursue Physics.

# End Punctuation Rules

There are three ways to end a sentence, but they are used for different effects.

## Period

Use a period to end an independent clause that constitutes a sentence.
    You can use the period to end any ordinary statement, a mild command, or a question embedded in a statement. The word following

a period will be a capital. In contrast, the word following a semicolon is only capitalized if it is a proper noun.

Examples:

Hong saw both chickadees and nuthatches at the feeder. (ordinary statement)

Please shut the window. (mild command)

I've often wondered *how a modem works*. (embedded question)

Students whose first language is not English should look particularly carefully at the embedded question in the final example. A common error in statements with embedded questions occurs when students use normal question word order in the statement. The above example would then read "I've often wondered *how does a modem work*." We deal further with this common error on pages 147–150 and 195, but you need to remember just one thing: **never use question word order in a statement**.

Use a period to end common abbreviations. Use periods with common abbreviations, but watch for exceptions:

| | | |
|---|---|---|
| Alta. | CIBC | Mr. Mrs. Ms. |
| a.m. | Cres. | Mt. |
| A.M. | Dr. | Ph.D. |
| B.A. | i.e. | St. |

Note three things:

1. Canada Post has a system of writing provinces without periods, e.g., NB, PQ, ON, MB. The above Alta. becomes AB in the new system.

2. Metric units of measurements are used without periods: km, cm, MHz, kg, and many recipes no longer use periods with oz, lb, tsp, or tbsp.

3. Required punctuation follows the period of an abbreviation. Contrast the examples below.

   • After you find the books, newspapers, journals, etc., you can use your note cards.

   • You can use your note cards after you find the books, newspapers, journals, etc.

You do not use periods within acronyms such as UNICEF, AIDS, TOEFL, CBC, or the RCMP. Acronyms are words formed by the initial letters of an organization or phenomenon's name and often result in a pronounceable word. Some people now carefully name their organization so that it will have a meaningful acronym. Some acronyms, such as radar and scuba, have now entered the language as normal words and do not require capitals.

## Question Mark

1. **Use a question mark to end a sentence that asks a direct question.**

   Why did you do it?

   When did you do it?

   Where is it?

   How can I fix it?

   Should I just throw it out?

2. **Use a question mark to end an abnormally structured sentence that asks a direct question.**

   An inversion of the subject and an auxiliary verb marks the usual question word order. However, you will often hear, and sometimes read, questions phrased in an abnormal, colloquial manner. The examples below still require question marks; indeed, without them, the intended meaning would be lost.

   He got to class on time?

   You finished the final report?

   Kim got a scholarship?

3. **Use a question mark to end a sentence interrupter that asks a direct question.**

   To interrupt a sentence with a question, use parentheses or dashes and include the question mark.

   Gordon—why does he always do such things?— left the keys in the car!

   I saw that cute guy (what is his name?) who works in the weight-training room.

   Should we use that song—how does it go?—about a little teapot?

## Exclamation Point

1. **Use an exclamation point to end an independent clause forming a sentence that expresses strong feeling.**

   You use an exclamation point when the sentence expresses strong feeling or requires special emphasis. Note in the final example below that we use an exclamation point instead of a question mark because we want to show intense feeling.

   After three tries, my friend finally passed the TOEFL!

   Watch where you're going!

   Is it really alive!

2. **Use an exclamation point to end an interjection or interrupter expressing strong feeling.**

   "Well!" Manjit said, "I hope you're satisfied now!"

   Gee whiz! Can you blame me?

   Douglas found the keys—can you believe it!—in the sugar bowl!

   Teresa asked Mayumi (she's only known her for a month!) to be maid-of-honour.

   When you have read over the above sentences, you may feel a bit over-stimulated. Using a great many exclamation points creates a format more suitable to a comic book. If all sentences end with exclamation points, all emphasis is lost. Claire limits her first year composition students to one exclamation point per semester, but grants that they can use them much more often in friendly letters or e-mail to friends. In general, use the exclamation mark sparingly!

## Exercise 32: End Punctuation

Use appropriate end punctuation in the following sentences, removing the punctuation that is there if you have to.

1. There's no way I can finish before quitting time

2. Do you know what time it is

3. It took a hint from Mrs. Jacobi's grandson before she realized that 80 km translated to just 50 mph; then, she felt a lot less like a drag racer

4. Jamie asked her if she would like to go for lunch

5. The whole group—can you believe it—fit in that small boat

6. I wonder why the newspaper isn't here

7. An aphelandra has attractive yellow stripes on its leaves, and it gets a beautiful flower

8. On the CBC morning show, I heard a UN diplomat speaking about all the great work that UNESCO and UNICEF accomplished in the '50s

9. Mr and Mrs Liang have planned a trip to Canada when Catherine gets her B Ed

10. Hurrah, we are famous

# Interrupt Punctuation

## Dashes

1. **Use dashes sparingly. If you use a great many, people will suspect that you don't know how to use other punctuation properly.**

2. **Use dashes—two typed hyphens—to set off parenthetical material or a dramatic shift in thought or tone. Do not space before, between, or after dashes. Dashes can be used in a pair or as a single.**

   Reiko left before 8:30—yet she missed the 9:00 bus!

   Jeremy thinks—and who can blame him!—that he will win Saturday.

   Just as the dawn was breaking near Lawrencetown Beach, as the mist was drifting in off the Atlantic, Kevin—who, don't forget, is some woman's son—and I drove silently and not at all unpleasantly in our separate, though no doubt not lasting, peace.

3. **Phrases set apart by dashes receive an emphasis not apparent in the same phrases set apart by commas. The latter example below is more emphatic.**

   Everything he eats, for breakfast, lunch or dinner, is white!

   Everything he eats—for breakfast, lunch or dinner—is white!

4. **Use dashes to set an appositive noun or a noun phrase that contains commas apart from the rest of the sentence or to prepare for a list.**

   I shared his lunch sandwich—provolone and cucumber with mayonnaise on white bread—before I went back to work.

   His planned dinner sounded unappetizing—cod, shredded daikon, rice, and blanc mange with white chocolate sauce.

## Exercise 33: Dashes

Put dashes where needed in the following sentences:

1. I know what I need pencils, pens and erasers.

2. Boris ate can you believe it? a whole roasted-garlic pizza.

3. She did creative writing poetry and short stories although she was working on her degree in Physics.

# Parentheses

1. **Always use parentheses (round brackets) in pairs. Do not put a comma before a parenthetical phrase.**

2. **Use parentheses to enclose afterthoughts, cross-references, non-essential material, or mild digressions. In contrast to dashes and even to commas, parentheses de-emphasize, rather than emphasize.**

   Barbara (the friend I mentioned before) will edit our tape.

   We deal further with question word order in Chapter Five (pages 147–150 and 194–195).

## Exercise 34: Parentheses

Put parentheses where needed in the following sentences:

1. Going home last night after the concert, I met my former boss David Kee on the LRT.

2. Boris ate a whole roasted-garlic pizza the large.

3. Trevor a big Woody Guthrie fan wanted to see the Billy Bragg concert because Bragg would be playing songs from the album of Woody's words and Billy's music.

# Brackets

1.  Use brackets, [   ], to add something that clarifies the meaning of a quotation while maintaining the writer's original intent. You usually leave out the word(s) that you are clarifying. The brackets signal the readers that something has been changed, and if they wish, they may check the original. Here, for example, is the sentence a writer wants to quote:

    "Eventually, he became Premier in 1944."

    The writer can add clarity using brackets:

    "Eventually, [Tommy Douglas] became Premier in 1944."

    As another example, a writer wants to quote the following:

    "Overfishing of Coho, Chinook, and Sockeye will mean the demise of the species on the West Coast."

    To add clarity, he or she can write,

    "Overfishing of Coho, Chinook, and Sockeye will mean the demise of [salmon] on the West Coast."

    The rest of the quotation remains word for word; the quotation marks remain in place; and the meaning of the original is maintained and clarified.

    It is important to note that the writer cannot alter the quotation as it has been altered below because to do so changes the intent of the original passage.

    ✗ "Overfishing of Coho, Chinook, and Sockeye will mean the demise of [all fish stocks] on the West Coast."

2.  Still dealing with quotations, you would enclose *sic* in brackets and use it when there is an error in the sentence that you want to quote. The Latin word *sic* means "so," so you are saying "I found this word (or idea) so, just like this." Let's suppose that some author made a Spell-check error in our first example above and that no editor had picked it up. The book came out with a sentence reading:

    "Eventually, he became Premiere in 1944."

    If you use this sentence, you want your readers to know that this silly mistake is in the original. Sometimes you can skirt around the error or paraphrase the material rather than quote, but if you want to use this sentence, this is how you tell your readers the mistake is not your own: put *sic* in brackets immediately after the error.

"Eventually, he became Premiere [sic] in 1944."

## Ellipses

Ellipses ( ... ) are used in quotations. An ellipsis is three spaced periods indicating an omission, four if what you omit passes a period or other end punctuation. There is a space both before and after an ellipsis.

When you use a quotation, use an ellipsis to show omission, but leave a recognizable English sentence and retain the author's meaning.

We can use the above paragraph to illustrate the use of ellipsis. Here is our quotation, properly worked into a sentence of our own devising.

De Pledge and McKenzie state that when you "use an ellipsis to show omission, ... [you must] retain the author's meaning."

## Quotation Marks

Clearly, quotation marks are important pieces of punctuation, for we have talked about them in relation to many other pieces of punctuation from commas to ellipsis. Now we will talk about quotations marks in their own right.

1.  **Use quotation marks with direct quotations.**

    a) Note that indirect quotations do not use quotation marks. Contrast the following pair of sentences:

    Petra said, "Richard won't be able to attend the semi-annual meeting, but he has read the report and will give us written feedback." (direct)

    Petra said *that* Richard won't be able to attend the semi-annual meeting, but that he has read the report and will give us written feedback. (indirect)

    b) Note, too, that if a quotation is interrupted by a phrase designating the speaker, the word following the interrupter is lower case, unless it is a proper noun.

    Examples:

    "Richard won't be able to attend the semi-annual meeting," said Petra, "but he has read the report and will give us written feedback."

"Although he won't be able to attend the semi-annual meeting," said Petra, "Richard has read the report and will give us written feedback."

c) If there are two or more speakers, conventional use calls for a new paragraph for each speaker.

Example:

Dimitri, obviously agitated, leaped up from his chair and paced around the room, stopping suddenly to face Carmella. "But where," he said, "should we hide the package? It's dangerous to leave it in this room!"

"Why not put it in the laundry basket? No one ever goes near it." Scowling, Dimitri picked up the package and ...

Remember that this rule concerns *dialogue*. Do not, as some writers of research papers have done, start a new paragraph every time you use a quotation.

2.  **Use quotation marks with quotations from an outside source.**

Whether your source is primary, from an interview, or secondary, from a book, magazine, journal, video, newspaper, the Net, etc., you must enclose word for word quotations within quotation marks. In addition, you should integrate a quotation into your own sentence rather than use it in isolation. See pages 337–338 for much more information on conventions to follow when you write a paper that incorporates quotations. In the meantime, look at the following quotation from *The Government of Canada* by the late R. MacGregor Dawson.

> "The late Mr. Woodsworth once enumerated at some length the directorships held by certain senators, and the list is still long and impressive."

A writer including this quotation in a research paper would do it something like this:

> This situation is not a recent one; for example, referring to conditions before the seventies, Dawson tells us that "the late Mr. Woodsworth once enumerated at some length the directorships held by certain senators, and the list [was] still long and impressive" (298).

In the above example, we quoted the whole sentence, but the same rules apply to partial quotations in a formal paper. Integrate the quotation, and give the source. In the following example, the writer has used only part of the quotation:

> Even in the forties, when the head of the CCF "enumerated at some length the directorships held by certain senators," we can see that the trend was well established (Dawson 298).

Note that because the writer did not use Dawson's name as she integrated the quotation, she included his name with the page number in the citation.

3. **Use single quotation marks to show a quotation within a quotation.**

In one of the exercises on colons, we used single quotation marks to show a quotation within a quotation:

> This is my favourite line in Austen's *Sense and Sensibility*: "'It is not everyone,' said Elinor, 'who has your passion for dead leaves.'"

If you quote dialogue when you write essays about literature, you will use this technique of single quotation marks within double quotation marks often unless you use block quotations. See pages 335–336.

For information about the difference between end punctuation with block quotation and embedded quotations, also see Chapter Seven: Organization, pages 337–338. For information about how to use quotations and commas, refer to page 213.

4. **Use quotation marks around the titles of works found within other works.**

Titles of poems, short stories, essays, articles in newspapers, magazines, or journals, and songs are put in double quotation marks. They are published as part of greater works whose titles are underlined or italicized.

Therefore, you would italicize the name of an anthology but put the names of a poem or short story within it in quotation marks. The name of a newspaper would be italicized, but the title of an editorial would be in quotation marks. The name of a CD would be italicized, but the name of an individual song would be in quotation marks. Norma's rule of thumb says, "If it's on the cover, it's italicized; if it's between the covers, it's in quotation marks."

5. **Use quotation marks to draw attention to a word being defined in a special sense.**

Use this rule very sparingly, and do not, for example, put quotation marks around slang in your essays. If the slang term shouldn't be there, it is inadvisable to draw attention to it. If it is appropriate in context, you have no need to apologize for using it.

Here is an example of quotation marks signalling a special sense of the word friend.

A "friend" is someone with whom you can share comfortable silences.

## Exercise 35: Quotation Marks

Use quotation marks and other punctuation where appropriate in the following sentences.

1. I was wondering said Hannah how we can carry this carpet down the mountain.

2. The River Merchant's Wife: a Letter, a poem by Ezra Pound, is a translation of a poem by an 8th century Chinese poet, Li Po, but for some strange reason, Pound uses Japanese names in the poem.

3. My father has a valuable, very breakable record of the Beatles' first release of I Wanna Hold Your Hand which he bought as a teenager in London.

4. In *The Moonstone*, one of Sergeant Cuff's more cutting lines is There's also such a thing as making nothing out of a molehill in consequence of your head being too high to see it.

5. Watermelon and corn on the cob Algernon said should never be eaten in polite company.

6. Ken needs to know about squelch to understand why his FM receiver cuts out when it receives noisy signals.

7. Most religions have a dictum similar to do unto others as you would have them do unto you, a simple but effective idea.

8. My favourite part in Louise Erdrich's *Love Medicine* isn't the title story, though it's wonderful, but the very end of The Good Tears, after Lulu has her cataracts removed, and Marie goes to help her.

9. Who could have known what that courier service thinks prompt means! They say the parcel will get there in two weeks.

10. In *The Woodlanders*, Creedle gets some great lines such as And I don't care who the man is, I says that a stick of celery that isn't scrubbed with a scrubbing brush is not clean.

## Exercise 36: Brackets, Ellipsis, and Quotation Marks

Here is an excerpt from page 306 of a composition text by U. Burne and I. Browne. Read it carefully.

> If the material is long or complicated, you should probably use note carts. Use one card for each note and carefully record the source: the author, the place of publication, the date, and the page. If a quotation crosses a pagr, indicate this in your note by a single or double slash.

1. Quote the first sentence, but leave out the words "you should probably."

2. Quote the third sentence, and change "your" to "the."

# Hyphens

A hyphen is an odd sort of staple, capable of both joining and separating words or parts of words. Put a space neither before a hyphen, nor after it.

## Hyphenated words

1. **Use a hyphen to separate compound nouns.**

   If both nouns are of equal importance to a concept, put a hyphen between them:

   Mr. Halakoski was a member of the CCF-NDP for a total of fifty-five years.

   He acted as secretary-treasurer for twenty-four years.

2. **Use a hyphen to join two or more nouns and other parts of speech to create a word.**

   Some words are composed of many parts and held together by hyphens.

   | | |
   |---|---|
   | coat-of-arms | editor-in-chief |
   | do-it-yourselfer | hole-in-one |

   Do not, however, hyphenate military or governmental titles such as Brigadier General, Chief Petty Officer, Lieutenant Governor, or Prime Minister.

3. **Use a hyphen to make certain verbs nouns or adjectives.**

A number of verbs contain prepositions. To make these words nouns or adjectives, you must add a hyphen.

| | | | |
|---|---|---|---|
| hand out | hand-out | strike out | strike-out |
| write off | write-off | take off | take-off |
| set up | set-up | hang up | hang-up |
| put down | put-down | slow down | slow-down |
| drop in | drop-in | pick up | pick-up |

4. **Use a hyphen if a compound modifier precedes the noun.**

Terrance Harvey is a well-known expert in hydroponic gardening.

but

Terrance Harvey's expertise in hydroponic gardening is well known.

5. **Use hyphens with prefixes before a proper noun.**

| | |
|---|---|
| ex-Prime-Minister | pseudo-Gothic |
| anti-Communist | neo-Conservative |
| post-Romantic | all-Canadian |

6. **Use hyphens with prefixes that modify the same one root.**

He pre- and post-dated cheques, then left the country.

7. **Use hyphens with prefixes "great" and "in law."**

My great-grandma's brother-in-law was a colonel in the Seaforth Highlanders, and her son-in-law, my great-uncle, served under him.

8. **Use hyphens to separate prefixes from nouns or from suffixes connected to one or two letters.**

Percival's parents were ex-hippies, so his tie-dyed T-shirts were fine with them.

The fashion police recommend that you re-do your hairdo.

9. **Use hyphens with the word "self" as prefix.**

Except for "selfish," "selfless" and "selfsame," use the prefix "self" followed by a hyphen.

| | | |
|---|---|---|
| self-assured | self-confidence | self-deluded |
| self-esteem | self-government | self-sufficient |

10. **Use a hyphen to avoid awkward double (or triple) consonants or vowel combinations.**

   If double (or triple) consonants or vowels occur in nouns or modifiers, separate the elements with hyphens. Look at these examples.

   co-op work term    bell-like tone    re-entry orbit    anti-insect

11. **Use a hyphen to make the meaning of a word clearly distinguishable from another possible meaning.**

   Some words do double duty in English, and, for some, you must clearly distinguish between them with hyphens. For example, you recover from your exam, but you re-cover your text book.

   Let me re-cap the bottle, and then I'll recap the argument.

12. **Use a hyphen to increase clarity.**

   With some modifiers, you will need to use hyphens to avoid ambiguity or add clarity. The following sentence, for example, is unclear.

   The daycare can now handle six year old children.

   In contrast, hyphens make both of the following sentences clear.

   The daycare can now handle six-year-old children.

   The daycare can now handle six year-old children.

13. **Use a hyphen to separate a word of more than one syllable at the end of a line.**

   If a word comes at the end of a line, separate the word with a hyphen at the end of a syllable. You must, however, never use a hyphen to separate a word that is already hyphenated, even if it falls at the end of a line. In general, adhering to Churchill's philosophy, try to avoid hyphens.

   Clearly, more things should be dreamt of in Horatio's philosophy if he is to understand everything.

## Hyphens with Numbers

1. **Use a hyphen to separate compound numbers and compound fractions.**

   Separate compound numbers such as those from twenty-one to ninety-nine with a hyphen.

   Ling wanted twenty-three doughnuts, not two dozen.

   Separate compound fractions, especially when they are used as adjectives, i.e., one-half cup butter.

   Two-thirds of the audience was under twenty-five.

   Separate words describing decades with hyphens.

   In the nineteen-twenties, women bobbed their hair.

2. **Use hyphens to indicate time when written in words.**

   Danny said he would be there at seven-thirty, but he didn't arrive until eight-fifteen.

3. **Use hyphens to separate compound adjectives containing numbers.**

   The eight-year-old girl was taller than her ten-year-old brother.

4. **Use hyphens to show a range of numbers.**

   Please read pages 67-92 very carefully.

**6**

# Developing Ideas

## Learning Outcomes

### This Chapter will help you to

- consider the audience and purpose for your writing.

- identify methods of development that are most appropriate to your ideas.

- use prewriting strategies to develop your ideas effectively.

# Prewriting

Prewriting involves exploring. It is that stage at which writers search for some facet of the topic that they care about. They find out what they know and don't know. They figure out what they would like to know. The difficulty for many beginning writers is that, as with all exploring, the purpose of freewriting is discovery. Therefore, it requires that, for a while, the writer suspend her or his need for certainty and accept the fact that, at the outset, explorers don't know what they're going to find in the end.

We believe that the prewriting stage is *crucial* to good writing. In order to write prose that has energy, writers *must* find some facet of the topic they care about. Failing to do so results in essays that are pedestrian and boring, not only for the reader, but for the writer.

This chapter will provide you with a repertoire of strategies for generating ideas for writing. None of them will be appropriate for every writing situation, and none of them will give you a finished product. Rather, they are designed to help you discover and create raw material from which you can begin to draft.

The strategies you choose will depend on the demands of the particular assignment and on your personal learning and writing styles. However, we recommend that you try out a number of the strategies described here, including those that don't appeal to you at first. Different strategies actually cause us to think in different ways, so an unfamiliar strategy can have surprisingly positive results.

## Reading Strategies

### The Thank-you Strategy

The "Thank-you" strategy involves approaching a text in a focused way so frequently that it begins to *mean* differently. It also involves thinking and writing about the shifting meanings.

Try repeating the words "thank you" twenty times in succession. For most people, the exercise has the effect of changing the way the words mean. Some people experience a change in the order of the two words. By repetition nine or ten "thank you" becomes "Ku thang."

Others experience a sensation of the sound disconnecting from the meaning. For the first time, you may hear "thank you" as harsh and grating. The experience can leave you wondering if English sounds harsh to people who don't speak it. The point is that the very act of repetition changes your interaction with words, often causing you to hear or experience them in new ways.

College and university writing assignments sometimes require that you respond to an unfamiliar text. It may be advertising copy, an historical royal proclamation, an editorial, a poem, a short story, an executive summary, a news report, or an analysis of foreign policy. Many students express frustration that, having read the text, they don't know what to say. Some students express the opinion that there is nothing more to be said: the text says it all. Some worry that they don't know what their instructor *wants* them to say, so they write gingerly, afraid of saying the wrong thing.

What students sometimes need is an approach to the text that enables them to get inside it. Lacking a strong engagement with the text, they may write superficial essays, stating the obvious but showing little insight or originality.

When you repeated "thank you" twenty or more times, the act of repetition probably deflated the meaning of the words. However, it may also have triggered questions that you hadn't considered before. Repetition helps you see connections where you previously saw none. It can alert you to contradictions or shifts of tone. It can trigger emotion and memory. It can uncover crescendos and decrescendos, subtleties of a text wholly overlooked in first readings.

## Drawbacks and Advantages

The thank-you strategy involves learning some complex reading and observation skills. Therefore, at first, it is time-consuming and can be used successfully only with short texts. However, with practice, most of the repetitions can be eliminated. Once you have mastered the skills, you will be able to process information from the bulk of a long text on the run, having learned to identify which short passages warrant several readings. In the long run, the strategy saves time because it teaches you what to pay attention to and gives you confidence in your own ability to write an insightful response to a text.

## Step I

1. Read a text or passage once to get a general overview. If the text is a story, you might read for plot. If it is an article, you might read for the main point. If the text includes pictures or graphics, remember that reading includes examining the pictures and their captions carefully as well.

2. Take 10 to 15 minutes to write down your general impressions. Start your writing with the following words: "My most dominant impression of this text is . . . ."

**Step II**

1. Reread the text with the idea of verifying whether your first impressions accurately capture the spirit of the text. As you read, notice words or phrases that support your impression or cause you to expand, refine, or alter it. You may wish to underline faintly in pencil. Later, you can erase all marks.

2. Take 10 to 15 minutes to write an expanded version of your general impressions. Start your writing with the following prompt: "On second reading, I think . . . ."

**Step III**

1. Read the text a third time. Your job, this time, is to circle words or phrases that are starting to stick in your mind: powerful or surprising images, diction that has powerful connotations, phrases that reveal tone, words that amuse or offend you, concepts that make you nod or squirm. If the text has pictures, note the elements that stick in your mind there, too: colours, proximity of shapes, sharpness of focus, character of shapes, for example, geometric shapes or organic shapes; and notice your emotional response to them.

2. Reread the words you have circled, and write for ten to fifteen minutes about those words. Begin your writing with the following prompt: "When I review the words that I circled, the connections among them that I notice are . . ."

**Step IV**

1. Reread the text one last time. This time, look for connections between the text and the world outside the text. Every time you think of a connection, make a pencil notation in the margin. For example, the text might make you think of another text you have read, or an historical or current event, a place you've visited, a character in a story, a person you know, an experience you've had, a memory, a belief you hold, or one you disbelieve, a value or any kind of connection.

2. Reread your notations. Take ten to fifteen minutes to complete the following prompt: "When I read this text, it brings to mind . . . ."

## Activity 1: Creating a point of comparison

This activity is designed to help you compare the effect of the Read-once-and-start-writing method with the thank-you strategy. In number 1, you will read a sight passage once only, and then draft an introduction to an essay. In number 2, responding to a different sight passage, you will work through the thank-you strategy step by step.

Read Passage 1 beginning "Calm takes over when you least expect it to," and then generate a topic for a short essay about the passage.

**Passage 1**

Calm takes over when you least expect it to, when you see your arm severed from your body in your own basement for example, by the ripping blade of a table saw. Suddenly the world is silent; you no longer hear the scream of machinery; you don't feel pain. You're mesmerized by things that, prior to that moment, didn't matter, weren't connected: the stitches on the neckline of your husband's vest, the knife-edge of a skate blade hanging from a hook beside the furnace. Time hasn't stopped, but it's been fiercely shoved aside by the seething details of indiscriminate reality, which are sharper and more insistent now than they have ever been before. Your hand is vivid on the concrete floor, the palm upturned, the fingers slightly curled. Your life line and your heart line intersect and it dawns on you that you have never taken stock of that before and that it is enormously significant; but then the sawdust in coagulating blood looks like toasted coconut and you know that when you were ten and your grandfather took you to the slaughter house three days after Christmas, you got blood in the tread of your running shoes and the patterns they made on your bedroom floor were tire patterns, not coconut, and suddenly you wonder if you should call your mother—because you think that today may be her birthday and you haven't made a cake.

You don't scream or run out of the room. You have no sense of urgency. You're buffered by an envelope of dead, hermetic air, yet beyond it, you can see electrons spinning. They say that when one of our senses is compromised, the others compensate. So it is with this. Sensation is now paralyzed, but your vision has gone manic. You cannot stop the flood of details coming in; neither can you feel them; nor can you send a single impulse out. They record themselves upon an empty screen. Your nervous system has shut down.

Shock is not a sudden, violent blow, an impact or collision, or a fierce encounter. It's the collapse of all the circuits between your knowing and your being. It's a state in which cause is severed from effect, impetus from action. It's the failure of all frames of reference, the place of no response, a phantasmatic place of calm.

from "A Phantasmatic Place of Calm," *A Room of One's Own*, Summer 1998. Vol. 21: 2.

## Activity 2: Working through the thank-you strategy

Most people will see Passage 2 as being more challenging than Passage 1—perhaps even intimidating; nevertheless, we believe that with the help of the thank-you strategy, you will feel confident about generating and narrowing a topic that responds to the excerpt.

Read Passage 2 and follow the steps of the thank-you strategy before writing a thesis statement and a list of ideas for an essay responding to the text.

**Passage 2**

Silent. Accordingly my personal experience which I had mention earlier. Because definitely broken language, I think. Must be. Comparing to your language which loud and strong, and demonstrate no doubt always. Like stand up tall and hero, in picture book. Like you talking speech give true meaning. Me listening listening. Waiting for hear right answer. Then you giving. Always for sure and no doubt.

Trying to think strength thought, like you. Stand up and tall thought. But accordingly my personal experience, failing on knowing for definite. Because I found a cruelty, which many answers for one question only. So no true meaning because true is only one answer. Like adjective, third degree. Put *the* in front. No one look anymore afterthen. Is finish. This, similar you can do for sure, with no worries. Although I am still look, but so don't ever had final answer. Not yet.

[ ● ● ● ]

So I am falling into a sad. Because my thinking is not forgetting even after trying trying please forget. Which you are replying: very beetle-wit addle-pate, no difference from oyster shell and bit of grit, feed to chicken. So, agreeing to your replying, I talk myself once more time which I say: Only stupid write a unimportant because comparing to your language which stand up tall and loud. I am say, Leave this for person got knowing for definite and clear. Leave this for person got one true answer for sure. Therefore I am shake my head with critical which is: Why I waste my time, woman? and I am talk myself a feeling of no flinch. Finally, I am chastise me with a severe. So after all, I am satisfying this finish. No more needle needle make me thinking write down little thinking. Therefore I have been able to learn the correct knowledge.

So my chastise is bring me to a quiet. And for sure this time now I am decide turn away and make some busy occupy to other thing. Make some adding for my bank account for serious job job business, do some sensible as order cloth for sewing, organize for work, help small daughter learn from school arithmetic and right spell word. Stop she silly making painting every page for notebook. Help she think for sensible. This is make me to forget my foolish thinking.

from "Accordingly my personal experience and also very thank you" Tillie Olsen, *The Malahat Review*, Fall 1998. No. 124

---

### Activity 3: Comparing the two methods

You have now read passage one, once, and written an introduction. You have read passage two, four times, working through the thank-you strategy. Compare the experiences:

|  | Phantasmatic | Tillie Olsen |
|---|---|---|
| • level of confidence I feel about making claims about the text | | |
| • depth of insight I have about the text | | |
| • my awareness of patterns in the text | | |
| • number of connections that come to mind between the text and other texts or experiences | | |
| • length of time required for the activity | | |

As we noted at the beginning of this section, the thank-you strategy has the drawback of taking a significant amount of time. It has the advantage that it usually increases confidence and depth of understanding. Depending on the difficulty of your assignment and on your confidence about a text, this strategy may work well for you.

## The Connect-the-Dots Strategy

Imagine that you are required to write an essay on a novel about a man who dies unknown. On the first page, a sentence notes that the hardship of the character's life is "recorded in his face." Then, a few pages later, an image appears saying that the character's back bears the scars of a whipping he received as a boy. Already, you have the start of what may prove to be a theme in the book: the man's body bears a record of his life.

If you do not read with a purpose, you may read past important "clues" without attending to them. As a result, you may not notice patterns or recurring themes. In fact, you may arrive at the end of the novel with only a general understanding of the plot but no idea what to write an essay about.

We've called this strategy "Connect-the-Dots" in honour of the puzzles you probably remember doing as children. When you first looked at those puzzles, the dots appeared to be random on the page. If the puzzles were at all complex, until a pattern was made visible by connecting the appropriate dots, the page had no meaning.

While you can readily follow the plot of most texts, when you begin reading a book, it's impossible for you to know whether early images or ideas form part of a pattern that is central to the meaning of the text. If you use the connect-the-dots strategy, patterns will make themselves visible to you as you go.

We suggest that you invest in an inexpensive notebook. Dedicate each page to one image or concept by summarizing the concept in a few words at the top of the page. As you go, you may need to revise your original summary, as we have done below. Therefore, using the example described in the first paragraph of the connect-the-dots strategy, page one of your notebook might say the following:

*life is recorded in his face*

*page 1. The passage talks about his hardships, says the lines on his face record the hardships.*

Soon you might add another entry, causing you to refine the original heading:

*life is recorded in his face on his body*

*page 1. The passage talks about his hardships, says the lines on his face record the hardships.*

*page 6. Scars on his back.*

As you read, whenever you notice the recurrence of an image or an idea, write it down on the page dedicated to that subject. Include the page number on which the idea appeared in the novel as well as four or five words that will remind you of the passage. We recommend that you also use pencil to underline the passage in the text.

By the end of the first fifty or so pages of the novel, you may have as many as ten to twenty concepts to which you've dedicated pages in your notebook; but as you progress through the text, you'll find that only a few of the lists really grow to any appreciable size.

By the time you've finished the novel, you may have three or four lists that include substantial numbers of entries. The chances are extremely good that those three or four concept lists represent major themes in the novel. By the time you are ready to begin to write, you will have a strong sense of some of the patterns that give meaning to the story. You should be in a position to make some claims about the recurrent concerns of the text. You may be able to discuss how those concerns affect the characters and the development of the plot. Moreover, you will have a record of where to find the details supporting your claims.

## The Summary Strategy

Sometimes the reason that students have trouble developing ideas to write about is because they have not done or do not know how to do the required pre-reading. Whether you intend to write about a text or a general topic, it is not enough to read either primary or secondary sources in the same manner that you would read a book for pleasure. You need to become familiar enough with the material to be able to make some generalizations about it. Otherwise, you will have nothing to say that is not self-evident or superficial. Developing a sophisticated argument or piece of exposition requires comprehension of material, analysis, and synthesis.

Summarizing is particularly useful to help you understand and synthesize material if you are required to do a research paper. Good summaries require that you read closely, identify main ideas and key phrases, rephrase in your own words, eliminate any material that is not essential, and condense details and examples. Summarizing, therefore, helps you to assimilate and synthesize material.

# Writing Strategies

## The Freefall Strategy

This strategy, variously called *freefall*, *freewriting*, and *no-edit journalling*, has much in common with stream-of-consciousness writing. It involves exploring your thoughts rather than your responses to a text. It is a useful tool for finding out what you know and don't know about a topic and—what can be more surprising—your attitudes and biases, which are not always what you thought them to be.

There are only two rules for freefall: don't edit, and don't stop. If you can think of nothing to write, write "I can think of nothing to write. I can think of nothing to write. I can think of nothing to write," until your thoughts begin to flow again. Some books will tell you not to use punctuation. We believe it doesn't matter whether you do or not. Just try not to get in your own way. Let your thoughts make whatever connections and leaps they will. Your job is to follow them wherever they want to go. The writing merely traces the path of your thoughts. You will sift the material for ideas later.

## First Jump

Look at the freefall started with the word "colour."

---

**Freefall: Colour**

I'm looking at blue right now. Pale blue and sky blue. Both about the same blue to tell the truth. Both bright. Nothing "blue" about them. Summer colours. Summer colours are airier than other colours. Tinged by sunshine. Nothing is blue when the sun is shining. Winter blue is not the same. sombre more like grey. Closer to the ground. Bright blue, summer blue makes breathing easier. Hard is not hard if the sun is shining. What has this got to do with colour? I can't think of anything else. colour, colour, colour, Other colours I can see...Green and shadows under the trees. Light green and dark green. I love the golden green near the end of the afternoon in summer, under trees when the light is long. Thick creamy light. You don't get those colours in winter.

---

### Activity 4: Now, you try it.

Read the excerpt from "A Phantasmatic Place of Calm" again. Then write a "First Jump" response in which you allow your unedited ideas and responses to the text to unfold on paper.

Freefall on "Phantasmatic"

_____

_____

_____

_____

_____

_____

_____

_____

As we've already pointed out, prewriting activities are explorations. You don't know what you might find in them. Before drafting, you need to sift through the ideas generated by the prewriting activities, pick out those that have potential, and explore their potential. For example, after rereading the "Colour" freefall, you might find that the sentence "hard is not hard if the sun is shining" appeals to you. That sentence might become the prompt for your "second jump."

## *Second Jump*

The "Second Jump" of freefall involves identifying key ideas or words that arose in your first freefall text. Once you have discovered which idea is nudging at you to be developed, take a second jump. Begin by writing a sentence that sums up one idea that stands out in the freefall. When you freefall this time, bring a little more discipline to the exercise. If you can't think of anything to say, write the summary sentence again. If you still can't think of anything to say, try the Reporters' Questions which you'll find in the "Journalists' Strategy," on pages 260–262.

Here is an example of a second jump, selected from "Freefall: Colour," above:

---

**Second Jump: Colour**
Summary sentence: Bright summer colours affect my mood.

When I think about it, I know its true. I guess it's like — what do they call it? Seasonal light disorder? Is that the name? I guess if that's what I'm going to write about, which it may not be, I'd better look it up. Why is everything termed a disorder. Why can't we just say that when it's light and cheery I feel light and cheery, instead of saying I don't feel light and cheery when all the colours out my window are grey, so I must have a disorder. Actually, I think what I'd like to write about is both the idea brightness/lightness affects our moods and in our culture, we're so obsessed with labelling that everybody has some disorder or another. I wonder what a "normal" person would look like? Not too fat, not too thin, not too just right, not too active, not too passive, not too sun-loving, not a mole, not working too hard, and not watching too much TV. I wonder if that would be all right for me to write about? Start with the differences in summer colours and winter colours and their effect on me; then talk about seasonal light disorder, or whatever it's called, and move from that to questioning the obsession we have with disorders in our culture so that everything, even things that are just "normal" differences between people, ends up being a problem that people have to feel bad about. I wonder if that would work?

---

## Activity 5: Freefalling

Choose one of the following broad topics and freefall for 4–5 minutes. Remember, the only rules are don't edit, and don't stop.

- invisibility
- rules
- racism
- play
- green
- image

## Activity 6: Sifting

Reread your freefall and find the one idea that stands out or interests you most. If no idea stands out, ask a peer to read the text and tell you what he or she thinks is the most compelling idea.

## Activity 7: Second Jump

Write a summary sentence that describes the main idea arising from your first freefall. Then jump again for 4–5 minutes. Remember, this freefall has a clearer objective than the first one. Rather than writing "I can think of nothing to say," when you come to a blank wall, write the sentence that describes your main idea again.

## The Journalists' Strategy

Headline journalism almost always asks the four questions "Who? What? Where? When?" Investigative journalism usually attempts to answer the questions "Why?" and "How?" in addition to the basic questions.

By applying the journalists' questions to a broad subject, and truly allowing your mind free rein, you will generate a range of possible essay topics. Then, if you talk over the questions with someone else, you will probably spark another line of questioning. When Norma generated the first version of the list of questions below, the list was about two-thirds its current length. Claire read the list and added "When did crayon companies start having more than one "skin" colour." That question sparked several more questions, opening even more alternatives.

Below is Norma and Claire's list of questions, generated in response to the prompt, "colour."

## What?

- What do I know about the properties of colour?
- What makes colours seem light and bright or dark and sombre?
- What do people who are colour-blind see when I see red?
- What effect do differing intensities of colour have on our eyes? Our brains?
- What are the different connotations of, say, white, across several different cultures?
- What makes some light seem thick and creamy while other light seems light and airy?
- What ingredients are used in natural dyes?
- What are some of our prejudices or assumptions about colour?
- What are some of the ways we organize our lives to maximize our enjoyment of light and colour?
- What are some of the experiments that explore the effect of colour on mood?
- What evidence is there that drivers of red cars get more tickets?
- What is Seasonal Affective Disorder? What is its correct name?
- What's the difference between SAD and having a down day?
- What proportion of the population is colour-blind? Is the proportion the same cross-culturally?

## Who?

- Who is renowned for her/his use of colour? Photographer? Painter?
- Who discovered how to produce colour photographs?
- Who is affected by SAD?
- Who is born with colour-blindness?
- Who first made coloured crayons for children?

## When?

- When do we first see colour? Are we born with the ability to differentiate between subtle gradations of colour?
- As we grow older, does our colour acuity deteriorate like our eyesight or our sense of smell?
- When did house paints, as we know them, become readily available? How long have we been able to easily apply colour to our homes?

- When did crayon companies start having more than one "skin" colour?

- When did colours that used to be very rare, like indigo, become mass-producible?

- When did indigo become the colour of royalty?

**Where?**

- Where could one find a thriving industry in the manufacture of natural dyes?

- Where is colour registered in the brain?

- Where can I get information about colour receptors?

- Where is colour used by human beings for other ends than decoration? (e.g., camouflage, visibility, marketability ???)

**Why?**

- Why does colour affect the way we feel?

- Why do some animals lack pigment, e.g. some cave fish? (Is it possible for a plant not to have colour?)

- Why do car colours come in "years"?

- Why did indigo become the colour of royalty?

- Why do more blue-eyed females get glaucoma than brown-eyed females?

**How?**

- How do they decide which colours to use in hospitals or public buildings? That is, what kinds of experiments are done to test the effect of colour?

- How do different colours affect us? Does red really have a different effect on us than green or white?

- How did the development of commercial paints evolve?

- How are natural dyes manufactured?

- How do colour-blind people's eyes work differently?

- How do blind people "feel" colour?

# Picturing Strategies

Visual learners learn best when they see or create visual representations of ideas. Visual representations can range from idea balloons, such as cartoonists use, to formal outlines, which use several levels of indentation to show the shape and continuity of a text.

The following strategies capitalize on visual representations. Even if you do not consider yourself to be a visual learner, we suggest that you try some of these strategies because using unfamiliar learning styles can result in surprisingly original patterns of thinking.

We divide the picturing strategies into two categories:

- Graphic Organizers, which include all those types of charts and graphs that represent connections visually.

- Outlining, which involves text-driven strategies, usually used to visually represent the organization of a piece of writing rather than its ideas.

## Mapping

Mapping represents visually the connections between ideas, evidence, arguments, or concepts. You begin a map either by jotting down ideas or questions at random or by selecting ideas from a brainstorm or a freefall. In the example below, we have done the latter, using the earlier freefall about colour. As we identified connected ideas, we clustered them around the appropriate key idea.

---

**Mapping**

Second Jump
Summary sentence: **Bright summer colours affect my mood.**

When I think about it, I know its true. I guess it's like—what do they call it? **Seasonal light disorder?** Is that the name? I guess if that's what I'm going write about, which it may not be, I'd better look it up. Why is everything termed a **disorder?** Why can't we just say that when it's **light and cheery** I feel light and cheery, instead of saying I don't feel light and cherry when all the colours out my window are grey, so I must have a disorder? Actually, I think what I'd like to write about is both the notion **brightness/lightness affects our moods** and in our culture, we're so obsessed with **labelling** that everybody has some disorder or another. I wonder what a **"normal" person** would look like? **Not too fat, not too thin, not too just right, not too active, not**

*continued*

---

**Mapping** *(continued)*

**too passive, not too sun-loving, not a mole, not working too hard,
and not watching too much TV.** I wonder if that would be all right for
me to write about? Start with the differences in **summer colours and
winter colours** and their effect on me; then talk about seasonal light
disorder, or whatever it's called, and move from that to questioning
the obsession we have with disorders in our culture so that everything, even things that are just "normal" differences between people,
ends up being a problem that people have to feel bad about. I wonder
if that would work?

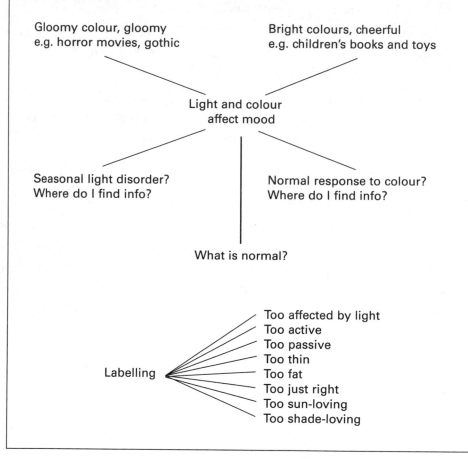

Gloomy colour, gloomy
e.g. horror movies, gothic

Bright colours, cheerful
e.g. children's books and toys

Light and colour
affect mood

Seasonal light disorder?
Where do I find info?

Normal response to colour?
Where do I find info?

What is normal?

Labelling

Too affected by light
Too active
Too passive
Too thin
Too fat
Too just right
Too sun-loving
Too shade-loving

## Sociograms

A sociogram is a specialized kind of map that shows connections between people or characters. The following sociogram offers one way of thinking about the relationships between the characters in Alice Munro's story, "Boys and Girls."

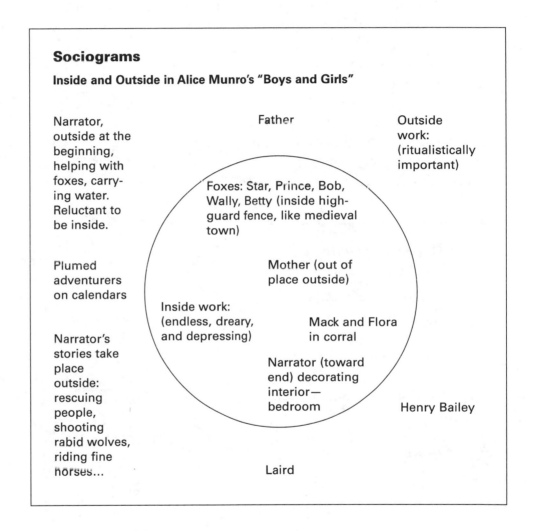

**Sociograms**

**Inside and Outside in Alice Munro's "Boys and Girls"**

Narrator, outside at the beginning, helping with foxes, carrying water. Reluctant to be inside.

Plumed adventurers on calendars

Narrator's stories take place outside: rescuing people, shooting rabid wolves, riding fine horses...

Father

Foxes: Star, Prince, Bob, Wally, Betty (inside high-guard fence, like medieval town)

Mother (out of place outside)

Inside work: (endless, dreary, and depressing)

Mack and Flora in corral

Narrator (toward end) decorating interior—bedroom

Outside work: (ritualistically important)

Henry Bailey

Laird

# Tree Charts

Tree Charts are usually upside-down trees in which each successively smaller branch represents a subdivision of a larger concept. The familiar family trees used in genealolgy show the spreading branches of a family. Tree charts are also used in biology to show systems of classification.

We use a variation on conventional tree charts—to trigger ideas rather than to sort them, though sorting, too, happens as a result of using this strategy.

Students beginning a research paper, for example, may start with a very broad or vague interest in a subject such as Australia. Using a tree chart can help them to conceptualize main divisions and subdivisions of the subject, triggering ideas that narrow their topic to manageable proportions. The branching effect guides them along particular pathways of thought, requiring that they become more and more specific with each step.

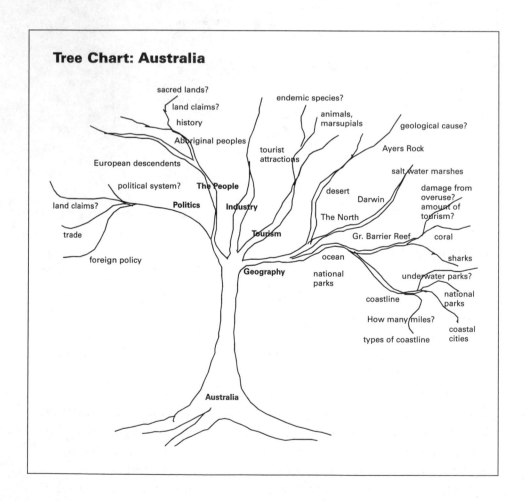

**Tree Chart: Australia**

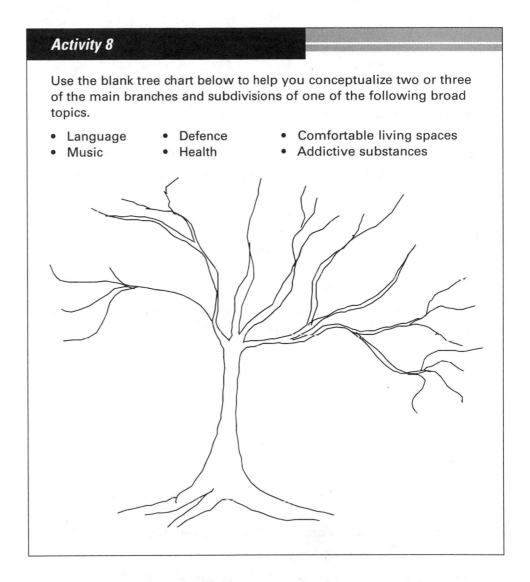

**Activity 8**

Use the blank tree chart below to help you conceptualize two or three of the main branches and subdivisions of one of the following broad topics.

- Language
- Music
- Defence
- Health
- Comfortable living spaces
- Addictive substances

## Graphs and Charts

Now that computers have made professional-looking graphing and charting easy, graphs and charts are common features of business and technical writing. In business and technical communication, their function is, normally, to organize complex or confusing information in an eye-catching and simplified manner.

However, graphs and charts can help you to develop ideas too. For example, you may be required to distill a large amount of information, identify which information is pertinent and which is not, and write an analysis. Then charts and graphs can help you to refine your focus, enabling you to develop only those ideas that are most important.

In the box below is the text of an assignment that you have been given in a Technical Writing Course. Following the text entitled "Inn on the Water: Client Dissatisfaction," we have charted and graphed the information in three ways to demonstrate how graphing and charting can help you to develop a plan for writing the report.

*Technical Writing 275*
*Assignment #4*
*Analytical Report and Recommendations*

Louanna Bjork, General Manager of Inn on the Water, a fictitious, 128 room, luxury hotel located in one of Canada's major urban centres, has directed you to analyse, report on, and make recommendations regarding the series of incidents that occurred two weeks ago at the hotel. The incidents have resulted in a threat by the Great Northern Bears hockey team to terminate their contract because of the hotel's failure to provide contracted services.

## INN ON THE WATER: CLIENT DISSATISFACTION

### The Hotel:

- 128 guest rooms

- fifteen conference and banquet rooms

- restaurant

- bar and lounge

- bulk of the revenue from conference and large-group business.

### The Management Team and Staff involved:

- Hotel Manager: Louanna Bjork

- Manager of Conference Services : Bernice Capaz
  Duties: plan catering for large groups; work with group and conference leaders to plan menus, and book space to best serve the client; identify most appropriate room settings: classroom setting, conference table setting, etc.; identify equipment needs such as sound systems, overhead projectors and screens, flip charts, etc.; allocate banquet and conference rooms, to make optimum use of hotel facilities; ensure that all Banquet Orders are complete and accurate; supervise the system through which Banquet Orders are delivered.

- Banquets Manager: Hewatt Olam
  Duties: work closely with Manager of Conference Services implementing all arrangements identified on "Banquet Orders"; arrange staffing for group functions; ensure adequate numbers of porters and servers to cater all conferences taking place in the hotel on any given day.

*continued*

## INN ON THE WATER: CLIENT DISSATISFACTION *(CONTINUED)*

- Duty Manager, Bob Newbiggings
  Duties: oversee all hotel operations in the absence of the General Manager.

- Assistant Executive Chef: Len Gosh
  Duties: Oversee food purchasing, staffing, and operation of kitchen in the absence of Chief Executive Chef, Lee Arez. Has volunteered to stand-in for Bernice Capaz in Capaz's absence, should any problems arise. (Capaz wears pager at all times, even when on vacation.)

- Porters
  Duties: set up the banquet rooms according to the settings specified by Conference Services Manager; install chairs, equipment, deliver tableware, and glasses, arrange podiums and whatever is necessary.

- Servers
  Duties: serve the food. Their jobs may involve simply rolling a trolley of plates and glasses, and another of sandwiches, muffins, juice, tea, and coffee into the conference room; or it may involve formal dinner service.

- Reservations Clerks: Magda Selwyn (new employee) and Manon Boudreau
  Duties: check-ins, walk-in reservations, check-outs, balancing cash prior to going off-duty.

- Switchboard operator: Rosemary Loggins

- On annual vacation at the time of the incident:
  Bernice Capaz
  Hewatt Olam

- On regular weekend schedule:
  Louanna Bjork

### The Client:

- Great Northern Bears Minor League Hockey Team

- Sales team signed three-year contract with them last year

- 7 dates each winter

- 12 double rooms per visit. All rooms to be adjoining or on the same hall.

- Contract specifies availability of early check-in when necessary (11:00 am) (no extra charge)

- Contracted arrival: late morning on game days

- Contract includes pre-game dinner (full course, two choices) for 21, plus optional 4 extra dinners to be charged as required

*continued*

## Inn on the Water: Client Dissatisfaction (*continued*)

- Buffet brunch on morning of departure

- Food service in private banquet space

- Total value of contract: $8000+

- Hotel's contact with team: Jim Bates, Team Manager

### Sunday, January 27th visit:

- Historically one of the slowest weekends of the year.

- Clients on middle game of a three-game road trip.

- Slated arrival time, game day, 1:00 pm, Sunday, January 27. Actual arrival time, Saturday, January 26.

- Team Manager Bates did not arrive with team. Team members informed reservation desk clerk that Bates would arrive the following morning. Reservation desk clerk, Magda Selwyn, was not aware that Bates was the team manager.

- Twenty team members checked in.

- Client subsequently claimed hotel had been notified by phone of the change of plan. Bates produced a phone log, indicating that a call had been made to the hotel reservations desk from the team office on Friday, January 25. Bates said he personally spoke to a reservations clerk at that time, requested, and confirmed all changes. She does not remember the call. No reservation change or confirmation number was recorded in the computer. Hotel has no record of notification.

- Reservations staff were able to arrange accommodations because of slow weekend, but unable to provide adjoining rooms.

- Only two additional events in hotel on Sunday, both small. Planned staffing to cover both events, one server. No porters on duty.

- Reservations Desk on skeleton staff (one clerk).

### Reports from management personnel on duty at the time:

Reservations clerk, Magda Selwyn: relatively new employee with the hotel working alone for the first time. Selwyn reports that the GNBs were checked in without incident and directed to proceed to the Diefenbaker Room for 6:30 serving of dinner. Team seemed very pleased. Selwyn assumed that the game date had been changed. She contacted Assistant Executive Chef Len Gosh to notify him of the change of date. She did not attempt to contact Bernice Capaz or to inform anyone that there was no record of a request for change of

*continued*

## INN ON THE WATER: CLIENT DISSATISFACTION (CONTINUED)

arrival in the computer. She did not realize that there was a problem since she was able to find rooms for all team members and since Gosh was available to make changes to meal plans.

Gosh checked Banquet Orders to verify the menu, checked stores to ensure that everything was in order, then called on help from the restaurant kitchen staff. Together, he and restaurant staff prepared the pre-game dinners, which provided for a choice of steak or chicken.

Gosh notes that he is new to this hotel and has worked under a somewhat different system in the past. Moreover, the Banquet Orders are not something that he normally deals with on a day-to-day basis.

Experienced Head Waiter Ben Bentley's note on Banquet Order: served pre-game meal: 17 steak, 3 chicken. Team seemed pleased with food; no hitches.

Leo Hollirock, porter, did the tear-down of the Diefenbaker Room and the 3 set-ups for the 27th, including the GNBs' 11:30 brunch in the Diefenbaker Room. Locked all banquet rooms and left the hotel at 9:30pm. No porters on duty on Sunday, January 27.

GNB team members reportedly arrived Diefenbaker Room at 7:00am, Sunday, January 27. They were scheduled to be at the arena by 8:30 for an early practice because ice time was tied up until game time for the rest of the day.

GNB found door to the Diefenbaker Room locked. 7:15, team captain approached Reservations Desk Clerk, Manon Boudreau, who had just come on duty. Boudreau was not yet aware of the early arrival of the team. She asked to talk to team manager. Was told he would arrive later. Checked computer for reservation change confirmation number. Found none. Contacted Duty Manager Bob Newbiggings. Newbiggings contacted Len Gosh at home. Gosh contacted the kitchen and directed Chef Mayra Lenca to check Banquet Order. Was informed that a brunch Order was there but dated for the 28th. Gosh instructed Lenca to change the date of the Banquet Order and begin preparations. Gosh left immediately for the hotel.

8:05 am, Ben Bentley served brunch of muffins, rolls, jams and cheese, cold cereals, juice, and tea and coffee. Team members who had not already left to get breakfast in a restaurant downtown stated that they required ham, eggs, sausages, or pancakes and steak for energy. They refused the brunch and left.

Later team members reported that players who went to a restaurant were late for practice, for which they were fined. Others arrived at practice on time but without breakfast. (Gosh explained that most restaurants are ill-equipped to deal with an influx of 15 or more big eaters all at once on a slow weekend.)

11:00 am, Team Manager Jim Bates had still not arrived. Duty Manager, Bob Newbiggings, tried unsuccessfully to contact him or

continued

## INN ON THE WATER: CLIENT DISSATISFACTION *(CONTINUED)*

any other representative of the team in their home city. Finally directed Len Gosh to prepare a second pre-game meal.

Newbiggings called in porter Leo Hollirock (at time and a half) to tear down after the brunch and set up for the dinner.

3:00 pm, Jim Bates, Team Manager, checked in. Expressed dissatisfaction that rooms were not blocked. Told desk to phone all team members and tell them to meet immediately. Diefenbaker Room was made available.

4:30 pm, two hours before the game, Ben Bentley served hot smorgasbord. Bates became very angry. Asked where pre-game steak was. Was told it had been served the night before. Bates said he had expressly stated that team members would be on their own for dinner Saturday night. Said the hotel was in error and GNBs would not pay for two pre-game meals.

Team members ate the meal but expressed extreme dissatisfaction.

A second brunch was served prior to the team's departure Monday morning.

Subsequently, communication from GNBs management produced a phone log which, they claim, provides evidence that arrangements had been made with the hotel. They also state that the organization refuses to pay for three of the meals since two of them were never ordered and one was inappropriate. They express extreme anger at what they describe as the shoddy treatment of their players and the bad management of the hotel.

In order to write your report on this incident, you must first sort through a great deal of information to identify which ideas you want to focus on and develop.

A flow chart, such as the one below, provides you with a visual representation of the flow of communication and responsibility at the time of the GNBs' visit. Such a chart may help you to decide whether or not you will need to include a discussion of lines of communication in your report.

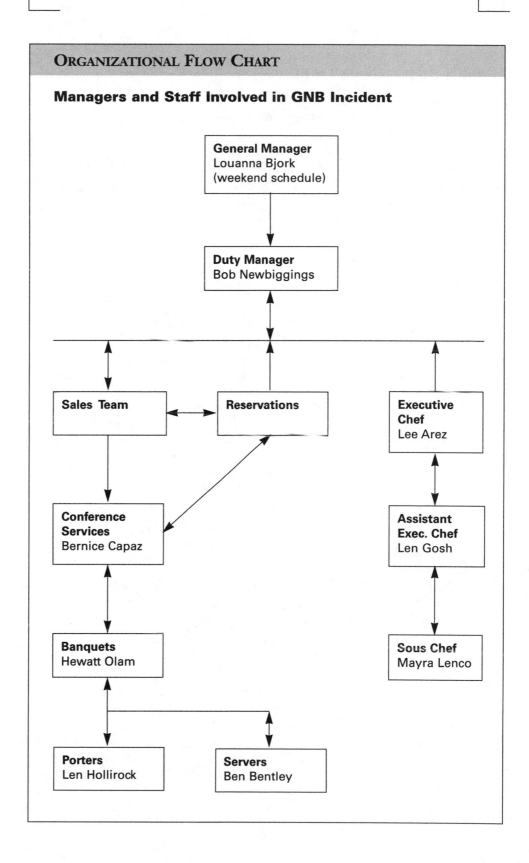

ORGANIZATIONAL FLOW CHART

**Managers and Staff Involved in GNB Incident**

**General Manager**
Louanna Bjork
(weekend schedule)

**Duty Manager**
Bob Newbiggings

**Sales Team**

**Reservations**

**Executive Chef**
Lee Arez

**Conference Services**
Bernice Capaz

**Assistant Exec. Chef**
Len Gosh

**Banquets**
Hewatt Olam

**Sous Chef**
Mayra Lenco

**Porters**
Len Hollirock

**Servers**
Ben Bentley

## Detail Analysis Chart
## Great Northern Bears Contract

A detail analysis can help you to identify and rank elements of the
problem you wish to concentrate on in your report.

| POSSIBLE FACTORS LEADING TO GNB'S DISSATISFACTION | SOURCE OF PROBLEM | POSSIBLE SOLUTION |
|---|---|---|
| Communication breakdowns | • no confirmation of change of arrival (source of problem still uncertain)<br>• failure to contact Conference Services Manager, B. Capaz, as soon as team arrived unannounced<br>• failure to contact Banquets Manager Hewatt Olam re: decision to change Banquet Order dates and add meals to scheduled BOs | |
| Staffing | • Conference Services Manager and Banquets Manager both on vacation at the same time<br>• inexperienced staff on Reservations Desk at time of GNBs' arrival<br>• Len Gosh, covering for Bernice Capaz, new to hotel and not thoroughly familiar with Banquet Orders system | |
| Physical plant | • block of guest rooms unavailable<br>• doors locked on Diefenbaker room on Sunday morning | |

*continued*

| POSSIBLE FACTORS LEADING TO GNB'S DISSATISFACTION | SOURCE OF PROBLEM | POSSIBLE SOLUTION |
|---|---|---|
| Food service | • Sunday brunch inappropriate for pre-practice meal<br>• unconventional Sunday pre-game hot buffet<br>• two meals served to team that were never contracted in writing | |

## Activity 9: Developing and ranking ideas for writing a problem analysis report

Working in small groups, imagine that your assignment is to write a report on a problem that has arisen in your organization. Select one of the problems below and then give the organization a name, and give each of the members of your group a role. Using the roles you have chosen, rough out a flow chart of the chain of communication. Then make up a detail analysis chart, including all information that you feel will be necessary for the report.

Problems

1. You work in a gym that caters to wealthy, middle-aged, and older clients. They sign lucrative six-month and one-year contracts with you. You contract to provide trained specialists to do individual assessment of exercise needs and develop personal exercise schedules; professional on-site support and safety supervision; coaching for continuity and optimum health gains; state-of-the-art, well-maintained facilities and equipment. In that past month, three clients have been injured, and several have expressed dissatisfaction. Your job is to analyse the problem and make recommendations regarding how to regain client satisfaction and avoid injuries in the future.

2. You work for a government ministry that receives a great deal of correspondence from the public. The correspondence takes the form of complaints, inquiries, demands for changes in government services, and pleas for help. Because all replies are signed by the minister, they must be very carefully worded to ensure that nothing is said that could be interpreted as a promise or that could lead to litigation or other complications. As a result, all letters go through five levels of approval prior to being signed, and most letters are turned back at least three or four times and must begin the process

*continued*

**Activity 9: Developing and ranking ideas for
writing a problem analysis report (continued)**

of climbing the approval ladder again each time. The result is
extremely low morale among the correspondence writers and
extremely high costs per letter. Your job is to analyse the situation
and make recommendations to reduce the costs and improve
morale.

3. You are teachers in a small highschool that has recently been
designated a "Community School." The new mandate of the school
is to make it a hub of the community, involving community
members of all ages and in all walks of life in the day-to-day
activities of the school in order to foster a sense of pride,
community, and belonging in students. Also part of the mandate is
to try to counter the feelings of alienation that many community
members have expressed since the community's business centre
has shrunk and the town has become a bedroom community for a
nearby city. The school board has left it to the school to figure out
how this change is to be accomplished, and the principal has
handed the problem over to the staff.

Your job is to consider possible solutions: how members of the
community might be able to contribute to the programmes at the
school, and what teachers would have to do in order to facilitate the
inclusion of outsiders in classrooms and programmes. You are then to
report and make recommendations for beginning the new
programme.

# Outlining Strategy

Outlining is a method of representing visually the organization of a
piece of writing rather than its ideas. The following outline, for
example, proides a visual representation of the organization of an essay
by Kerry Patriarche, "Why Do the Doula Hula?" The full text of
Kerry's essay is included in Chapter Seven.

I. Introduction: A doula's experience, education, and position outside
both the medical hierarchy and the emotions of the family allow her
to provide comfort and confidence to parents at the time of a birth.

II. A doula's knowledge of hospital environment and language makes
her an invaluable help to both parents.
   A. Couples often do not know hospital environment.

   B. Excitement and distractions of hospital can confuse the couple.

   C. Important decisions like abandoning labour in favour of Caesarean
section need to be based on accurate information, not fear.

III. A doula's knowledge enables her to clarify for the father what is expected of and needed from him so that he can support the mother.

    A.  The father is often expected, inappropriately, to know what to do to help.

    B.  The mother is usually too preoccupied to communicate her needs clearly to her partner.

    C.  Partners often retreat when their attempts to help are ineffective or met with irritation.

    D.  With the help of a doula, these breakdowns of communication can be bridged, thereby reducing the likelihood of further complications.

IV. Conclusion: Neither distressed by fears nor distracted by joys, the doula has the focus and knowledge to assist parents to have a birth experience that is positive for everyone concerned.

## Talking Strategies

### Formulating a Question

If you have a clear question in mind to act as a compass bearing, it is much easier to write a research paper. The question keeps you on track each step of the way. For example, a former student of Norma's, Danny Jaswal, whose research essay we have included in Chapter Seven, asked the question "Does the movie *Outbreak* accurately represent the nature of the Ebola virus and its threat to human populations?" Danny's question established a direction that made the steps in the development of the essay virtually inevitable. He had to tell his readers how the virus was characterized in the film, he had to describe the way the virus behaves in reality, and he had to compare the two and draw conclusions. A good question made the path of Danny's research clear.

    The following strategy uses discussion to help you develop a question to guide you along the path of your research.

### Step I

Having settled on a broad topic, write a one-sentence summary of it on a clean sheet of paper, and set it aside for a moment.

### Step II

On a separate sheet of paper, take five to ten minutes to freewrite everything you know and everything you don't know about the topic. Remember, a freewrite has two rules: don't stop, and don't edit.

## Step III

Working in pairs, exchange your one-sentence summaries. Now do a five-minute freewrite on your partner's topic. This time, use the following two questions to guide your freewrite: "What common knowledge do I have about my partner's topic? If this were my topic, what potential problems do I see?"

## Step IV

In your pairs, decide whose topic you will address first. For the time being, set aside all writing on the other topic. Then exchange and read the two freewrites on the topic under discussion. For example, let's say one of you intends to write on the tobacco industry, and the other intends to write on kayaking. If you have decided that you will address the topic of kayaking first, exchange and read each other's freewrite on kayaking.

Once you have each read your partner's freewrite, your job is to discuss the topic using the following questions as prompts. Keep in mind that you are trying to work toward developing a question that limits the topic and gives the writer a strong sense of direction for his or her research. The partner whose work is under discussion should make notes.

### Possible Discussion Questions

1. What's interesting to each of you about this topic?

2. What seems to be the focus of the original freewrite?

3. Does this topic appear to be a dead end or a dead bore?

4. On the other hand, is it too huge, or would it require research that it would be impossible for the researcher to do in the time available?

5. Is there an angle that would make this topic come alive or give the researcher a clearer sense of direction?

6. What aspect of this topic is merely common knowledge?

7. What skepticism might the writer anticipate from her or his audience?

8. What is the purpose of this essay likely to be: to inform, to persuade, or to analyse?

9. What questions leap to mind about this topic?

## Step V

Switch pairs and repeat.

*Step VI*

Draft your question, again keeping in mind that you want a question that limits the topic and gives the writer a strong sense of direction.

*Step VII*

Form groups of four. Number off to decide the order in which you will discuss the questions. Your job is to share each group member's question and suggest logical section topics in the essay. For example, the section topics in Danny's essay on *Outbreak* were the characterization of the virus in the film, the real behaviour of and threat represented by the virus, and a comparison of the two.

If, as a group, you find no agreement on what the section topics of the essay would be, or you find dozens of topics that could be included in the essay, it may be that the question is too vague or too broad. In those cases, make suggestions for refining the topic.

Christy, one of Norma's students, started her research essay with the question, "What do dreams mean?" At first, she identified three possible section topics: dream images as symbols giving insight into the unconscious, dreams as paranormal events that can predict the future, and dreams as records of and interpretations of recent experiences. However, as Christy began to research and write, she found that she had little more than a list of dream images and someone's interpretation of them.

As a result of talking to her group, Christy expanded her list of possible dream topics to include beliefs and cultural interpretations of dreams, types of dreams such as lucid dreams and nightmares, differences between women's and men's dreams. Those additional ideas spurred a shift in Christy's question.

The final version of her question was, "What are dreams?" On the basis of that question, the section topics became clearer to her: a) What is the physical phenomenon of dreaming? b) What are some types of dreams (e.g. lucid dreams and nightmares, and c) What do we make of dreams? Once Christy's question was finalized, Christy's essay unfolded easily.

## Brainstorming

Brainstorming is a familiar talking strategy in which one person records ideas as a group suggests every idea that comes to mind on a topic. Frequently, an idea from one individual will often trigger another idea that no one would have thought of alone. It is the interaction of thoughts that makes brainstorming work. Therefore, the goal of brainstorming is simply to get all the possible ideas out on the table in the hope that some will be useable and that others will trigger more ideas. Therefore, all ideas are recorded. No attempt is made to edit or censor. Sorting and selection comes later.

# Factors That Influence Your Choices

## Audience

In 1963, when Martin Luther King, Jr. was in prison, eight Alabama clergymen made a public statement regarding "a series of demonstrations by some of our Negro citizens." In their statement, they expressed the concern that the demonstrations were instigated in part by "outsiders." They urged "our own Negro community to withdraw support from these demonstrations" and instead to have patience and to press for their demands "in the courts and in negotiations among local leaders, and not in the streets."

Martin Luther King, Jr., in prison as a result of those demonstrations, wrote a reply in which he argued that "justice too long delayed is justice denied." As an "outsider" and leader in the struggle for civil rights in Alabama, he was "in Birmingham because injustice is here." In support of his argument, he called on the authority of the Hebrew prophets, the Apostle Paul, St. Augustine, Shadrach, Meshach, and Abednego, the Old Testament figures who braved a fiery furnace rather than bow to a false god, St. Thomas Aquinas, and on the example of Christ himself. If you remember that King's audience was eight Alabama clergymen, you may agree that he could not have enlisted more compelling authorities than those to whom his audience turned for moral guidance.

The choice of details to include in an essay depends in part on the audience. I heard someone say that before Stephen King begins to write he searches for a photograph that he can identify as his audience for the new book. He then writes to and for that person. Whether the Stephen King story is true or not, just thinking carefully about who your audience is can help you to generate ideas for writing.

## Purpose

Rhetorical purposes are described as expressive, expository, or argumentative. If the purpose of a piece of writing is expressive, the writer attempts to deliver to readers the immediacy of a felt experience by evoking emotional responses. An expressive purpose is achieved by a variety of means including imagery, connotative language, humour, irony, suspense, climactic arrangement of details, and carefully orchestrated plots. While we normally think of creative writing as being more expressive than expository or argumentative writing, nevertheless, a strong argument or a clear piece of exposition often calls upon expressive text to bolster a claim.

The main purpose of an expository text is to inform. It does so primarily through the presentation of carefully organized information. Frequently, an expository text is analytical, investigating the nature of a problem, sifting through data, determining essential elements, and drawing conclusions. In contrast, the goal of an argumentative essay is to persuade. It marshalls evidence and logic to support its position. However, none of these purposes is discrete. Though one will tend to be primary and the others secondary or subordinate in an essay, most essays will include a mix.

By identifying your purpose, you will establish some limits as to what belongs in your essay and what does not.

Most students are familiar with the standard list of Methods of Paragraph and Essay Development. With some variation, they usually include

| | |
|---|---|
| Definition | Cause and effect |
| Comparison and contrast | Process analysis |
| Examples and illustrations | Classification |
| Details | Reasons |
| Narration | |

Unfortunately, beginning writers sometimes try to force their ideas to conform to an arbitrarily chosen method of development. The result can be strained and unsatisfying. Methods of development are not straitjackets to be used to restrain your thoughts. Try to understand them as descriptions rather than prescriptions: descriptions of the various patterns that thoughts fall into.

If we allow them to, our thoughts tend to fall into logical patterns, by themselves. If you give your ideas the time and conditions necessary to germinate, and if you respect the results of that germination, you will often discover that the ideas themselves beg to be developed by particular methods. You will also discover that, in a single essay, you will use several methods of development according to the needs of the section topic at hand. Our advice is that you be aware of these different methods, and that you allow your topics to choose the appropriate ones.

# Methods of Development

## Definition

To test that claim, return to the ideas that you generated in response to "Accordingly my personal experience. . . ." (page 254) It may be that two phrases particularly caught your attention: *broken language*, and s*tand up and tall thought*. Maybe your questions included "What is *stand up and tall thought*? How does the speaker define it? How does the speaker define *broken language*? What are the connotative meanings of these two expressions?" In other words, you may have discovered that your response to the entire passage hinges on the definitions of these two terms. If so, your ideas are dictating the method of development that most suits them.

Classical definitions include a noun, the class or category into which it fits, and its special features. For example, *salt* (noun) is a chemical compound (class) that dries up slugs (special features). Or, *stand up and tall language* (noun) is a an authoritative system of communicating (class), which has the power to intimidate because it seems so right (special features). You might contrast that definition with a definition of *broken language*. Once you have the definitions pinned down, more questions may come to mind: Who speaks the *stand up and tall language* (special feature)? How does speaking a *stand up and tall language* affect the speaker (special feature)? How does it affect a person who cannot speak it (special feature)? Who most strongly feels the power of the *stand up and tall language* (special feature)? Who takes it for granted (special feature)?

When the method of development you choose is right for your ideas, the ideas not only slide naturally into position, but the method itself can be a framework for extending the ideas you already have. By systematically considering the methods of development until you find the one that mirrors your thinking process, you enlist the power of the form to bolster the power of your own ideas.

---

### Activity 10: When the organizational pattern of definition mirrors your thinking

We feel that the following two topics lend themselves to the organizational pattern of definition. Select one and develop it.

1. Different people mean different things by the term "hard work."

2. There are three kinds of campers: the don't-forget-the-tv campers, the if-you-can't-get-it-on-your-back,-you-don't-need-it campers, and the once-was-more-than-enough campers.

---

**Activity 11: Developing topics**

List two topics that you feel would lend themselves to development
by definition and provide brief definitions of the element(s) you would
define.

1. _____

_____

2. _____

_____

---

# Comparison and Contrast

Perhaps when you worked through the thank-you strategy with the
excerpt from "Accordingly my personal experience and also very thank
you Tillie Olsen," your ideas clustered around the language itself.
Perhaps you found it frustrating or strange or intriguing or bizarre or
simply wrong. In short, you found that the language was different from
"normal" language. Maybe you wrote about the impact of that
difference on you as a reader. Maybe you wondered why anyone would
write a story like that. Maybe you thought, "What's the point of using
that language?" In other words, for you, the most salient feature of this
text was the contrast between the language it uses and standard English.

In that case, it seems that your ideas are begging to be developed by
comparison and contrast. If so, capitalize on the features of the method.
Think about the kinds of comparisons and contrasts you can make. You
might, for example, "translate" the passage into standard English and
compare and contrast the two versions. You might ask questions like the
following: What's the difference in the length of time it takes to read
each version? So what? What's the difference in the emotional intensity
of the two versions? Why? Does the broken language add anything that
the standard English lacks, or vice versa? Does the meaning change
when the passage is translated? What kinds of changes occur?

If your focus was the language itself, comparison and contrast may
lend itself with ease to fully developing your thoughts.

## Activity 12: When the organizational pattern of comparison and contrast mirrors your thinking

We feel that the following three topics lend themselves to the organizational pattern of comparison and contrast. Select one and develop it.

1. A piece of classical music and a rock song affect me in different ways.

2. My experience as a waiter in a small, family-owned restaurant was very different from my experience working for a big restaurant chain.

3. Whether in the tropics, the temperate zones, or the arctic, I love the season of summer best of all.

# Cause and Effect, and Reasons

Maybe your explorations of the excerpt from "Accordingly my personal experience and also very thank you Tillie Olsen" reveal that you identify with the speaker's experience of inadequacy. Perhaps you too have kept silent on occasion rather than expose what you believed to be your "beetle-wit addle-pate, no difference from oyster shell and bit of grit, feed to chicken" ideas. Maybe your essay will move away from the text, using it as evidence for an argument about what causes people to keep their silence rather than expressing themselves.

## Activity 13: When the organizational pattern of cause and effect mirrors your thinking

1. Using the excerpt from "Accordingly my personal experience and also very thank you Tillie Olsen," page 254, respond to the following topic: "Sometimes people are afraid to speak up even though they have very good ideas."

2. Using an experience of your own, write about a circumstance, factual or fictional, in which you hesitated to express yourself because of the circumstances you found yourself in.

If you wrote the report on accidents in the gym, in the activity "Developing and ranking ideas for writing a problem analysis report," you would be expected to uncover the causes of the accidents. You may need to begin by describing the details of each accident, including where staff were located, relative to the accident victim, what equipment was involved, the age of the individuals who suffered injuries, and any other details that are pertinent. Those details may help to reveal the cause of the problems. As you offered solutions, you would need to provide reasons why you think your solutions are sound.

**Activity 14: Finding reasons and solutions**

Reread problem 1 on page 275. Make up whatever details you need to complete the scenario. Then write a paragraph in which you explain the causes of the accidents and offer solutions to the problem.

# Examples and Illustrations

This type of paragraph or essay development provides samples or specific instances of a particular idea. An example is like a specimen. It provides readers with something concrete that they can imagine. If, as a result of using a tree chart to guide you to a topic, you decided to write an essay about Australia's underwater parks, you would probably need to include examples of several of the parks, describing their unique features, and possibly comparing and contrasting them.

**Activity 15: When the organizational pattern of examples and illustrations mirrors your thinking**

List three topics that you feel would lend themselves to this type of development. Briefly outline the examples you would use to develop each topic.

1. _____          _____
   _____          _____
   _____          _____
   _____          _____
   _____

2. _____          _____
   _____          _____
   _____          _____
   _____          _____
   _____

*continued*

**Activity 15: When the organizational
pattern of examples and illustrations
mirrors your thinking (continued)**

3. _____          _____

_____          _____

_____          _____

_____          _____

_____          _____

# Narration

Narration tells a story. It is often, though not always, organized
chronologically. Though most commonly thought of as the main
strategy of fiction, in small doses it is a frequent partner in expository
and persuasive writing. An anecdote can have powerful emotional appeal.
Even in your report on the gym, you might use a short narrative
segment to describe graphically what happened and how distressed the
injured victim was. Such a story could convince your audience that the
expensive solution you have recommended is justified because emotional
distress felt by clients can have a very negative impact on business.

**Activity 16: When the organizational pattern of
narration mirrors your thinking**

Write the narrative described in the paragraph above. Include details
that will create empathy for the injured victim.

# Process Analysis

Whenever your project involves an explanation of how something works
or how to accomplish something, your ideas will most likely fall into the
pattern of process analysis. Process analysis either takes the reader
through the steps involved in making buttonholes or writing a thesis

proposal, or it tells the reader how tornadoes form or how a lightbulb works. Again, if process analysis is appropriate for your topic, your topic will choose it if you just allow the internal logic of the subject to play itself out.

---

### Activity 17: When the organizational pattern of process analysis mirrors your thinking

We feel that the following topics would lend themselves to development by process analysis. Select one or more of them and list the steps necessary to accomplish the objective stated in the topic.

1. How to cope with incessantly humid weather.

2. How to pack a parachute.

3. How to sneak up on a rattlesnake.

4. How to back away from a rattlesnake.

5. How to treat a rattlesnake bite.

---

### Activity 18: When the organizational pattern of process analysis mirrors your thinking

Write a list of five things that you would like to know how to do. These topics would probably lend themselves to development by process analysis.

---

## Classification and Division

Classifying is simply a method of grouping ideas or information. Dividing is a means of separating groups of ideas into categories. You will find that certain topics logically demand to be organized using these principles. If, for example, after using a tree chart to tease out your ideas about Australia, you decided to write about Australian animals with tourist appeal, you might want to classify the animals according to particular classes: marsupials, of course, flightless birds, parrots and cockatoos, and lizards and skinks. If you decided to write about eggs, you might want to divide the topic into types of eggs: bird eggs, reptile eggs, insect eggs, etc.

## Activity 19: When the organizational pattern of classification or division mirrors your thinking

Select one of the three topics below, and list two or three different ways to classify or divide the topics. For example, if given the topic "breads," you might write four entirely different essays, depending on how you subdivided the broad topic of "breads":

Breads     types of breads by countries of origin
             types of breads by ease of baking
             types of breads by ingredients
             types of breads by celebratory uses

Buffet lunches     _____

                      _____

                      _____

                      _____

Wines     _____

                      _____

                      _____

                      _____

Whines     _____

                      _____

                      _____

                      _____

## Wrap-up Activity: Letting the topic find its method

Select one of the following essay questions and brainstorm a list of section topics that might appear in the essay. Then, on the basis of your list, identify the method of development that seems to lend itself most readily to each section.

1. What are the human and economic costs of cigarette smoking in my home city?

2. What does modern-day witchcraft or wiccan have in common with historical practices that were described as witchcraft?

3. Who can be held responsible for the decline of the fishing industry on the east or west coast of Canada?

4. Do the economic benefits of controlled clearcutting warrant the environmental costs?

5. Do women and men dream differently?

6. Have our attitudes toward sickness and health led us to be a nation of pill-poppers?

None of the strategies outlined in this chapter will produce a finished essay for you. They are, in the main, prewriting strategies—strategies designed to help you establish a focus and direction for your writing and to generate ideas. In Chapter Seven, we offer you strategies for organizing the raw material.

*Chapter*

# 7

# *Organization*

## Learning Outcomes

**This Chapter will help you to**

- write a well-constructed paragraph.

- write a well-constructed essay.

- use transitions to link your ideas smoothly.

We devote Chapter Six to developing ideas, but in this chapter we would like to talk first about organizing those ideas into paragraphs, then about gluing the paragraphs into essays, and, finally, about organizing those essays. In this chapter, we provide the structures that will hold your ideas and give them a recognizable shape.

We know that the organizational principles that we present here may be very different than the ones some of you learned in your home countries. If, however, you learn this rather linear form of development, where essay organization echoes paragraph organization, and the main ideas are always up front, we believe that you will be able to see the logic of this approach and apply it in essays, exams, business letters, and reports.

# Organizing the Paragraph

A paragraph focuses on one main, controlling idea, a meaningful point, whether it is part of a persuasive essay, a process paper, a narrative, or a business letter. The most common pattern for a paragraph is the following:

- the main idea

- the development of the idea

- the restatement of the main idea (the wrap)

## Topic Sentences and Wraps

A topic sentence of a paragraph has two very important functions:

- it tells the reader the paragraph's main point

- it provides a transition from the idea in the last paragraph

A **topic sentence** fulfills these tasks whether it comes at the beginning of a paragraph or at the end, as it would if you were developing the paragraph by using inductive reasoning. For instance, an inductive paragraph, where you pile up evidence that leads to an inescapable conclusion, could be part of a letter to the editor about the need for increased bus service. After reading all the evidence, the reader would be prepared to read your final topic statement that "Bus service must be improved if we are to be kind to the environment." In expository essays, ones containing an explanation or argument, however, the topic sentence, the clear statement of a paragraph's main point, begins the paragraph. These essays are the ones you most often write at college or university. The idea is developed, and then the paragraph is wrapped up. The paragraph ends not with an example, but with a wrap that relates to the main idea presented in the topic sentence.

The topic sentence not only sets out the main idea but also communicates the writer's attitude toward the subject. (This idea of establishing the writer's attitude toward a subject comes up again when we discuss an essay's thesis statement.) For instance, on the one hand, if someone writes "The most common pet in Canada is the cat," this is simply an irrefutable fact. If, on the other hand, his or her topic sentence reads "Although cats are the most common pet in Canada, they are not the most rewarding," the reader knows what the writer's attitude toward the subject of cats is and has a pretty good idea of what to expect in the details sections of the paragraphs: evidence that cats can be a pain! Topic sentences without attitude are ineffectual.

Similarly, very narrow topic sentences are inadequate. If someone writes, as a topic sentence, "Robertson Davies was born in Thamesville," or "Mary is the youngest of the three Elliott daughters," the reader would be tempted to say "So what??" The ideas in these topic sentences, nonetheless, could be made meaningful. The sentences "Robertson Davies' birthplace, Thamesville, influenced his later depiction of small town life," or "Because Mary was the youngest of the three Elliott daughters and without a mother's guidance for the longest, she is childish in speech and actions," are focused without being too narrow, and the main ideas are developable, arguable ones. These sentences, less constricting than the originals, then, make effective, focused topics.

Just as too narrow topic sentences are problems, so are very broad or vague ones. A topic sentence that states "Margaret Laurence uses a lot of imagery," is not nearly as effective as one that suggests "Similes drawn from nature give us insight into Hagar's character." To illustrate further, "The report has a lot of problems," needs a more specific focus. "The report needs to be revised to remove jargon," has a much clearer focus, and if you have more to say about the report, each of your main ideas should occupy its own paragraph. Here are two possibilities: "In making this report more readable, reducing wordiness will be as important as reducing the amount of jargon," and "More important than the language issues, the report's structure must be reorganized to conform to persuasive format." The topic sentence needs to make an explicit statement about its subject.

Naturally, the **wrap** refers directly to the explicit statement the topic sentence makes about the subject, so it keeps the main idea clearly in your reader's mind. Therefore, a paragraph's final sentence should never end with an example, which is just a piece of supporting evidence.

Wraps keep both the writer and reader focused. Stream-of-consciousness writers who sail happily from interesting idea to interesting idea, for example, will find that the use of a wrap sentence will alert them to the places where they drift off topic. With the aid of the wrap, both the writer and the reader have an easier time concentrating on the main point.

Obviously, the last sentence of a paragraph should not make a transition to the idea in the next paragraph, for the content of that sentence could not wrap back to the idea presented in the topic sentence. Moreover, such a sentence would destroy the unity of your paragraph. To preserve unity, writers of academic papers, reports, or business proposals, must ensure that a paragraph discusses one main idea and that all details in that paragraph contribute to the development of that idea.

## Exercise 1: Finding a Secure Wrap

The following are the first, topic sentences, and last sentences of the paragraphs in which they occur. Put a check beside sentences that wrap properly to the main idea presented in the topic sentences.

1. Mystery permeates my favourite restaurant's atmosphere.

   _____ After the door swings shut behind me, I am back in a world without mystery.

2. After Sylvie Berdine joined our team, we won more games.

   _____ Having a female goalie changed some of the team's attitudes toward what had been considered appropriate locker-room behaviour.

3. Having to name a child is a big responsibility, and one that most new parents take very seriously.

   _____ Naming a child is one of the new parents' first important tasks.

4. The annual meeting dealt with three important issues.

   _____ The consensus was that the quality of the loan portfolio had deteriorated because of weaker economic conditions and the rising number of bankruptcies.

5. Rhythm reinforces the feeling that the words suggest.

   _____ The poem's rhythm reinforces the poem's tone of joy.

6. Basic English was proposed as an international language in 1932.

   _____ Esperanto has never been a great success either.

Although narratives do not usually have paragraphs with topic sentences and wraps, they, like expository paragraphs, must have a main or controlling idea. Each detail in such paragraphs should contribute to the overriding theme of the narrative. Tone, sentence structure, and word usage must all be appropriate to the overall idea. Similarly, it doesn't matter whether the narrative occurs in chronological order, starts at the end and moves to the beginning, or starts in the middle and uses a flashback technique. Each paragraph must have a point, and the details must be presented in a logical order.

The main idea that you present in a paragraph's topic sentence can be developed in many ways or combinations of ways. In the inductively organized paragraph on buses that we mentioned above, the evidence could be concrete examples drawn from your own experience or that of others, or statistics from government publications, or a logical sequence of ideas moving from causes to effect, etc. Of course, in other paragraphs, you can use still other organizing techniques. For example, if you were describing a room, you might move from right to left recording the details. In another essay or draft of a presentation, you could start with an abstraction and move to concrete examples or vice versa. You could compare and contrast or describe. In a paragraph, you could have one developmental tactic or a combination of many, and Chapter Six helps you investigate these strategies.

As you write papers, essays, and reports, keep in mind the basic elements of paragraph structure. Two concepts should govern your paragraphs: **unity** and **coherence**. We have already talked about unity, for this means simply that you develop one main idea per paragraph. Coherence concerns the development of that idea. Coherence demands that the sentences developing the main idea stick together in a logical way. We deal further with the idea of coherence in Chapter Four: Sentence Structure and Punctuation, and show you that transitions— which always contribute to coherence—fulfill different functions. See pages 136–137.

Nonetheless, as coherence is very important to both paragraph and essay organization, we discuss transitions in the next section of this chapter as well. Before we move on to these important elements of paragraph construction, we need to take time to reinforce what you have already learned.

## Exercise 2: Choosing Writable Topic Sentences

Put a check mark beside the topic sentences that have an attitude or a developable idea.

1. _____ My favourite horse's name is Lois Mane.

2. _____ Having a female goalie changed some of the team's attitudes toward what had been considered appropriate locker-room behaviour.

3. _____ Naming a child is one of the new parents' first important tasks.

4. _____ February 14, Valentine's Day, is not a statutory holiday.

5. _____ My Grade 10 math teacher's method of teaching Algebra was very odd.

6. _____ Marvin is Hagar's elder son.

7. _____ The first meal I cooked for company was memorable.

8. _____ Writing good memos and letters is important.

9. _____ "Easy as pie" can be a meaningful cliché if you just follow these steps.

10. _____ The poem's rhythm reinforces the poem's tone of joy.

## Exercise 3: Choosing Writable Topic Sentences

Put a check mark beside the topic sentences that have an attitude or a developable idea.

1. _____ The Aztec capital Mexico-Tenochtitlan became Mexico city.

2. _____ Arranged marriages could strengthen family bonds.

3. _____ Qi Gong reduces the incidence of respiratory illnesses.

4. _____ Marty first shows her ability to sacrifice when she cuts her hair.

5. _____ Living in a small town also has many advantages.

6. _____ Cooking is an interesting hobby.

7. _____ One must first establish the purpose of the essay.

8. _____ The poem's rhyme scheme is regular: abba acca adda acca.

9. _____ The Hindu astronomer, mathematician, and writer Aryabhata was born in 476.

10. _____ Tai Chi is a beneficial system of exercise.

## Activity 1: Writing the wrap

Here are three separate paragraphs: Write appropriate "wrap" sentences for each paragraph.

1. Similarly, although you communicate with your audience in words, you also communicate non-verbally. An "Uhmer," for example, might unknowingly communicate a number of things: lack of confidence, shyness, or lack of preparation. Speakers who mumble can send similar messages or one that suggests they do not value their audience. In addition, you have probably noticed that speakers who speak in a monotone communicate a sense of boredom and monotony that rubs off on their listeners. In contrast, speakers who use appropriate volume and vary their tone project energy and animation. A receptionist, for example, who answers the phone with a smile in his or her voice will project a positive image of the company.

2. In *The Stone Angel*, we can see some parallels to the stories of the biblical Hagar, but we mustn't stretch them too far. Hagar does become a housekeeper, a kind of servant, but Mr. Oatley is no Abraham. Hagar is as bound by chains as a slave might be, but her chains are metaphorical. She is bound by convention, by pride, by fear of expressing her emotions, and by fear of what others might think of her.

3. The writer must guide the reader logically through the report if he or she expects the report to have maximum impact. Because the report may have more than one reader, and because they may be of differing interests and expertise, the writer should help the reader to skim or read selected parts thoroughly. The writer should use headings and subheadings and, of course, include their pagination in the table of contents.

## Activity 2: Writing assignment

Choosing one of these subjects, write a paragraph of 100–150 words on one of them. Focus on getting a strong topic sentence and a firm wrap as well as narrowing the subject and developing the idea fully.

1. Your first time cooking for company

2. Your first paid job

3. Your first car

4. Your first day in Canada

5. Your first day on campus

In the paragraph in Activity 2, you will have to use past tenses of varying kinds, so before you begin, read over pages 53–68. Your essay will also probably include some of the tricky prepositional phrases that trip people up, so after you have finished your first draft, underline the prepositional phrases and check them against our lists on pages 341–359. If we haven't included a phrase that you used, check it with a native-born English speaker for accuracy; if it is correct idiomatically, add it to your list of idiomatically correct phrases in your Idiom Log, page 387. If it is not, get suggestions from your classmate or your instructor for an idiomatically correct phrase, and then add it to your list.

## Transitions: Gluing Ideas Together

It is essential that your ideas and paragraphs have **transitions** to link them. Although we discuss useful transition words to use between ideas on pages 135–137 in Chapter Four, in this chapter, we are more concerned with transitions between **paragraphs** than between ideas. Naturally, you can use mechanical transitions such as *first*, *second* and *third* to begin each of your body paragraphs. Such mechanical transitions, however, appear more appropriate to a process paper when you are explaining how to do something or how something works. Smooth, rather than mechanical, transitions contribute to stronger writing.

The smoother way to make transitions is to refer to the idea you have just discussed in the topic sentence of the next body paragraph and to then introduce the new idea. If, for example, you have just written a paragraph about ball games played by the ancient Romans, the new paragraph could begin "As well as ball games, games with dice were popular." As another example, if you have just written about the Indonesian economy in the '90s, you could then write "Unlike the conditions in Indonesia, the Malaysian situation ..." In both of these examples, the idea discussed in the former paragraph appears in the topic sentence and the new one is introduced. If you have a thesis containing specific points and strong topic sentences and wraps, you have automatic transitions between the introduction and the first body paragraph and between the last body paragraph and the conclusion. Transitions between paragraphs ensure that your reader progresses smoothly through your paper, essay, or report.

When you concentrate on one main idea in each paragraph, you will achieve **unity**; when you link your ideas together with transitions, you will achieve **coherence**. When you structure your paragraphs with strong topic sentences and firm wraps, your reader will be sure to remember your main points. Then, as a bonus, after learning the basic unit of the paragraph, you can apply many of the same principles to organizing an essay.

## Activity 3: Writing assignment

Add a paragraph to the one that you wrote on the writing assignment on page 296. Pay particular attention to the topic/transition sentence that begins the second paragraph. In both paragraphs, be sure that you have strong topic sentences, well-developed ideas, and firm wraps.

As you did earlier, you will have to use past tenses of varying kinds, so before you begin, read over pages 353–366. After you have finished your first draft, underline any prepositional phrases. As always, we advise that you check the phrases you used with our list or with a native-born English speaker for accuracy; then, add any new ones to your list of idiomatically correct phrases in your Idiom Log.

## Activity 4: Writing transitional/topic sentences

1. **The topic sentence of paragraph one was "Clearcutting is an indefensible practice even from an overall economic point of view."**

   The new idea for paragraph two is that clearcutting endangers the complex eco-system under which we all live by destroying the balance of nature.

   Write the topic/transitional sentence.

2. **The topic sentence of paragraph one was "Some people change their names, believing in the power of words to change their lives."**

   The new idea for paragraph two is that advertisers use the power of words to change our spending habits.

   Write the topic/transitional sentence.

3. **The topic sentence of paragraph one was "A common romantic motif is love at first sight."**

   The new idea for paragraph two is that sometimes the people who eventually became romantically entangled start out feeling very antagonistic toward each other.

   Write the topic/transitional sentence

*continued*

## Activity 4: Writing transitional/topic sentences (continued)

4. **The topic sentence of paragraph one was "Paragraphs with vivid concrete details capture your reader's interest."**
   The new idea for paragraph two is that you can add interest to your writing by using figurative language such as similes, metaphors, and personification.
   Write the topic/transitional sentence.

5. **The topic sentence of paragraph one was "Reviewing employee goals and aspirations must become part of the annual employee evaluation."**
   The new idea for paragraph two is that the company must act in ways to help the employee achieve his or her goals and aspirations.
   Write the topic/transitional sentence.

6. **The topic sentence of paragraph one was "Violence in adult soccer influences children."**
   The new idea for paragraph two is that fans can have negative impact.
   Write the topic/transitional sentence.

As a last word on transitions, here is a poem by Canadian poet Eli Mandel:

**First Political Speech**

first, in the first place, to begin with, secondly, in the second place, lastly

again, also, in the next place, once more, moreover, furthermore, likewise, besides, similarly, for example, for instance, another

then, nevertheless, still, however, at the same time, yet, in spite of that, on the other hand, on the contrary

certainly, surely, doubtless, indeed, perhaps, possibly, probably, anyway, in all probability, in all likelihood, at all events, in any case

therefore, consequently, accordingly, thus, as a result, in consequence of this, as might be expected

the foregoing, the preceding, as previously mentioned

as already stated

"First Political Speech" from *Crusoe* © 1973 by Eli Mandel. Reprinted by permission of House of Anansi Press Limited.

# Paragraphs: The Body of the Essay

Later in this chapter, we will discuss in detail how to write a good thesis statement and develop an introduction and conclusion to an essay. However, the work you have just completed on paragraphs is particularly important to remember when you write the body of your essay. Therefore, the next activity skips forward, briefly, to the body.

Each paragraph in the body of an essay should respect the conventions for good paragraph writing, described above. The following activity gives you an opportunity to review those conventions and to apply the criteria you have learned.

## Activity 5: Ranking paragraphs

Below is an introductory paragraph that will introduce you to a topic. The idea for this activity started with an essay written by one of Norma's students, Tom Woodsworth. Both the introduction and the best paragraph are his. Following the introduction are three body paragraphs, numbered 1, 2, and 3.

1. Rank the three body paragraphs: best, second best, least effective.

2. Discuss what makes the best paragraph effective and what makes the other two less effective.

3. Then, make a list of criteria for a good paragraph.

**Introduction**
A time capsule is a device used to demonstrate to a future generation how a present society lives and what cultural values and beliefs it holds. Typically, a time capsule includes items that reflect the good, not the bad, aspects of a society. However, if I were to make a time capsule, I would include in it three items, all of them negative, to demonstrate the state of our society today. Those three items would be . . . .

**Body Paragraph, Version 1**
I would put a glass heart into the time capsule to represent a loving, fragile, and useless era. Our era loves everything. Everybody is trying to help out people who are down on their luck. If a country tries to take over another country, the rest of the world tries to help out the country that is the underdog. Our era is fragile because of many things. One thing that shows our fragility is the fall of the Asian markets. This affected people not only in Asia, but all over the world. The glass heart represents uselessness. Our era cannot stop simple things like the destruction of the rain forest or things like the depleting ozone layer. I would put a glass heart into the time capsule to represent how our era is.

*continued*

**Activity 5: Ranking paragraphs (continued)**

**Body Paragraph, Version 2**

A reader might wonder how my first item, a pair of brand name shoes could represent a society—and represent it negatively at that. To clarify the significance of the shoes, I would include with them a picture of the woman in Indonesia who constructed them. Beside her picture, I would write the amount of money she received for her labour. To make my point even more clear, on the back of the picture I would glue a photograph of an athlete who endorses those shoes in Canada and the U.S., and beside his face, I would write the amount of money he makes yearly from the endorsement. When citizens of the future opened the time capsule, the shoes and the pictures would reveal to them the gross inequity, crass consumerism, and ridiculous hero worship currently condoned in our society.

**Body Paragraph, Version 3**

Computers are used a lot by people today. That's why I would put a computer in the time capsule. If you can't use a computer, you are handicapped. The problem with computers is they change so fast that you need to be constantly buying a new one or else yours is out of date, which is very expensive. The Internet is another thing about computers. It has lots of good information, but it also has pornography and violence, and it could be harmful if children get addicted to surfing the net. Also, with some computers, they give off radiation that is harmful to your health. On the other hand, where would we be without computers? They are in our microwaves and our cars and even in our banking machines, so they have both good and bad aspects.

# Organizing the Five-Hundred Word Essay

Writing an essay resembles writing a good, satisfying story. Both should have a beginning, a middle, and an end. In an essay, the beginning is usually called the introduction, and the end the conclusion. While a research paper is longer, the normal first-year English composition is about 500 words.

The introduction and the conclusion paragraphs can be called non-substantive because they do not contribute to the main ideas or argument in the essay. That function belongs to the middle or substantive paragraphs, the body. These paragraphs, using a number of different methods such as examples, definition, description, classification, cause and effect, analogy, analysis, or narration, develop the main idea of the essay, the thesis.

# The Introduction

Your paper's introduction begins your essay in general and then literally comes to the point of the essay, the thesis. Together, the introduction and the thesis lead your reader into the main part of your essay, just as the topic sentence led into the body of the paragraph.

The functions of an introduction are important:

1. The introduction should gain the reader's interest and attention. It should try to provoke a response: surprise, recognition, laughter, dissent, wonder, etc. It should be clear and reasonable. It can be provocative, but not pugnacious or patronizing.

2. The introduction should establish your essay's tone. Will the tone be serious? satiric? informal? humorous? emotional?

The introduction should establish your attitude toward your subject. Will the essay criticize, describe, praise, define, or analyze its subject? The last sentence of the introduction, the thesis, makes your attitude clear.

# The Thesis

The thesis is the sentence that gets to the point. Like the topic sentence, the thesis should be neither too narrow, nor too broad. Again, like the topic sentence, it should be one sentence only. The thesis leads directly into the main ideas of your essay, the material that you will develop in the body, or substantive, paragraphs.

Although it is just one sentence, the thesis (usually) contains the main points in the order that you intend to discuss them, always presenting the most interesting or important point last unless there is a compelling reason to use another kind of organization. An example of a paper that requires another method of organization would be one devoted to explaining a process, whether it was telling the reader how to do something or explaining how something works. In all cases, a carefully wrought thesis statement can organize the entire essay, so crafting a good one is definitely worthwhile.

# Thesis Traps

Because the thesis statement is so important, you should be on the alert for problems that could confuse your reader and obstruct your efforts to develop clear ideas.

## Exercise 4: Choosing a Writable Thesis

Look carefully at the following theses, and think about why they would be hard to develop:

1. Albert Einstein was an American citizen.

2. Albert Schweitzer was the most wonderful man in the world.

3. Her ideas are interesting, but they are disorganized.

4. I prefer knitting to crochet or sewing.

5. In this essay, I will show the cultural, political, and economic effects of free trade.

6. It is the opinion of this writer that political polls generate boredom, focus on inconsequentials, and demean the democratic process.

7. My friend's best qualities include care, concern, and love.

8. Post-secondary education develops social, interpersonal and scholarly growth.

9. Shakespeare is a really great writer.

10. Sports develop coordination, discipline, and good sports.

11. Television affects the family, the individual, and the society.

12. Television promotes violence.

13. The cultural factor is important. The political aspects are vital. The most significant influence, however, is economic.

14. The prime minister was ineffective in cabinet, but he was a great statesman.

We think that you'll agree that trying to write on many of the above theses could be very frustrating. Broad or vague statements such as "Albert Schweitzer was the most wonderful man in the world," are impossible to substantiate. Statements such as "Shakespeare is really a great writer," are both vague and inane: the thesis begs for a "because." Similarly, and perhaps ironically, overly narrow theses such as "Albert Einstein was an American citizen," also need to be expanded so that the main idea of the thesis can be developed: "Albert Einstein's American citizenship influenced his ..." or "Because Albert Einstein was an American citizen, he ..." would lead to a more focused essay.

Theses composed of compound sentences also need better focus. It is unlikely that both ideas are of equal weight, so the writer should take a stand. For instance, either "Although the prime minister was ineffective in cabinet, he was a great statesman," or "Although the prime minister was a great statesman, she was ineffective in cabinet," make better theses than "The prime minister was ineffective in cabinet, but he was a great statesman." In the complex sentences, the reader understands the focus and attitude of the essays.

"A university education develops social, interpersonal, and scholarly growth" provides another example of theses that would lead to problems with development. After finishing the paragraph on social growth, the writer would find it difficult to differentiate this idea from interpersonal growth and have little to say. Having undifferentiated main points is clearly a graver problem than having non-parallel main points as did the thesis "I prefer knitting, to crochet, and sewing." The former concerns development and the latter concerns grammar. Nonetheless, as the kind of thesis you will most often write contains a list of three main points, in other words, items in a series, remembering to check for parallelism is an excellent idea.

Other kinds of faulty theses could, nonetheless, like a non-parallel thesis, be easily developed in the body paragraphs. Some people write an introduction that is just a series of topic sentences. Such a thesis composed of many sentences may have sound ideas that could be easily and completely developed, but, as with non-parallel points, the ideas simply need to be rephrased. The problem lies with sentence structure rather than with concepts.

An announcement shows us yet another kind of thesis that may be developed easily. Instructors in some disciplines encourage this kind of thesis because the main idea is clear, but this kind of announcement is never appropriate in an English essay.

Finally, incorrectly ordered points can leave the reader with a feeling of anti-climax or even confusion, though the points themselves may be valid. Taking time to ensure that your thesis is correctly phrased is worthwhile. Ending your thesis, and your paper, on the best or the most developed point will leave the reader satisfied and impressed. If, accidentally, you write an essay in which all of your points are equally brilliant, original, and well developed, however, be assured that no instructor will penalize you.

We suggest that you develop the all-important thesis before you write the introduction that precedes it. We will illustrate the process later in this chapter.

## Activity 6: Revising the thesis

Here is the introduction in the first draft of Rebekkah's essay on Science Fiction. You'll see that the thesis is a series of sentences rather than a statement. Rewrite the ideas in these sentences into one thesis statement.

Science Fiction can be so much more than just "space opera." The genre is trying to shake its pulp-fiction image, but the many strong works, new and old, in Science Fiction are often dismissed with the weak. Good Science Fiction can make fascinating observations about the interaction between humanity and technology. Writers of science fiction must research their works and take care when creating plot and character, like writers of any other fiction. Science Fiction is also great fuel for the imagination.

# Prescription

### The Thesis

- Don't make sweeping generalizations.
- Don't make announcements.
- Avoid self-evident statements.
- Avoid overlapping main points.
- Do make your thesis just one sentence.
- Do order your points to create proper emphasis.

## From Abstract to Specific: Narrowing Your Thesis

The word "essay" comes from the French, meaning "to try." Professional writers make many tries as they conceptualize, draft, refine, edit, and proofread an essay. Writers rarely start out with an ideal thesis; rather, as they work through their drafts, the thesis gains clarity and focus. Look at this variety of draft theses that respond to the question "What did you learn on your summer job?" Observe the way the writer has clarified and focused her originally vague and abstract idea.

1. *I learned much of value while working this summer.*

This thesis is very vague and abstract. The thesis statement could apply to any job in the world. If fifty-thousand students from fifty countries wrote using this thesis, however, probably not one essay would resemble another.

2. *While working last summer, I learned tent pitching, bug killing, and tree planting.*

The second thesis, more concrete and specific, still has room for more specifics. You don't know, for example, whether the bug killing that went on protected the tree seedlings, the established trees, or the worker. Perhaps the tree planter was a budding entomologist collecting rare specimens. Although each of the fifty-thousand students would have topic sentences referring to the same aspects of tree planting, again there would still be a huge variation in the details that fleshed out the paragraphs.

3. *When I worked as a tree planter last summer, I learned to choose the best camping site, to pack and unpack my tent and my belongings, and to assemble my home in ten minutes.*

4. *As a tree planter last summer, I learned to cut appropriate holes in various soils, select micro-sites for different seedlings, and plant at the correct density.*

The third and fourth theses take one point of the second thesis and then expand on it. In other words, what would have been one of three body paragraphs in the second essay becomes an entire essay in number three. We have moved a long way from the vague generality of the first thesis. Although the fifty-thousand essays would still be unique, we would find similarities in the concrete details supplied by the tree planters of various regions.

The more concrete and specific your thesis, the easier you will find it to organize your paper and supply meaningful concrete details to develop the body paragraphs.

---

**Activity 7: Honing the thesis**

Work to make the given ideas more concrete, specific, and focused. Taking more than one step if necessary, as in the examples above, write a thesis that gives your readers a clear idea of the structure of your essay.

1. Student loan policy in Canada is a big mess.
2. Multiculturalism is a benefit to everyone.
3. Television is a bad influence on the young.
4. Eating in fast-food restaurants is a pain.
5. Pets can change your life.
6. Computers help us in every way.
7. Eating disorders are really scary.
8. Learning how to prepare for exams is essential.
9. You can easily figure out who your real friends are.
10. X was the best (worst) movie I saw last year.

---

# Generating Introductions

Remember that the introduction presents your subject in general terms and establishes your tone. Remember, too, like the conclusion, the introduction is a non-substantive paragraph. Save your argument, the substance of your essay, report, or paper, for the body paragraphs.

One way to generate an introduction is by picking a word or a form of the word from the thesis and generalizing about it. Usually, the word will be a noun. Do not, however, choose one of the specific points that you intend to discuss later. If, for example, your thesis is "Gardening provides good exercise, good food, and good mental stimulation," you would pick up on the word "gardening" and say something in general about it. You could, for example, tell a little anecdote about your first garden or talk about the increasing number of people, even those in apartments, who have begun to garden. Do, however, remember that, although important, the introduction should not be the best-developed, most interesting part of the essay. That's a sure way to create an unhappy reader. In an essay of 500 words, the introduction should be just 50–80 words, allowing you to fully develop your ideas in the body paragraphs.

## Sample Introductions

Here are a set of six introductions using the technique of picking a word from the thesis to generalize about. In additions, the introductions use specific strategies—pro-con, examples and definition—to develop the paragraph. The first set of introductions concerns an essay about the advisability of wearing school uniforms and the second set concerns arranged marriages.

## Uniforms

1. **Introduction using pro-con**

   *At bus stops or in convenience stores, we can tell instantly if students from private schools are there. Their uniforms make them hard to miss. Some parents and school trustees think that all school children should be wearing uniforms. Although many students feel horrified at the idea, they would soon find that uniforms are economical, convenient, and morale-boosting.*

2. **Introduction using a concrete example/anecdote**

   *In junior high school, we all wore uniforms. The guys wore long grey itchy trousers, a never-very-clean, never-very-pressed white shirt, ugly black shoes, a green cap, and a green, long-sleeved cardigan without pockets. The girls wore slightly cleaner and better pressed white blouses, grey jumpers or skirts, the same kind of pocketless sweaters and ugly black shoes. Because uniforms are uncomfortable, ugly, and inconvenient, no child should have to wear them.*

3. **Introduction using a definition**

   *Uniform just means "the same." McDonald's restaurants all over the world make uniform Big Macs. Pickets in a fence are uniform as are the hanging baskets along downtown streets. Why do students get so upset if someone says that they should wear school uniforms? Usually, it is because they believe uniforms are ugly and uncomfortable. The definition of uniform, however, does not include these ideas. In fact, public schools uniforms could be economical, fashionable, and comfortable.*

## Arranged Marriages

1. **Introductions using pro-con**
   a) *Arranged marriages may survive into the 21st century. Existing in many cultures, arranged marriages often ensure that marriage partners come from compatible backgrounds and have similar values, so why do we oppose this traditional marriage arrangement with its long history and potential advantages? We oppose arranged marriage because it leaves out the heady experience of romantic love; it offends our idea of personal choice and autonomy; and the normally effective process may be damaged by unscrupulous parents or matchmakers.*

   b) *Nowadays, marriages arranged by parents are diminishing in most countries; however, in some parts of the world, a new kind of arranged marriage is rising, a collective religious marriage in which a religious leader designates the marriage partners. Traditionally, arranged marriages have focused on families' economic, social, or dynastic interests, but this new kind of arranged marriage differs fundamentally from the traditional.*

2. **Introduction using a concrete example**
   *Because I just met the love of my life, last week I asked my grandmother when and how she first met my grandfather. She replied that she first met him on their wedding day. How could such a marriage last, as my grandparents' has, for over fifty years? Because I am interested in romance and family, I have had to learn about what makes an arranged marriage succeed.*

3. **Introduction using a definition**
   *An arranged marriage occurs when the parents, sometimes using a go-between, arrange a union of their offspring and other families' children. Sometimes, these marriages are arranged at birth, but in other cases, the principals can be university graduates. These marriages often succeed because the marriage partners come from similar backgrounds, hold similar views about important issues, and have similar beliefs about the role of the family.*

The above examples all use the technique of finding a thesis first, then choosing a word from it to generalize about. They show, as well, a variety of techniques that you can use when you generalize.

Because the focus of this chapter is organization and because we devote a whole chapter to development, we are going to presume that you have developed the ideas presented in your thesis, supporting them with analogy or analysis, cause and effect or classification, definition or description, examples, or narration. This means that we can now talk about your conclusion.

## The Conclusion

After you develop the points mentioned in the thesis within the body paragraphs, you should properly conclude your essay, not simply put your pen down or close the file. You should also not introduce new ideas. Finally, you need to remember that, like the introduction, the conclusion should be relatively short.

Begin your conclusion with a restatement of the gist of the thesis statement. Neither merely repeat it nor reiterate your topic sentences, for such repetition is boring and annoying. Instead, mention the key words, forms of them, or synonyms in a sentence that reinforce your argument. You should then write a concluding thought or two about the subject. For instance, you could reinforce your subject's significance, or you could make a suggestion for improvement, present a solution, point to consequences, or suggest an area for further study.

For example, if you were writing a conclusion to the essay whose thesis was "In fact, public schools uniforms could be economical, fashionable, and comfortable," your conclusion might be something like this:

> School uniforms can please both parents and students, for they can be not only easy on the budget but also stylish and comfortable. Therefore, uniforms are a triple win. Students feel happy with style and comfort; parents feel happy with economy and ease of care; and schools feel happy with students who look and feel proud of their school's reputation.

## Writing Conclusions

Imagine that the following is the outline of an essay that you have just written.

**Your topic was**

*The city of Halifax has something to satisfy the demands of every type of tourist.*

**The body paragraphs** covered the following information:

1.  **the active/sports tourist**

    *In this paragraph, you talked about one or more of the following activities available to active tourists in the Halifax area: hiking, sea kayaking, cycling, "polar bear" swimming, diving.*

2.  **the budget traveller**

    *In paragraph two of the body, you talked about facilities and entertainment available to this group of people: the youth hostel, free parks such as Point Pleasant and the Public Gardens, Maritime scenery, free open-air concerts.*

3.  **the couch potato, luxury, or sedentary traveller**

    *Here, you described theatres, museums, restaurants, including the Historic Feast in the Historic Properties, afternoon tea at MacDonald House near Lawrencetown Beach, and singing at O'Carroll's famous piano bar with Frankie or Leo Arab at the keyboard.*

## Possible Conclusions

### Conclusion #1

This conclusion mentions the general subject of each of the body paragraphs in the opposite order from which they appeared in the essay. Then it reiterates those general ideas more specifically, and ends on a positive generalization.

*Whether the traveller wants luxurious surroundings, shoestring accommodation, or physical challenge, Halifax and the surrounding area can satisfy her needs. With its beautiful scenery, its wealth of restaurants and museums, its bracing climate and welcoming people, Halifax is the traveller's dream.*

### Conclusion #2

This conclusion presents a new piece of information, a survey that supports the argument of the entire essay.

*Last week, Tourism Nova Scotia conducted a survey at Citadel Hill. Six-hundred-and-seventy tourists in all, from Baghdad, London, Chartres, Melbourne, Houston, Ottawa, and Anchor Drive in Halifax, were asked to complete a short questionnaire. Ranging in age from seven weeks to ninety-one years of age, the visitors (or their moms and dads) expected to spend between six dollars and fifteen-hundred over the next twenty-four hours, diving, dozing, dancing, dining, and gingerly dandling their toes in the ocean. Every one of them seemed to have found something that he or she was looking for. That's high praise for Halifax, a city for all travellers.*

## Activity 8: Now you try it.

Write a conclusion for the essay about professional wrestling outlined below.

Your topic is summed up in the following sentence from your introduction:

More than merely infantile posturing and staged violence, professional wrestling is a modern variation on the morality play, bringing the archetypal battle between good and evil into viewers' living rooms every Saturday afternoon.

The body paragraphs of your essay covered the following information:

1. The bad guys:
   Here, you claimed that in professional wrestling, evil—in the form of treachery, deceit, betrayal, greed, malevolence, corruption, irrationality, and hatred—is simplified and distilled into a single, clearly identifiable character whom the viewer can see as very different from himself or herself.

2. The good guys:
   Here, you talked about how the good guys are characterized as more rational, more attractive, more normal, more like us. Therefore, the viewer can identify with the good guys and with the values they defend.

3. The conflict:
   Here, you presented examples demonstrating that the good guys win honourably whereas the bad guys win by cheating. You then claimed that underlying this conflict convention is a message that the forces of evil lack the character, skills, moral fibre, or righteousness to triumph on their own.

Your conclusion:

_____

_____

_____

_____

_____

_____

In the next section, we use examples to guide you through the process of writing a thesis, generating an introduction, and writing a conclusion.

# Procedure: Four Examples

In the normal sequence of essay writing, you will be given a subject or will be allowed to choose one from a number of choices. Sometimes the question or subject will be very specific: "Discuss the major industries of British Columbia," or "Analyze the causes of the Three Mile Island disaster," or "Compare and contrast the characters of Emma and Elizabeth." At other times, the subject will be only a word or two: discuss *skateboarding*, or *drunk drivers*, or *photography*, or *grading versus marking*. For these subjects, you must narrow the topic to a manageable size.

As we mentioned previously, a normal first-year English in-class essay averages about 500 words. Knowing the word length and having chosen your subject or having been given one, you should determine, on scrap paper, your approach and attitude.

Mull the subject over. Ask yourself questions about it. Do you have a lot of information about it? Can you get some from primary or secondary sources? (Obviously, if it is an in-class essay, you will have to go with your own resources.) Is it a serious subject? Is it a subject about which many people disagree? Is it a subject that engages your emotions? If so, can you find a way to write about it in a reasonable, rather than a rabid, fashion? Can you reduce the broad or vague subject you were given to manageable proportions? Can you find at least three good points to support your attitude? If so, you have a thesis, and your essay now has a form.

The following four examples take you step by step through the procedure outlined above.

## 1. Skateboarding

Jot down what comes to your mind........ ☞▌

*Boards are expensive.*

*They're dangerous.*

*Skateboarders get hurt.*

They need safety equipment.

Other people get hurt.

Skateboarders should not be on downtown sidewalks.

The skateboarders are nearly always guys.

They are often very skillful.

Skateboards are very popular.

Use strategies from Chapter Six: Developing Ideas to generate more ideas.

## Skateboarding: The Thesis

On the whole, although you have mentioned some positive things about skateboarding, your attitude seems negative. Try a thesis: "Skateboarders are irresponsible and dangerous, but skillful." Wait a minute! That order is bad: it ends on a positive when your overall attitude is negative. Try again. "Although some skateboarders are very skillful, many are irresponsible and dangerous." That's pretty good. Conceding good things about what you criticize makes you sound like a reasonable person, but your essay will still end with paragraphs discussing irresponsibility and danger, leading properly into your conclusion.

## Skateboarding: The Introduction

Having developed the all-important thesis, you can now write the introduction that precedes it. It introduces the subject in general terms and establishes your tone. As we said earlier, you can generate an introduction by picking a word or a form of the word from the thesis and generalizing about it. Usually, the word will be a noun. Probably, in this essay, you will choose "skateboarding." Your tone will be serious and fairly formal because you want your audience to take your criticism seriously.

Try an introduction for your thesis:

Most of us pay little attention to skateboarders or skateboarding. Therefore, we may be unaware of the cost this sport exacts from us. We taxpayers pay a great deal of money, not for safety equipment or boards, but for broken teeth and bones. The reason is clear. Although some skateboarders are very skillful, many are irresponsible and dangerous.

If you aren't happy with this introduction, you can try a different one:

*Skateboarding forces itself on one's attention. Whether one strolls down a suburban sidewalk in summer, drives a car on a city street, or parks in a civic parkade in winter, one sees skateboarders. They defy gravity as they shoot up skateboarding ramps or defy our reaction times as they skate between cars and up over curbs. Although some skateboarders are very skillful, many are irresponsible and dangerous.*

## Skateboarding: Body Development

You can develop your main points with personal examples or newspaper stories, with statistics, or with vivid concrete details. You will concentrate on the serious effects or consequences of dangerous, irresponsible skateboarding. See Chapter Six for more ideas about developing ideas.

## Skateboarding: The Conclusion

Finally, you can write your conclusion, beginning with the gist of your thesis, then broadening out. In the following examples, the gist of the thesis is underlined.

*Skateboarders cannot continue to develop their skill at the expense of others; they must become more responsible and more safety conscious. Safety and skill programmes similar to those for motorcycles should be mandatory for skateboarders.*

This conclusion sounds a bit cranky. It makes no concessions to people who love to skateboard, does not acknowledge their skills, and has an aggressive tone. Perhaps you could soften it a bit.

*Nobody can deny that some skateboard enthusiasts show athletic prowess, but many show lack of responsibility on city streets and endanger themselves and others. The Capital Regional District should provide more supervised facilities where proper safety measures could be enforced and skills could be honed. In this way, both the athletes and the public would be satisfied.*

Although the paper has discussed a problem, this conclusion has a polite tone. It grants, for example, that skateboarders are athletes rather than hooligans. Moreover, it provides a solution that should be agreeable to both the public and the skateboarders.

## 2. Drunk Drivers

Your attitude on this one comes easily: you're against them. You know that something should be done. Start jotting ideas down. Remember the strategies in Chapter Six: Developing Ideas.

......... 🖎

*There should be greater deterrents—but what??*

*Long jail sentences?*

*Community service?*

*Stiffer fines?*

*Permanent loss of licences?*

*Are fines practical?*

*Is confiscation of licences possible?*

*Society pays a lot of money to keep someone in jail.*

*How much does it cost to keep someone in jail?*

*Jail risks criminalizing him or her.*

*What about electronic monitoring?*

Keep thinking. Even if you scratch that "long jail sentence" solution, you should remember to find out the figure about jail costs. Remember electronic monitoring? How much does that cost? How about those fines? Aren't they unfair? A $2000 fine weighs much more heavily on a person making $20,000 a year than on someone making $90,000. But maybe fines could be levied as a percentage of income, 10 percent of $20,000 would be $2000 and 10 percent of $90,000 would be $9000. Keep thinking! The brainstorming process can eliminate the fuzzy ideas and leave the valuable ones.

Find your three workable, supportable points. Your subject is serious. A humorous approach would offend your audience, and sarcasm or irony would take considerable finesse on your part.

### Drunk Drivers: The Thesis

a) *Drunk drivers should pay large fines, spend community service sentences in hospital emergency rooms, and lose their licences permanently on the second conviction.*

You can try a completely different thesis. Ask yourself why drunk drivers concern us.

b) *Drunk drivers must be stopped, for they harm not only themselves but also their families and our society.*

## Drunk Drivers: The Introduction

For thesis a): *We all worry about the epidemics that can sweep through our community while authorities try desperately to find cures. This year, for example, a big worry was toxoplasmosis. Shouldn't we also worry, however, that last year five Sudbury children under ten years died, victims not of disease, but of drunk drivers? Authorities need to take action now.* <u>*Drunk drivers should pay large fines, spend community service sentences in hospital emergency rooms, and lose their licences permanently on the second conviction.*</u>

For thesis b): *People who drink too much seldom worry about drunk drivers, nor do they worry much about road conditions, traffic lights, or speed limits.* <u>*Drunk drivers must be stopped, for they harm not only themselves, but also their families and our society.*</u>

## Drunk Drivers: The Body

In this essay, whether you write thesis a) or b), we think that you can use both logical and emotional arguments in your body paragraphs as you suggest your solutions to this problem. Logical methods would include citing statistics about how many accidents or deaths are caused by drunk drivers, how much insurance is paid out, ultimately out of all our pockets, to the victims, etc. For thesis a), you could play these ideas off against the large fines you want the drivers to pay. Emotional reasons could include personal experience, always very powerful, a graphic newspaper account of an accident caused by a drunk driver, or a transcript of a victim impact statement. These strategies would work particularly well for thesis b).

## Drunk Drivers: The Conclusion

Restate the gist of your main ideas in the opening of your conclusion.

For introduction a): <u>*Substantial fines, perhaps one quarter of the offender's gross income, enforced emergency room service, and licence confiscation seem reasonable measures.*</u> *We must change drunk drivers' lives before they change ours.*

For introduction b): *Drunk drivers endanger us all, not just themselves, and they must be stopped. Drunk driving is our most costly social disease.*

## 3. Photography

How much do you know about cameras or photography? Let's suppose you know hardly anything—but the other subjects on the in-class essay are worse, and you've got to write on photography. You do *like* photographs and have numerous albums, but many of the pictures came from friends because yours often don't turn out. Why is that? Think about your favourite almost-great pictures. Are there common denominators in their failure?

### Photography: The Thesis

a) *Good photographs require proper lighting, careful composition, and, above all, patience.*
You have little knowledge about the subject, with dozens of prime examples of photographic disasters to prove it, but you also have a thesis. Those failed photographs that caused you so much expense and embarrassment will fill your paragraphs with lots of great concrete details that will interest, and perhaps amuse, your audience. Your tone, then, could be lighthearted as you write an interesting essay on the topic you knew little about.

Let's suppose, instead, that you know quite a bit about cameras. Your thesis would be quite different: for example, you could try the following:

b) *Today, although new technology has created interesting equipment for those who like to see the future in their viewfinders, most people still choose a pinhole, an automatic focus, or single lens reflex camera.*

### Photography: The Introduction

Now pick a noun from your thesis, and generalize about it to generate your **introduction**:

For thesis a): *Good cameras cannot guarantee good photographs. In many cherished albums, one finds headless children holding birthday presents, shadowy forms pointing at deeper shadows, and coloured streaks showing where the Christmas kitten was. Good photographs, however, require proper lighting, careful composition and, above all, patience.*

k—or even the purple and pink ink that some teachers use—
 feel queasy and reduces your assignment's look of
e and expertise. But then you remember that not all the red
cize your work. Some make suggestions; some give
n; some say "good point!!" or "well-developed paragraph."
nformation and suggestions on a C paper that looked as
eone had bled over every paragraph, for example, you got
 next one. Obviously, we can have very different ideas about
ers with letter grades or papers with comments are more

tudents are of mixed emotions, what would teachers rather
assignment and put a letter grade at the end based on their
 what was expected and what was produced, or wear out
pens a semester writing voluminous comments that they
eople never read? A letter grade seems easier for the
uch a grade seems to offer nothing really helpful to you,
Vhat is the difference between a high C+ and a low B-?
 a grade help you? Is a mix of grades and remarks the
 idea?

## us Marking: The Thesis

*ore effective than grading, provides specific and helpful advice.*

 approach the subject from a slightly different angle:

*arbitrary and useless.*

## Marking: The Introduction

ld use the same introduction for thesis a) or b). For
ld write:

*d to sympathize with a student who got a lab, an essay, or a term
 just an A at the end? Maybe you found sympathy hard to feel or
— on the same assignment. Nonetheless, often such a student,
crazy, or hypocritical, has a right to be upset.*

## Marking: The Body

hoose lots of good persuasive arguments, adding
 using concrete examples drawn from your own

For thesis b): *Today in camera shops and dr*
*everyone. Young children can have fun with simple*
*experiment with the newest apparatus and gadget*
*Although new technology has created interestin*
*the future in their viewfinders, most people stil*
*single lens reflex camera.*

You could create a different kind
"new technology" and beginning you
latest advances available to photogra

## Photography: The Body

The **body paragraphs** could be de
thesis a) you can have a lot of fun
b) you could compare and contras
a different essay still based on co
kinds of photography at which th
photographer excel.

## Photography: The Conclusi

To write a conclusion to the ca
the thesis and then broaden ou

a) *Amateur photographers who*
*lighting, careful composition, and pa*
*notice the change when people, look*

b) *From the simple pinhole t*
*cameras make photography a plea*
*provide such ageless pleasure, d*
*the art and the artist. Camera*

## 4. Grading Versus

You may have very mixe
quite different from no
an assignment back wit
lots of time to correctl
professional; and the

Red in
makes you
competen
marks criti
informatio
Using the
though son
an A on the
whether pa
gratifying.
Well, if
do—read an
knowledge o
two or three
know some p
teacher, but s
the student.
How can such
most practical

## Grading Vers
Try a thesis:

a) *Marking,*

Perhaps you ca

b) *Grades are*

## Grading Versu
Probably you cou
example, you cou

*Have you ever h*
*project back with*
*give if you got a B*
*not self-satisfied,*

## Grading Versus
Here's a chance to
emotional appeal by

experience. Even if you remove yourself from the examples and write about "one student" or "a student in first year," the emotion you feel will be communicated to your reader.

## Grading Versus Marking: The Conclusion

After you've developed your ideas and linked them smoothly, you can write the conclusion.

*Any student happily accepts an A, but, in truth, even such a sought-after grade offers no specifics and gives no help for the future. Grades will never disappear: transcripts, for example, will never be pages of edifying remarks. Our labs, assignments, and essays, though, can have both comments and A's. Who would quarrel with that?*

---

### Activity 9: Transitions between paragraphs

For each of the essays in the Procedure section (Skateboarding, Drunk Driving, Photography, and Grading Versus Marking), write transitional sentences to go between the first and second, and second and third body paragraphs.

Remember that if you have organized with a thesis containing specific points and have strong topic sentences and wraps, you have automatic transitions between the introduction and the first body paragraph and between the last body paragraph and the conclusion.

Remember that the sentences you write should contain both the transition from the previous idea and the topic of the new paragraph. Check with your neighbour to see if you wrote similar sentences.

---

# Organizing Fact-Based Essays

We can go back now and look at a couple of the topics that gave you less leeway than the one-word subjects that we worked with above. With the above one-word topics, a creative student could write an in-class essay without having had any idea beforehand what the subject was. There are essays, however, that will be based on lecture material and/or on research material. For these essays, you will be expected to read a variety of sources, some contradictory, and come to a thesis based on your analysis.

We could look, for example, at the topic about the main industries of British Columbia. You might think that your thesis statement might be a bit cumbersome if you listed agriculture, forestry, fishing, mining, and tourism in it. You could, however, write simply, "All but one of British Columbia's major industries is resource based," or "In the 1990's, income from fishing and forestry greatly declined, revenues from mining and agriculture remained stable, and return from tourism increased." Even if your thesis stated simply, "British Columbia has five major industries," you would set up your paragraphs as though your thesis had laid out each point, one paragraph each for agriculture, forestry, fishing, mining, and tourism.

The following is one paragraph fom Marc's 750-word in-class essay concerning the state of the British Columbia economy in 1998:

> Although tourism has remained a relatively bright sector in the economy compared to forestry, British Columbians should not be complacent because the makeup of our tourism has been changing as a result of the global economy. The number of Japanese tourists, for example, has declined 12 percent. It is true that the number of American tourists has increased, but studies suggest that American tourists spend less time and money (50 percent less) than overseas tourists. Our fellow Canadians spend even less. Clearly, if tourism is to remain a bright spot, we need to focus more energy on getting our American cousins to stay longer and spend more.

The above paragraph is well organized, with a topic sentence, supporting details, and a wrap. Marc has remembered concrete details to back up his main point about tourism. If he were writing the same essay at home, however, he would be expected to cite where he got this information.

The kind of organization we have discussed provides freedom within its basic structure. Although the above strategies mostly concern writing a typical 500-word composition, the kind that often appears on an exam or an in-class essay, you can apply the same techniques in a 5000-word essay or in a book. In the case of a book, for example, your introduction would present your main ideas, your approach, and your attitude, while each of your main points, for instance, the British Columbia industries mentioned previously, would appear as a chapter. In the conclusion, you would call attention to your main points and their implications. It's the basic structure that makes your work accessible to your audience.

## Hints on Writing Analytical or Research Essays

1. **Narrow and focus** the subject.
2. **Use primary and secondary sources** to find information.

3. **Use note cards** as you record information, and clearly include the source, the author, title, place of publication, publisher, date of publication, and the page number.

4. **Clearly indicate the kind of information on the note card:** summary, paraphrase, or direct quotation.

5. **Construct a working thesis**, knowing it may change.

6. **Sort your file cards** into piles conforming to the main points in your thesis, **label them**, and use them to supply concrete details and evidence in your paper.

7. **Use only relevant quotations**, i.e., ones that back up a major point.

8. **Cite your sources** whether you are using an idea, a paraphrase, or a summary.

9. Make sure that your body paragraphs **have strong topic sentences and wraps.**

10. **Revise** to ensure that the paper is clear, concise, concrete, and correct in sentence structure, punctuation, and grammar.

The following first-year university paper is a 1500-word research essay about the accuracy of Hollywood's portrayal of the threat and symptoms of Ebola in the movie *Outbreak*.

**Sample Essay #1: Toying with Emotions**
by Dharmvir Singh Jaswal

> A rare killer virus from the jungles of Zaire has taken hold in a California community. It knows no boundaries. Its mortality rate is 100 percent. And some say the only way to stop its spread is to fire bomb the town and everyone in it.
> (*Outbreak* 1995)

The above quotation expresses the central idea behind the movie *Outbreak*: the virus Ebola Montaba. Could this scenario be true? Is it possible for a virus to have the strength to wipe out a whole community? According to the write-up on the jacket of the video, apparently so. And unfortunately, to the uneducated and unaware, Hollywood's portrayal of the Ebola virus and its potential effects on humanity may be accepted as truth, no questions asked. Research into the Ebola virus, however, shows Hollywood's representation of the virus to be predominately misleading. One can speculate about the intrinsic motivation behind making the movie, *Outbreak*, in such a manner. By presenting only half the facts and adding its own interpretations and extrapolations, Hollywood has been able to create an intense and dramatic motion picture whose success is based on the ability of the audience to become emotionally involved with the movie. In the movie, the over-dramatization and the intensification of the effects of the Ebola virus allowed Hollywood to play on the emotions of the audience and thus capitalize at the box office.

To effectively show the misrepresentations of Hollywood's portrayal and its effect on the audience, we must first learn about the background of this deadly virus. Named after a river in Zaire where it was first discovered, "the Ebola virus is one of the most pathogenic viral agents known to man" ("Identifying Ebola's Natural Host Reservoir" 101–102). It is found, coincidentally, where poor medical facilities exist, as attested to by outbreaks in Central Africa, in both Zaire and Sudan. There are four strains of the virus known: Ebola Zaire, Ebola Sudan, Ebola Reston, and Ebola Tai (Ornstein and Mathews 2). Causing victims to bleed to death internally, this blood-born pathogen kills 80 to 90 percent of its victims. Despite its virulence, however, research indicates that only 800 people have died from Ebola since it was first identified in 1976 ("First Case of Deadly Ebola Virus Diagnosed in S. Africa" 1–2).

We can now turn our attention to how Hollywood inaccurately portrays this deadly virus. The first inaccuracy in Hollywood's portrayal of the Ebola virus begins with the symptoms. In the movie, symptoms include flu-like symptoms and Hemorrhagic fever, followed by the presence of lesions all over the body. Pustules of blood and pus also appear all over the body, and in a matter of two or three days, the body becomes "mushy to the touch." By the end of the third day, the movie claims, the vital organs begin to shut down and their eventual liquefaction leaves the patient dead *(Outbreak)*.

Indeed, research shows that the symptoms of Ebola are frightening:

> Persons develop fever, chills, headaches, muscle aches, and loss of appetite. As the disease progresses, vomiting, diarrhea, abdominal pain, and chest pain can occur. The blood fails to clot and the patient may bleed from injection sites as well as in the gastrointestinal tract, skin, and internal organs. (Ornstein and Mathews 2)

However, Hollywood sensationalizes the disease with the addition of liquefying organs. In addition, the movie claims that the infected patient dies within two or three days; however, research indicates seven to fourteen as the average incubation period for the virus (Ornstein and Mathews 2). This intensification of the virulence of the virus, achieved by shrinking the time frame, is one way Hollywood captivates the audience and draws them into the movie. The more virulent the virus appears to the audience, the more viewers will be affected emotionally.

A second example of how Hollywood misleads and emotionally affects the audience is in the transmission of the virus. The movie claims that the sole carrier of the virus is a monkey that a trafficker brings over to the United States from Central Africa. The infected monkey spreads the virus at two different points in the movie. The first time, the monkey spits saliva into the mouth of the man who is transporting him. The man later spreads the virus to his girlfriend when she meets him at the airport. The second infection occurs once the monkey has been given to a pet store owner. While the owner is opening the cage, the infected monkey scratches the shop owner's arm (*Outbreak*). Because the Ebola virus is spread through personal contact with an infected individual, usually through the transmission of blood or bodily fluids, this portrayal of the transmission is an accurate one (Ornstein and Mathews 3). However, what the movie fails to show is that while the monkey is a host for the virus, it is also a victim. In *Time* magazine, Andrew Purvis writes that "chimps seem as susceptible as people to the pathogen" (39). In other words, the infected monkey is also suffering and would presumably have been dead before it reached the pet store, had it been infected with the Hollywood version of the virus. Moreover, monkeys do not appear to be the source of the "natural reservoir" for the virus. Rather, researchers believe that the real natural reservoir of the virus is a small, forest-dwelling rodent. They also speculate that mosquitoes and other insects can transfer the virus (Purvis 39). While this example does not directly relate to the emotional distress of the audience, it does mislead the audience into thinking that monkeys are the carriers of this disease.

While Hollywood's portrayal of the transmission of the virus through the exchange of blood and bodily fluids is accurate, its claim that the Ebola virus can also spread through the air is false. There is a very dramatic scene in the movie where, at a movie theatre, an infected person coughs and the virus is shown travelling through the air and landing in the breathing path of the other people in the theatre (*Outbreak*). Unfortunately for Hollywood, in order to become airborne, the Ebola virus would have to undergo numerous complex genetic mutations, both internally and externally. It would have to mutate in such a way as to change not only its outer protective coating of proteins, but also its structure to allow infection to spread through the respiratory system. Also, while there is no measurement of the rate of mutation, research suggests that the probability of the virus undergoing the required mutations is very low (Ornstein and Mathews 4). Therefore, showing the virus travelling through the air and infecting others is not very realistic. However, such dramatic images effectively capture the audience and keep it focused intensely on the movie.

A final example of how Hollywood's portrayal of the Ebola virus is inaccurate is found at the end of the movie. Conveniently enough, Hollywood is able to find a cure for the virus. The cure comes in the form of a vaccination serum made from the antibodies found in the host organism's blood. In the movie, the doctors take the infected monkey's blood and separate the plasma from the blood. They then make a serum from the plasma. Within a matter of seconds of locating the host, the infected monkey, the assistant doctor injects the serum into the infected patients and prevents their deaths (*Outbreak*). By finding a cure for the virus, Hollywood can mislead the audience into believing that there is, in fact, a cure for the Ebola virus, and once again present a happy ending. In reality, researchers have been trying to develop a cure for almost twenty years, since the first outbreak was identified. Unfortunately, because the initial host is still unknown, developing an effective antiserum is a difficult process ("Ebola Kills 13 in Gabon" 1–2).

One has to question Hollywood's motives in making movies like *Outbreak*. Is it to inform the public about emerging epidemics such as the Ebola virus, or is it to sell tickets and make big money by toying with the emotions of audiences? Evidence found in the research suggests that the latter is the case. Over-dramatizing the symptoms makes the audience feel vulnerable; characterizing the virus as airborne gives the viewer a feeling of paranoia; isolating the host gives the audience a feeling of hope; and finding a cure creates a sense of relief. While the sensationalizing of the Ebola virus is beneficial to Hollywood, it is misleading to the public. If Hollywood is going to take on such serious, real-life issues as deadly pathogenic viruses, it should tell more facts and create less fantasy. As it stands, if we believe everything we see on the big screen, we will only know what is necessary to sell movie tickets.

Works Cited

"Ebola Virus Kills 13 in Gabon." <http://www.cnn.com/WORLD/9602/ebola/index.html>. February 1996.

"First Case of Deadly Ebola Virus Diagnozed in S. Africa." <http://www/cnn.com/WORLD/9611/16/safrica.ebola.ap/index.html#top>. November 1996.

"Identifying Ebola's Natural Host Reservoir." *Public Health Reports 111* (1996): 101–102.

Murphy, Dr. Fredrick A. "Electron Micrographs of Viruses." <http:/www.gene.com/ae/WM/NM/murphy_EMs.html>. October 1996.

Ornstein, David, and Kai Mathews. "Frequently Asked Questions About Ebola." <http://www.outbreak.org/cgi-unreg/dynaserve.exe/Ebola/faq.html#symptoms>. July 1996.

*Outbreak*. Dir. Wolfgang Peterson. Prod. Arnold Kopelson. Warner Bros. 1995.

Purvis. Andrew. "Where Does Ebola Hide?" *Time* magazine. 147.10 (1996): 39.

# Hints on Writing Literary Essays

1. **Use a strong thesis**, preferably containing the specific points that you will discuss in the body of the essay, **solid topic sentences** and **firm wraps** to keep your main points clear in the reader's mind.

2. **Be objective.** Use evidence from the work itself to back up your ideas and interpretations.

3. **Be conscious of the author's technique**—how does he or she shape your perception of the work, the characters? What **mood** is created?

4. **Distinguish between denotation and connotation**, the dictionary definition and the emotional, suggestive meanings.

5. **Separate the author from the narrator or from any of the main characters.** You may write that "the narrator suggests," or "the hero believes," or, in a poem, that "the persona feels elated," or "the speaker wants to die." The narrator, the persona, or the speaker is the voice speaking in a literary work.

6. **Be aware of context**—time, place, patterns—and how these affect the characters and the action.

7. **Avoid plot summary**—"and then, and then, and then."

8. **Assume an intelligent reader** has read the work once but needs you to highlight the finer points and deeper meanings.

9. **Analyze**, don't merely describe. Ask yourself specific questions and find the answers. For example, do I like this character? Why? What techniques does the author use to make me understand the characters? Why does the author repeat this image? When does my feeling about this character change? Why? How? Why did the poet start or stop using rhyme? What does the setting add?

10. **Set the context** for any quotations that you include to support your main points **and write using present tense**, e.g., "The town is swamped by the influx of tourists, and the young girl loses her sense of connection with the whales." Do not merely float out a raft of quotations and expect your reader to figure out where they come from.

The following at-home essay written for a first-year literature course is on *The Moonstone* by Wilkie Collins. Look carefully at the organization of this essay: its thesis, topic sentences, and wraps. Note that Rob supplies evidence for his claims and that, far from just giving a plot summary, he doesn't even reveal the name of the thief! Note that his main point, in fact, is the author's technique and how Collins encourages us to read on. If you are already aware of the desirability of conciseness and of the technique of zapping isys to help you achieve this goal, then you can check this essay for its isy quotient and see if you can find any easy zaps that Rob missed.

### Sample Essay #2: Wilkie's Way, the Right Way, Right Away
by Rob Flemming

Wilkie Collins, by writing *The Moonstone*, defined a style of literature. This work, the first British detective novel, established writing techniques which have since contributed immeasurably to the entertainment of people all over the world. Later novels of similar style, such as Conan Doyle's Sherlock Holmes, have adopted many of its prototype elements. Any good detective novel draws the reader into its pages through the fabrication of mystery and suspense. Wilkie Collins mastered this skill in his first attempt. Wilkie Collins establishes suspense in *The Moonstone* with an engrossing prologue; maintains it with dangling chapter ends; heightens it by delivering the narration through concealed observers; and sustains it excruciatingly toward the end of the novel by delaying the communication of key information.

The prologue to *The Moonstone* serves as an exciting introduction to the story, casting a villainous light on the character of John Herncastle and establishing an aura of mystery and legend surrounding the stone. The thrilling and violent taking of the stone is punctuated by the oath of its dying Indian guardian: "The Moonstone will have its vengeance on you and yours" (37). If this curse should fail to arouse interest in the fate of those who may come into close proximity with the Moonstone, the opinion that follows probably will not. Wilkie Collins means for the reader to take the belief to heart "that he will live to regret it, if he keeps the Diamond; and that others will live to regret taking it from him, if he gives the Diamond away" (38) . The suggestion to "let our relatives . . . decide for themselves" (38) surely invites the readers' opinion as well. The prologue immediately captures the readers' attention and involves them in the tale from the beginning.

Throughout the first and part of the second narrative, the author uses the simple but effective trick of dangling chapter endings to keep the reader in a state of perpetual anticipation. Outright statements by Betteredge, the narrator, of what follows, like "Read on . . . and perhaps you will be as sorry for Rosanna Spearman as I was, when I found out the truth" (60), or "that chapter shall take you straight into the thick of the story" (93) usually close a chapter. A less obvious conversation also serves the same purpose when placed at the chapter's end: "'Wait a little' said the Sergeant. 'The pieces of the puzzle are not all put together yet'"(143). Miss Clack's narrative has dangling chapter endings as well. Chapter four ends with Godfrey's statement "I'll do it to-day!" (275), and no indication, until later, of what the deed may be. The last sentence of almost every chapter in the first and second narrative poses a question or leaves the reader hanging in anticipation of further revelation.

A more subtle technique for producing suspense involves the unusual perspective of an observer and narrator concealed behind curtains. This method of writing adds the risk of discovery to whatever excitement the main action generates. As Miss Clack "noiselessly arranged the curtains so that [she] could both see and hear" (276), the reader enters an anxious state simply by imagining the furtiveness of the concealment. The shameful means of observation doubles the impact of the proceeding proposal. Later, the climactic experiment that solves at least part of the mystery has three concealed observers who watch with "breathless interest" (476). Again the reader is excited by imagining "Mr. Bruff looking eagerly through a crack in the imperfectly-drawn curtains of the bed. And Betteredge . . . peeping over Mr. Bruff's shoulder" (476). Wilkie Collins has the skill to draw the reader almost personally into the tale. He takes full advantage of this ability by placing the reader in precisely the position that will generate the greatest thrill.

As the novel approaches its climax with quickening pace, Wilkie Collins still manages to prolong and heighten the reader's suspense by delaying the delivery of important evidence. The first opportunity he takes to torment the reader involves the letter, addressed to Franklin Blake, containing the last words of Rosanna Spearman. Although this letter appears very early in the novel, Limping Lucy insists on holding it for months. Upon discovery of its existence, Franklin wishes to "go back and get it at once" (350), but must wait until the next morning. The delays increase as the mystery further unfolds. Ezra Jennings makes this astonishing statement to Franklin: "I believe the vindication of your innocence is in my hands" (431). However exciting this revelation may be, to characters and readers alike, he cannot reveal the facts because it is "too serious a matter to be explained in a hurry" (432). Franklin must wait to hear the news "in two hours time" (432). Collins takes one more opportunity to stretch suspense, before finally revealing the identity of the criminal. After the Diamond is removed from the bank and secretly passed to the thief, Gooseberry disappears. Franklin, Bruff, and the hired men assume that he may have followed the right man but have "seen nothing of him since [they] left the bank" (489). Franklin misses Gooseberry that night and must wait for him to "come back tomorrow morning" (490) between 9:00 and 10:00. At 9:30 the next morning, Sergeant Cuff arrives instead. Not until he has given Franklin a letter, instructing him to "compare the name of the guilty person with the name that I have written in that sealed letter" (492) does Gooseberry arrive, to help them finally solve the mystery completely. Wilkie Collins knows that the reader will expect Gooseberry, an endearing character, to find the solution, and so delays his return just long enough to dare the reader to make one final guess on the identity of the true villain.

Wilkie Collins generates suspense in *The Moonstone* with a gripping prologue, uniquely exciting perspectives, and a skillful rein on the delivery of clues and information. These elements, combined with interesting characterizations and a believable narrative format, make for a thoroughly entertaining 'who-dunnit' read. Not surprisingly, later storytellers have borrowed heavily from this style. Few writers have improved on it. Such a complete prototype renders improvement unnecessary and even impossible. Rarely do humans prove to be so inventive, and, when they do, rarely do they get it so right the first time.

### Activity 10: Writing about literature

Write a thesis sentence for a potential essay about your favourite book. If you are not a reader, draft a thesis sentence about your favourite (or unfavourite) movie.

In any essay, on any topic, in any subject, you should keep in mind the significance of what you write. Why does it matter? What are the main ideas you want to leave your reader thinking about? In order to convince your reader to respect your ideas, you will need to present them in an organized way, provide evidence, and keep your main points clear.

## More Sample Essays

The following essay, which uses Classification as an organizational strategy, was written by an imaginary student, Imagene A. Monniker.

### Sample Essay #3. When My Fingers did the Walking Through the White Pages

At about ten, I became interested in my own names, what the characters meant and why my parents had chosen them. Since coming to Canada, I have again become very interested in names. A look in my phone book showed me many names from many countries. I decided to look for names from only the British Isles and to put them into categories.

A small but interesting category included personal or physical characteristics: Goodfellow, Goodenough, Longfellow, Armstrong, Strong, Strongman, Barefoot, Smiley, Blackman, Coward, Dearman, Drinkwater, Cruickshanks, Hardy, Hopewell, Jolly, Lovejoy, Lovelady, Newlove, Truelove, Wiseman, and Young. These names made me wonder what people might choose to name me. Perhaps they would choose Slowtyper or Quietperson. Personal or physical traits make interesting names.

Place names formed a major group. These names included names of the countryside such as Green, Garden, Field, Meadow, Forest, Fallowfield, Woods, River, Ford, Burn, Brook, and Lake. Some of the names like Castle, Barnes, House, Chapel, and Church concerned buildings. Another group contained features of the area: Lea, Grove, Hill, Bridges, or Wells. Still other place names include Street and Lane. Some of these names could be combined to create others such as Churchill, Fieldhouse, or Greenwood. It seems that where people came from provided a good way of identifying them.

Another category useful in identifying people is occupation names, but it had some surprises for me. Some—like Gardener, Carpenter, Baker, Priest, Barber, Butler, Carter, Cook, Farmer, Miller, Taylor, and Hunter—I discovered easily. I eventually found the Wrights and Wainwrights, Plowrights, and Cartwrights too. Other occupation names like Archer, Bowman, Fletcher, Thatcher, Turner, Tanner, Palmer, Chamberlain, Sawyer, Chandler, Baxter, Chapman, and Cooper had to be pointed out to me by other people. I laughed when I realized that Smith, a name that occupies more than thirteen columns in my phone book, was an occupation name. Although some of these occupation names such as Laird, Squire, Knight, Earl, Prince, King, Baron, Queen, Abbott, Bishop, and Pope seem more like titles, clearly, occupation accounts for many of the names from the British Isles.

One more major category that I found in the phone book was "offspring of" names. For example, all the "son" names like Robertson, Richardson, Thompson, Peterson and Davidson fit into this group. "Kin" names fit here too: Perkins, Thompkins, Hawkins, Dawkins, and Watkins. Imagine how I felt when I discovered that the Fitz's fit here as well: Fitzgerald, Fitzwilliam, Fitzsimmons, and many more. I also located "O" names like O'Brien, O'Connor, O'Hara, O'Leary, O'Neil, and O'Rourke. Actually, in my phone book there is an O'Nions, but I think, although the people are undoubtedly real, that this name is the same kind of "offspring" name joke as MacHinery, a name that my friend Donald Macdonald asked me to pronounce. It turned out to be "machinery" with a Scots accent. Donald's name—with all the other Mc's and Mac's such as McCrae, MacDougall, McEwen, MacFarland, McGregor, MacInnes, McKenzie, MacLaughlin, McMaster, MacNulty, McPherson, and McWhirter—fit in here too. "Offspring" names appear in the phone book in many guises.

During my adventures with my phone book, I found several categories under which to file names: personal and physical characteristics, place, occupation, and "offspring" names. I know that there are other categories of names such as ones derived from names of seasons, animals, birds, or fruits, and maybe you can think of others. Let your fingers do the walking in the white pages, and have some fun with names.

---

## Activity 11: Revising for tone

The preceding essay is informal in tone.

1. Write a more formal thesis statement for this essay.

2. Revise the topic sentences for body paragraphs four and five to make them more formal.

3. Rewrite the conclusion to increase the level of formality.

---

## Activity 12: Writing about names

1. Write an essay of about five-hundred words on categories of surnames from another cultural group.

or

2. Write an essay of about five-hundred words on important things in your culture to think about when naming a baby.

or

3. Write an essay of about five-hundred words on what your names mean and how well the names suit you.

In the following essay, the writer uses an extended definition as the main organizational strategy.

**Sample Essay #4. Why Do the Doula Hula?**
by Kerry Patriarche

Should a woman engage a doula to attend her baby's birth? Isn't that just introducing an extraneous person into the already busy birth scene? No, it's not. The doula's experience, education, and position outside both the medical hierarchy and the emotions of the family allow her, during the birth process, to provide the comfort and confidence others cannot always be expected to offer.

Many couples come to the hospital without any previous experience in that institutional setting. In the excitement, couples can have trouble understanding the hospital dialect; fathers can sometimes be attracted to the technology, watching fetal monitors instead of their wives; and mothers may find themselves inexplicably compliant. When all that's at stake is where the father can go to the bathroom, there's no need for interpretation. The decision to abandon labour and give the mother a Caesarean section, however, results in a distressing explosion of activity and an influx of personnel in the birth room that parents invariably interpret as an indication of extreme danger for the mother and child. In fact, the bustle is related to the need to secure precious operating room time. Because she knows the hospital environment, a doula helps parents to ask for information and to understand what they are told, reducing their confusion and defusing their feelings of panic.

A doula's knowledge of the birth process and of strategies for easing labour aids her in supporting the father's role as helper and in increasing everyone's level of confidence. Though the post-Lamaze popular understanding acknowledges that a woman needs help while accommodating the different stages and sensations of her labour and that medical interventions should be minimized, it expects her partner to recognize what is needed. Nonetheless, many women are too preoccupied by their sensations to communicate their needs before they feel desperate. Moreover, inexperienced birth partners commonly retreat when proffered comfort appears ineffective or, worse, is met with irritation. This leads to an increased likelihood of medical interventions like narcotics, as well as a general loss of faith in the process. A doula models new or modified strategies and offers support to the birthing couple.

In conclusion, the doula provides comfort and confidence to both partners participating in a birth. A father's emotional response to the unfolding drama of birth can make him less than helpful to a mother who needs him to be a calm and encouraging anchor in a sea of sensation. Nurses, though willing to help, have other patients and endless paperwork, leaving them little time for personalized care. A couple is challenged in labour not only by hard work, lack of sleep, and a strange setting, but also by the difficulty of changing roles in public. In contrast, not distressed by fears nor distracted by joys, the doula, having learned about the parents and helped them learn about themselves before the birth, has the focus and knowledge, during labour and delivery, to assist the parents to build a good foundation. She helps them to attain their common goal, a birth experience that everyone feels is the best one possible for all concerned.

---

### Activity 13: A definition essay

Kerry's essay on the role of a doula is essentially an extended definition.

Write a similarly structured essay about another occupation, role, or profession.

**Suggested Subjects:**
a disc jockey, a master of ceremonies, a bridesmaid/best man, a piano tuner, a proofreader, a sous chef, a bus person, a pharmacist, a sales clerk.

---

The following essay, by imaginary student, Bea Chef, uses Process Analysis.

**Sample Essay #5. Starving Student Soup**

It happens to all of us now and then. One day in the midst of doing research or working on an impossible computer assignment, students realize that they are starving: not just starving, but tired and broke. How can they solve such a complicated problem? They, and you, can find a solution in the infinitely variable, but quick and easy, Starving Student Soup. You will need some basic utensils, simple ingredients, and the following easy method.

The equipment you need is basic. Find a pot, with a lid or foil to cover it, big enough to hold about eight cups of water. You'll need a sharp knife and a spoon, one long enough to get your hand well above the steam. Chopsticks could also perform this function. With these few simple utensils, you are off to a good start.

With your utensils ready, you can now think about ingredients. The limp carrots and the wilted celery that you would never put in a salad or stir fry will work well in your soup. Cabbage, broccoli, sui choy, potatoes, peppers, or even lettuce will be great additions. Of course, it is nice if you can start your soup with a nice big onion. Now, look for seasonings. You are bound to find salt and pepper, but if you can find basil, garlic, or oregano, your soup will smell more cheerful. Perhaps you will find Worchester sauce, soya sauce, ketchup, half a tin of prepared soup or gravy, or maybe even a half a jar of curry or spaghetti sauce. Look for hidden treasures: leftover sausages, baked beans, or barbecued pork. You might as well use the depressed-looking salad too. You can see that the ingredients are not only simple but also very variable.

Slice or dice the treasures that you rescued from the fridge. Now, put your big pot on the stove element about medium high and add about two table- spoons of oil. Add your onion and any spices you found to the hot oil. When they start to smell good, you can add all the rest of your ingredients and cook them until they are heated through. Now add about six cups of water and anything you found to make that water more like a broth. What you use will determine how much to put in. Pour and taste until you feel satisfied. Finally, bring your pot full of ingredients to a boil, turn the heat down to low, and clap on the pot lid or foil top.

The soup uses simple equipment and ingredients. If you nibble along the way, you could probably get another chapter read or another math problem done while your soup simmers. At any time, you can add finishing touches like a handful of rice or noodles, or some tofu. It's your soup. Serve it with bread or crackers if you have some. You'll probably have some soup left over to fuel another day's studying.

### Activity 14: Writing about cooking

The above essay is an in-class essay of 500 words. Write a similar essay telling someone how to make a simple dish.

In the following essay, Rebekkah has written a persuasive essay that makes use of concrete examples.

### Sample Essay #6: It's No Space Opera
by Rebekkah Patriarche

Science fiction can be so much more than just "space opera." The genre is trying to shake its pulp-fiction image, but the many strong works, new and old, in science fiction are often dismissed with the weak. Good science fic- tion provides fascinating observations about the interaction between humanity and technology, enlists careful research leading to strong plots and characters, and offers great fuel for the imagination.

Science fiction can examine the interaction between humanity and technol- ogy, present possible futures, and make interesting social commentaries. Its focus has changed to include more than just inter-galactic wars between heroic spacemen and technologically advanced, but ultimately flawed, humanoid aliens. "The Golden Helix," Theodore Sturgeon's classic short story, begins in a spaceship, then continues on to introduce the reader to a beautiful yet frightening planet and tell the story of its five accidental colonists. Describing the planet's wildlife and the anomalies that obsess one of the colonists, Sturgeon goes into detail, to craft a fascinating story with no fighting. Like most SF works, "The Golden Helix" is set in the not-too- distant future, a time which many writers have used to tell stories with strong cautionary themes. George Orwell's *Nineteen Eighty-Four* is a well-known example of the type, as is Robert A. Heinlein's *Stranger In A Strange Land*. *The Lathe of Heaven* by Ursula K. LeGuin could be cited as a story with an unusual focus, but the plot of the book merely serves to present its theme: any attempt to create perfection is destined to fail. Some works provide witty satires on the current state of world affairs, pointing out what may happen if certain situations persist. Science fiction is the medium through which many authors attempt to improve the future.

Like any other fiction, science fiction can be carefully researched and painstakingly crafted. Special attention must be paid to character and plot, but also, often, to world-building. Hal Clement's *Mission of Gravity* is an incredible example of this. The author has taken the time and trouble to give the planet his book takes place on a certain mass and atmosphere, and has carefully determined how these factors affect native life, as well as visiting humans. Although Clement is an extraordinary case, most other writers do research their work carefully, and use detail where detail is necessary.

Characters play a large role in any story, so a good author cannot afford to ignore their revelation and development. John Wyndham's characters in *The Chrysalids* are very true-to-life. They muddle along as best they can in the midst of their problems and, like living people, win some battles and lose others. At the end of the book, the reader is left with the feeling that he or she knows the characters intimately. This same intimate knowledge is important when it comes to non-human characters as well, and a book that demonstrates the power of lifelike characters in this way is Katie Waitman's *The Merro Tree*. The extraterrestrial characters in this book range from nearly human to almost incomprehensibly alien, but all of them have real, well-developed personalities.

While science fiction uses character development well, many books in the genre, including most of the works of Isaac Asimov, are still plot-driven. However, many of these plots are far from the usual. "—All You Zombies—" by Robert A. Heinlein involves a man with a time machine who searches for his parents and finds a strange truth. *The Death of Sleep* by Anne McCaffrey and Jody Lynn Nye tells what might almost be considered a "Rip Van Winkle" story about a woman who gets lost in space while in suspended animation—several times. These examples are only a few of the great books that have been written.

In addition to being well written, science fiction can fuel the imagination. It can stimulate the mind in a concrete, scientific way. There are many scientific developments and inventions that have been inspired by or anticipated by science fiction works. One of the most notable of these is the Waldo, an artificial "arm" which is used in nuclear plants and similar places, and was inspired by the device in Heinlein's short story by the same name. Perhaps the most famous examples are the inspired fantasies of Jules Verne, who predicted the invention of television, the airplane, the submarine, and guided missile. Inventions, however, are not the only things which science fiction can enkindle in the brain. Most of the people who read science fiction do so for the exciting plots and insightful observations the books can give them. Books like *Brightness Falls From The Air* by James Tiptree, Jr. and *The Looking Glass Factor* by Judith M. Goldberger are great escapist fiction, without missing out on the other qualifications of a good book. *The Looking Glass Factor* is set on Earth in the near future, where a girl and two members of a genetically-engineered race of sentient cats investigate an experimental scientific technique that may be better left alone, combining elements of suspense and mystery with scientific fact to create a marvelous story. In *Brightness Falls From The Air*, nine humans have gathered on a planet to witness the final night of light from a nearby star-gone-nova and to see the planet's stunningly beautiful native race. The story proceeds to a frightening close as poachers and alien races become involved in this placid paradise. Both are exciting novels for many reasons.

Although "space opera" is not entirely a thing of the past, science fiction has a lot more to it than just "Spaceman Kevin vs. Gorgle the Bug-Eyed Monster." Character development, strong plots, well-researched worlds, and interesting, well-developed themes are as much a part of the genre as excitement and adventure. It is science fiction's job to present possible futures, and the future of science fiction is more than "pulp fiction."

## Activity 15: Defending your turf

Write an essay of 400-500 words defending something you like very much from those who attack it. Be sure to be concrete and specific in defence of your preference.

**Suggested Topics:**
country music, big truck derbies, haggis, rap music, spinach, Harlequin Romances, horror movies, skateboarding, fast food, comic books.

# Suggested At-Home Essay Format

## Format

1. If your essay has a title page, centre the title 1/4 to 1/3 down the page. Put your name, the course name and section, the instructor's name, and the date either at the bottom right side or the bottom centre.

2. If the essay has no title page, in the upper left of page one, starting 1" (2 1/2 cm ) from the top, write your name, the course name and section, the instructor's name, and the date. Double space, then centre the title on the page. Quadruple space before starting your essay.

3. Use one side only. Keyboard or write clearly using a dark ink on clear white paper.

4. Double space.

5. Leave margins of 1 1/2" (3 1/2—4 cm) at the top and left. Use 1" (2 1/2—3 cm) margins at the right and bottom.

6. To begin a paragraph, indent handwritten papers about one inch (3 1/2 cm) and typewritten ones five spaces, or leave double spaces between paragraphs. Even if you indent, the double spaces between paragraphs are reader-friendly.

## Numbering

7. Do not number page one. Instead, begin 1/4 or 1/3 down the page.

8. If you wish to number preliminary pages or appendices (a précis, notes, Works Cited, etc.) separately from the body in a long report such as a business report or proposal, centre Roman numerals at the bottom of the pages.

9. Place other numbers, unadorned, at the top centre or the top right.

## Titles

10. Create your own title. Do not, for example, simply use the title of a book or poem that you are writing about.

11. Do not put your title in italics, or underline it, or use quotation marks around it. If your title contains the title of a poem or book, use normal conventions for the title of the work.

12. Do not make your title a sentence or put a period after it.

13. Do not capitalize unimportant words such as articles, conjunctions, or prepositions with fewer than five letters unless they are the first or last words.

## Punctuation

14. Except for quotation marks and occasionally a dash or an ellipsis, punctuation should not begin a line.

15. In typed papers, leave two spaces after terminal punctuation such as a period or question mark. A dash—two typed hyphens—has spaces neither before nor after it, but an ellipsis does.

16. When you are using quotations, use ellipsis ( ... ) to show omission, but leave a recognizable English sentence and retain the author's meaning.

17. Use square brackets to add, to change, or to comment on a quotation.

18. Change, if necessary, the case of the first letter of an integrated quotation without the use of brackets to make it fit into your sentence.

19. Use [sic] to show that an error occurs in the original quotation.

20. Work each quotation into your own sentence.

21. If there is a quotation within a quotation, use single quotation marks around it.

22. If a poetic quotation exceeds two or three lines, indent it about eight or ten spaces on the left.

23. If a prose quotation exceeds more than four typed lines, indent it about eight or ten spaces on the left. Block quotations only have quotation marks if the quotation marks appear in the text. It is not necessary to single space a block quotation.

24. Wrap your paragraphs using your own words. Do not end them with quotations of someone else's words.

25. If you have an alphabetized Works Cited at the end of your essay, all that your reader needs in order to find where you got your information or quotation is (Name and the page number), e.g., (DePledge and McKenzie 105).

# Chapter

# 8

# Idiom

## Learning Outcomes

**This Chapter will help you to**

- recognize and use phrases commonly used in English.

- recognize and use idiomatic sentence patterns.

- differentiate between similar or the same words used idiomatically in different ways.

What exactly is idiom? It seems as though it is really a set of possibilities concerning how words are used. One kind of idiom involves long lists of sayings that may sound like nonsense to someone learning English but be quite meaningful to a native speaker. Although some of the idiomatic sayings may be called clichés because they have been repeated so often ("Birds of a feather flock together"), others may be called proverbs, wise sayings meant to guide your actions ("A stitch in time saves nine"). Idiom may also include using a word differently in one country than another or in one part of the country from another. Perhaps we can simply define idiom as "the customary way that words are used in a particular area."

Although this chapter is primarily for non-native speakers of English, we recognize that all across Canada, because of French Immersion, thousands of native-born English speakers also make idiomatic mistakes. To them, we say welcome, as their appreciation of idiomatic differences will help us all. Using idiom is not a situation where logic helps us, so it's best to live and learn.

One thing that we quickly learn is that idiom differs widely from English-speaking country to English-speaking country. We can give you a couple striking examples of idiomatic differences between Canada and England. A Canadian-born English speaker might, for example, meet some surprises when travelling in Britain. If, for instance, she wants to buy a sleeveless dress that could have a blouse or sweater worn under it, she will probably ask for a jumper. In return, the sales clerk might well bring her a selection of sweaters. If a newly-met British friend says he has a four-foot pot plant in the kitchen, our traveller may decide to stay elsewhere, fearing a drug-bust. A more experienced traveller may realize at once that the pot plant is probably a begonia or an ivy, grounds for admiration rather than arrest. Our traveller will also have to learn that to "knock up" a girl in England means that you rouse her out of bed. In contrast, if you "knock up" a girl here in Canada, you have made her pregnant. Clearly, understanding the idiom of a particular country is both important and challenging.

There are whole books devoted to common idioms such as "dyed in the wool," "in a pig's eye," and so forth. We encourage you to buy a book of idioms and to read through a page or so everyday for fun and, incidentally, to improve your understanding of this kind of idiom.

We, however, using a bit of idiom, have other fish to fry. This chapter, based on our long experience teaching writing to non-native speakers of English, concerns sentence-structure patterns, some of which defy logic. Our idiom concerns workaday problems: what preposition to use after what verb, when to use a present participle and when to use a past participle as modifier, how to distinguish between "because of" and "due to." Our collection of idiomatic phrases should help you to home in on the ones that cause you difficulty. Your other partner, your instructor, can help by identifying certain errors as idiomatic and referring you to the appropriate pages in this text, but the major responsibility is yours. You will find exercises to reinforce many of the entries that, we again emphasize, are best learned as "patterns."

Native speakers need to hear from non-native English speakers that it is okay to stop them and say "This is how we say that." Often, because the message is clear, native speakers feel that correcting someone who may speak three other languages is impolite and insulting. Therefore, some idiomatic mistakes become fossilized. A highly successful business person with twenty years in Canada, for example, might still be saying "I'm returning back your call." It would have been so much easier to have learned in his or her first years in Canada that the "re" already contains the meaning "back," so "returning back" is redundant. Native speakers can be a major help in reducing the number of idiomatic mistakes a non-native speaker makes. For once, native speakers aren't expected to know "rules." It's enough to say simply, "This is what we say."

Because idioms are second nature to native speakers, the exploration of idiom is an area in which native speakers and ESL speakers can work effectively together. As many non-native English speakers know, many idioms involve those prepositional phrases that became so important when English lost most of its inflections. (See page 409.) For this reason, we are starting this chapter with a wealth of common prepositional phrases alphabetically arranged to make them easy to find. When you make a mistake with one of these phrases, you could highlight it, write it in an idiom log, and pay special attention to the phrase when you read it over. In addition, practising using the phrases in conversation and in papers will help you gain mastery over them.

Idiomatic errors made by ESL speakers are seldom careless errors. Instead, they often result from careful thought, sometimes based on the logic that works in a learner's native language. We have provided an **Idiom Log** at the end of this chapter. As you make mistakes, add the corrected phrases to your log. Reading over the correct forms every couple of days will ensure that the right patterns get imprinted.

## Common Phrases with Prepositions

As many of us are painfully aware, many of the idiomatic errors that people make when learning a language involve prepositions. Logic seldom helps. Below we include many of the most common phrases and give you examples of their use. Using your **Idiom Log**, isolate the phrases that you are most likely to use (you can probably get the list down to a dozen or so). Look at the lists for phrases relating to School Stuff and The Work Place following this section for an idea about how your lists will look. If you are studying criminology, your list may be very different from that of your friend who is studying commerce. Add relevant phrases that you hear. Read the phrases over, and practise making sentences with them. Soon, the phrases will simply sound right to you, and they will, in fact, *be* right.

to be according **to** (consistent with)

> Sue played <u>according to</u> the rules.

to be accountable **for** [actions/things]

> Natasha was <u>accountable for</u> the errors in the final draft.

to be accountable **to** [a superior]

> Natasha was <u>accountable to</u> the vice-president in charge of marketing.

to be accused **of** [something]

> She was <u>accused of</u> being too picky.

to be accused **by** [someone]

> She was <u>accused by</u> Natasha, of course.

to adapt **from** (to have modified the original)

> The pattern was <u>adapted from</u> one used by Kimiko's mother twenty years ago.

to adapt **to** (to comply with or conform to)

> Ben quickly <u>adapted to</u> the conditions.

to adhere **to** (to stick to)

> Vikram <u>adhered to</u> his principles.
> The gum <u>adhered to</u> his shoe.

to be afraid **of** (to be fearful of)

> Jason was <u>afraid of</u> owls.

to agree **on** [a plan, terms]

> They <u>agreed on</u> a publicity campaign.

to agree **to** [consent to another's idea]

> Oscar <u>agreed to</u> come home early.

to agree **with** (to be in concord)

> The verb must <u>agree with</u> the noun.
> Jasmine <u>agreed with</u> Ada.

to be angry **about** or at [a thing or a person]

> Ravinder was <u>angry about</u> the article.
> He was also <u>angry at</u> the person who wrote it.

to be angry **with** [a person]

> Penelope was <u>angry with</u> Percival.

to apply **for** [a position, a job]

> Ted <u>applied for</u> a job as a programmer.

to apply **to** an institution

> Raven <u>applied to</u> four universities.

to approve (to authorize)

> The faculty <u>approved the change</u> in the calendar.

to approve **of** (to think or speak favourably of)

> The class <u>approved of</u> the change in the exam's date.

to argue **about** [an issue]

> They frequently <u>argued about</u> politics.

to argue **with** [a person]

Jim argues a lot with David about buses.

to ask for something **for** someone

Please call and ask for Jonathan.

to ask **about** something (to inquire)

Benji asked about the length of the report.

to be aware **of** [someone/thing]

Were you aware of the late penalty?

to be **on** the phone

I can never get on the phone at work because my supervisor never gets off.

to get **off** the phone

Please get off the phone before dad gets home.

to blame someone/thing **for** something

The heavy rain was blamed for the lack of attendance.

to care **about** (to be concerned about or to be fond of)

Mary cared a lot about her parents.

to care **for** (to look after)

He went to the apartment to care for the plants.

to catch up **with** (to overtake someone/thing)

Sam caught up with Joan before she reached the store.

to catch up **on** (to finally do what should have been done before)

Anne caught up on her homework during Reading Break.

to catch on **to** [verb] (to understand)

> Fred finally <u>caught on</u> to the joke.

to compare **to**/to compare **with**

> <u>Compared to</u> last night's meal, this is really great!
>
> <u>Compared with</u> Toronto drivers, Peterborough drivers are real slowpokes.

to complain **about** [an issue]

> June <u>complained about</u> the dog's barking.

to complain **to** [a person]

> June <u>complained to</u> the woman next door.

to comply **with** (to conform to)

> They <u>complied with</u> the dorm's rules.

to conform **to** (to comply with or adapt to)

> The report <u>conformed to</u> the guidelines.

to be consistent **with**

> This grade is <u>consistent with</u> Gail's other marks.

to contrast **with**

> The outcome <u>contrasted with</u> their expectations.

Note that the above "contrast" is a verb. Another use of contrast is the following:

in contrast **to** (a noun, object of preposition "in")

> The outcome was <u>in contrast to</u> their expectations.

to cope **with** (deal with successfully)

> Jonathan <u>coped very well with</u> the new operating system.

to correspond **with** [a person] (to communicate in writing)

> Carolyn corresponds with many people.

to correspond **with** (to be in agreement)

> This number corresponds with the previous research.

to correspond **to** (to be in agreement)

> This number corresponds to that in the previous research.

to deal **with** (to concern)

> The plan deals with the amalgamation.

to deal **with** (to discuss, to handle)

> Next year, we have to deal with the amalgamation.

to depend **on** (rely on)

> Claire depends on Crawford for technical assistance.

to differ **about** (disagree about something)

> Joy and Gay differed about whether to continue wearing matching outfits.

to differ **from** [a thing]

> Your painting differs from your sketch in mood.

to differ **from** (be different)

> Koji differed from his big brother.

to differ **with** (disagree with someone)

> Koji differed with his little sister.

to disagree **with** [someone]

> Koji disagreed with his little sister.

to disagree **on** [a plan, an issue]

> They <u>disagreed on</u> the benefits of tofu.

to divide **among** (to distribute to more than two people)

> They <u>divided</u> the cookies <u>among</u> the class.

to divide **between** (to distribute to two people)

> They <u>divided</u> the cookies <u>between</u> the teacher and the principal.

to engage **in** [an activity]

> Michael <u>engaged in</u> stamp collecting.

to be engaged **to** [a person]

> Agnes is <u>engaged to</u> Algernon.

to be grateful **to** [a person]

> Hing was <u>grateful to</u> his uncle.

to experiment **on** (See page 368)

> Louis never <u>experimented on</u> lab animals.

to experiment **with** (See page 368)

> Lori always <u>experimented with</u> spices.

to be grateful **for** [a thing]

> Marcus was <u>grateful for</u> the advice.

to be impatient **about** [something]

> Patrick was <u>impatient about</u> the delay.

to be impatient **with** [someone]

> He was <u>impatient with</u> the manager.

to be **in** a hurry (to be rushed)

James is always in a hurry at the end of term.

to hurry **up** (to act more quickly)

You'd better hurry up, or the soup will be cold.

to have an impact **on**

The speech had an impact on Mr. Lee.

to be inferior **to**

This blue chair is definitely inferior to the red one.

to be interested **in**

Bryan was interested in anthropology.

to interfere **with**

The tunnel interfered with the car's radio reception.

to look down **on** (to scorn)

He looked down on people with pen-holders.

to look up **to** (to respect)

Nicole looked up to her grandma.

to make up **for** (to compensate)

The flowers made up for the rain.

to make up **with** (to reconcile)

Penelope made up with Percival.

to object **to**

He will object to the ticket.

to proceed **with** [a plan, an action]

> We can <u>proceed with</u> the meeting.

to proceed **to** (to begin)

> She <u>proceeded to</u> laugh out loud.

to protect **against**

> The wax <u>protects against</u> water damage.

to protest **against**

> They will <u>protest against</u> the tax increase.

to put up **with** (to tolerate)

> They can no longer <u>put up with</u> the noise.

to reason **with** (to employ logic to convince)

> You can't <u>reason with</u> that guy.

to rely **on** (depend)

> We all <u>rely on</u> our friends.

to make a remark [noun] **about** (to comment about)

> Ling <u>made a remark about</u> the beautiful colours of the sunrise.

to remark [verb] **on** (to comment on)

> Jay <u>remarked on</u> the colour of the trees.

to reply **to**

> I am <u>replying to</u> your letter of application.

to be responsible **for** [a thing]

> Kay is <u>responsible for</u> doing the graphics.

to be responsible **to** [a superior]

He is <u>responsible to</u> the deputy minister.

to have respect **for**

Robin has a great deal of <u>respect for</u> his landlady's artistic ability.

to search **for** (to look for someone/thing, see page 382)

Susan was <u>searching for</u> a working pen.

to search **through** (to look through things: papers, houses, boxes, see page 382)

You'd better <u>search through</u> your suitcases.

to be sensitive **to**

Marc's eyes are <u>sensitive to</u> light.

to be superior **to**

This vintage is <u>superior to</u> that one.

to be surrounded **by** [people]

The Prime Minister was <u>surrounded by</u> the media.

to be surrounded **with** [things]

Erin <u>surrounded</u> the piece of cake <u>with</u> whipped cream.

to take advantage **of** (to make use of an opportunity or to exploit a weakness)

Jeremy took <u>advantage of</u> the sale price on the car.

The con-artist took <u>advantage of</u> Jenny's kind nature.

to take care **of** (to take responsibility for)

Joe said he would <u>take care of</u> the tip.

to talk **to** [a group]

Isabelle <u>talked to</u> the committee.

to talk **with** [a person]

> Ken had a <u>talk with</u> Bill's brother.

to be thankful **for** someone/thing

> Bob was <u>thankful for</u> the good advice.
> They were <u>thankful for</u> responsible, hard-working parents.

to wait **at** [a place]

> <u>Wait</u> for me <u>at</u> the Student Union building!

to wait **for** someone/thing

> Joy <u>waited for</u> the bus.

to work **on**

> Dana <u>worked on</u> the year-end report.

to worry **about**

> Don't <u>worry about</u> the leak until tomorrow.

The following phrases concern work and school. Although not all of these commonly-used phrases contain prepositional phrases, you will note that most of them do.

## Phrases Relating to the Workplace

to be according **to** (consistent with)
to be accountable **for** [actions/things]
to be accountable **to** [a superior]
to agree **on** [a plan, terms]
to agree **to** (consent to another's idea)
to agree **with** (to be in accord)
to apply **for** [a position, a job]
to be **on** the phone/to get **off** the phone
to catch up **on** (to finally do what should have been done before)
to **come in useful**, to **come in handy**
to complain **about** [an issue]
to complain **to** [a person]
to comply **with** (to conform to)
to cope **with** (to deal with successfully)

to correspond **with** [a person]

to correspond **with** (to be in agreement)

to correspond **to** (to be in agreement)

to deal **with** (to concern)

to deal **with** (to discuss, to handle)

to have an impact **on**

to look forward to **doing** something

to proceed **with** [a plan, an action]

to proceed **to** (to begin)

to rely **on**

to reply **to**

to be responsible **for** [a task]

to be responsible **to** [a superior]

to take advantage **of** (to make use of an opportunity or to exploit a weakness)

to take care **of** (to take responsibility for)

to talk **with** [a person]

to talk **to** [a group]

to work **on**

## Phrases Relating to School

to apply **for** a student loan/scholarship

to apply **to** a college, university

to arrive **at** the campus **of** Seneca College

to attend UBC, or to attend **the** University of British Columbia

to be late **for** class

to borrow/get a book **from** the library

to get a book **out of** the library

to **do** an assignment, an essay, a lab, a paper

to drop a course

to drop **out** of school/college/university

to enter Carleton University, or to enter **the** University of Ottawa

to get/receive a good/bad mark

to get/receive a degree

to go **to** kindergarten/school/college/graduate school

to go to UVic, or to go to **the** University of Victoria

to graduate **from** school/college/university

to have office hours

to live **in** or **on** residence

to live **on**-campus/**off**-campus

to register **for** a class

to be registered **in** a class

residence = housing

residents = people living in housing
to take a course
to write a makeup exam
to write a makeup
to write a paper

## Prepositions With Units of Time

When you do something that is governed by prepositions relating to time, such as "in," "at," and "on," you need to practise the phrases until they begin to sound "right."

If you want rules to help you learn these idiomatic phrases, you can remember the following:

**At** is mainly used for

- specific points of time: **at** ten o'clock, **at** midnight, **at** noon.
- holidays: **at** Thanksgiving, **at** Easter.
- phrases: **at** night, **at** that time, **at** that point in time.

**On** is mainly used for

- days: **on** Wednesday, **on** Friday, **on** Saturday night.
- dates: **on** July 1st, **on** the 15th of every month.
- specific times: **on** a sunny evening, **on** the first Thursday of the month.
- habitual actions: I have night classes [**on**] Thursdays.

**In** is used mainly for

- a more extended period of time: **in** the evening, **in** the late afternoon, **in** the 18th century, in May.

**During** is also used when the action occurs over a period of time

- **during** the early 1800s, during the French Revolution, **during** Reading Week, **during** the 20th century.

**For** is used to indicate duration of an action.

- Helenè has been working **for** twelve hours.
- Polly has lived here **for** 17 years.

**Since** is used with a definite time in the past.

*   Helenè has been working **since** six o'clock.

*   Polly has lived here **since** 1983.

**Note** the following particularly illogical idiom:

*   to do something **in** the evening, but to do something **at** night

Note, that if you use the word "beginning" or "end" in a prepositional phrase and if there is a prepositional phrase following it, the preposition preceding "beginning" or "end" should be "at." If there is not a prepositional phrase, then use "in."
Contrast these sentences:

<u>At the beginning of</u> the programme, Mischa felt intimidated, but he gained confidence quickly.

In the beginning, he felt unsure.

<u>At the end of</u> the twentieth century, Canada's population was more diverse than it was in mid-century.

In the end, we decided to leave the garden the way it was.

## Exercise 1: Prepositions With Units of Time and Place

Use the most appropriate prepositions to fill in the blanks. Look at this example: Tim has a class _____*at*_____ eight o'clock _____*at*_____ night.

1.  Barbara has three classes _____ Friday _____ Malaspina College.

2.  She has the first class _____ 8:30 _____ the morning and the last one _____ 3:00 _____ the afternoon.

3.  _____ Thanksgiving, she will enjoy the extra day off.

4.  Besides, her birthday is _____ the day before Thanksgiving.

5.  Although she seldom goes out _____ night, Barbara and Steve plan to go out _____ that evening,

6.  _____ her last class _____ Friday afternoon, she day-dreamed about what they would do.

7.  If they caught the 6:00 ferry, they would arrive _____ Vancouver _____ 7:40.

8.  She expected that they would arrive _____ downtown _____ 8:30.

9. Their favourite restaurant is located _____ the corner _____ Broadway and Pine, but after a long day _____ school, she did not think that she would want to eat.

10. If their friends pick them up _____ the bus depot, she will be happy just to go _____ home for some tea.

## Prepositions with Verbs Relating to Speech or Thought

to think, talk, speak, or argue
    "Think," "talk," "speak," and "argue" are followed by the preposition "about."

    to think **about** something

    to talk **about** something

    to speak **about** something

    to argue **about** something

    They <u>thought about</u> leaving early, but instead they <u>talked about</u> baseball, <u>spoke about</u> their favourite players, and <u>argued about</u> the players' salaries.

to bring up, discuss or mention
    Note that "discuss" and "mention" are very similar to "talk" and "speak." Nonetheless, "discuss" and "mention" are **not** followed by "about." Nor is "bring up," which means to introduce a subject.

    ✗ to discuss about something

    ✗ to bring up about something

    They <u>discussed</u> baseball, hockey, and football and mentioned their favourite players.

to comment or remark [verb]
    You comment or remark **on** something.

    Renata remarked on the beautiful tablecloth and dishes, and Richard <u>commented on</u> the great food.

to make a comment or remark about
    In this pattern, comment and remark are nouns: the use of the article shows that "comment" and "remark" are countable nouns.

Renata <u>made a remark about</u> the beautiful tablecloth and dishes, and Richard made <u>a comment about</u> the great food.

## Exercise 2: Prepositions With Thinking and Speaking

Use the most appropriate prepositions to fill in the blanks. Look at this example: Tara and James discussed ____*on*____ the new lab procedure and remarked _____ the increased safety.

1.  Barbara likes to talk _____ what special dishes they will eat on her birthday.

2.  Steve's birthday is on October 13, so he likes to discuss _____ his favourite dishes too, and he loves to bring up _____ how much he would like a barbecue.

3.  Actually, you shouldn't mention _____ the word barbecue in front of Steve.

4.  Barbara learned a long time ago not to talk _____ barbecues.

5.  When someone mentions _____ a barbecue, Steve always has to say _____ how he can never have a barbecue on his birthday because it is in October.

6.  Barbara has talked _____ the problem with other friends, and they all think _____ that it is possible to have a barbecue in October.

7.  Barbara always says, and the other friends agree, _____ that the barbecue should be a surprise.

8.  When she mentioned _____ the idea of a barbecue to Steve's mother, Mrs. Bérubé said she'd thought _____ this idea too.

9.  Mrs. Bérubé and Barbara talked _____ the plan on the phone.

10. They both think _____ that beach umbrellas can work very well as rain umbrellas.

## Prepositions Related to Going, Getting, and Being Places

### Transportation

> **to take** a plane, train, bus, ferry, car
>
> to ride **in** a plane
>
> to ride **on** a train
>
> to ride **on** a bus

to ride **on** a ferry

to ride **in** a car

to get **on** a plane

to get **on** a train

to get **on** a bus

to get **on** a ferry

to get **in/into** a car

to get **off** a bus, plane, train, ferry, to get **out of** a car

How did you get there? <u>By</u> car/bus/ferry/train/plane.

## Arrival

to go **to** a city, country, continent

to arrive **in** a city, country, continent

to arrive **at** a airport, bus depot, train station, Eaton's, a movie

✗ to go to downtown          ✗ to arrive at downtown

✓ to go downtown             ✓ to arrive downtown

Where are you staying? <u>In</u> a tent/motel/hotel/apartment/small village.

Something **is located** downtown/at Yates and Douglas/in Victoria.

Never use "locates" unless it means "finds."

He *locates* missing jewellery using a metal detector.

She *locates* books for her friends.

## Departure

to leave/depart **from** a city, country, continent

to depart/leave **from** a airport, bus depot, train station

## Living somewhere

to live **in** a town, city, country, or specific continent

to live **on** an island containing the word "island" or "isle"

**on** the Isle of Wight, **on** Ellesmere Island, **on** Prince Edward Island to live **in** an island that does not contain the word "island"

**in** Newfoundland, **in** Madagascar

to live **on** the coast or **on** the prairies

to live **in** the Maritimes or **in** the mountains

to live **in** a house, in an apartment, or **in** a tent

## Exercise 3: Going to and Getting Places

Write the appropriate preposition in the blanks. Look at this example:
Steve arrived ___*in*___ Toronto ___*at*___ May 24.

1. Earlier in the evening before going _____ the airport, Ling had had dinner with her family and her two best friends.

2. The restaurant was _____ downtown.

3. She and her parents and two brothers took a cab _____ the airport.

4. Ling arrived _____ Kai Tek airport at 10:30 at night.

5. She had never been _____ a plane before, although she had been _____ the subway when she was only five days old.

6. Ling had also been _____ a train _____ China and a ferry to Macao.

7. _____ the airport, Ling saw a friend, Yan, that she hadn't seen since school got out on July 15.

8. Yan was going to go _____ school _____ Vancouver.

9. Ling was going to go _____ UVic _____ Victoria _____ Vancouver Island.

10. Like Ling, Yan had never been _____ Canada before.

## Exercise 4: Going To and Getting Places

Write the appropriate preposition in the blanks. Look at this example:
Virgil arrived ___*in*___ Toronto ___*at*___ the bus depot where we picked him up.

1. Neither Ling nor Yan knew what to expect _____ Canada, but they both hoped to see snow.

2. They knew that you could ski near Vancouver, but they weren't sure if there was snow _____ Vancouver in late August.

3. After they arrived _____ British Columbia _____ the Vancouver International Airport, Ling's journey hadn't ended.

4. Nonetheless, she felt relieved not to be _____ the plane any more.

5. Her friend Teresa met her _____ the airport, and she helped her to get her luggage _____ the car.

6. When Ling arrived _____ the car, she saw some of her fellow passengers waiting with all their baggage to get _____ a bus.

7. Teresa drove Ling _____ the ferry.

8. Ling got _____ the ferry by following many people down a long ramp.

9. When she arrived _____ Sidney _____ Vancouver Island, her friend Elaine picked her up.

10. Although she was glad to be _____ Canada, Ling was quiet as they drove _____ downtown through such strange, tree-lined streets.

# Useful Patterns

## Index to Useful Patterns

The following patterns are alphabetically arranged to make them easy to find. They represent the most common idiomatic errors that we have seen when reading papers of non-native speakers of English. We would like non-native English speakers to browse in this section every day, focusing on the structures that seem "foreign" or useful. Even five minutes a day would be enough to improve your use of idiom dramatically.

allow, force, cause, and compel

Allow, force, cause, and compel are followed by full infinitives. Note that these words are very similar to "let " and "make," which are followed by bare infinitives. Clearly, "allow" means the same as "let" while "force," "cause," and "compel" mean the same as "make."

Nonetheless, *allow, force, cause,* and *compel* are followed by full infinitives.

Sarah allowed Joe <u>to finish</u> the wine.

She forced him <u>to put</u> the pretty bottle in the recycling.

He was compelled <u>to hide</u> the bottle in the garage.

another
>   This word must be followed by a singular word, and you never use "the" before it.

>   I want <u>another pen</u> like the one I had last semester.

other
>   This word is followed by a plural word.

>   The <u>other pens</u> I have had always made blotches.

to appreciate [verb]
>   You appreciate (value) something.

>   Sean <u>appreciates</u> fine cooking.

>   I <u>appreciate</u> your help.

appreciative [adjective]
>   This adjective follows a linking verb.

>   Nicolas <u>was appreciative</u> of the pianist's skill.

appreciate it if...
>   To be thankful if something should happen.

>   I would <u>appreciate it if</u> you could finish this page.

attention [noun]
>   You pay attention **to** something or someone.

>   He <u>paid a lot of attention</u> to his work.

to give someone/something your full attention

>   Tim <u>gave the speaker his full attention</u>.

to get/gain attention

>   Yasu <u>tried to get the driver's attention</u>.

because/because **of**
>   "Because" means "since" or "for the reason that." (However, don't ever use "for the reason that." It is awkward and wordy!)

>   <u>Because</u> the bus was early, Norman missed it.

"Because of" means "as a result of" or "on account of."

Jean and James went to the matinee <u>because of</u> the inexpensive ticket price.

to blame, emphasize, and stress
The *verbs* "blame," "stress," and "emphasize" appear in a particular pattern that contrasts with the pattern of the *nouns* "blame," "emphasis," and "stress."

When the **nouns** are used, they are preceded by transitive verbs like "put," "lay," or "place" and followed by the preposition "**on**."

| | | |
|---|---|---|
| | (lay blame) | |
| to | (place emphasis) | **on** something/someone |
| | (put stress) | |

When the **verbs** are used, you follow them immediately with their objects.

| | | |
|---|---|---|
| | (blame) | |
| to | (emphasize) | something |
| | (stress) | |

Yuko <u>blamed</u> <u>the</u> <u>weather</u> for the poor turnout at the picnic. She emphasized that <u>having a picnic in December</u> was not entirely reasonable.

to blame someone for doing something

Charles <u>blamed the cook</u> for his broken tooth.

to bring up (to mention)

Hideki <u>brought up</u> the possibility of taking the train instead of a bus.

to bring up (to regurgitate, throw up)

The baby suddenly <u>brought up</u> all the strained peaches and spinach.

"by" at the beginning of sentences
Make sure that if you start a sentence with "**by**," you do not have two subjects. (See pages 178–180.)

By studying over Reading Break, it will make the rest of the

subject

subject

semester easier.

By studying over Reading Break, you will have an easier time during
the rest of the semester.   subject

**to call on/upon** (to visit someone in person)

I will call on you at the office on Tuesday.

**to call up** (to reach someone by telephone)

Harry called Tai up but got the answering  machine.

Tai called up Harry the next day.

**to care for** (to look after)

He went to the apartment to care for the plants.

**to care about** (to be concerned about or to be fond of)

Mary cared a lot about her parents.

Sarah cared a great deal about Joe.

Oswald cared about his grade point average.

Algernon cared about wearing coordinated clothes.

**to take care of** (to be responsible for)

Jacques said he would take care of the tip/the windows/the phone
bill.

Grandma asked me to take care of the salad dressing/ the kids/the
carburetor.

**to take care that** [imperative] (to be alert, to be careful)

Take care that you proofread carefully.

**catch** [noun] (a drawback, something undesirable)

They said I had won a car, but I knew there was a catch to it: I had
to go to Russia to pick it up.

to catch up **with** [verb] (to overtake someone)

Sam caught up to Joe before he reached the store.

to catch up **on** [verb] [to finally do what should have been done before]

Anne caught up on her homework during Reading Week.

to catch on **to** [verb] (to understand)

Fred finally caught on to the joke.

to catch **on** [verb] (to become popular)

Thai peppers caught on with many Canadian cooks in the 1980's.

to cause or dare
"Cause" and "dare" are followed by infinitives.

He dared her to jump, and Henrietta caused him to regret his words.

to come in useful or to come in handy (to be useful)

This wrench will come in useful and the drill will come in handy, too.

to compare (to find similarities)

1. It is difficult to compare Pepsi and Sprite.
2. When comparing cities, you must consider size.
3. Compared to a dog, a cat is more independent.

Note that in sentence two, after the participial phrase, you must have a subject that is doing the action. If you write "When comparing cities, Montreal is much quieter than New York City," you have created an error called a dangling modifier as Montreal, a city, is incapable of the action of comparing.

In sentence three, the subject has to be what is being compared. Writing "Compared to a dog, you will enjoy a cat," would be a big error.

## Exercise 5: Using Compared and Comparing
In the following sentences, put the correct form of compare in the blanks.

1. _____ to Vancouver, Edmonton gets little rain.

2. _____ Vancouver and Edmonton, statistics tell us that the latter gets less rain.

3. _____ to dogs, cats are more independent.

4. Josie spent time _____ the two universities.

5. _____ the two universities was interesting.

6. _____ to ice cream, cheesecake is an expensive dessert.

7. I think that _____ to a Cavalier, a Sprite is much easier to park for a beginner.

8. After _____ the two stores, the manager decided to keep the smaller one open.

9. Most people spend little time on English _____ to what they spend on Computer Science.

10. Why is it that _____ to writing letters, sending e-mail seems to provide little challenge?

**Activity 1: Write pairs of sentences in whIch each first sentence uses "comparing" and each second sentence uses "compared."**

Compare two movies.

1. _____

2. _____

Compare you and your best friend.

1. _____

2. _____

Compare two courses.

1. _____

2. _____

Compare spring and fall.

1. _____

2. _____

Compare Macs and IBMs.

1. _____

2. _____

*continued*

**Activity 1: Write pairs of sentences in which
each first sentence uses "comparing" and each
second sentence uses "compared." (continued)**

Compare Wendy's and Macdonald's.

1. _____

2. _____

Compare two tourists.

1. _____

2. _____

Compare your favourite food and your least favourite food.

1. _____

2. _____

to be concerned **about** (to be disturbed or worried about something)

Sarah was <u>concerned about</u> driving at night.

Joe is <u>concerned about</u> taking a taxi.

to concern oneself **with** (something to be interested or involved in something)

Sarah <u>concerns herself with</u> her Tai Chi club.

Joe <u>concerns himself with</u> his garden.

## Exercise 6: Using *Concern*

Using a word or phrase that incorporates a form of the word "concern," fill in the following blanks.

1.  The new group's focus _____ neighbourhood safety.

2.  Meeting for the second time, the group _____ about a new subject after the minutes of the last meeting had been read.

3.  Percival Peterson had taken the minutes at the last meeting, and many members _____ about the way that they were written.

4.  Under "New Business," the first item on the Agenda _____ the minutes.

5.  On the one hand, Mr. Lindros _____ that, for an hour's meeting, there were six pages of minutes.

6. On the other hand, Mrs. Oglethorpe _____ that there were thirty exclamation marks.

7. In addition, Judy Chang and Raymond Pelletier _____ that using words like "stupid" and "ridiculous" to describe suggestions from the members of the group was unprofessional.

8. Percival stated that he had _____ about accurately representing what had gone on at the meeting.

9. Erin Irish showed the group a newspaper item that _____ how to write clear, concise minutes.

10. Gratefully, the group asked Ms. Irish to read the information that she had found _____ how to record minutes properly.

**to contact [verb] someone but to make contact [noun] with someone**

It took David ages <u>to make contact with</u> Simon by letter, but Evelyn <u>contacted</u> him immediately by e-mail.

**despite/in spite of [preposition]**

Remember to distinguish between "despite" and "in spite of," which mean exactly the same thing. ("In spite" must always be followed by "of.") "Despite" is slightly more formal in tone.

✓ in spite **of** something:

They went out in spite <u>of</u> the snow.

✗ despite ~~of~~ something:

They went out despite ~~of~~ the snow.

**to do something for or to**

To do something **for** someone or something is a positive thing.

What Sam made <u>for</u> Yuki's desk was very efficient.

To do something **to** someone or something is a negative thing:

What the wind did <u>to</u> the flowers and shrubs was terrible.

**to be done by hand (to do something without the aid of machines/technology)**

The computer wasn't working. I had to write the letter <u>by</u> hand.

even, an extreme case

I like all animals, <u>even</u> goats.

He passed all his courses, <u>even</u> Chemistry.

even though and although [subordinate conjunctions]

These words mean the same thing: "in spite of the fact that" or "even if." Just as you will rarely write a sentence with a comma immediately after "because," you will very seldom have a sentence with a comma immediately after one of these words. You would, in fact, need two commas because otherwise you would break the rule that says you must not separate subject and verb by just one comma. Look at the following examples.

- ✗ Although, I knew that it would rain.
- ✓ Although, despite my misgivings, I took the old road through the forest, I arrived safely.

"Even though" and "although" are subordinate conjunctions, not conjunctive adverbs like "however," "nonetheless," and "nevertheless."

<u>Even though</u> Ian enjoyed the movie, he liked the book better.

<u>Although</u> Ian enjoyed the movie, he liked the book better.

In contrast, conjunctive adverbs can begin a sentence and have a comma immediately following them.

<u>However</u>, Ian took Murray to the movie.

<u>Nonetheless</u>, Murray refused to read the book.

to experiment **with/on** something:

Remember to distinguish between "experimenting **with**" and "experimenting **on**."

experimenting **with** (to dabble in, to investigate)

experimenting **on** (something has a more scientific—and sometimes sinister—feeling, as though you plan to prove something)

If you experiment <u>with</u> drugs, you will probably get in trouble with the law.

If you experiment <u>on</u> drugs, you probably work in a lab.

Experiments done <u>on</u> human subjects are carefully regulated by law.

to feel like it/feel like doing (to have the desire to do something)

> Kimiko <u>felt like going</u> to a movie, but her friends didn't <u>feel like it</u>. They stayed home and watched a video.

find/find out (to discover or recover something)

> I <u>found</u> that a three-hour class was OK.

> You can <u>find</u> lots of synonyms in a thesaurus, but you must be careful about the words' connotations.

> To "find out" means to discover, learn or confirm the truth of something. It is often followed by "about" when it means to learn about something.

> Kendrick wanted to <u>find out about</u> his schedule. When he went to the registrar's office, he <u>found out that</u> his schedule would be quite different from last term's.

> To "find out" can also mean to solve something.

> Darren <u>found out</u> how to open the trunk without the key.

## Exercise 7: Using *Find/Find Out*

Fill in the blanks in the following sentences with either "find" or "find out."

1. We've looked all over, but we can't _____ the umbrella.

2. Were you able to _____ whether Monday's class is cancelled?

3. By watching the Knowledge Network, you can _____ information about nature and history.

4. If you want to _____ an address, try looking in the phone book.

5. The little girl became frustrated because she couldn't _____ how to start up her mother's computer.

to get **into/out of** bed

> Once Harry finally <u>got into bed</u>, he knew that he wouldn't get out of bed until the noon whistle blew.

to give **in**/to give **up**

Distinguish between these two phrases.

To "give up" means to stop doing something.

Yoshi tried to make the part fit, but he had <u>to give up</u>.

To "give up" can also mean to admit defeat or to admit that you can't guess an answer.

"What's the square root of 389,728?"

"<u>I give up</u>."

to "give **in**" (to yield)

After we argued all night, I <u>gave in</u>: we're going to the West Edmonton Mall.

to go downstairs/upstairs or to be downstairs/upstairs

Please <u>go downstairs</u> and see if the paper is there.

to hang **on**/to hang **up**/to hang **up on** [verbs]

To "hang **on**" means to wait.

<u>Hang on</u> a minute, and I'll find the folder.

To "hang **up**" means, as a verb, to terminate a phone call.

Sandra was so annoyed at his tone that she <u>hung up</u>.

To "hang up **on**" means to terminate a phone call abruptly, rudely. "Hang up **on**" is always followed by a person.

Sylvie was so angry that she <u>hung up on</u> Algernon.

hang-up [noun] (to have a definite preoccupation with something)

Percival <u>has a hang-up</u> about food in his car.

to be **in** a hurry (to act with haste, quickly)

Rebekkah was <u>in a hurry</u> to get to the concert.

to hurry **up** (move quickly)

Hurry up! The bus is coming around the corner!

to impress [verb] someone *but* to make an impression [noun] **on** someone

Although the book didn't impress Helen, it made a big impression on the critics.

in or into

"In" is usually used with a verb that describes a stationary situation.

We sat in the car by the pond for twenty minutes waiting for Jeffrey.

"Into" is usually used with a verb that describes movement.

Jeffrey finally got into the car carrying a large box of turtles.

**in** other words

"In other words" is always in the plural, even if what follows is one word.

When I asked if I could borrow the car, Dave said, "You stayed out until two the last time you borrowed it, you left it full of junk, and you didn't fill the gas tank. In other words, no!"

We cannot hand the essay in tomorrow. In other words, we will have to miss lunch today.

to involve or immerse or engage

In one pattern, "involve" and "immerse" are followed by "in" plus a gerund. Someone is **involved** or **immersed** or **engaged in doing** something. "Immersed," probably not a word you will use often, means "heavily involved or absorbed."

Ina is immersed in making kites. She and Jaime are involved in creating a new kiting programme.

In a second pattern, someone is simply **involved** or **immersed in** something.

Michelle is involved in Guides. Asher is immersed in his book.

In a third pattern, **"involve"** or **"immerse"** are followed by **reflexive pronouns** plus **"in."**

Barbara involved <u>herself in</u> many volunteer activities.

## Exercise 8: Using *Involve, Immerse, Interest, Engage,* or *Concern*

Fill in the blanks with the most appropriate form of the word in the brackets.

1. Simon experiments _____ (involve) different foods.

2. Before they came to the University of Guelph, Simon was always _____ (involve) cooking.

3. Besides, he liked to do things _____ (involve) other people.

4. Now, Maria _____ (concern) herself with the shopping.

5. Maria is _____ (involve) in making the food lists and in shopping, but she lets Simon and their friends _____ (concern) themselves with the cleaning up.

6. Simon often _____ (immerse) himself in recipe books.

7. Maria frequently _____ (engage) in speculation about what kind of food Simon will choose: Chinese, French, Italian, or Mexican.

8. Simon always _____ (concern) himself about nutritional content.

9. Choosing a recipe means that Simon is _____ (involve) in an almost scientific analysis of the recipes.

10. Maria _____ (interest) herself more in how the food will taste.

to keep (stay) away **from**
> These phrases mean the same thing.

> His mother told Tom to <u>keep away from</u> hard rock and to stay away from soft drugs.

lack
> Be sure to determine whether "lack" in your sentence is a verb or a noun. Only if it is a noun do you use "lack **of**."

> I <u>lack</u> (verb) skill in hockey.

> This dish <u>lacks</u> (verb) salt.

My brother has a <u>lack</u> (noun) of skill in baseball.

<u>Lacking</u> salt, the dish tasted bland.

Note that "lacking salt," the participial phrase above, must be followed by a subject that lacks salt, or the phrase dangles.

**to let or to make**
"Let" and "make" are followed by bare infinitives.

(to let)

someone do something, e.g., to **make** a giraffe run

(to make)

Sarah <u>let</u> Joe <u>finish</u> the wine.

She <u>made</u> him <u>put</u> the pretty bottle in the recycling.

**to live on your own/to live by yourself**
These phrases mean the same thing; however, note the difference in prepositions.

Wing had looked forward to living <u>on</u> her own, but living <u>by</u> herself was a mixed blessing.

**look**
This word is used in two common phrases that mean the same thing. Problems arise when half of one phrase is combined with half of the other.

✓ I wonder <u>what he looks like</u> as a blonde.

✓ I wonder <u>how he looks</u> as a blonde.

The tendency is to write "I don't know how he looks like." This is incorrect.

**to look forward to**
This phrase is followed by a gerund.

Kim <u>looks forward to</u> getting Simone's letters.

**to look down on**
To have a bad opinion of.

Percival <u>looks down on</u> people who didn't finish college.

## Words that Denote Units of Distance, Money, Weight, or Time

A major group of words falls into this category. When a unit of distance, money, weight, or time is used as a modifier, you don't use an "s."

He walked six miles.

*but*

He had a six-mile walk.

Wayne spent twenty dollars for the ticket.

*but*

Wayne bought a twenty-dollar ticket.

The cat weighed twenty pounds.

*but*

It was a twenty-pound cat.

She was ten years old.

*but*

She was a ten-year-old girl.

Sean paid fifty dollars for a ticket.

*but*

Sean bought a fifty-dollar ticket.

## Words that Appear to be Plural

To form the plural, most nouns in English add "s." However, when a noun is used as an adjective in English, it does not add "s," even if it seems to be plural.

Two cars were involved in an accident on the Trans-Canada Highway outside Kenora this morning.

There was a two-car accident on the Trans-Canada Highway outside Kenora this morning.

Many people feel we must have stricter gun controls in Canada.

Some people feel we must have stricter gun control laws in Canada.

## Exercise 9: "S" Nouns as Modifiers

Fill in the blanks with the appropriate word.

1. Pong bought a new _____ (jeans or jean) jacket.

2. That dog weighs 150 _____ (pounds or pound).

3. Kisha borrowed my pair of _____ (scissors or scissor).

4. Under the proposed law, new _____ (drivers or driver) would be subject to slightly different regulations from old drivers.

5. Do you have a _____ (pants or pant) suit to wear on the bus?

6. Brian had blue striped _____ (pyjamas or pyjama), but Bryan had a red _____ (pyjamas or pyjama) top and a green _____ (pyjamas or pyjama) bottom.

7. Nancy bought a six _____ (ounces or ounce) cup of coffee.

8. Under the proposed law, new _____ (drivers or driver) regulations would undergo some changes.

9. The _____ (scissors or scissor) cut on his index finger was infected.

10. Five _____ (tractors or tractor) were in a _____ (tractors or tractor) rodeo.

## Exercise 10: "S" Nouns as Modifiers

Fill in the blanks with the appropriate word.

1. Riders of _____ (motorcycles or motorcycle) are often people who enjoy being outdoors.

2. Please send me 24 six _____ (dollars or dollar) passes.

3. (Sports, sport) _____ enthusiasts are often people who enjoy being outdoors.

4. He likes to go 100 _____ (kilometres or kilometre) an hour.

5. Wool _____ (trousers or trouser) are itchy.

6. Kitty had ten pairs of _____ (socks or sock) and five pairs of _____ [tights or tight] in her _____ (socks or sock) drawer.

7. Barney gave the five _____ (years- or year-) old girl the two _____ (pounds or pound) of cherries.

8. I love to study _____ (economics or economic) theory.

9. Last night, there was a _____ (cats or cat) fight right outside my window.

10. Please put this plate in the _____ (plates or plate) rack in the dining room.

*On*

    to do something **off and on** (sporadically)

    to do something **on and on** (at great length: tiresome)

    to have an **impact on** something (have an effect on)

    to **work on** something (to be continually working)

*One of, Each of, a Few of, Many of*

These words will always be followed by a plural. See Definite and Indefinite Groups on page 373.

    Example:

↑

each of my fingers

## Exercise 11: Using, *Many, Some, All, A Few*

In parentheses at the start of each question, you will find a pair of expressions. Select the appropriate expression to complete the sentence and write it in the blank provided.

1. (Many of the, Many) We have students from all over the world in my geography class. _____ students in the class have lived in the countries we are studying.

2. (Many of the, Many) _____ Canadians visit their doctors every time they feel a little headache.

3. (some of the, some) Until recently, Rebecca couldn't figure out what was causing her hands to itch. Finally she discovered that _____ dishwashing liquids give her eczema.

4. (a few of the, a few) The exam questions on the mid-term were taken from the textbook, but _____ questions on the most recent test were on material that we hadn't seen before.

5. (some of the, some) Glaciation varies at different lattitudes; therefore, _____ mountains have huge glaciers while others have only a light dusting of snow that disappears each summer.

6. (some of the, some) Although _____ mountains in the Rockies are more than twenty-five hundred metres high, the snow on their peaks disappears in summer.

7. (All of the, All) _____ Canadians have certain rights under the Charter.

8. (a few of the, a few) I don't think we will have enough seats for everyone. I wonder if we could rent _____ folding chairs.

9. (All of the, All) _____ times and locations will be listed beside the course names and numbers on the exam schedule.

10. (All of the, All) _____ other reindeer used to call Rudolf names.

---

We used to think that "one" and "one of the" fit into the above pattern, but we have come to the conclusion that, usually, they are interchangeable.

For example, look at the following sentences:

- The organizing committee for the Fall Fair announced that
  __one of the__ outstanding citizen(s) will be honoured at the annual banquet.

- The organizing committee for the Fall Fair announced that
  __one__ outstanding citizen will be honoured at the annual banquet.

- Few of the band members at Lambrick Park High School have time to participate in more than one band; however, __one of the__ boy(s) in the concert band also play(s) in the stage band.

- Few of the band members at Lambrick Park High School have time to participate in more than one band; however, __one__ boy in the concert band also play(s) in the stage band.

---

"Or" with Negative Verbs

When your verb is negative, use "or" to join the objects of the verbs.

✓ Agnes doesn't like cats <u>or</u> dogs.

✗ Agnes doesn't like cats and dogs.

✓ Elvira won't eat clams, scallops, <u>or</u> oysters.

✗ Elvira won't eat clams, scallops, and oysters.

## Present and Past Participles as Modifiers

When **present or past participles** (verbals ending in "ing" or "ed" acting as adjectives) **follow a linking verb**, they modify the subject of the sentence.

The present participle describes the person or thing *causing* an experience. In other words, the noun that it modifies *causes* something to happen.

> The paragraph was confusing.

In the above sentence, the present participle "confusing" modifies "paragraph." The noun "paragraph" is active: it is **causing** confusion.

The past participle describes how the person or thing **undergoing** the experience feels. It describes a subject that is passive rather than active. The subject is being acted upon by something or someone.

> The students were confused after reading the paragraph.

In the above example, the past participle "confused" modifies the subject "students." The students are not active: they are being confused by something, the paragraph.

> The movie [cause] was amusing, and Sarah and Joe were amused [result or effect].

> The dog was annoying [cause], and the cat was annoyed [result or effect].

## Exercise 12: Using Present and Past Participle Modifiers

Read the following story and then fill in the blanks in the sentences on the next page.

Paul and Danielle felt restless and unsatisfied. The television programmes that they were watching could not hold their interest, although some of the commercials were creative and amusing. Finally, the discontented couple decided to go to a movie.

They caught a bus. They felt happy because, although the bus was crowded, they found two empty seats. They sat beside someone who was tapping not quite in time with the music from his boom box. Danielle was irritated, but Paul has no sense of rhythm, and he liked the music. When they arrived at the theatre, he was still humming.

Later, Paul was again humming on the bus. This time, it was the movie's theme song, and soon he and Danielle began to discuss the movie. They agreed that it certainly was not monotonous or predictable. The plot was intricate and hard to follow. Because Danielle had slipped out for popcorn, for example, she did not know how the hero and heroine survived the crocodile attack in the poisoned whale tank. She was startled to find out that the hero's aftershave, not only neutralized the poison, but also killed the crocodiles. The incident was not very believable, but at least it was not as terrifying as the one when the heroine was lassoed by a giant spider and imprisoned in its scary, bone-lined underground cavern.

Although they were not bored by the movie, it was not very realistic, so Paul and Danielle found it unsatisfactory. They decided to rent a video camera and to have fun while making their own interesting movie.

Fill in the following blanks with the appropriate form of the participle.

1. (bored, boring) Danielle and Paul felt _____.

2. (bored, boring) The television programme was _____.

3. (interested, interesting) The commercials were _____.

4. (annoyed, annoying) Danielle was _____ by the boy with the boom box.

5. (annoyed, annoying) Although Danielle was _____, Paul did not find the music _____.

6. (excited, exciting) Paul and Danielle thought that the movie was _____.

7. (confused, confusing) They thought that the plot was _____.

8. (confused, confusing) Danielle was _____ about what happened in the whale tank.

9. (surprised, surprising) What happened in the whale tank was _____.

10. (convinced, convincing) The incident was not _____.

11. (frightened, frightening) Danielle was _____ by the giant spider.

12. (frightened, frightening) The spider's bone-lined cavern was also _____.

13. (unsatisfied, unsatisfying) Paul and Danielle thought that the movie was _____ because it was not believable.

14. (interested, interesting) Danielle and Paul were _____ in trying to make a home movie, so they decided to rent a video camera.

15. (rewarded, rewarding) Making a simple home movie was a
_____ experience as it taught Paul and Danielle a great
deal about the need for a coherent plot line.

**to put up with** to tolerate

How can you <u>put up with</u> Algernon's silly jokes?

**relationships**

**Family** is generally regarded as non-countable, so you would say
"My whole family—three brothers, two sisters, my parents and my
grandparents—**is** coming to visit me at mid-term."

As you would with other collective nouns that are regarded as acting
as a unit, if the family members act as individuals rather than as a group,
you will use a plural verb: "My family **are** going to vacation separately
this year."

**Parents** are countable, but many people just have two.

My parents are coming to visit at mid-term!!

**to get married**

Joe and Sarah <u>got married</u> two years ago.

**to be married**

They <u>were married</u> at her parents' home.

**to be divorced**

Agnes' parents <u>were divorced</u>.

**to get divorced**

They <u>got divorced</u> when Agnes was three.

**to search** something or someone (to examine carefully)

Looking for lost loonies, Anne <u>searched</u> her car.

**to search for** something or someone (to try to locate)

Anne <u>searched</u> for loonies in her car.

## Exercise 13: Using *Search* and *Search For*

Complete the blanks in the following sentences by using forms of the words "search" or "search for."

1. (searched, searched for) Mikey _____ the pockets of all the jackets in the coat closet, hoping that he might find enough change to buy an ice cream from the ice cream truck.

2. (searched, searched for) The kind police officer helped _____ the neighbourhood looking for Simon's lost cat.

3. (searched, searched for) The other police officers _____ the bank robber.

4. (search, search for) Use the "Find" command to _____ specific words in a document.

5. (search, search for) They planned to go to Treasure Island to _____ gold doubloons and pieces of eight.

### to stop or prevent

The words "stop" or "prevent" mean that you ensure that something does not happen. Both these words are followed by the word "from" if you use a gerund.

(to stop)

someone/something **from** doing something

(to prevent)

Ms. Martin stopped the race <u>from</u> continuing.

Jeffrey prevented the car <u>from</u> rolling into the crowd at the racetrack.

If you just use a noun or noun phrase as **object** after "stop" or "prevent," you do not use "from."

Louise <u>stopped</u> <u>the meeting</u> by yelling.

She <u>prevented</u> <u>the speaker's</u> being heard.

## Stress that Changes the Meaning of Words

The following words change their parts of speech depending on whether the first or second syllable is stressed.

| noun | verb |
|------|------|
| address | address |
| confines | confine |
| conflict | conflict |
| consent | consent |
| convict | convict |
| defeat | defeat |
| permit | permit |
| produce | produce |
| rewrite | rewrite |
| recall | recall |
| record | record |
| refuse | refuse |
| suspect | suspect |

Some words that were once probably in the above pattern have lost the differing pronunciation: **demand, display, export,** and **transfer.**

Some words differ in pronunciation between verbs and adjectives:

| verb | adjective |
|------|-----------|
| address | address [also noun] |
| record | record [also noun] |
| transport | transport |

to be thankful for (to be grateful for)

I am thankful for the nice weather.

They were thankful for the teacher's help.

to say thank-you [noun] (a show of gratitude)

He said a big thank-you to his grandparents.

She said thank-you to the friends who visited.

Note that a hyphenated thank-you is a noun. When you are using a verb as in "Thank you for replying so soon" ("I thank you for replying so soon") you do not use a hyphen—even though your spell check may suggest that you should.

thank-you [adjective]

Sarah plans to send a thank-you card to Ling.

thanks [noun]

> Joe and Sarah gave <u>thanks</u> for the great weather.
>
> <u>Thanks</u> for the chocolate.
>
> (I give you **thanks** for the chocolate.)

thanks to (because of)

> <u>Thanks</u> to all the studying, he got an A+.

thankless (not worth doing, unappreciated)

> It was a <u>thankless</u> job.

thankfulness (gratitude)

> Their <u>thankfulness</u> was apparent from their faces. 🐱 🐱 🐱

to throw something **to** or **at**

To throw something **to** someone or something is a positive thing: you expect the person to be able to catch the object or make use of it.

> Gilles threw the ball <u>to</u> Gabrielle.
>
> The woman threw the life preserver <u>to</u> the boy in the water.

To throw something **at** someone or something is a negative thing: you expect to cause a problem or damage. Contrast the following sentences.

> The gorilla threw a bunch of bananas <u>at</u> Tarzan.
> (The gorilla was mad at Tarzan.)
>
> The gorilla threw a bunch of bananas to Tarzan.
> (Tarzan was hungry, and the gorilla was kind.)

update [transitive verb] (to bring something up-to-date)

> Please <u>update</u> your records.

up-to-date [adjective] (current, up-to-the minute)

> Jim has an <u>up-to-date</u> library list of books on Elvis.

updated [adjective]

>   I have an <u>updated</u> version of her résumé.

to wait **for** someone or something

>   Sarah <u>waited for</u> Joe.
>   They <u>waited for</u> the restaurant to open.

to wait in a lineup or a line 🐞 🐞 🐞

>   They waited <u>in a lineup</u> that was half a block long.

worth [noun] (value or importance)

>   The diamond was of <u>great worth</u>.

worth [preposition] (good to do, beneficial or useful to do, important enough to justify)

>   It is <u>worth</u> doing this job very well in order to get a recommendation.
>   This course is <u>worth</u> taking.
>   Proofreading is <u>worth</u> doing.

to put in one's two cents' **worth** (to make a comment)

>   After she <u>put in her two cents' worth</u>, she remained absolutely silent.

worthy [adjective] (admirable or commendable)

>   You have a <u>worthy</u> opponent in Jason.
>   (He has great skill or is of admirable character.)

worthwhile [adjective] (worth the effort or beneficial)

>   Doing the practice test was <u>worthwhile</u>.

worth it [adjective] (means the same as "worthwhile" but is informal)

>   She spent a lot on her dress, but it was <u>worth</u> it.

# Learning Log: Idioms

We realize that we can't possibly list every idiomatic phrase used in English. Therefore, as you identify the idiomatic phrases that you have trouble with, write their corrected forms in this log. We recommend that you, with your instructor's permission, keep your log open beside you as you write so that you can practise these phrases often.

# *Diction*

## Learning Outcomes

***This Chapter will help
you to***

- write with more
  clarity.

- improve your
  spelling.

- understand how
  English has
  evolved and will
  continue to
  evolve.

# Levels of Usage

Diction refers simply to your choice of words. Specifically, it means choosing the most appropriate words given your audience and purpose. A poor choice of usage level, in fact, can greatly undermine very well organized and grammatically perfect writing. Therefore, you should carefully choose from the following levels to make your writing more effective in convincing your audience and achieving your purpose:

slang                              informal

technical                         formal

colloquial

Thesauruses used in conjunction with dictionaries are very helpful in differentiating between levels of usage. They can, for example, help you to find more formal words for the slang terms that you are most familiar with. Conversely, depending on your purpose and audience, you may want to use a thesaurus to change formal language to slang.

## Slang

Slang expressions tend to be lively and vigorous, yet they are frequently short-lived. Some slang terms live such a short time that they never make it into a dictionary. Other words, such as "cocksure," "balderdash," and "sham" have been in the language so long that they have become standard. Think about other colourful words like "nincompoop" that people use to describe someone who has done something stupid: "dimwit," "dope," "dork," "nitwit," "twit." Do you detect a generation gap? What about words to describe an event that was a lot of fun? Do you know people who say it was "a blast," "a gas," "a hoot," "a riot," "a bomb?" Are these people the same age? Yes, slang can date people. There is, for example, a "neat" or "peachy keen" generation, a "right on" generation, an "awesome" and "outrageous" generation and a "stylin" generation. There is an "on the same wave length" group and an "on the same page" group. Take a minute, and think what generation you are. What words do you use now that will turn into fossils so that your grandchildren can "date" you? Will "road rage" label you as a "fuddy-duddy?"

## Jargon

Some slang is specialized. Group or profession related slang is termed jargon. Such slang, then, is not at first readily understood by outsiders but can be learned. The advent of computers, for instance, has added jargon that infiltrates our language. As well as gaining words that have never existed before, such as "bytes," "baud," "e-mail," "modem," "CD Rom" and "the Internet," we use old words in new ways: "interface," "access" (as a verb), "bolded," and "spell-checked."

Although each sport has specific jargon, an example of jargon used across many sports comes to us from the Olympics when we hear people speaking about "medalling" in a sport. Unfortunately, many of us think that the sport in which we participate is one of the few that has no jargon. It takes an outsider to draw to our attention to the fact that terms such as "running back," "quarter back," "convert," "stealing a base," "foul ball," "bullpen," "hat trick," "scrum," "between the pipes," "bogeys," "birdies," and "eagles" are not immediately clear. If you don't know the basics of cricket, for example, having someone explain it is equivalent to culture shock.

Pop psychology spreads jargon to the masses: "meaningful dialogue," "identify with," "significant other," "co-dependent." Government and business, too, create a great deal of jargon, particularly words ending with "wise," "ize," and "ization." "Finalize," "situation-wise," "prioritize," "privatize," "public relationswise," "prioritization," "bureaucratization," "patronization," "marginalization," and "strategization" are some examples.

We can learn to avoid this kind of language while recognizing that all people in all kinds of jobs use technical language appropriate to their purposes and audience, in this case a group with shared expertise. In an era of increasing specialization, however, we should also recognize that workers must carefully consider the language they use when addressing others who specialize in different areas. Why? Because when we fail to do so, technical language, which provides fast, efficient, and effective communication between those with shared expertise, degenerates into jargon and becomes an expensive, inefficient hindrance to understanding.

Only when the user and audience work or play in or on the same field, or when they share a specific interest can jargon be efficient, effective language. Your aim as a writer is to communicate your ideas as clearly and concisely as possible to your chosen audience. Jargon will often obscure that goal.

Distinguishing between slang and formal English is not always easy. Even dictionaries do not agree. Your audience will help you determine your language level. In general, if you are going to err, err on the side of formality.

**Activity 1: Slang**

Change these formal terms into slang:

1. annoyed
2. beautiful
3. a young man
4. a young woman
5. a juvenile delinquent
6. ugly
7. intoxicated
8. defraud
9. to talk
10. a stupid person

**Activity 2: Slang**

Change these slang terms into more formal language:

1. to ream out
2. booze
3. crazy
4. to ditch
5. nerd
6. jerk
7. cheapskate
8. to face the music
9. to freak out
10. lame

**Activity 3: Slang**

Write two 100-word paragraphs, one from a letter to your best friend, one from a letter to your grandmother or grandfather, describing a party you recently attended.

## Colloquial Language

"Colloquial language" is not a derogatory term, but a descriptive one. It doesn't, for example, mean vulgar or substandard. In fact, the Latin root of "colloquial" means "to speak." Colloquial language, then, is just our ordinary spoken language, the language you hear in cafeterias, stores, airports, and arenas. It is the language parents speak to their children, that most instructors use in the classroom, and that business people use in the boardroom. It lies on a mid-ground, higher than slang, lower than the English that you might hear the recipient of the Nobel Prize use, or that many instructors expect you to write.

If we wanted an example to illustrate the three levels, we could use that Nobel Prize winner we mentioned above. To her colleagues, she might say, "Cool! I scored the Big One!" On a radio programme, she might say, "I am grateful for such an honour." In her acceptance speech, she might say, "I am gratified to have had my work acknowledged with such a prestigious award." The meaning here is much the same: the level of diction differs.

Our Nobel Prize winner may have given you the wrong impression: formal diction doesn't necessarily use more words to express meaning. To illustrate, you might say, "I used to live here when I was a little kid," but if you were writing a formal paper, you would probably write, "I resided here as a child." As another example, imagine that you are the member of the Prime Minister's office in charge of travel arrangements and have received a letter inquiring about the Prime Minister's fruit preferences from your counterpart in Malaysia. The Prime Minister might tell you, "I can't stand papayas, but mangoes are super!" On the phone to the Malaysian Travel Coordinator, you might say, "The Prime Minister likes mangoes a lot better than he likes papayas." This is colloquial. If you write a letter in reply, you may write, "The Prime Minister prefers mangoes to papayas," both more formal and less wordy than the other two levels of diction.

## Informal Language

Informal language is what we use in this book. For the most part, we sound as though we are talking to you. For example, we use contractions and use a few exclamation points. We also tend to use familiar vocabulary. In addition, we refer to you as "you," rather than "the student." Nonetheless, we do obey all grammar rules and are very careful to have independent clauses before we use a colon. This level of diction, then, is relaxed but still correct.

## Formal Language

We use formal English mostly in writing, rather than speech. Generally, your instructors expect you to write papers and essays using this level of diction. You would also use formal English in a letter of application for a job or in a letter of reference that you write for someone. "You" is seldom found at this level, and "one" makes an appearance. There are very few exclamation points! The language is more controlled. Instead of employing ordinary parallel structures, for example, you may use parallelism to create rhetorical effects. In addition, you may use more precise and polished vocabulary, and your sentence structures may be of greater variety and length than those you normally write. Naturally, you won't use contractions or abbreviations in formal writing. In general, whether in an academic paper, a business proposal, or a technical manual, the effective formal writer is clear, concise, correct, and cultivated, exhibiting her or his expertise in expression as well as in knowledge,

Your audience will help you determine the level of language you should use. As communicators, in order to be effective, you should choose the most appropriate diction level given your audience. You will not be effective speaking at a high school if you choose to speak as our Nobel Prize winner did when she accepted her award; however, you might not do so badly if you used the level she did when she spoke to her colleagues. The more you know about language and sentence structure, the more you have the ability to choose the correct, effective level of diction.

Most people realize that contractions and abbreviations are not appropriate in formal English, but some people have yet to learn that formal diction does not mean pretentious words. The misunderstanding, however, has existed a long time. Shakespeare's *Love's Labour Lost* shows us an example of pretentious Latinate diction contrasted with clear concrete diction as a character says "Remuneration! O, that's the Latin word for three farthings."

You can readily see that "It was his diurnal habit to begin with ablutions and then, with assiduity, to sit down to his matutinal repast" is not good English, nor is "Her erstwhile orthography had demanded remediation, so she engaged in perfervid lucubration." Moreover, people who use pretentious, polysyllabic diction or very sophisticated or archaic terms sometimes make mistakes that turn their supposedly elegant prose into a comedy of errors. Perhaps you have noticed that Shakespeare loves to introduce characters who, attempting to be impressive, unintentionally mangle the language. Clear and concise language is most effective and, therefore, most impressive.

# Sentence Cloggers

Clarity in diction includes choices of more than just formal or informal words. For example, you should avoid using euphemisms, clichés, or vague generalizations. These enemies of clarity and conciseness clog your sentences with ineffective words.

## Euphemisms

Euphemisms are mild, indirect, vague ways of expressing something thought to be harsh or distressing. "He took early retirement," when translated, may simply mean that he was fired. Sometimes, therefore, people think euphemisms are a sign of refinement, for brutal reality is softened. To illustrate further, "I lost my husband five years ago," is a euphemism that native speakers of English can very readily understand as a woman's way of avoiding saying "My husband died five years ago." The expression's vague mildness, however, may confuse a non-native English speaker and engender a look of surprise rather than of sympathy. Indeed, most euphemisms should be avoided because their gentle imprecision can obscure meaning, but, occasionally, in order to conform to good taste, you may want to use one.

---

### Activity 4: Euphemisms

Supply equivalents for these euphemisms:

| | |
|---|---|
| 1. negative progress | 6. collateral damage |
| 2. in the family way | 7. between jobs |
| 3. restrooms | 8. ethnic cleansing |
| 4. downsizing | 9. impaired |
| 5. underprivileged | 10. growth cycle slow down |

---

## Clichés

Some euphemisms are already clichés, trite or worn out expressions. "She has gone to meet her maker," is such an expression. Although some clichés began as lively, interesting similes or metaphors, because of overuse, they have become predictable and boring. Such clichés include "busy as a bee," "fast as a speeding bullet," and "nipped in the bud."

Some other clichés are wordy, familiar, prefabricated phrases like "last but not least," "when all is said and done," "in no way, shape, or form." Some of the worst offenders are not only trite and boring but also redundant: "above and beyond," "first and foremost," "few and far between," "over and above." A cheerful thought for non-native speakers of English is that they can use what might be a clichéd phrase in their native language and have it sound fresh and interesting in English.

### Exercise 1: Clichés

Finish the following clichés:

1. black as ...

3. gentle as a ...

2. cool as a ...

4. sadder but ...

5.  sharp as a ...                       8. moment of ...

6.  blushing ...                         9. seeing is ...

7.  good as ...                          10. growing by ...

Sometimes clichés can be used for humorous effect or have life poured back into them, but thoughtless use of clichés leads to weak and wordy writing.

## Wordy Prepositional Phrases

Like outworn clichés, jargon, and euphemisms, strings of prepositional phrases can make your writing less effective than it can be. We know that you don't always have the luxury of being able to do drafts of an essay. When you do, after your ideas are down on paper, you can start looking, on the second draft, for the cloggers that make your writing less clear and concise than it should be. You aim is not to get rid of all prepositional phrases. That would be an impossible task, as prepositional phrases play an important role in English (see page 410). Instead, your goal is to reduce awkward overuse.

We can give you an example that we got rid of ourselves as we were writing this book. Claire wrote, "The problem of the use of apostrophes in plurals begins as students take a specific rule and broaden it to embrace all plurals." Then she looked at the string of prepositional phrases, "of the use of apostrophes in plurals," and rewrote the sentence to read, "the problem of using apostrophes in plurals begins ..." We think that a reader, not being bumped from prepositional phrase to prepositional phrase, has an easier time understanding the meaning. In the process of reducing bumps, we also reduced the number of words in the sentence. The rewritten sentence is less awkward and more concise.

Before doing the following exercise, you should make sure that you will recognize the prepositional phrases. If you are unsure, reread the section on prepositions in Parts of Speech, page 21, and glance through the list of "Common Prepositional Phrases" in Chapter Eight: Idiom.

### Exercise 2: Strings of Prepositional Phrases
Reduce the number of prepositional strings and clichéd phrases in the following sentences. Do a word count for your sentences.

1.  At about twelve o'clock on Tuesday, the fire alarm in the cafeteria went off.  15

2.  In view of the fact that the consensus of opinion is against me, I will resign.  17

3. This chart is meant to be for the purpose of keeping track of Josephine's winnings.  16

4. Due to the fact that the temperature of the water in this glass is almost below freezing, I think that I will skip the ice.  23

5. Henry has the capacity of being a success in any area of his choosing.  15

6. In light of the fact that he is of the opinion that the book was better than the movie, we should make an effort to read it.  28

7. Fortunately, we have Marie Benoit in the position of being an expert in LAN systems, so she can oversee the way in which the new system is set up.  30

8. The buskers always try to stand in close proximity to the front doors of the bookstore.  18

9. In the not-too-distant future, the place in which we work may change in dramatic ways.  18

10. In view of the fact that many jobs ask for experience, students should be aware of the fact that work in volunteer positions can be of assistance to them.  30

## Exercise 3: Strings of Prepositional Phrases

Reduce the number of prepositional strings and clichéd phrases in the following sentences. Do a word count for your sentences.

1. In view of the fact that she is in the habit of being late, I think that we should just leave.  22

2. In the event that someone is in the position of not being able to walk, a scooter can be of great help.  23

3. Manuel received a letter to the effect that, on the grounds that he was so late in handing in his essay, his grade was recorded as incomplete.  28

4. In spite of the fact that the approval of the project was delayed, Barrison Brothers are of the opinion that they can finish it by the first of March.  30

5. At the end of the novel *The Stone Angel* by Margaret Laurence, the character of Hagar begins to reach out in a physical and in an emotional way to others.  31

6. The leadership of the union has reached a consensus of opinion that the attitude of the new government is one of hostility toward a hike in wages.  27

7. All of us had a taste of the new wine made by the Vinearts' Vintners. 16

8. In order to increase the accessibility of the product, we should make the way in which it is opened more visible. 22

9. The study of economics is an investigation of the production, distribution, and consumption of goods. 16

10. You should be aware of the fact that one of the laptops is missing. 15

# Isys

Although you have encountered isys before (see pages 86–88), we want to remind you that needless use of "to be" *(is, am, are, was, were)* and disguised isys *(seem, appear, become, remain)* will clog your sentences with unnecessary words. On a first draft, you should be working on getting your ideas down on paper. On a second draft, you can look for isy-loaded sentences in the same way that you look for strings of awkward prepositional phrases.

We work this way too, going back to check for sentence cloggers. For example, the first draft near the beginning of Wordy Prepositional Phrases read, "We are aware that you don't always have the luxury of being able to do drafts." The second draft read, "We know that you don't always have the luxury of being able to do drafts." "Are aware that" was reduced to "know," a more efficient use of language. Try the following exercise to refresh your memory about how to zap needless isys.

## Exercise 4: Isy Zapping

Reduce the number of needless isys. Do a word count for your sentences.

1. When you get home, you will see there is a big parcel that is just for you sitting under the tree. 22

2. The biggest problem with the report is that it is not coherent. 13

3. The meeting is going to be chaired by the woman who is manager of the Credit Union. 18

4. It is necessary that the switch be fully engaged before the lever is pulled. 15

5. It is obvious that the reason for Peter's getting great grades is because of his ability to study effectively even when he is living in residence. 26

6. It is essential that you determine what the bias of the author is.  14

7. It is obvious that this is the fuse that is responsible for the failure of the computer.  18

8. The reason for the delay in your grades is because the new operating system is creating problems.  18

9. It is clear that Vicky is the one who is going to be best at creating interesting graphics.  19

10. Rock climbing is the reason why he is much fitter than he was last year.   18

Probably when you corrected the sentences in the above exercises, you accidentally did a good thing and made passive sentences active. This is one of the bonuses of zapping isys. For example, if, for Exercise 4, number 3, you wrote "The manager of the Credit Union will chair the meeting" or for Exercise 4, number 8, "Problems with the new operating system caused the delay in your grades," you made the sentences active, with the doers of the action as the subjects of the sentence. See pages 166 for a reminder about passives.

# Concrete and Specific Language

Being concrete and specific makes writing more clear, more concise, and more meaningful. A specific word defines and limits a general term. In other words, a specific word designates a particular member or members while a general term designates a class. "Visitor" is a general term; "Aunt Sally" or "a skunk" is more specific. "Small town" is a general term: "a town with fewer than 2500 people" is more specific.

**Abstract** words denote intangible things: ideas or qualities. "Human nature," "sorrow," "campaign," and "democracy" are abstract terms. "Virtue" is another abstraction. "Honesty," more specific, is, neverthe-less, also an abstraction.

When you make your writing more concrete, it becomes more precise and conveys greater meaning. You can take a general or an abstract term and make it progressively more meaningful:

desk       wooden desk; oak desk; oak school desk; nineteenth-century oak school desk

fine art   painting; oil painting; West Coast oil painting; oil painting by Emily Carr; oil painting of a bird by Emily Carr; Big Raven by Emily Carr

---

### Activity 5: Concrete language

Make the following words progressively more concrete as we did in the above examples:

1. rich
2. a car
3. a piece of furniture

4. campaign
5. a ride
6. paper

---

# Precision

Sometimes, writers use words imprecisely because they make lazy choices, not bothering to check which of two or three words is correct or most apt. Such writers might incorrectly say, "Just before my guests arrived, the potatoes boiled over and the aroma of burnt starch dissipated from room to room," instead of "... the smell of burnt potatoes spread from room to room." They might imprecisely write, "Fishing includes many challenging aspects," instead of "Fishing entails many challenging skills." Imprecise diction makes writing flabby and uninteresting.

In other cases, a writer's thinking itself, rather than her or his word selection, is lazy. Lazy thinking occurs when a writer has not figured out what he or she really means. In lieu of thinking, the writer uses catch-all phrases, those that George Orwell in his essay, "Politics and the English Language," calls "ready-made phrases." These phrases are usually abstract and so vague that they "perform the important service of partially concealing your meaning even from yourself." They tend, even, to conceal the fact that what you have written really has no meaning.

Observe how a writer moves from a flabby, essentially meaningless topic sentence containing two abstractions to one that contains concrete details and a developable idea.

*The book has one interesting aspect.*

*The book has a surprising main character.*

↓

*The book has a surprising main character, a woman.*

↓

*The book has a surprising main character, Minnie Haughha.*

↓

*The book's main character, Minnie Haughha, illustrates that beauty can be only skin deep.*

Finally, the writer has said something of significance and now has a topic sentence that can easily be developed.

---

### Activity 6: Thesaurus and precision activity

The following short paragraph contains several common, ready-made phrases that entirely obscure any intended meaning.

Read and then rethink the paragraph, clarifying in your mind what Mandy was like before and after the change, and what "the episode" was. Then, use the thesaurus entries we have created for you (pages 401–403) to help you find words to express your thoughts clearly and precisely. As Orwell says, "Let the meaning choose the word, and not the other way about."

Once you have thought through what you want the paragraph to mean, rewrite it, using concrete examples and precise diction to make Mandy's change and its impact clear to your readers. In your paragraph, you may include words from the *Ersatz Thesaurus*, or you may merely use the *ET* to stimulate your thinking.

*The change in Mandy was really noticeable. In the past, she was always different, but after the episode at work, she was nothing like she used to be. Her change affected the atmosphere in the office and had an impact on everyone who worked with her.*

---

## ERSATZ THESAURUS

In most good thesauruses, words are listed alphabetically in the last half of the book. You first look up a word in the alphabetical listings, where you will find generalized meanings. Each generalized meaning provides you with an entry reference number, referring to detailed entries in the front half of the book. In those entries, you will find lists of words associated with the generalized meanings.

In our **ERSATZ THESAURUS**, we have located the alphabetical listings first, so you can see what they look like immediately. Detailed entries follow.

**affect**

| | |
|---|---|
| negatively | 16.1 |
| positively | 15.1 |

**difference**

| | |
|---|---|
| dissent | 84.11 |
| tensions | 83.6 |
| positive difference | 37.6 |

**different**

| | |
|---|---|
| nonuniform | 26.1 |
| novel | 26.8 |
| abnormal | 45.10 |
| eccentric | 44.9 |
| uncommon | 12.1 |

**noticeable**

| | |
|---|---|
| great | 21.7 |
| visible | 3.1 |

**(some) unpleasant traits**

| | |
|---|---|
| bossy | 94.7 |
| gossipy | 94.8 |
| stingy | 24.9 |
| silly | 38.1 |
| critical | 92.6 |
| lazy | 29.4 |
| self-important | 3.9 |
| sneaky | 77.9 |
| tardy | 36.2 |
| obsequious | 7.5 |
| paranoid | 19.1 |

**(some) pleasant traits**

| | |
|---|---|
| friendly | 95.7 |
| trustworthy | 89.1 |
| generous | 25.9 |
| thoughtful | 41 |
| industrious | 30.6 |
| open | 55.3 |
| punctual | 37.1 |
| self-assured | 20.2 |

**3.1** **visible:** easily seen, clear, perceptible, obvious, apparent, conspicuous, recognizable, exposed to view, naked, revealed, stark, high-profile

**3.9** **self-important:** haughty, arrogant, high-handed, overbearing, conceited

**7.5** **obsequious:** servile, fawning, grovelling, snivelling, abject, sycophantic

**12.1** **uncommon:** rare, exceptional, extraordinary, above the ordinary, scarce, outstanding, valuable

**15.1** **make better:** improve, bolster, unite, calm, increase productivity, rectify problems, affect positively, promote, enhance, invigorate, brighten, warm, repair, prune, correct, purify, refresh, inspire, uplift, organize, restore, cure, rejuvenate, remedy

*continued*

**16.1 damage:** affect negatively, cause dissent, divide, undermine, embitter, impair, erode, botch, endanger, poison, threaten, contaminate, break up, infect, destroy, prejudice, spoil, hamstring

**19.1 paranoid:** suspicious, fearful, timid, faint-hearted, apprehensive, hysterical, eccentric

**20.2 self-assured:** confident, plucky, self-reliant, determined

**21.7 great:** large, remarkable, distinguished, important, superior, admirable, of consequence, of merit, imposing, serious, eminent.

**24.9 stingy:** cheap, selfish, parsimonious, miserly

**25.9 generous:** charitable, benevolent, indulgent, philanthropic, soft-hearted

**26.1 nonuniform:** varying, nonconforming, erratic, changing, changeable, different, unusual, irregular, inconsistent, impulsive, capricious, maverick

**26.8 novel:** new, fresh, modern, unprecedented, original, striking, unusual, odd, intriguing

**29.4 lazy:** slothful, indolent, idle, loafer, non-cooperative, careless

**30.6 industrious:** business-like, professional, active, enterprising, diligent, hard-working, bustling, busy, occupied

**36.2 tardy:** late, slow, sluggish, apathetic, phlegmatic, deliberate, snail-like

**37.1 punctual:** prompt, regular, methodical, steady

**37.6 positive difference:** alternative, altered, options, suggestions, selections, opportunities, choices, preferences, original, imaginative, unconventional, genuine

**38.1 silly:** gullible, simple, childish, blundering, feeble-minded, dull, infantile, puerile, fatuous, bewildered, inept, giddy

**41 thoughtful:** perceptive, thinking, pensive, reflective

**44.9 eccentric:** peculiar, erratic, idiosyncratic, foolish, odd, abnormal, unusual, screwball, outlandish, bizarre, quaint, freakish

**45.10 abnormal:** not conforming to rules, deviating, delinquent, exceptional, peculiar, aberrant, wrong, inappropriate, incorrect, unnatural, odd, eccentric

**55.3 open:** unaffected, sincere, frank, guileless, direct, truthful

**77.9 sneaky:** furtive, stealthy, skulking, secretive, uncommunicative, taciturn

**83.6 tensions:** arguments, disagreement, contradiction, quarrel, defend, deny, hatch, blame, rebut, justify, explain, smooth over, refute

**84.11 dissent:** disagreement, discord, discontent, quarrel, disapproval, disharmony, dissonance, antagonism, clash, controversy, negativity, fractiousness

*continued*

**89.1 trustworthy:** truthful, sincere, honest, scrupulous, guileless, virtuous, fair, honourable, even-handed, dependable

**92.6 critical:** disparaging, abusive, sarcastic, cynical, sharp, cutting, censorious, carping, hypercritical, meddling

**94.7 bossy:** domineering, tyrannical, dominant, imperious, influential, authoritative, officious

**94.8 gossipy:** babbler, talkative, flippant, glib, garrulous tattletale

**95.7 friendly:** congenial, courteous, polite, mannerly, soft-spoken, winning, good-humoured, cordial, gracious, amiable, affable, neighbourly

Concrete words can be perceived by one of the five senses. Giving back a wallet that you found is a concrete example of "honesty." Tears are a concrete example of "sorrow." Concrete details, besides giving more factual information, deepen and define attitudes. "Sarah bought some stuff after work," is general and not very interesting. "Sarah bought groceries after work," is more specific but still not very interesting. "Sarah bought two steaks, some asparagus, and a bottle of Blue Nun after work," is not only more concrete and specific, but also richer in meaning. Concrete language makes your work both clearer and more interesting.

### Activity 7: Concrete writing: A camping trip

The following essay is correct in organization, punctuation, and grammar, but an instructor may assign it a grade of C+ or B– simply because the content lacks the kind of meaningful concrete details that give life to writing. Add the concrete and specific details about who, what, where, when, why, and how that will turn this boring piece of prose into something meaningful.

#### A Camping Trip

A few years ago, an old friend and I planned a short camping trip. Neither of us had much experience, but we were optimists. We borrowed some equipment from my family and from my friend's family. My old car was pretty small, but we crowded all our necessities into it. We were quite pleased with our planning: we had stuff to sleep on or in, food to eat, and ways to cook.

We drove for quite a while before we found a place where we wanted to camp. Actually, we drove quite a bit further than we

*continued*

## Activity 7: Concrete writing: A camping trip (continued)

had planned. We passed three campgrounds, but each had something wrong with it. It was a relief to find one that we both liked. We selected a site that overlooked the water.

Pitching the tent was a bit of a hassle. Because we got quite tired and did not feel like cooking, our first meal was very strange. As a result, we ended the first day somewhat disillusioned about the holiday. However, in the morning, we started off the day right with a great breakfast. The only flaw was that a kid from the next campsite sat and watched us eat. Then, he said something to his mom that made me blush. Sound carries well outdoors.

Fortunately, the child's family decided to move on, and my friend and I enjoyed the rest of our time at the campsite. The weather stayed pretty nice almost the whole time, so we engaged in many activities—not all of them athletic. In fact, once we became more adept at camping, we had lots of time left every day to amuse ourselves.

When we loaded up the car again, we included a lot of good memories of our camping trip, and the car did not seem at all crowded.

## Activity 8: Concrete writing

The following paragraph is almost completely abstract. Its vocabulary and the complexity of its sentence structure may mislead you into thinking that it is sophisticated. In fact, it is simply vague. Rewrite the paragraph making it concrete and specific.

Some adults contend that young children should be denied access to certain toys because, through interaction with those toys, children learn certain attitudes. This concern is valid. Particular types of toys do impart particular values, which have a potential impact on everyone, not least of all, on the children. However, the argument that these toys are responsible for causing certain behaviour or attitudes is insufficient. In reality, many factors in our society contribute to the formation of attitudes and values. Children are bombarded with input everyday, toys comprising only a small part of it. A broad range of input affects their view of the world. Toys alone cannot be blamed for the attitudes of children.

We understand that sometimes you need to use abstract words; we just want you to recognize that, to make sure that your reader understands the import of what you say, you need to include concrete illustrations or details. Suppose that you are a reporter writing for the school newspaper, and you are writing about a student who felt so lonely in first year that, in second year, he started a campus club called Lonely-No-Longer. You realize that "lonely" is an abstraction that means different things to different people. Therefore, you need to communicate the kind of loneliness this student experienced that made him resolve to do something about it, and you do this by being concrete and specific.

Was the student lonely sitting in a lecture hall week after week with 299 other students, not one of whom he knew? Was he, one of a family of eight, lonely coming home to a small, cold apartment with no one to greet him, to cook with, or to talk with? Was he someone who moved into residence on his first day in Canada and found that nobody understood his accent or what difficulties he was having adapting to such a different educational system and language? When you are concrete and precise, your readers will gain an understanding of what motivated your interviewee. The details that you use may cause the readers to look at first year students in a new way or may cause them to rethink how they would define, or deal with, loneliness. Opening new ways for your readers to think is an exciting prospect.

Working with language and communicating your ideas to others makes writing a pleasurable and exciting experience. The English language contains many riches for us to explore. As we briefly outline the development of the language, you will understand from whence the riches came and why they continue to come.

# English Roots and Growth

Language, like a tree, has many forms. In addition, just as a tree loses its leaves and grows others, a language loses words and gains new ones. New generations with new experiences and new speakers of the language continually feed and enrich it.

Because words differ with the user, time, place, and situation, language cannot be a closed system with words that express the essence of things. Nonetheless, language is the tool that enables us to communicate with other human beings and helps to distinguish us from other animals. We can nourish our own use of language by widening our first-hand experience or by enjoying vicarious experience as we explore the world through books, magazines, and other media.

In the development of English, an Indo-European language like Greek, Iranian, and Sanskrit, we commonly recognize three periods: Old English, Middle English, and Modern English. All these periods contribute to the language that we speak today, and some of the oddities of our present language are explained if we briefly explore the legacy of the earlier periods.

## Old English (450–1100)

Romans ruled the Celtic tribes of Britain from about AD 43, although the peoples of what became Scotland, Wales, and Ireland remained free from Roman domination. Even in England, unlike in Gaul or Spain, people rejected Latin in favour of their own Celtic language.

As the power of the Roman Empire waned about the 5th Century, there were three major influences on English. First, around 450, the Angles, Saxons and Jutes, who had had sufficient contact of their own with the Roman Empire to pick up a few words like "church," "pipe," "kettle," "butter," "wine," and "cheese," brought Germanic languages into Celtic Britain. These Low German speakers from northern Europe are commonly called Anglo-Saxons. The predominant language in England became a Germanic one, and it is this period, until about the 11th Century, that we term Old English.

Second, in 597, Christianity brought to England not only Latin but also the ability to record language, for missionaries brought the alphabet. At this time, words like "abbot," "alms," "hymn," and "litany" entered the language. It is about this time that the poem Beowulf was written. The poem gives an example of the English used during this time:

> Fyrst forð ġewāt: flota wæs on ȳðum,
> bāt under beorge, Beornas ġearwe
> On stefn stigon,—strēmas wundon,
> sund wið sande.

---

"Beowulf," *England in Literature,* Macbeth edition, Scott, Foresman and Company.

Of the passage, we recognize the words "stremas" (streams) and "sande" (sand), and with a little coaxing, we recognize "wid," meaning "against." We still use the word in this way when we say, "I had a fight with my brother." Clearly, however, we must struggle to understand most of the vocabulary and syntax.

Third, Scandinavian or Norse attacks and settlements in the 700s and 800s also provided a Germanic-based influence. It is likely that these new settlers and the Anglo-Saxons understood much of each other's language, and we can see many "borrowings" in this period.

From these people, English gained the useful adjectives "both" and "many." It also gained nouns such as "fellow," "husband," "dirt," "leg," and quite a few "sk" nouns: "skill," "sky," "skirt," and "skin." In addition, English gained some verbs such as "crawl," "die," "give," and "take." Some Scandinavian words, such as "take," replaced existing English words, but others just took their place alongside them as synonyms. "Skin," for example, joined the English "hide;" "raise" joined "rear;" and "ill" lay side by side with "sick." The languages of the newcomers enriched Anglo-Saxon.

In the last half of the 9th Century, Alfred the Great championed learning. In 970, for example, a book of poems, *The Exeter Book* was written. In addition, many books were translated from Latin into English. Alfred the Great himself, in 885, translated Gregory's *Cura Pastoralis* into English, and less than ten years later, the Bishop of Sherborne wrote *The Life of Alfred the Great*.

To set the flowering of English writing at this time in a very brief cross-cultural perspective, the first full translation of the Bible into English wasn't until 1385, although parts had been translated dating from about the 7th century. In Germany, as early as 381, however, the Bible had been translated into Old High German, but until 1100, the most important works were still translations from Latin. Before the 9th century and 12th centuries, Latin was also the literary language of France and Italy respectively. By the 1100s in France and Germany, minstrels were writing long poems about Christian knights and courtly love. By 961, the Norwegian epic poem "Eyvind Skaldaspillir" appeared.

In the East, before 600, in Korea, a 100-volume history appeared. In 984, there was a 1000-volume Chinese encyclopedia. In about 900, an anthology of the preceding 150 years of Japanese poetry, *Kokinshu*, was published. In the year 1000, Sei Shonagan wrote her diary of life at the Imperial Japanese court, *The Pillow Book*. This book was written at about the same time as the English epic poem, "Beowulf," that we mentioned before.

"Beowulf" brings us back to the Anglo-Saxon Period in England. Anglo-Saxon pronunciation, grammar, vocabulary, and spelling differed from our own, yet some words are recognizable:

| | |
|---|---|
| bedd | he |
| on | hus or huse |
| God | mannum |

The letters *eth*, ð, and *thorn*, þ, common in this era, were eventually replaced by th, but we see their remnant in signs like "Ye Olde English Sweete Shoppe" and "Ye Olde British Fishe and Chippe Shoppe."

Moreover, these letters that we replaced explain the two pronunciations of "th" because thorn, þ, unvoiced, is the ancestor of the "th" in "thin," "thick," and "thought" while eth, ð, voiced, is responsible for "these," "then," and "therefore." Once we find out about *thorn* and *eth*, some Old English words that seemed unintelligible reveal their familiar bones.

The Anglo-Saxon word order is more strange to us than the words themselves, some of which we recognize and some of which we can guess at, though their spellings are different from ours. In the Old English period in the language's development, words were inflected; that is, they indicated the part they played in a sentence, whether nouns were subjects, possessives, direct or indirect objects, for example. Therefore, word order was not as important as it is to us.

The beginning of the Lord's Prayer, in Old English looked like this:

"Faeder ure þuðe eart on heofonum si þin nama gehalgod."

We now say, "Our Father who art in Heaven, hallowed be thy name."

Old English words also had endings that made present tense verbs plural to agree with their subjects, more like verbs in French, Spanish, or Portuguese than those we now write in English. The Bible gives us an example of the kind of inflection that was required. Here is a passage from "The Book of Ruth" to show some typical inflections of pronouns and verbs: "Whither thou goest, I will go; and where thou lodgest, I will lodge: thy people shall be my people, and thy God my God." Although this passage is written later, during the Renaissance, we have used it to give you an easily understood passage where you would not have to decipher which part of speech went where, what the unfamiliar letters sounded like, or what words lay beneath unfamiliar spelling.

Their spelling was different, and their inflections are unfamiliar to us; however, nouns describing close family relationships and parts of the body derive from Old English:

| | | | |
|---|---|---|---|
| man | woman | child | father |
| mother | sister | brother | head |
| hair | eye | ear | nose |
| mouth | bone | hand | chin |

Old English also gave us nouns to describe natural phenomena:

| | | | |
|---|---|---|---|
| sun | earth | tide | north |
| moon | fire | day | east |
| star | water | night | west |

In addition, *corn*, *wheat*, *meadow*, *tree*, *hill*, and *stream* are all Old English. Common animal names are also Old English: *cow*, *bull*, *sheep*, *lamb*, *bear*, *deer*, *fox*, *hen*, *sow*, and *horse*.

Most of our numbers, basic colours, adjectives, and verbs are Old English.

| | | | |
|---|---|---|---|
| two | thousand | white | little |
| thirteen | black | yellow | slow |
| forty | green | empty | thick |
| hundred | red | great | build |
| come | go | set | stand |
| cut | sell | sleep | walk |

Except the Scandinavian *they*, *them*, *their*, and *theirs*, all our pronouns, including demonstrative (*this*, *that*, *these* and *those*), interrogative *(who, whose, what)*, and relative *(who, that, which)*, come from this Old English period. Finally, the common prepositions, such as *at*, *by*, *for*, *from*, *under*, *with*, *before*, and *out*, date from this period.

In general, words from Old English are short, one syllable, and native, rather than borrowed. Of the 1000 most commonly used words, about 60 percent are native English. About one quarter of the words in our dictionaries will be Old English or derived from it.

---

### Activity 9

Choose a passage of about three lines from one of your texts or of this book; then, rewrite it using þ or ð for the th's you find there.

---

## Middle English (1150–1500)

Middle English developed gradually around the time of the Norman invasion of Britain in 1066. As their name suggests, the Normans were also at one time from the North, just another group of successful Scandinavian raiders. Early in the 900s, they had established themselves in Northern France and began speaking a variant of French, a Romance rather than a Germanic language.

From 1066 to 1350, English disappeared as the language of government, business, law, education, and religion. The lower classes, however, continued to speak English, and finally, as the middle class gained strength, English gained in prestige over Norman French.

Both the Scandinavian and the Norman invasions helped erase some of the inflections on English words. Word order became more important. The absence of inflections didn't really simplify the language, for as any learner of English as a second or additional language can testify, the "new" reliance on prepositional phrases to indicate case creates its own complexity.

Although Latinate church-related words such as *abbot, disciple, mass, monk, nun*, and *priest* existed in English from the 6th Century, the Norman French brought many more, including abstract terms:

| | | | |
|---|---|---|---|
| angel | confess | faith | parson |
| piety | preach | sermon | virtue |
| conscience | convent | miracle | |
| pity | religion | vice | |

In addition, Norman French brought many words related to government, law, and business:

## Nouns

| | | | |
|---|---|---|---|
| parliament | council | throne | wage |
| traitor | sovereign | budget | tax |
| nation | homage | salary | |

## Verbs

| | | | |
|---|---|---|---|
| obey | fine | seize | arrest |
| sue | acquit | pardon | command |

Norman French gave us words to describe what had been prepared from the Old English *cows, pigs, sheep*, and *deer: beef, veal, mutton, bacon, pork*, and *venison*. They also gave English words to say how to cook: *boil, broil, fry, roast*, and *stew*. We can see from these words that the Norman French came as masters, landlords, or rulers. They were the eaters of the food raised and prepared by the conquered English.

Colours became more vibrant with the influx of Norman French: *blue, vermillion*, and *scarlet* entered the language. *Dance, chess, conversation*, and *leisure* along with *story, romance, poetry*, and *literature* also took their place in Middle English.

Although Chaucer wrote using Middle English, he was not able to take advantage of one of the greatest influences on the English language, the printing press, developed in 1475. Books became cheaper, and consequently, more common; more people learned to read and write; and spelling became more regular. The advent of television and radio in the 20th Century had a similar kind of standardizing effect on language in the English speaking world.

## Modern English

Modern English dates from about the beginning of the 16th Century. Shakespeare, therefore, wrote in Modern English. By 1500, except in rituals and in poetry, the use of *thee*, *thy*, and *thine* had disappeared. (Note that some wedding services still use "Wilt *thou* take this man to be thy lawful wedded husband.") Words and spelling became more standardized partly because the government recognized the need for standard forms. Not until the 18th Century, however, did English grammars begin to appear, mostly based on Latin grammars. This Latin base accounts for some of the oddities in English grammar. For example, for centuries, English-speaking children were taught that they must never split an infinitive because it was impossible to do so in Latin, or in French or Spanish for that matter.

The first English dictionary, containing 2500 words, was published in 1603. During the English Renaissance, educated English speakers divided into two camps—those who felt that Greek and Latinate words dignified and improved English and nationalists who believed that such words corrupted English. In *Loves Labour Lost*, Shakespeare shows his awareness of this linguistic tension. Recall the "remuneration" that equalled "three farthings," for example. Of course, the group that approved of borrowings won, and English speakers have appropriated words from other languages ever since.

In fact, the most striking feature of Modern English is its large vocabulary. English speakers not only continue to borrow but also to create new words using Greek or Latin roots. We speak of this phenomenon later on page 414. An example of a recent borrowing is the Swedish "ombudsman." In most parts of the English speaking world, in an effort to be gender neutral, this word has now been modified, and we speak quite naturally of "the ombudsperson." This process shows how English borrows, changes, and grows.

Now, more than a quarter billion people speak English. The opportunity for diversity continues to grow. George Bernard Shaw, a prolific British playwright very interested in language, once wrote that "England and America are two countries separated by the same language." Even Canada shows, however, the diverse nature of English, for if we travel from British Columbia on the Pacific to Newfoundland on the Atlantic, we will encounter different accents, pronunciation, and vocabulary. Indeed, Newfoundland's English alone has a dictionary of over 600 pages devoted to it. If we think of the English spoken to the south, we again recognize the differences that highlight the vast similarities in English. In Canada, Britain, The United States, India, Malaysia, and Hong Kong, English flourishes and changes. Even the twelve volume *Oxford English Dictionary* cannot hold the wealth of the language.

The following exercises will help you appreciate how much English has gained from other languages and encourage you to recognize that the language will undoubtedly continue to grow and change wherever it is spoken.

# Dictionaries

Before you begin the exercises, we'd like to tell you about some helpful and interesting dictionaries that we discovered. We suggest that, some afternoon, you do what we did: sit on the floor of the bookstore and read dictionaries for a couple hours. In each dictionary, look for words relevant to your specialties. If they are missing or defined in ways that you find unclear or inaccurate, then that is not the dictionary for you. If English is not your first language, check to see if most entries have sentences showing the words in action and to see if they make helpful comments about idiom. Note if they tell you that a word is archaic or obscene. If pronunciation is your concern, ensure that the pronunciation guide is helpful. You will probably have a dictionary for ten years or more, so taking time to check it out thoroughly will definitely be worthwhile.

*American Heritage English as a Second Language Dictionary.* (Houghton Mifflin)

*Collins Cobuild English Dictionary.* (Whole paragraph explanations, for example: "right: You can refer to people who support the political ideals of capitalism and conservatism as *the right*. They are often contrasted with *the left*.")

*Collins Paperback English Dictionary.* (Contains sample sentences. Good value for the money.)

*Longman's Dictionary of Contemporary English.* (Excellent for ESL. It contains pictures with vocabulary items identified, for example, a kitchen and appliances, etc.; cartoons depicting different types of walking such as strolling or striding. It also contains good example sentences.)

*Oxford Advanced Learner's Dictionary.* (Good sentences, some pictures.)

*Oxford Dictionary of Canadian English.* (Includes many "Canadianisms." Also includes a lot of place names, along with their derivations, and names of prominent people.)

*Oxford Dictionary of Current English.* (Contains sample phrases and some sentences. Contains a spell-it-right guide.)

*Oxford Paperback Dictionary.* (Contains phrases.)

## Activity 10: Word derivations

Look up the following words in a dictionary and ascertain their origin. Write the definition of any unfamiliar word.

1. blood
2. brandy
3. bull
4. candle
5. daughter
6. model
7. skirt

6. husband
7. chipmunk
8. run
9. second
10. shrine
11. hustings
12. brown

## Activity 11: Word derivations

Look up the following words in a dictionary and ascertain their origin. Write the definition of any unfamiliar word.

1. duck
2. shawl
3. flesh
4. important
5. night
6. skunk
7. ginger

8. one
9. poor
10. season
11. skin
12. snow
13. golf
14. whinge

## Activity 12: Word derivations

Look up the following words in a dictionary and ascertain their origin. Write the definition of any unfamiliar word.

1. bungalow
2. gung ho
3. patio
4. tsunami
5. vodka
6. mandarin
7. cyclone

8. typhoon
9. umbrella
10. studio
11. smithereens
12. thug
13. miniature
14. mackinaw

## Activity 13: Word derivations

Look up the following words in a dictionary and ascertain their origin.
Write the definition of any unfamiliar word.

1. incognito
2. magic
3. ketchup
4. hazard
5. canyon
6. yoga
7. anthology

8. naive
9. lemon
10. casino
11. bonanza
12. boomerang
13. chocolate
14. checkmate

## Activity 14: Writing the world's English

Choosing words in one of the above activities, write a narrative
paragraph of 100–200 words containing all of them. Be sure to review
your definitions before you begin to write. If necessary, you may
change the form of the word: for example, you could make a noun
plural or possessive, or you could change the verb's tense or make it
into a gerund. (Note that writing with the words from Activity 12 is
not for the faint of heart.)

# Prefixes, Roots, and Suffixes

Most dictionaries provide the derivation of the words. We have just
shown some examples of other countries' words that English has
adopted and adapted to enrich its vocabulary. English also enriches the
language by employing Greek or Latin prefixes, roots, and suffixes to
create new words.

If you know the prefixes, one or more elements preceding a root
word, and suffixes, one or more elements following a root word, you
have tools to understand words you have never seen before. In addition,
inventors and scientists have ways to describe new phenomena. On a
more mundane level, recently, a prefix, "mega" has come into use as a
word on its own, while preserving its meaning of "great" or "large."
"How much did that sweater cost?" says Algernon. "Mega!" groans
Percival. But then, people have been saying "Super," another prefix, on
its own for many years. How many of you have heard of the "micro-
mini," a skirt or dress composed solely of prefixes? These extreme

examples show that we continue the process of creating new uses for Greek and Latin prefixes. We intuit the meaning of many prefixes, roots, and suffixes and can enhance our understanding of language by studying the rest.

A root or base word cannot be divided into smaller parts, but we can add to it to create new words. The noun "mark" is a root word, meaning "to take note of or to heed." We may want to relay to someone else the thing that we "marked." Therefore, we make a "remark." If we add a suffix, "able" to "remark," we have a new word, an adjective, that expresses our feeling that what we communicated was worthwhile, or "remarkable."

Everyone can benefit from knowledge of prefixes and suffixes. ESL speakers, for example, noticing the suffixes on words, will know "ance" or "ence" signals a noun while "ous" signals an adjective. As you noticed, this skill in recognizing word endings is so important in correctly using vocabulary that we included it in the chapter on Parts of Speech (see pages 45–46). As another example, non-native English speakers who recognize the meaning of "re" may realize without anyone telling them that they shouldn't say "I'm returning back your call," and native speakers may stop saying "I'm returning the book back to the library." Everyone will realize that, as "re" contains the meaning of "back," to say "returning back" is both wordy and redundant. Again, if everyone learns that "a" means "without or not," when he or she meets the words "amoral" or "asymmetrical" for the first time, there is a clue to understanding them. Therefore, this section offers clues to help you to make better use of the vocabulary that you already know, ways to recognize the unfamiliar, and ways to extend your use of language.

Most good dictionaries recognize the importance of the common prefixes, roots, and suffixes, by listing them and their meanings and giving examples. Here, we have arranged these elements, as we encouraged you to do with transitions, according to their functions. Prefixes, of course, come first.

## Prefixes

### Negation, Pejorative, or Opposition Prefixes

| Prefix | Meaning | Examples |
|--------|---------|----------|
| a or an | not, without | amoral, asymmetrical |
| anti | against | antiperspirant, antiwar |
| contra | against, opposing | contradict, contraband |
| counter | against, in opposition to | counter-argument |
| de | removal, take away from | deforest, debase |

| Prefix | Meaning | Examples |
|--------|---------|----------|
| dis | apart, away | dissimilar, disapprove |
| il | not | illogical, illegal |
| im/in | not | impatient, inept |
| ir | not | irrational, irreverent |
| mal | bad, wrong | malcontent, malfunction |
| mis | mistaken, wrong | misspelling, mistaken |
| non | not | nonaligned, nonagression |
| pseudo | false, imitation | pseudonym, pseudopod |
| un | not | untidy, unappreciated |

## Time, Order, Space, and Size Prefixes

| Prefix | Meaning | Examples |
|--------|---------|----------|
| ante | before | antebellum, antecedent |
| arch | highest or worst | archbishop, archenemy |
| circum | around, about | circumcise, circumvent |
| e or ex | out of, from | emit, excrement |
| ex | former | ex-model, ex-husband |
| fore (English) | before | foremothers, foretell |
| hyper | over | hypertext, hyperbole |
| hypo | under | hypothesis, hypokinesia |
| inter | between, among | intermarry, intercept |
| mega | large, great | megavolt, mega-movie |
| micro | small | microcosm, micro-organism |
| mini | little | miniscule, minimum |
| neo | new | neoclassic, neo-nazi |
| out | to the greatest extent | outlast, outdo |
| post | behind, after, later | postwar, postmodern |
| pre | before, in front of | pretest, preconscious |
| pro | before, projecting | proficient, proboscis |
| re | back, again | return, reinvent |
| sub | under, inferior | submarine, substrata |
| super | above, beyond | superlative, superscript |
| sur | over, above | surname, survive |
| syn | with, together | synonymous, synthesis |
| trans | across, over | transliterate, translucent |
| ultra | extremely, beyond | ultraviolet, ultranationalism |

## Number Prefixes

| Prefix | Meaning | Examples |
|---|---|---|
| uni, mono | one | uniform, university |
| bi, di | two | bilingual, bi-annual |
| tri | three | triathlete, trimester |
| tetra | four | tetrameter, tetravalent |
| penta | five | Pentagon, pentagram |
| hex | six | hexagon, hexangular |
| scpt | seven | sextuplet, septuagenarian |
| octa | eight | octopus, octave |
| nona | nine | nonagon, nonagenarian |
| multi, poly | many | polygram, polygamous |

## Attitude Prefixes

| Prefix | Meaning | Examples |
|---|---|---|
| anti | against | antiwar, antiphony |
| co | with, together | cooperate, cohabit |
| col, com, cor | with, together | collaborate, commune, correlate |
| con | with, together | concur, concord |
| pro | on the side of | pro-democracy, proponent |

## Other Prefixes

| Prefix | Meaning | Examples |
|---|---|---|
| auto | self | autograph, automobile |
| biblio | book | bibliography, bibliophile |
| demi | lesser, half | demigod, demitasse |
| mcta | of a higher order | metaphysics, metanarrative |
| pan | world-wide, all | pan-African, pan-Pacific |
| pedi/o | foot | pedicure, pedicab |
| proto | first, original | prototype, protogenesis |
| semi | half | semicolon, semiformal |
| stereo | solid | stereotype, stereography |
| vice | deputy | viceroy, vice-president |

Just as knowing prefixes is an aid to vocabulary building, so too is knowing some of the common roots. We showed you in the introduction how a French root like "mark" could grow as we added prefixes and suffixes to it. English is filled with words that have common Greek or Latin roots. In some of the examples, you will notice that we have used prefixes from the above list, and in others, you will see two roots words combined to form words. Knowing the roots will strengthen your grasp on the English language.

## Root Words

| Root | Meaning | Examples |
|---|---|---|
| audi | hearing, sound | audiophile, audiology |
| bene | good or well | benefactor, beneficiary |
| bio | life | biology, biosphere |
| duc(e) | lead or make | produce, deduce |
| gen | production of | generator, generation |
| gen | race, descent | genetics, gene |
| geo | the earth | geology, geography |
| graph | to write | cartography, calligraphy |
| jur, jus | law | jurisdiction, justice |
| log(o) | word, speech | logograph, logotherapy |
| luc | light | translucent, lucid |
| manu | hand | manuscript, manufacture |
| mit, mis | to send | transmitter, transmission |
| path | feel, suffer | sympathy, empathy |
| phil(e) | love | bibliophile, pedophile |
| photo | light | photosynthesis, telephoto |
| port | to carry | transport, portable |
| psyche | soul | psychology, psyched out |
| scrib/script | to write | scribble, transcription |
| sent | to feel | resentful, sentimental |

## Suffixes

### Noun Suffixes

| Suffix | Meaning | Examples |
|---|---|---|
| **people** | | |
| er/or | inhabitant | teenager, Newfoundlander |
| er/or | one who | instructor, plumber |
| eer | one who | engineer, volunteer |
| ster | worker, agent | webster, gangster |
| ese | nationality | Chinese, Japanese |
| (i)an | pertaining to | Canadian, Acadian |
| ite | member of a | socialite, Mennonite |
| ist | community, a party | socialist, guitarist |

| Suffix | Meaning | Examples |
|--------|---------|----------|
| **small** | | |
| let | small, insignificant | Piglet, booklet |
| ette | imitation | leatherette, flanellette |
| ette | small, compact | Chevette, roomette |
| ess | female | waitress, actress |
| ie/y | relatives | auntie, daddy, mummy |
| | | |
| **status, class, position** | | |
| dom (English) | rank, state | freedom, kingdom |
| ery | condition, place | slavery, nunnery |
| ism | doctrine, political theory | fascism, Darwinism |
| (ocr)acy | governmental system | theocracy, democracy |
| ship | condition, position | leadership, friendship |

## Other Noun Suffixes

| Suffix | Meaning | Examples |
|--------|---------|----------|
| ful | amount contained by $x$ | spoonful, cupful |
| ing | composition of $x$ | panelling, heading |
| ity | quality of | equity, tenacity |
| ment | condition of | excitement, detriment |
| ness | state of | kindness, stubbornness |
| sion/tion | state of being, action | transmission, exaltation |

## Verb Suffixes

| Suffix | Meaning | Examples |
|--------|---------|----------|
| age | activity or result | drainage, suffrage |
| al | action | dismissal, renewal |
| ant | agent, instrument | defendant, sextant |
| ate | cause to be | detonate, consecrate |
| ation | state, action | demonstration, domination |
| ation | (collective noun) institution | organization |
| ee | passive | employee, divorcee, licensee |
| en | cause to become | strengthen, whiten |
| ify, fy | cause to become | falsify, satisfy |
| ing | (forms gerunds) | sitting, smiling, smoking |
| ize | cause to become | revolutionize, magnetize |
| ment | state, action | government, inducement |

## Adjective Suffixes

| Suffix | Meaning | Examples |
|---|---|---|
| al (ial, ical) | pertaining to | glacial, logical |
| able | capable of being | writable, doable |
| ed | having the quality of the preceding verb | rented, lightened |
| esque | appearing like | grotesque, arabesque |
| ful | having a quality of | dreadful, mirthful |
| ible | capable of being | incredible, edible |
| ic | pertaining to | panic, Hispanic |
| ian | pertaining to | Calgarian, ruffian |
| ish | having a quality of | reddish, selfish |
| ive | having a nature of | creative, relative |
| less | without | careless, moonless |
| like | having a quality of | child-like, meat-like |
| ly | having the quality of | womanly, saintly |
| (i)ous | having a quality of | contagious, outrageous |

# Spelling

The cheerful news is that most of us spell correctly most of the time, and that's quite remarkable. A few basic strategies help us to do this. Some people compare what they have just written on the page with the "picture" in their minds of what the correct word looks like. These are the people who mutter, "That doesn't look right," as they proofread for spelling. When you ask these people how to spell a word, they often write the word in the air or on a desk with their finger so that they can check the "picture." Another strategy that some people use is to "sound the word out." In other words, they use phonetics, either what they learned in school or their personal version. These people murmur "an-al-y-sis" or "soph-is-ti-cate." Both these strategies work well for many people, yet they are certainly not foolproof.

Some dyslexics tell us that either of these strategies taken to the extreme can collapse. On the one hand, people take such careful pictures that they see discrete components very clearly, and as long as all those components make it to the page, these people feel satisfied. For them, *order* is not important. The *components* of the "picture" are. These people do the classic switching of letters, syllables, or even words. On the other hand, some people take "sounding the word out" to its logical conclusion. They might spell "to," "two," and "too" all as "to" on one day or "too" on the next. If they were asked to spell "phonetics," they might write "foneticks" or "fonetix." Therefore, unless we understand our own spelling challenges, our natural strategies can sometimes cause problems.

In this section, we provide you with Spell Checkmates that give some ways to differentiate between words that people often confuse and, therefore, misspell. Later, we present a list of commonly misspelled words, ask you to analyze the mistakes you make, and give you a few rules.

## The Technological Proofreaders

Naturally, we expect that you will use a spell-check programme to help you hand in a mechanically correct paper. You may even use a grammar check for the same reason, and we appreciate your care. Nonetheless, we know that these programmes are fallible. Just for fun, Claire did a grammar check on an agreement exercise, and the programme failed to pick up any of the errors but drew her attention to an agreement error that didn't exist. Of course, such programmes also regularly draw attention to sentence structures that they think are passive although they are not. Ironically, the people who can benefit from these technical aids are the people who know most about grammar and sentence structure—and we hope that that is you. This book should give you the tools to make grammar checks safe to use at the same time that it makes them redundant.

## Spell Checkmates

In general, although spell checkers help in picking up typos, they cannot help with some of the most commonly misspelled words. Actually, grammar checks are a bit more helpful in this area, as they may say something like "This word is often confused with X." Still, that puts the responsibility right back with you, the writer. You have to know which word is appropriate.

Fortunately, as we've already mentioned, most of us spell correctly most of the time and just have a few dozen words about which we are unsure. Frequently, these words have mates, sometimes homonyms, words that sound the same as they do, that we confuse them with. Below is a list of Spell Checkmates, frequently confused words that spell checkers cannot help you with. When we can, we give you mnemonic devices to help you remember how to spell the word you need. We mark these aids with a 🐾 . (See page 432 for our rationale.) We also supply rhyming words to help in differentiating the pronunciation.

Naturally, you can also create your own mnemonics. Make an effort to learn your trouble words, for technology cannot do this for you.

Follow these suggestions when you identify the Spell Checkmates that plague you:

- When we identify a word as being a countable noun, you can make it plural. Write a few different sentences using the plural, e.g., *The effects of the fire were devastating.*

- If the word is uncountable, then be sure to use it without any article.

- Verbs, on the other hand, can be made past tense, so write a few sentences using the past tense, e.g., *The fire affected the neighbours' houses too.*

Writing these sentences should help to implant the right patterns in your mind, and when you want to use the word, the sentences that you wrote should come to mind. Add your problem words to your spelling log.

| Word | Comment and Example |
|---|---|
| **accept** | a verb |
| **except** | a preposition, it will be followed by a noun/object |
| | *If you accept this proposal, we will paint everything except the ceiling.* |
| **advice** | an uncountable noun, it will be a subject or an object, rhymes with "mice." |
| **advise** | verb, to give advice, counsel, it rhymes with "surprise." |
| | *We advise you to accept the advice of your lawyer.* |
| | These words, with "c" in the noun and "s" in the verb are the same pattern as **apprentice/apprentise, device/devise, licence/license, practice/practise, prophecy/ prophesy.** "Defence/defense" is not in this pattern, "defence" merely being the preferred British spelling of this noun. |
| | *We advise you to practise before trying for your licence.* |
| | *This advice about practice will ensure you get your licence on the first try, and when they license you, you will feel proud.* |
| **adolescence** | noun, the state of being becoming mature. |
| | *His adolescence was prolonged by a serious illness.* |
| **adolescent(s)** | noun, someone in the process of becoming mature. |
| | 🐾 Perhaps you can think of that "t" as "teenager." |
| | adjective, immature |
| | *Calling the team's behaviour adolescent gave real adolescents a bad name.* |

| | |
|---|---|
| **affect** | a verb in normal usage, it can be a noun meaning "emotion" or "feeling," but only people in psychology use it this way. |
| **effect(s)** | usually a noun, it will be a subject or an object. If the questionable word follows "the," you know, unless you are taking psychology, that "effect" is the word you need. |
| | *When Harry took the pill, the effect was startling: it affected his vision.* |
| | As rarely as you will use "affect" as a noun, you will use "effect" as a verb when you mean to produce an effect or to accomplish something. |
| | *If we are to effect a solution, we will need the backing of all staff.* |
| **alot** | This is never, under any circumstance, a word! |
| **a lot** | These words can mean either "much" or "many," so they can be used with either countable or uncountable nouns. You can have a lot of monkeys or a lot of trouble. Some instructors prefer that you avoid the term entirely and use "much" or "many" or something more specific (twenty-three) instead. |
| **allot** | verb, meaning to apportion, distribute, or give |
| | *Janice allotted each child a lot of play dough.* |
| **anecdote(s)** | noun, a short narrative, not necessarily funny, but, one hopes, at least interesting |
| | *The speaker began the presentation with an anecdote about her adventures in Peru.* |
| **antidote(s)** | noun, something that prevents or counteracts something bad or injurious, like a poison |
| | *The doctor began her speech with an anecdote about finding an antidote for the disease that killed most of the children in a small African village.* |
| **bare** | verb, to reveal, to expose |
| | *She bared her innermost feelings.* |
| | adjective, naked, uncomplicated, simple. |
| | *In his defence, he said only the bare minimum.* |
| **bear(s)** | noun, the animal or a crabby person |
| | verb, present tense, to give birth, to carry, to be patient. |
| | *The bear bore two cubs that spring, and we couldn't bear to disturb her.* |

| | |
|---|---|
| **brake(s)** | noun, a device for stopping or separation |
| | *Because Vincent wasn't used to driving a standard, he used the emergency brake when he was going up hill, coming to a stop at a traffic light.* |
| | verb, to slow down, to prevent, to stop |
| | *Jennifer braked hard before the curve.* |
| **break(s)** | noun, a change, a pause, a stroke of luck |
| | *Give me a break!* |
| | transitive verb, to be changed, damaged, to discontinue, to interrupt |
| | *She was afraid she would break the crystal vase.* |
| **breath(s)** | noun, an intake or outflow of air, rhymes with "death" |
| | *His breath smelled of licorice.* |
| **breathe** | verb, inhale, respire. This word rhymes with "seethe." |
| | *I can't breathe in this stuffy room.* |
| **choose** | verb, present tense. This word rhymes with "news." |
| **chose** | verb, past tense. This word rhymes with "nose." |
| | *It was hard to choose, but eventually, Martin chose the dark beer.* |

Try to associate these words with their rhymes in your mind. For example, "Choose to read good news now," could reinforce the pronunciation while emphasizing, with "now," that it is present tense. "Choose ordinary oranges," could alert you to the two o's. "Joe chose hard toes," helps with the pronunciation of "chose." Use this technique with other word pairs.

| | |
|---|---|
| **coarse** | adjective, meaning "rough" in texture or "unrefined," "vulgar." Movie censors refer to "coarse language." |
| | *The coarse sandpaper gouged nasty scratches into the fine veneer.* |
| **course(s)** | noun, a programme or a route |
| | *Shelley dropped the course.* |
| **complement** | verb, meaning to *complete* something or noun, something that has completed something |
| | verb |
| | *This colour will complement the colour of the sofa.* |
| | noun (countable) |
| | *Roger thinks wine is a complement to a good meal* |

| | |
|---|---|
| **compliment(s)** | transitive verb, to flatter, to commend |
| | verb |
| | *May I compliment you on your presentation!* |
| | noun |
| | *Harriet loved to receive compliments on her wit.* |
| | Perhaps you can remember the difference by thinking "**I** like to receive compl**i**ments." |
| **comprehensible** | adjective, meaning capable of being understood |
| | *His handwriting was barely comprehensible.* |
| **comprehensive** | adjective, meaning having a large range or scope |
| | *The report on the amalgamation was comprehensive, answering all our questions.* |
| **conscience(s)** | noun, inner sense of right and wrong. Some people do well with this word just muttering "con *science*." |
| **conscious** | adjective, alert, attentive, able to feel |
| | *Because of her social conscience, she was conscious of the difference in wages for what appeared to be equal work.* |
| **consul(s)** | noun, a government official |
| **council(s)** | noun, a group of people, often elected, e.g., a strata council or a city council |
| **counsel** | noun, advice |
| | *He received excellent counsel from his doctor.* |
| | noun, one who gives legal advice, countable |
| | *Martha was counsel for the defence.* |
| **counsel** | verb, to give advice |
| | *Peter counselled first-year students each September.* |
| | *The strata council hired legal counsel, which counselled them to sue the roofing company.* |
| ***desert(s)*** | noun, stress the first syllable, a dry, arid region or emptiness |
| | Think of the one "s" as being the Sahara. |
| **des*ert*** | verb, stress the second syllable, to abandon, flee |
| | *The soldier deserted just before the final battle.* |
| **dessert(s)** | noun, pronounced like the verb above. Think of the two "s's" in the middle of the word as meaning strawberry shortcake. |
| **decent** | adjective, honest, considerate |
| | *Earnest is a decent sort of fellow.* |

**descent(s)**   noun, fall, course (path going downward), ancestry

*The descent was so steep that they took two hours to get back to the camp.* (course)

*Annika was of Danish descent, and Peter was of Dutch descent.* (ancestry)

**dining**   noun, eating

*The dining room was too small for the whole family.*

**dinning**   noun, a loud, confused noise. Never in our combined years of teaching has a student had to use this word. Perhaps, you should think of the "nn" as being "not necessary!" The word is related to "din," so if this is the meaning that you want, use "din" rather than "dinning."

**does**   verb, rhymes with "was," another verb. The confusion between "does" and "dose" is slight, but it does turn up frequently in word-processed papers (as does confusion between "from" and "form.") For most of us, these are typos rather than misspellings; nonetheless, there is a problem here that spell checkers cannot help with. Therefore, you must always proofread the printed page watching for these words if they spell trouble for you.

**dose(s)**   noun, a quantity of medicine, rhymes with "gross," often a quality of medicine

*How does a good dose of medicine sound to you?*

**forth**   adverb, forward or onward, in older books often preceded by the verb "sally" (to set out energetically on a trip or excursion)

**fourth**   noun or adjective, coming number four in a sequence

*They sallied forth on their fourth expedition, not knowing that the colony was now wracked with civil war.*

**hear**   verb, to perceive by ear, to listen. Think about that "ear."

**here**   adverb, in this place, at this point

*Please put the tarantulas in here.*

or to call attention to something

*Here is the antidote.*

**heroin**   noun, a drug

**heroine(s)**   noun, the main character in a literary work

*The heroine left her boyfriend as soon as she found out that he was using heroin.*

**its**   possessive pronoun. Like other possessive pronouns such as *hers*, *theirs*, and *ours*, this word does not have an apostrophe.

**it's**        contraction of "it is" and, but not very often in Canada, "it has."

*It's a shame that its head gasket went just days before they were going to sell the car.*

*It's been a pleasure working with you.*

**later**        adverb, happening after something else, rhymes with (Christian) Slater. Remember that it has the word *late* in it.

**latter**       noun and adjective, meaning second in a sequence of two, rhymes with "matter." 🐀 Associate the necessity of "two" with the two "t's." The partner of the latter is "the former."

*Later, Erin will deal with the latter section of the report.*

**lead**        verb, present tense. This word rhymes with "weed."

*The path leads to a small bridge that crosses the creek at a narrow point.*

noun (countable), a clue or direction

*Give me a lead! Who were the victim's enemies?*

noun, metal. This word rhymes with "dead."

*The presence of the lead pipe was a lead suggesting that Mr. Body was killed in the kitchen.*

noun (countable), what we call that which is found in the middle of a pencil, even though we know perfectly well that it is graphite.

*During the exam the lead in my pencil broke twice!*

**led**        verb, past tense, rhymes with "dead"

*I was led to my bed, and I slept like the dead until noon.*

**loose**       adjective, rhymes with "noose." 🐀 Try to see those two "o's" as two hula hoops circling loosely around someone's waist. 🐀 Alternately, if you are in a bad mood, envision a noose with two loose knots in it being put around someone's neck.

*Trevor shouldn't make his noose so loose.*

**lose**        verb, present tense, to mislay, rhymes with "shoes." 🐀 Associating these two words should help you with pronunciation, and the "s" in "shoe" can remind you of the one "s" in "lose."

*If she loses the locket, she'll have no picture of Sam.*

**loss(es)**     noun, a debit or expense, or something that has been lost, rhymes with "boss"

*The loss annoyed Tai's boss.*

| | |
|---|---|
| **lost** | adjective, missing or bewildered |
| | *Ben was lost in thought.* |
| **meet** | verb, present tense, to encounter or to come together, rhymes with "treat" |
| | *Can we meet for lunch next week?* |
| | noun (countable), an assembly, a contest, a tournament. |
| | *Betty had to go to three track meets.* |
| **met** | verb, past tense, to encounter or to come together, rhymes with "get" |
| | *Betty met Pete at the meet, but she didn't meet his brother.* |
| **miner** | noun, someone who works extracting ore in a mine |
| | *Miners have faced unsafe working conditions for centuries.* |
| **minor** | noun or adjective, inferior or not important. |
| | *The miner had a minor complaint about a piece of his safety equipment, but he immediately got a new one.* |
| **moral(s)** | noun, lesson or precept |
| | *The morals in movies are seldom surprising.* |
| | adjective, virtuous, honest, ethical |
| | *Al is a very moral person.* |
| **morale** | noun, team spirit or frame of mind |
| | *The team's morale rebounded after the no-hitter, and they celebrated with a flagon of ale.* |
| | 🐷— You could think, although incorrectly, that "ale" was a kind of spirit like whiskey to help you remember how to spell "morale." |
| | *The moral of the story seemed to be that good morale must precede success rather than follow it.* |
| **passed** | verb, past tense, to go by, to complete successfully, to approve of |
| | *The council passed a motion to amend the parking bylaws.* |
| **past(s)** | noun, former times, a personal history, tense |
| | *The old men, preferring to speculate about the future, seldom talked about their pasts.* |
| **patience** | noun, endurance, tolerance |
| | *Lawrence's patience was remarkable.* |
| **patient(s)** | noun, a sick person |
| | *The patient had both legs in a cast.* |
| | adjective, enduring, tolerant |
| | *The patients in the waiting room were very patient.* |

**personal** adjective, particular, private, relating to self

*Patrick's personal pet peeve is privacy, lack of.*

🐷— Perhaps, you can think of the person, Al.

**personnel** noun, staff or work force, or adjective, as in personnel officer, someone looking after the needs or interest of the personnel in a company or institution

*The personnel voted unanimously in favour of accepting the agreement.*

**principal(s)** noun, chief, educator or, for those with mortgages, the amount of money owed without considering the interest.

🐷— Many people are taught that a princi*pal* is your *pal*.

*After she won the 649, the principal of Jake's school was able to pay down $100,000 on the principal of her mortgage.*

adjective, chief, main

*The principal reason Kenji is leaving is that the bus service is inadequate.*

**principle(s)** noun, a belief, a rule

*Michael's principles and ability ensure that he succeeds.*

**quiet** noun, peace, order, lack of noise or disturbance or adjective, peaceful, calm, silent

*The quiet neighbourhood appealed to Sylvie.*

🐷— Perhaps you can envision ET, with that long finger in front of his mouth, saying "Shhhhh! Qui*et*!'

**quit** verb, to abandon leave

*Sally quit her job.*

**quite** adverb, to a degree, very

*The tie was quite loud, so Algernon changed his plaid shirt.*

**set** transitive verb, to place, to designate

*Yu Chien set the flowers on the table.*

Also to "set the table," to put dishes, eating utensils, napkins, etc. on the table.

*Darlene set the table.*

**set** noun, countable, a collection of items

*When they got married, Rob and Sandra got five sets of towels, four sets of bedding, three sets of dishes, two sets of steak knives, and a partridge in a deep freeze.*

**sit** verb, present tense, to be seated

*They all like to sit in the front row.*

**sight(s)** noun, scene, marvel, range of view

*Of all the sights that they saw on the prairies, the sight of the vee of geese flying across the full moon would remain with them forever.*

| | |
|---|---|
| **site(s)** | noun, location, area |
| | *We found an inexpensive building site, but it was on a tremendous slope.* |
| | *The building site was a dreadful sight, with decrepit cars, rusty cans, and boards full of nails lying around.* |
| **cite** | transitive verb, to attribute or to acknowledge |
| | *You must always cite your sources when you are writing a paper.* |
| **stationary** | adjective, motionless, immovable, permanent |
| | *The bar was stationary, but the bartender moved around a lot.* |
| **stationery** | noun, writing paper, envelopes |
| | *The stationery had the company logo stretched down the left-hand margin.* |
| | — You could perhaps associate the "e" in "stationery" with "envelope." |
| **than** | conjunction, used in comparisons, rhymes with "can" |
| | *Stephen can run faster than Steven can.* |
| **then** | adverb of time, rhymes with "men" |
| | *The men then put the hen in the pen.* |
| | — Think of the "e" in "then" as meaning "era," a unit of *time.* |
| **their** | possessive pronoun/adjective. — Perhaps you can think of the *heir possessing* what he or she has inherited. |
| **there** | adverb of place, not here |
| | *Put the computer there.* |
| **they're** | contraction of "they are" |
| | *They're going to take their kites there tomorrow.* |
| | *They're going to fly higher!* |
| **to** | preposition and part of an infinitive |
| | *To go downtown or to go to the mall is a question sometimes decided on the basis of where one can park easily.* |
| **too** | adverb used to modify adjectives or other adverbs, meaning excessively or also. |
| | *The car was too big and too fast to make Kimiko feel comfortable.* |
| | — Norma's grade five teacher, Mrs. Adams, told her to remember that "too" has too many "o's". |
| | *James thought it was too big too.* |
| **two** | the number 2 |
| **weather** | atmospheric conditions |
| | *The weather during the summer was the hottest on record.* |
| | — Think of "*heat*" and good w*ea*ther. |

| | |
|---|---|
| **whether** | in any case, adverb |
| | *Charles is going whether we go or not.* |
| **were** | past tense, plural, of the verb "to be," rhymes with "her" |
| | *They were happy to see that the thieves had been caught.* |
| **we're** | contraction, "we are." If you have trouble with these words, pronounce the word "we're" to rhyme with the first part of "weird" or with "beer." |
| | *If we win the 649, we're going to buy two Harleys.* |
| **where** | adverb, in or at what place? rhymes with "care" or "bear" |
| | *Where did Yvonne put the Christmas decorations?* |
| **who's** | contraction, "who is," rhymes with "shoes" |
| | *Who's that knocking at my door?* |
| **whose** | interrogative or possessive pronoun, rhymes with "shoes" |
| | *Whose car did you put the alligator in?* |
| | *This is Amy, the former friend whose car we borrowed.* |
| **woman** | noun, one female person, generally pronounced "wumin" |
| | *The woman stepped from her car and strode down the sidewalk toward the pawnshop.* |
| **women** | noun, more than one female person, generally pronounced "wimmin." |
| | *The woman in red joined the three elderly women sitting in the far corner of the room.* |
| **you're** | contraction, "you are," rhymes with "cure" |
| | *You're the one I'll be waiting for.* |
| **your** | possessive pronoun, rhymes with "door" |
| | *Your purple door ensures that you're always going to be able to tell which townhouse is yours.* |

## The Common Spelling Errors

Should you make a mistake with the following words, unlike the Spell Checkmates above whose confusion technology cannot deal with, a spell checker will flag it for you. This is comforting and a great help to all of us.

However, we all have been or will be in situations where we write without the aid of technology. For many of you these experiences will be writing in-class essays or labs; for some of you, they will be quick memos on work terms; and for others, it will be letters or memos on the job when your computer system is down, and you have to write without its aid. At a meeting, you may be asked to jot down notes and give them to your boss immediately after. These situations create demands on our spelling ability. Another challenge for some of us is e-mail systems that don't have a spell-checking component.

For all these reasons, it is preferable to find out your problem words and learn them. Sometimes, you can mutter to yourself, "There is a rat in separate" to remember that "a" after the "p" or "Definite is finite" to get those two "i's." What you say doesn't have to make sense. You use it as a mnemonic device so that what your instructor or boss sees is correctly spelled. You can use your visual sense as well. Write out "separate" and draw a rat beside it. Print "definite" and draw eyes where the "i's" appear. Remember, the words that you misspell are comparatively few.

Your instructor may choose to use the following list as a pretest, and this is a fine idea. If, however, your class is one semester, and you have a great deal to get through, he or she may leave this section up to you. If you do the list as a pretest, the incorrect spellings will form the basis for your personal spelling list. You can add any words that you remember struggling over. If you are doing this on your own, go through the list and pick out the words that you know are troublesome for you. Start your personal Spelling Log, and add to it as you make errors in your work.

## Pretest or Your-test

| | | | |
|---|---|---|---|
| absence | outrageous | privilege | referring |
| knowledge | auxiliary | convenient | environment |
| accidentally | parallel | proceed | relevant |
| lieutenant | believe | curiosity | erroneous |
| accommodate | perceive | professor | repetition |
| maneuver | benefited | curriculum | exaggerate |
| (manoeuvre) | perform | pronounce | resistance |
| acknowledge | changeable | deceive | exhilaration |
| niece | permanent | pronunciation | restaurant |
| acquire | committee | definite | exist |
| ninety | perseverance | psychiatry | rhythm |
| amateur | comparatively | desirable | existence |
| noticeable | possession | psychology | ridiculous |
| analysis | conceive | dissatisfied | familiar |
| occasion(ally) | preceding | pursue | secretary |
| anxious | condemn | ecstasy | fascinating |
| occur | prejudice | receive | shepherd |
| apparent | conscientious | eighth | foreign |
| occurrence | prevalent | recommend | similar |
| athlete | consistent | embarrass | government |

| | | | |
|---|---|---|---|
| souvenir | guarantee | unnecessary | indispensable |
| governor | tragedy | humorous | writer/writing |
| supersede | guidance | vacuum | kindergarten |
| grammar | truly | (in)dependent | written |
| temperament | height | weird | |

## Your Personal Spelling List and Analysis

Once you have created your personal spelling list, you can start to group words and analyze your errors. You may find that you are quite consistent, struggling, for example, with the "*i* before *e* rule" and its exceptions, with *ent/ant* endings, or with double consonants in the middle of words. This kind of analysis gives you power.

### *i before e*

The "*i* before *e* rule: *i* before *e* except after *c* and when sounded like *a* as in *neighbour* and *weigh*," has exceptions:

| | |
|---|---|
| caffeine | neither |
| either | seize |
| feint | sheik |
| leisure | weird |

Here are examples that follow "except after *c*."

| | |
|---|---|
| ceiling | perceive |
| conceive | receive |
| deceive | |

Here are examples that follow "sounded like *a* as in *neighbour* and *weigh*.

| | |
|---|---|
| eight | veil |
| sleigh | weight |

If the sound is neither long *a* or long *e*, *ei* is normally used.

| | |
|---|---|
| counterfeit | height |
| foreign | heir |
| forfeit | their |

# Learning Log: Spelling

When you have done the pretest, (page 432) record your spelling
challenges here, adding to your list as other errors arise.

_____

_____

_____

_____

_____

_____

_____

_____

_____

_____

_____

_____

_____

_____

_____

_____

_____

_____

_____

_____

_____

_____

_____

_____

_____

_____

# Answer Key

## Chapter 1: Parts of Speech

### Pretest A (page 2)

2. <u>He</u>, personal pronoun; <u>who</u>, relative pronoun; <u>lead</u>, abstract noun; <u>running</u>, present participle
4. <u>Cowabunga</u>! interjection; <u>perfect</u>, adjective
6. <u>Who</u>, interrogative pronoun; <u>himself</u>, reflexive pronoun; <u>the</u>, definite article
8. <u>herself</u>, intensifier pronoun; <u>never</u>, adverb; <u>candy</u>, concrete noun

### Pretest B (pages 2–3)

2. <u>To be fit</u>, subject of verb "became"; <u>her</u>, modifier of noun "object"; <u>object</u>, predicate noun following verb "became"
4. <u>Fortunately</u>, adverb modifying the independent clause; <u>Letitia</u>, indirect object of the verb "gave"; <u>car keys</u>, direct object of the verb "gave"
6. <u>Wandering</u>, modifier of the noun "players"; <u>park</u>, object of the preposition "through"
8. <u>tripped</u>, verb of the independent clause; <u>sprawling</u>, modifier of the noun "dog"; <u>dog</u>, object of the preposition "over"

### Exercise 1 (page 4)

2. regards (abstract)
4. flock? (abstract, collective)

### Exercise 2 (page 6)

2. spider (countable)
4. chair (countable)

### Exercise 3 (pages 6–7)

2. Mr. Lopinski (object of the preposition "to")
4. sheep (object of the verb "gave")

### Exercise 4 (pages 7–8)

2. knowledge—abstract; student—concrete
4. counsellor—concrete; advice—abstract
6. Sarah—concrete; tea—concrete
8. coffee— concrete; tree house— concrete
10. teapot—concrete; microwave—concrete

### Exercise 5 (page 8)

2. pencils—common; floor—common
4. Christmas—proper; Thursday—proper
6. Woody Guthrie—proper; songs—common
8. Jergen's Lotion—proper; Perth—proper
10. PowerPoint—proper; computer—common

### Exercise 6 (page 9)

2. I myself (intensive)
4. Everyone (indefinite)
6. Who (interrogative)
8. this (demonstrative)
10. herself (intensive)

## Exercise 7 (page 10)

2.  They (subject of the verb "left")     4.  he (subject of the verb "managed")

## Exercise 8 (pages 10–11)

2.  its (one)          8.  their (boys)
4.  they (men)         10. their (teachers)
6.  his (instructor)

## Exercise 9 (page 12)

2.  mowed; lawn     4.  hit; homer

## Exercise 10 (page 13)

2.  cried     4.  walked

## Exercise 11 (page 14)

2.  remains (predicate adjective)     4.  was (predicate noun)

## Exercise 12 (page 15)

2.  Driving (present participle modifying "aficionados")
4.  driving (present participle, nonfinite verb)

## Exercise 13 (page 18)

2.  favourite   number     4.  print   easy

## Exercise 14 (page 20)

2.  clumsily (adverb of manner)
4.  After the snowplow passed (adverb of time)

## Exercise 15 (page 22)

2.  for polio (adjective phrase modifying "cure")
4.  into mailbox (adverb phrase of place)
6.  to building (adjective phrase modifying "entrance")

## Exercise 16 (page 23–24)

2.  but (CC joining two independent clauses)
4.  so (CC joining two independent clauses)

## Exercise 17 (page 25)

2.  Since     4.  since

## Exercise 18 (page 26)

2.  Not only, but also     4.  neither, nor

## Exercise 19 (page 30)

2.  ___, ___        6.  The, a          10.  ___, ___
4.  ___             8.  a, a, the, the

## Exercise 20 (page 31)

2.  the, a          6.  a               10.  the, ___
4.  ___, ___, the, ___     8.  the

**Exercise 21 (page 31)**

2. the, the      6. the      10. The, ___
4. The      8. ___

**Exercise 22 (page 32)**

2. a, the, the      6. The      10. the, ___
4. the, the      8. The

**Exercise 23 (page 32)**

2. ___, ___      6. the      10. ___, the
4. the, ___      8. the, the

**Exercise 24 (page 33)**

2. the      6. ___, the      10. the
4. the      8. the

**Exercise 25 (page 33)**

2. ___      6. ___      10. The
4. the      8. the

**Exercise 26 (page 34)**

2. the, the      6. the      10. the
4. The      8. The

**Exercise 27 (page 35)**

advice, was, information, was, work, clothing, was, weather, was, snow, traffic, was

**Exercise 28 (page 38)**

2. a few      4. few

**Exercise 29 (page 40)**

2. little, or a little      4. much, or any

**Exercise 30 (pages 40–41)**

2. ___      6. ___      10. ___
4. ___      8. ___, a

**Exercise 31 (pages 41–42)**

2. a, ___      6. ___, a      10. ___, a
4. ___, a      8. ___

**Exercise 32 (page 42)**

2. equipment      6. popcorn      10. furniture
4. machinery      8. knowledge

**Exercise 33 (pages 42–43)**

2. software      6. traffic      10. transportation
4. music      8. homework, housework

**Exercise 34 (pages 43–44)**

2. wines      6. gases      10. cheese
4. bread      8. sugar

### Exercise 35 Indefinite Nouns (page 44)

2. Louisa thoroughly enjoys movies. She went to a movie on the weekend. The movie was about a group of people who went on a holiday together and became entangled in a series of crimes because of their naiveté. That type of movie is Louisa's favourite. She says movies like that provide her with an escape whereas movies about relationships leave her tired from worrying about the characters. She doesn't like art movies either because movies with slow plots leave her bored. As a result of her taste in movies, Louisa says few of her friends will go with her to a movie. They say that the movies Louisa enjoys are a waste of time. Louisa says that's not true. Even silly movies often give you something to think about. In fact, Louisa claims, you can learn a lot from movies.

### Exercise 36 (page 45)

| picky | A | economic | A | concealment | N |
|---|---|---|---|---|---|
| spectacle | N | fussy | A | questionable | A |
| extravagance | N | attractive | A | dependent | A |
| pushy | A | friendship | N | freedom | N |
| vibrant | A | imaginary | A | various | A |
| surprising | A | tragic | A | drainage | N |
| concentration | N | gradual | A | refusal | N |
| mistaken | A | memorable | A | impression | N |

### Exercise 37 (page 46)

2. confidence
4. competent

6. violent
8. confident

10. confidence

## Chapter 2: Verbs and Voice

### Exercise 1 (page 57)

2. started
4. has been
6. have lived

8. has damaged
10. Has written

### Exercise 2 (pages 57–58)

2. (past indicative, past indicative) taught
4. (present indicative, present indicative) has smoked
6. (present progressive) takes
8. (present indicative passive, present progressive) is, committed, works
10. (present indicative, present progressive) have gone

### Exercise 3 (page 58)

2. has been, is
4. gave

6. has been, came
8. appreciate

10. enters

### Exercise 4 (page 59)

2. has worked
4. underwent
6. received

8. is, will be
10. have lived

### Exercise 5 (pages 59–60)

2. found
4. reveal

6. watch, do, think
8. sets

10. has taken, has become;
*or* took, has become

### Exercise 7 (page 63–64)

2. has received, has been
4. has expressed
6. has been investigating *or* has investigated
8. have been counting *or* have counted
10. has graduated

### Exercise 8 (page 66) *Suggested answers*

2. By the time Jiki's birthday arrived, he had already had two birthday parties. *or* One day after Jiki had had his first pre-birthday party, he had a second pre-birthday party. *or* Jiki had already had a surprise pre-birthday party when Sarah gave him a second pre-birthday party.

### Exercise 9 (pages 66–67)

2. tried
4. studied
6. moved, bought

8. correct, depending upon what precedes it
10. had written

### Exercise 10 (page 67)

2. have finished
4. has worked
6. had cooperated

8. have stopped
10. had given

### Exercise 12 (page 73)

2. was
4. were

6. were
8. were

10. was

### Exercise 13 (pages 74–77)

would have been, would have rocketed, would have been, had been, would have loved, would have appealed, had had, would have studied, have entered, would have turned, would have made, would not have gained, would have wheezed, would have rolled, would have been

### Exercise 14 (pages 78–79)

2. would not have become
4. would make
6. will fly

8. will have
10. will come

### Exercise 15 (page 79)

2. would have been
4. would have finished
6. will buy

8. would have become
10. would have been

### Exercise 16 (pages 79–80)

2. will call
4. will be

6. will be surprised
8. would phone

10. Do not forget

### Exercise 17 (pages 80-81)

2. would choose
4. would have ruined
6. would defend

8. would know (Notice that this verb is an exception to the common pattern.)
10. would have lost

## Exercise 18 (page 84)

2. <u>are mercilessly satirized</u> (<u>passive</u>) The author mercilessly satirizes all the political parties that have ever campaigned in Blossomtown.
4. <u>capitalizes</u> (<u>active</u>) Insider knowledge is, therefore, capitalized on by Nostram to spin a convincing yarn.
6. <u>is locked</u> (<u>passive</u>) For example, in the novel, an opponent locks Pearlie Lightfinger, who is a thinly disguised reproduction of mayor June Brightlight, in a file room for ten hours on election day.
8. <u>has enjoyed</u> (<u>active</u>) Enormous success has been enjoyed by Mr. Nostram's book.
10. <u>recommend</u> (<u>active</u>) It is recommended as a light-hearted, humorous read.

## Exercise 19 (page 85) *Suggestions:*

2. I gained self-reliance by driving a bicycle rickshaw for a summer in Winnipeg.
4. I also gained interesting information about my city by driving tourists to nooks and crannies that I didn't know before.
6. I have often often criticized tourists for being ignorant about the places they visit.
8. They entertained me with unfamiliar stories of incidents and individuals.
10. Because of my peddling summer, I acquired a more tolerant and respectful view of the world.

## Exercise 20 (page 87–88) *Suggestions:*

2. As I looked out the window, a ship pulled into the harbour.  12
4. Sales begin right after Christmas.  5
6. At university, athletic students often join sports teams.  8
8. The exam was too difficult.  5 *or* Most students agreed the exam was too difficult.
10. A person may lack confidence because she suffered ridicule as a child.  12

## Exercise 21 (page 88) *Suggestions:*

2. The manager keeps employees in suspense by threatening "downsizing."  9
4. As I walked past the park, the band played "Scarborough Fair."  11
6. The government voted to remove the tobacco tax.  9
8. The big dog chased the small rabbit across the road.  10
10. Probably, you will enjoy the exam because, as you synthesize the course material, you learn something new.  17

## Exercise 22 (page 90)

2. may, might

4. should, will

## Exercise 23 (pages 90–91)

2. cannot, must not, may not

4. could not allow

## Exercise 24 (page 91–92)

should keep/ought to keep/must keep, may be/might be, may experience/might experience, produce, is, must light, must be, places, may seem/might seem, do not need, do need, can cause/may cause, represents, can be, become, can immobilize, threaten, takes

## Pretest (pages 93–96)

2. hearing
4. studying
6. us to return/the tenants to return
8. him to faint/the woman to faint
10. to go
12. to accept
14. visiting

16. us to vote/the voters to vote
18. to complete
20. to convince
22. winning
24. us to leave/the students to leave
26. buying
28. us to run/the soldiers to run

| | |
|---|---|
| 30. to get | 48. fighting |
| 32. me to take/someone to take | 50. to receive |
| 34. fixing | 52. to stop |
| 36. to maintain | 54. to be |
| 38. working | 56. buying |
| 40. playing | 58. to think |
| 42. to remember | 60. hard to get |
| 44. us not to cross/the civilians not to cross | 62. cleaning |
| 46. taking | 64. losing |

## Exercise 25 (page 98)

| | | |
|---|---|---|
| 2. to get | 6. to make | 10. to plan |
| 4. to choose | 8. to do | |

## Exercise 26 (pages 98–99)

| | | |
|---|---|---|
| 2. to try | 6. to keep | 10. to update |
| 4. to beat | 8. to start/to mention | |

## Exercise 27 (page 99)

| | |
|---|---|
| 2. parallel parking | 8. ordering |
| 4. to consider | 10. to lock |
| 6. cutting | |

## Exercise 28 (page 100)

| | | |
|---|---|---|
| 2. to pay | 6. walking | 10. to say |
| 4. to bring | 8. borrowing | |

## Exercise 29 (page 100)

| | | |
|---|---|---|
| 2. to enjoy | 6. to know | 10. warned Sarah to be |
| 4. them to join | 8. had difficulty finding | |

## Exercise 30 (page 101)

| | | |
|---|---|---|
| 2. telling | 6. reading | 10. being |
| 4. having | 8. to consider | |

## Exercise 31 (pages 101–102)

| | | |
|---|---|---|
| 2. ordering | 6. to eat | 10. tasting |
| 4. eating | 8. to try | |

# Chapter 3: Agreement

## Pretest (page 110)

| | |
|---|---|
| 2. have | 10. is |
| 4. contributes | 12. require |
| 6. looks | 14. has |
| 8. are | |

## Exercise 1 (pages 113–114)

| | |
|---|---|
| 2. fax can travel | 8. Electronic messages are |
| 4. fax transmissions transmit | 10. Both e-mail and faxes are, Canada moves |
| 6. e-mail messages use | |

## Exercise 2 (pages 114–115)

2. correct
4. has

6. make
8. were

10. is

## Exercise 3 (pages 117-118)

The best strategy is to use the plural for both students and teachers.

All at university or college look forward to Reading Break, but they all have their own reasons. Teachers, for example, have good reasons to be happy. Using Reading Break to catch up on marking or, without pressure, to plan for the following weeks gives teachers reasons to be happy about their break. This break can help them survive the following weeks and allow them more time to spend with panicky students who are trying to cram three months into one week at end of term. If they are already such hard-working and organized people that all their planning and marking are done, then Reading Break can really be fun. Similarly, students who have all their assignments and reading up-to-date may take a couple days to relax or visit their friends and families. Reading Break, for them, is a pause that refreshes. In contrast, students who are behind or disorganized can use Reading Break to save themselves from disaster. If they are sinking in a sea of undone assignments and readings, Reading Break is like a lifeline they can use to pull themselves away from certain doom. Is it any wonder that, no matter whether you speak to teachers or students, they can always tell you when Reading Break will be.

## Exercise 4 (page 119)

Again, the best strategy is to use the plural.

One reason some teenagers quit school is to work to support their families. If they are the eldest children, the teens may feel an obligation to provide for the family, so they look for a minimum wage job. Unfortunately, the students often must work so many hours per week that they cannot give much attention to schoolwork. As a result, they grow discouraged and drop out. If teenagers feel that their families need more financial support, they should speak to their counsellors about the problem. Counsellors can provide proper referrals to appropriate services so that the students do not jeopardize their future for the sake of the family's present.

## Exercise 5 (pages 119–120)

For twelve months, Daniel dreamt about getting his driver's licence. He turned sixteen months later than Pat and Terry, his best friends. He had wanted to get his licence as soon as possible, so he was pleased when, on his birthday, his big, and only, brother Darren gave him a cheque to get it. He was pleased, but he was also a bit surprised. "Cool," he said, "I was afraid that you had had it with Daniel the Dreadful!"

For weeks before his birthday, Daniel had been studying the driver's manual every night after doing his homework. Disappearing into his room promptly after nine o'clock to study the book, he had been confident that he knew it all after just a week.

Then he had started phase two of the learning process. During the next few weeks, whenever his brother or either of his parents took the car out, he had asked to go along, asked his dad to drop him off at his friend Pat's house on his way to his poker game, asked his mother if he could go and watch her get a haircut, and asked his brother if he could go to a movie with him and Winona, his girlfriend. Some days, he managed four trips, and, on all the trips, he watched everything the driver did.

During these trips, much to his delight, Daniel could point out all the mistakes Darren and his parents made. He had warned his father three times to watch out for cyclists as he made a right turn, explained to his mother how to turn the wheels when she parked uphill on a street without a curb, and told Darren, who had been driving only four years, the penalty for driving only one kilometre above the speed limit in a school zone.

On the morning of the fourth day of phase two, when Daniel, whistling cheerily, had gone down to breakfast, he found a bus pass and a certificate in his cereal bowl. The certificate read "Official Back Seat Driver's Licence." Under the official looking red seal, his parents and Darren had signed as witnesses. It wasn't the kind of driver's licence he had dreamt of.

### Exercise 6 (page 121)

2. wants
4. lets
6. needs
8. leave
10. has

### Exercise 7 (pages 121–122)

2. is
4. has
6. communicates
8. contains
10. is

### Exercise 8 (pages 122–123)

2. a live game
4. The duration of the rain
6. the cause of the stalling
8. the men's group
10. the workers, Such lack of communication *or* Such low morale

### Exercise 9 (page 124)

2. This
4. this
6. It
8. this
10. It

### Exercise 10 (127–128)

2. Incorrect
4. Incorrect

### Exercise 11 (page 128) *Suggestions*

2. is
4. these settlers had to
6. its executive
8. were
10. he or she should report

### Exercise 12 (page 129)

2. are not conjugated
4. takes
6. favours
8. was available
10. it should have bee

### Exercise 13 (pages 129–130)

2. are
4. animals
6. come
8. is
10. they give us

### Exercise 14 (page 130)

2. makes
4. plan
6. had caused
8. have to be changed
10. criterion

### Exercise 15 (pages 130–131)

2. were
4. was
6. make
8. is
10. means

### Exercise 16 (page 131)

2. where there are
4. are
6. correct
8. Are
10. this allowed

### Exercise 17 (pages 131–132)

2. this is
4. is
6. correct
8. was swimming
10. is

## Exercise 18 (page 132)

2.  can soothe
4.  think

6.  is anecdotal
8   correct

10.  painkillers

## Chapter 4: Sentence Structure

### Pretest

2.  Percival yelled, so Penelope left.
4.  Percival yelled; moreover [furthermore], Penelope left.
6.  Although Percival yelled, Penelope left. *or* Penelope left although Percival yelled.
8.  Percival yelled; however [nonetheless] [nevertheless], Penelope left.
10.  Percival yelled; therefore [thus] [hence] [consequently], Penelope left.

### Exercise 2 (page 138)

| Coordinate Conjunctions | Prepositions | Subordinate Conjunctions |
|---|---|---|
| for | above | after* |
| and | across | although |
| nor | after* | because |
| but | before* | before |
| or | beside | since |
| yet | during | unless |
| so | | when |
| | | while |

*"After" and "before" can be both prepositions or subordinate conjunctions.

### Exercise 3 (page 140)

2.  It started to rain, but they went on a picnic.
    It started to rain, yet they went on a picnic.
4.  On the highway, Ming saw a large dark shape, and he decided to slow down.
    On the highway, Ming saw a large dark shape, so he decided to slow down.

### Exercise 4 (page 141)

2.  The squirrel leapt on top of the bird feeder; it swung there precariously.
4.  Ralph got B+'s in English; he got A's in History.

### Exercise 5 (page 141)

2.  Debbie started to giggle; moreover [however] [therefore], Frank began to laugh.
4.  Daisy felt a cold coming on; therefore [hence] [thus], she decided to go to bed.

### Exercise 6 (page 142)

2.  When the squirrel leapt on top of the bird feeder, he swung there precariously.
4.  When [because] Debbie started to giggle, Frank began to laugh.
6.  As [because] [since] Daisy felt a cold coming on, she decided to go to bed.

### Exercise 7 (page 143)

2.  After Joe ate a large pizza, he felt very full, so he fell asleep.
4.  Monique had a job interview, but she felt very prepared because she had researched both the business and its competitors.

### Exercise 8 (page 144–145)

2.  The instructor arriving fifteen minutes late, many members of the class had left.
4.  Brendan having the longest string of hits, the team made him captain.

layed

they

ves.
d man

d errors,

three

one).

ony.

[object]

ittle money

ores that reduce their staffing

a stickler for the rules, and a

ne that he has written?

four o'clock?

w his mother is feeling now.
o you know who did the

en wondering what Sam's

ll him when the next bus

estaurant is. Can you tell us

ou notice when the

nust ask everyone where

dy knows what country

r. Has anyone asked if you

d why there is no number

e, but they were late

against the motion, only

n and Patrick

her the neighbours

to finish the exam
.

## Exercise 15 (pages 152–153)

2. (While) Janet <u>played</u> on the swing, <u>Judy</u> <u>played</u> on the merry-go-round, and <u>Jim</u> on the slide.

4. (After) we saw the movie, <u>Peter and Jeanette</u> <u>read</u> the book (because) <u>they</u> <u>felt</u> that <u>had missed</u> some of the best lines when <u>people</u> <u>were laughing</u> so hard.

6. (Since) Gianni <u>moved</u>, <u>Marina</u> <u>has been able to play</u> the country music that <u>she</u> 

8. Throughout the lecture, including the two intermissions, the curly-headed blo in the front row <u>slept</u>.

10. (Whereas) Ping <u>wrote</u> long, interesting paragraphs filled with concrete details a the young <u>woman</u> sitting next to her <u>wrote</u> dull, perfectly correct ones.

## Exercise 16 (pages 155–156)

2. The oldest dog, (which) <u>is</u> now close to thirteen years old), is the mother of the others.

4. May I please borrow the book (that) I <u>gave</u> you for your birthday?)

6. Your friend, (whom) I <u>met</u> yesterday), is in my chemistry class.

8. When you find the room (where) the <u>food</u> <u>is</u>), tell Aaron.

10. Jay found a black toque, (which) <u>exuded</u> quite a different <u>feeling</u> than his yellow

## Exercise 17 (page 156–157)

2. <u>game,</u> <u>that</u> [subject]  The game assured it a place in the finals.

4. <u>house,</u> <u>that</u> [subject]  The house was damaged by the explosion.

6. <u>Bill,</u> <u>who</u> [subject]  Your cousin Bill behaved strangely during the whole cerer

## Exercise 18 (pages 157–158)

2. <u>outfit,</u> <u>that</u> [object]  The man wore the outfit.

4. <u>story,</u> <u>which</u> [object]  The teacher read the story aloud to the class.

6. <u>incident,</u> <u>that</u> [object]  You witnessed the incident last night.

## Exercise 19 (page 158)

2. The mid-term <u>that</u> [object]

4. The holidays, <u>which</u> [object]

6. The council members, <u>who</u> [subject]

8. After <u>we</u> escaped the traffic jam caused by the parade, we scrapped the plans <u>that</u> [object]

10. My son Pete, <u>who</u> [subject]

## Exercise 20 (page 159)

2. The quizzes <u>that</u> [object]

4. money <u>that</u> [object]

6. Can you lend me the vacuum cleaner <u>that</u> [subject]

8. After our trip to the Caribbean, <u>which</u> [subject] was our third, the plans tha

10. Did Jeremy see the house <u>where</u>

## Exercise 21 (pages 159–160)

2. I need the letter <u>that</u> was in the mail yesterday.

4. What time is the bus <u>that</u> goes uptown?

6. Most of the people living in the apartments are poor people <u>who</u> have very for repairs.

8. When there is an unknown person <u>that</u> comes to my house, my dog barks.

10. Some of the papers contained cryptic symbols <u>that</u> appeared to be ancient writing.

## Exercise 22 (page 160)

2. After they finish the courses that [subject] <u>are</u> [verb]
4. Many of the students ate in the cafeteria that [subject] <u>served</u> [verb]
6. Mr. Simms was impressed by the workers that were [verb, passive voice] hired
8. Bus drivers agree that kneeling buses that [subject] <u>improve</u> [verb]
10. My next-door neighbours are newcomers who [subject] <u>come</u> [verb]

## Exercise 23 (page 161)

2. (which <u>was</u> including me.)
4. (that <u>we can</u> sign up for in the Physical Education building.)
6. (<u>that we</u> drive to work every day)
8. (<u>that we</u> use to do word processing)
10. (<u>who</u> watch a lot of TV)

## Exercise 24 (page161)

2. There are many bookstores in downtown Regina that <u>sell</u> second-hand books.
4. This is the woman who <u>gave</u> me the right answers.
6. This is the book that <u>was</u> on the bestseller list for nine months.
8. There are many stores downtown that <u>sell</u> books.
10. Did you read about the pit bull that <u>rescued</u> a little girl?

## Exercise 25 (pages 162)

2. The Okanagan is a valley that <u>has</u> lots of orchards and vineyards.
4. Did you see the cloud that <u>looked</u> like an elephant?
6. There is the lectern that <u>has</u> a picture of superman on it.
8. Last winter I had a friend who <u>got stuck</u> in her house for a whole week during the blizzard.
10. Where is the boy who <u>looks</u> after the sheep?

## Exercise 26 (page 163)

2. Correct
4. which is what happens every year.
6. My mum, who loved the Ferrari best,
8. My birthday Volvo, which is dung brown and flat out at eighty kilometres per hour,
10. My Volvo, which I call Valerie,

## Exercise 27 (pages 163–164)

2. Correct
4. spinach, which was out of season.
6. Correct
8. door, which was draped with a fat lasagne noodle,
10. the dog, which I now call Lucky-to-be-Alive, or Lucky,

## Exercise 28 (pages 164–165)

2. My eldest sister, who married a doctor,
4. Correct
6. Correct
8. schedules, which are a little late this year,
10. restrictions, which were revised in June,

## Exercise 29 (page 165)

Correct by yourself or with a classmate.

## Exercise 30 (pages 170–171)

2. At the basketball clinic, Sam learned self-confidence, new skills, and good sportsmanship.
4. Andy found sand in the shoes, the pants, and the jacket.
6. Good analytical skills are necessary in studying not only science but also literature.
8. Eleanor thought that the car was too old, too ugly, and too expensive!
10. Sam had not decided whether to take the bus or to hitchhike.

## Exercise 31 (page 171)

2. Sarah admires people with gentle personalities, but firm ideas.
4. You can get to St. John's by boat, ferry, or airplane.
6. Jeremy ran up the steps, laughing, panting, and struggling to keep his knees straight.
8. The dog was not only long legged but also short tailed.
10. Samantha told her friend that she expected courtesy, tolerance, and honesty.

## Exercise 32 (page 172)

| | | |
|---|---|---|
| 2. Incorrect | 6. Incorrect | 10. Incorrect |
| 4. Incorrect | 8. Incorrect | |

## Exercise 33 (page 173)

| | | |
|---|---|---|
| 2. Correct | 6. Correct | 10. Incorrect |
| 4. Incorrect | 8. Incorrect | |

## Exercise 34 (pages 174–175)

| | | |
|---|---|---|
| 2. Incorrect | 6. Incorrect | 10. Correct |
| 4. Incorrect | 8. Correct | |

## Exercise 35 (pages 175–176)

| | | |
|---|---|---|
| 2. Correct | 6. Incorrect | 10. Incorrect |
| 4. Incorrect | 8. Correct | |

## Exercise 36 (pages 177–178)

2. Rarely do we go to movies.
4. Never did David eat eggplant.
6. Only when she was coaxed did Mary do her homework.
8. Nowhere did I see the elephant.
10. Under no circumstances would Sarah ride the camel.

## Exercise 37 (page 178)

Answers to this exercise will vary.

## Exercise 38 (page 179)

2. Students need somewhere quiet to study.
4. Cleaning out your desk drawers will get you off to a fresh start.
6. A lot of checkout clerks have health problems caused by repetitive movement syndrome.
8. An athlete should recognize the need for a healthy diet to nourish an active body.
10. Renting a video will be much less expensive, and you can make your own popcorn.

### Exercise 39 (pages 179–180)

2. Some movies have so many special effects that very little attention is paid to a good script.
4. Checking the forecast will give you a clue about whether to pack your bathing suit.
6. A language like English often has a variety of ways to spell the same sound.
8. The title page should include your name, your instructor's name, the course and section number, and the date.
10. The winning team just looked as though they could easily play another two periods, but we were exhausted.

### Diagnostic Exercise (pages 180–181)

2. Incorrect     4. Correct

### Exercise 40 (page 181)

2. It is hard for teenagers to understand their parents. It is easy for teenagers to understand their parents.
4. Swallowing a bad-tasting medicine is easy. Swallowing a bad-tasting medicine is hard.
6. Car fumes make it hard for people with asthma to breathe.
8. The high cost of tuition makes it hard for some students to pay for higher education.
10. Traffic jams make it difficult for a commuter to get home quickly.

### Exercise 41: (pages 182–184)

2. It is common for teenagers to enjoy different music than their parents.
4. It is foolhardy to eat wild berries if you don't know what kind they are.
6. It is delightful to sit on the rock beside the ocean on a summer's day.
8. Student loans make it possible for students without many savings to attend university.
10. Traffic jams make it difficult for a commuter to get home quickly.

### Exercise 42 (page 186)

2. Jane suggested that I read the textbook.
4. Joe recommended that I start a garden.
6. It is necessary that we eat the leftovers today.
8. Joe insisted that Sarah help him.
10. I move the meeting adjourn.

### Exercise 43 (page 186)

2. Sam recommends that Teresa take a sociology course.
4. She asked that the people have their pens ready.
6. It is important that the singers control their movement.
8. The usher insisted that they move to the front row.
10. Shelagh asks that he finish the book before Tuesday.

### Exercise 44 (pages 186–187) Answers will vary.

2. It is important that they take napkins to the barbecue.
4. I was advised that she must take the first ferry.
6. Joe insisted that Barbara try his home-made cider.
8. Yasu insisted that his friends come for breakfast.
10. She suggests that you practise once a day.

### Exercise 45 (page187) Answers may vary.

2. Correct     6. Incorrect     10. Correct
4. Correct     8. Incorrect

**Exercise 46 (page 188)** Answers will vary.

2. correct
6. very relieved
10. very steep
4. very warm
8. very glad

**Exercise 47 (page 188)** Answers will vary.

2. Peter was very glad that he had eaten before the concert.
4. On the way downtown, Yoshi and Elaine saw a very big accident involving three cars.
6. The speaker's "uhms" and "uhs" made it so hard to listen to the content of the presentation that some people left.
8. Proofreading a printed document is very important.
10. Ever since the blizzard, Mac was very conscious of carrying proper equipment.

**Exercise 48 (page 190)** Answers may vary.

2. Driving the car at 100 km, he found that the direction sign zipped past before it could be read.
4. When John was age three, the barber gave him his first haircut.
6. Not having practised, Algernon found the oral presentation was a pain rather than a pleasure.
8. As a student, I think that my computer is my greatest friend.
10. As we climbed through the dense bush and rocky terrain, the hill was formidable.

**Exercise 49 (page 191)** Answers may vary.

2. Working as a sales representative, you will find a good smile is a necessity.
4. As we walked through the Natural History Museum, the dinosaurs made the greatest impact.
6. As I am a lover of vegetables, my favourite is peas fresh from the garden.
8. Twice when Mariaye was three, her mother took her to *Cinderella* in a theatre.
10. While you are cleaning storm gutters, a sturdy ladder is a necessity.

**Exercise 50 (page 191)** Answers may vary.

2. Comparing the two cities, Maxine believes that Churchill is more exciting.
4. New learners of English can absolutely rely on native speakers, despite their lack of knowing any article rules, when they say "You need to use 'the' here."
6. Feeling headachy, Penelope thought that an aspirin seemed like a good idea.
8. As a manager, she found that customer satisfaction must come first.
10. Wanting to be first in line, he knew that a sleeping bag and a thermos of coffee would be a good idea.

**Exercise 51 (pages 193–194)**

2. When Craig came home from tree planting, he put a load of clothes that he had worn for a whole week in the machine.
4. Fred saw a man reading a book while riding his bike.
6. Last week, I read almost all of *A Fine Balance* because everyone recommended it.
8. I handed in a drawing of a girl, who wore pigtails and had a wart on the end of her nose to my teacher, Mrs. Howard.
10. Una left the dress that she had worn to graduation in the suitcase.

**Exercise 52 (page 194)**

2. Wanted by a recent immigrant, a three-bedroom house with a large backyard, a vegetable garden, and fruit trees.
4. The pint-sized poodle with a nine-inch bone in its mouth stopped in front of the car.
6. With its paws neatly tucked under its chin, the cat lay on the bed.
8. Jason, looking out his grandma's window, could see the rampaging bulls.
10. I slept for almost ten hours, so I feel great.

### Exercise 53 (pages 194–195)

2. While Joe cut the front lawn, in the backyard, Sarah, with a hoe, weeded the beds that contained the flowers and vegetables.
4. The boy carried a basket with a six-foot cobra hiding in it under his arm.
6. In my mind, the use of photo radar reduces accidents.
8. On January 1, Mercedes resolved to create a garden with both flowers and vegetables.
10. In a new gardening book, I finally found a compact shrub that likes shade and is evergreen.

### Exercise 54 (page 195)

2. Can you please tell me how I can get to Dawson City?
4. The team members refused to reveal who was responsible for the damage to the locker room.
6. I wonder what I can buy my father for his birthday.
8. I think we should consider how we are going to pay for all these presents if we buy them.
10. We still haven't discussed where the banquet will be held.

### Exercise 55 (page 197) Answers will vary.

2. Literacy is crucial to success and even to survival in our society because most of us read and write every day of our lives.
4. Within the next few years, many of our landfills will become full, so we must find innovative ways to deal with our garbage problems.

### Exercise 56 (page 202) Answers will vary.

2. Dedicated to competition, devoted to figure skating, and committed excellence, Elvis Stojko embraced the challenge of Nagano as he had faced all earlier challenges, refusing to be defeated by sickness.

### Exercise 57 (pages 203–204) Answers will vary.

2. When the first light of dawn sketched an outline of the hills in the east, and the birds began a tentative conversation, Jack crept out of the tent and headed for the lake.

### Exercise 58 (page 204) Answers will vary.

2. If we do not have the entitlement to say "No," we do not have the power to say "Yes."

### Exercise 59 (page 204–205) Answers will vary.

### Exercise 60 (page 205)

2. She was a creative genius, creating genius her passion.

## Chapter 5: Punctuation

### Exercise 1 (page 209)

2. Fortunately, the new catalogue offers new products, new prices, and new delivery policies.

### Exercise 2 (page 210)

2. Honga found a pencil, a red plastic toy truck, a pair of handcuffs, and two loonies under the couch cushion.

### Exercise 3 (page 211)

2. It has started to rain, so I think that we need to borrow an umbrella.

### Exercise 4 (page 211)

2. After the fire, the dinner party became much more interesting.

### Exercise 5 (page 212)

2. He lived in Penticton, a city at the south end of Okanagan Lake.
4. Rats, I forgot to bring my camera!
6. The committee agreed, therefore, to postpone the August meeting.

### Exercise 6 (page 213)

2. No one in the audience could understand a word of its long, tedious lecture.
4. The main gist of the lecture seemed to be that the normal biological clock of the alien was slowed down under the powerful pull of the earth's gravitational field.

### Exercise 7 (page 214)

2. "A mother is not a person to lean on," said Dorothy Canfield Fisher, "but a person to make leaning unnecessary."

### Exercise 8 (page 214–215)

2. My eldest sister, who married a doctor, lives in Kaleden.
4. A child who screams for attention should be ignored.

### Exercise 9 (page 215)

2. The cat, a study in concentration, sat in front of the birdcage.
4. The agency, lacking funds for new staff, decided to move to a four-day week.

### Exercise 10 (page 216)

2. On Friday, July 17, 1959, in Victoria, the 2nd Battalion of the Princess Patricia's Canadian Light Infantry trooped the colours for Queen Elizabeth II.

### Exercise 11 (page 216)

2. Because you are sending the letter out of the country, write the return address this way: 55 Galt Crescent, Freont, Manitoba W8H 4P6 Canada.

### Exercise 12 (page 217)

2. July 1, now known as Canada Day, was once called Dominion Day.
4. The good news that Enio had won made everyone cheerful.
6. The purse contained keys, glasses, pictures, but no identification.
8. The brochure had described it as cozy, but the room seemed claustrophobic.
10. In 1791, the British parliament divided Canada into two provinces, Upper Canada and Lower Canada.

### Exercise 13 (pages 217–218)

2. Sarah pulled the plug, and Sam pushed the machine into the other room.
4. Everyone who reads the book will want to try hypnosis.
6. Fiona left at 5:00, but Matthew stayed until 6:00.
8. Her old bike tires, worn and slender, made riding over the sidewalk grates an adventure.
10. Frances always gave the newspaper to Marge Quinlan, the woman next door.

### Exercise 14 (pages 218–219)

2. Canada Day, formerly called Dominion Day, is on July 1, Claire, Tony, and the twins' birthday.
4. On Canada's first birthday in 1867, Quebec, Ontario, New Brunswick, and Nova Scotia were its only provinces.
6. Joey Smallwood, the last Father of Confederation, was premier of Newfoundland when it became a province.
8. In honour of Alberta and Saskatchewan entering Confederation, thousands of people, including Prime Minister Wilfred Laurier, attended ceremonies in Regina and Edmonton.
10. Manitoba, preceding British Columbia, joined Confederation in 1870.

### Exercise 15 (page 219)

2. Although Vancouver Island had been governed by the Hudsons's Bay Company, it became a British colony in 1849.
4. The Hudson's Bay Company, in 1849, leased Vancouver Island back from the British government.
6. The Hudson's Bay Company had a trading monopoly, but it had to pay defence costs and encourage settlers.
8. Some of Vancouver Island lies under the 49th parallel, Canada's border with the United States.
10. Vancouver Island's major city Victoria, British Columbia's capital, was incorporated in 1862.

### Exercise 16 (pages 219–220)

2. Pruning in late winter or early spring, while a plant is dormant, won't adversely affect its vigour, but pruning at other times can rob it of stored food energy.
4. Such pruning can retard, stunt, or dwarf a plant and is not recommended unless a dwarfing effect, as in a bonsai, is the goal.
6. As the days shorten in late summer, growth slows, and sugars collect in the leaves.
8. Pruning in fall or early winter exhausts the stored food reserves needed to initiate spring growth.
10. Later, in the dormant season, sugars move farther down the plant, and they are less likely to be affected.

### Exercise 17 (pages 220–221)

2. In your video store, you should look for *Tampopo*, an amusing, appetite-stimulating noodle western.
4. The next time my parole officer says "Have a nice day," I may decide to return to prison.
6. Wah Lee, an excellent student, also excels at basketball.
8. Lashmi spent an hour committing her new address to memory: 7063 Flemming Crescent, Calgary, Alberta T3H 0X4 Canada.
10. Leaping down the stairs two at a time, Pierre got to the door before the courier rang the bell.
12. Mary said that she would pick up the hot dogs and buns on her way home.
14. Kelly Kramer is a fast-talking, super-slick salesperson.

### Exercise 18 (page 223)

2. You should remember to buy candles, cards, and paper at the drugstore; blueberries, whipping cream, and icing sugar at the grocery; and a cake pan, cake rack, and measuring cup at the hardware. (Rule 2)

## Exercise 19 (page 223)

2. Charlotte Bronte wrote *Jane Eyre*, although Emily Bronte wrote *Wuthering Heights*.
4. Your letter to the editor should be clear, concise, and courteous.
6. Correct
8. Correct
10. Correct

## Exercise 20 (page 224)

2. history;[3] so
4. 1497;[1] Vasco da Gama
6. chili;[2] romaine
8. page;[2] an, company;[2] your, rejected;[2] an analysis, graphs;[2] and
10. Watercress, a peppery herb often used in salads and occasionally in sandwiches in British detective novels, grows well in wet conditions;[3] so it is a bit of a surprise to find that it is related to the nasturtium, which seems to do perfectly well in dry conditions.

## Exercise 21 (page 225)

2. When you proofread a paper, check for any changes that should be made in your thesis or topic sentences;[2] make sure that all ideas are developed well, that the paragraphs wrap nicely, and that the essay ends strongly;[2] and finally, proofread for the more mechanical details, like spelling, punctuation, and grammar, for example;[2] and check that you have included a pleasing variety of sentence structures.
4. Correct
6. Major League Baseball now has two representatives in Canada, the Toronto Blue Jays and the Montreal Expos;[1] interestingly, both Toronto and Montreal were previously represented in a long-running international league, Montreal for 55 years and Toronto for 78 years.
8. In 1981, the Nobel Prize for Physics was won by Kai Seigbahn, from Sweden, and Nicolaas Bloembergen and Arthur Schawlow, from the USA;[1] the Nobel Prize for Chemistry was won by Kenichi Fukui from Japan and Roald Hoffman from the USA.
10. In some words, however, it is the British or Canadian person who writes a shorter form;[1] while the American writes "learned," "dreamed," and "spelled," for example, the British or Canadian person often writes, "learnt," "dreamt," and "spelt."

## Exercise 22 (page 226)

2. You have forgotten the following things: candles, cards, cream, a cake pan, and cake rack.

## Exercise 23 (pages 226–227)

2. Correct
4. Correct
6. She could have just said "no," but instead, we got a ten minute lecture.
8. She knew it was a mall, but Carol was still surprised after she ordered a Tempura Combo to be asked "Would you like fries or rice with that?"
10. A Cantonese speaking person may have difficulty differentiating between the words "sheep" and "ship," "back" and "bag," and "flight" and "fright."

## Exercise 24 (pages 227–228)

2. Correct
4. You'll need the following before you can apply for your licence: your birth certificate, a piece of picture ID, and two pieces of correspondence addressed to you at your current address.
6. The boss seems to feel that the new receptionist, although skillful, lacks one thing: personality.

8.  Medvedev would agree with this point for he wrote the following: "Science and technology, and the various forms of art, all unite humanity in a single and interconnected system."
10. Correct

## Exercise 25 (page 229)

2.  Students receiving D's need either to reduce the number of serious errors or to increase the development and organization of ideas.

## Exercise 26 (page 230)

2.  catalogue's prices                    4.  The Women's Caucus

## Exercise 27 (page 231)

2.  birds' nest                           4.  knives' sharpness

## Exercise 28 (page 232)

2.  Its length makes its analysis more difficult for Mr. Leung.

## Exercise 29 (pages 232–233)

2.  glass' stem          6.  Bryan's calculator        10. goodness' sake
4.  It's                 8.  dad's car

## Exercise 30 (pages 233–234)

2.  he'll                8.  goodness' sake, Can't
4.  its battery, it's    10. Let's, Hazel's Chocolate Chunk Cookies
6.  She'll, he'll

## Exercise 31 (page 234)

2.  dog's, Where's       8.  didn't, she'd
4.  We're, she'll        10. Denis' preoccupation
6.  A's, B+'s

## Exercise 32 (pages 237–238)

2.  Do you know what time it is?
4.  Jamie asked her if she would like to go for lunch.
6.  I wonder why the newspaper isn't here.
8.  On the CBC's morning show, I heard a UN diplomat speaking about all the great work that UNESCO and UNICEF accomplished in the '50s.
10. Hurrah, we are famous!

## Exercise 33 (page 239)

2.  Boris ate—can you believe it?—a whole roasted-garlic pizza.

## Exercise 34 (page 239)

2.  (the large)

## Exercise 35 (page 244)

2.  "The River Merchant's Wife: a Letter," a poem by Ezra Pound, is a translation of a poem by an 8th century Chinese poet, Li Po, but for some strange reason, Pound uses Japanese names in the poem.
4.  In *The Moonstone*, one of Sergeant Cuff's more cutting lines is "There's also such a thing as making nothing out of a molehill in consequence of your head being too high to see it."

6. Ken needs to know about "squelch" to understand why his FM receiver cuts out when it receives noisy signals.

8. My favourite part in Louise Erdrich's *Love Medicine* isn't the title story, though it's wonderful, but the very end of "The Good Tears," after Lulu has her cataracts removed, and Marie goes to help her.

10. In *The Woodlanders*, Creedle gets some great lines such as "And I don't care who the man is, I says that a stick of celery that isn't scrubbed with a scrubbing brush is not clean."

### Exercise 36 (page 245) *Answers may vary.*

2. Always remember "If a quotation crosses a pagr[sic], indicate this in [the] note by a single or double slash" (Burne and Browne 306).

# Chapter 7: Organization

### Exercise 1 (page 293)

2. Incorrect    4. Incorrect    6. Incorrect

### Exercise 2 (pages 294–295)

| | | |
|---|---|---|
| 2. Correct | 6. no | 10. Correct |
| 4. no | 8. Correct | |

### Exercise 3 (page 295)

| | | |
|---|---|---|
| 2. Correct | 6. no | 10. Correct |
| 4. Correct | 8. no | |

### Exercise 4 (page 303) *Answers will vary.*

# Chapter 8: Idiom

### Exercise 1 (pages 354–355)

| | |
|---|---|
| 2. at, in, at, in | 8. no preposition, at |
| 4. on *or* no preposition | 10. at, no preposition |
| 6. During, on | |

### Exercise 2 (page 356)

| | |
|---|---|
| 2. no preposition, no preposition | 8. no preposition, about |
| 4. about | 10. no preposition |
| 6. about, no preposition | |

### Exercise 3 (page 358)

| | | |
|---|---|---|
| 2. no preposition | 6. on, to | 10. to |
| 4. at | 8. to, in | |

### Exercise 4 (pages 358–359)

| | | |
|---|---|---|
| 2. in | 6. at, on or onto | 10. in, no preposition |
| 4. on | 8. on | |

### Exercise 5 (pages 364–365)

| | | |
|---|---|---|
| 2. comparing | 6. compared | 10. compared |
| 4. comparing | 8. comparing | |

### Exercise 6 (pages 366–367)

| | | | |
|---|---|---|---|
| 2. | was concerned | 6. | was concerned |
| 4. | concerned | 8. | had been concerned |

10. concerning

### Exercise 7 (page 369)

2. find out      4. find

### Exercise 8 (page 372)

| | | | | | |
|---|---|---|---|---|---|
| 2. | involved | 6. | immerses | 10. | interests |
| 4. | concerns | 8. | concerns | | |

### Exercise 9 (page 377)

| | | | | | |
|---|---|---|---|---|---|
| 2. | pounds | 6. | pyjamas, pyjama, pyjama | 10. | tractors, tractor |
| 4. | drivers | 8. | driver | | |

### Exercise 10 (pages 377–378)

| | | | | | |
|---|---|---|---|---|---|
| 2. | dollar | 6. | socks, tights, sock | 10. | plate |
| 4. | kilometres | 8. | economic | | |

### Exercise 11 (pages 378–379)

| | | | | | |
|---|---|---|---|---|---|
| 2. | Many | 6. | some of the | 10. | All of the |
| 4. | a few of the | 8. | a few | | |

### Exercise 12 (pages 380–382)

| | | | | | |
|---|---|---|---|---|---|
| 2. | boring | 8. | confused | 12. | frightening |
| 4. | annoyed | 10. | convincing | 14. | interested |
| 6. | exciting | | | | |

### Exercise 13 (page 383)

| | | | |
|---|---|---|---|
| 1. | searched | 4. | search for |
| 2. | (to) search | 5. | search for |
| 3. | searched for | | |

## Chapter 9: Diction

### Exercise 1 (pages 394–395)

| | | | |
|---|---|---|---|
| 2. | cool as a cucumber | 8. | moment of truth |
| 4. | sadder but wiser | 10. | growing by leaps and bounds |
| 6. | blushing bride | | |

### Exercise 2 (pages 395–396) *Answers will vary.*

2. Because everyone disagrees with me, I will resign. 8/17
4. Because the water in this glass is almost below freezing, I will skip the ice. 15/23
6. Because he thinks that the book was better than the movie, we should try to read it. 17/28
8. The buskers always try to stand near the book store's front doors. 12/18
10. Because many jobs ask for experience, students should recognize that volunteer positions can assist them. 15/30

**Exercise 3 (pages 396–397)** *Answers will vary.*

2. If someone cannot walk, a scooter can be a great help. 11/23
4. Despite the delayed project approval, Barrison Brothers think that they can finish it by March 1. 16/31
6. The union leadership thinks that new government is hostile toward a wage hike. 13/27
8. To increase the product's accessibility, we should make the opening more visible. 12/22
10. You should know that one of the laptops is missing. 10/15

**Exercise 4 (pages 397–398)** *Answers will vary.*

2. The biggest problem with the report is incoherence. 8/13
4. The switch must be fully engaged before the lever is pulled. 11/15
6. You must determine the author's bias. 6/14
8. Problems in the new operating system caused the delay in your grades. 12/18
10. This year, he is much fitter because of rock climbing. 10/18

# Index